Empire Builders Series: Masterclasses in Business and Law

From Idea to Empire

ALSO BY AUTHORSDOOR GROUP

Empire Builders Series: Masterclasses in Business and Law

From Idea to Empire

Abridged Edition

For entrepreneurs, students, or professionals who want a concise, practical guide.

L. A. MOESZINGER

AuthorsDoor Group
an imprint of The Ridge Publishing Group

Library of Congress Control Number: 2024922963

From Idea to Empire: Abridged Edition / by L. A. Moeszinger

ISBN 978-1-956905-37-3 (softcover)

1. Business & Economics / Entrepreneurship. 2. Business & Economics / Small Business. 3. Business & Economics / Management. 4. Self-Help / Motivational & Inspiration. 5. Business & Economics / Leadership. I. Title. II. Series

Printed in the United States of America

To all the dreamers and doers—may this guide be the blueprint that turns your ideas into empires.

Authorsdoor Group
Coeur d'Alene, Idaho

INTRODUCTION TO THE
AUTHORSDOOR LEADERSHIP PROGRAM

The AuthorsDoor Leadership Program, separate from the Builders Empire Series, is a new initiative designed to empower authors and publishers with the skills to effectively sell books. It features three tailored series: (1) AuthorsDoor Series: *Publisher & Her World*, (2) AuthorsDoor Advanced Series: *Publisher & Her World*, and (3) AuthorsDoor Masterclass Series: *Publisher & Her World*; each series is meticulously structured to guide participants from foundational concepts to advanced strategies in selling books, book by book, in a chronological format. The courses, offered for free on our YouTube channels—Publisher & Her World at Ridge Publishing Group, AuthorsDoor Group: Publisher & Her World, and Authors Red Door #Shorts—complement the books and workbooks, each providing unique and valuable teachings.

Explore additional resources to enhance your journey:

- Follow our blog at AuthorsRedDoor.com.
- Subscribe to our Newsletters at AuthorsDoor.com.
- Join our AuthorsDoor Strategy Forum Facebook Group.
- Connect with our Facebook Page at AuthorsDoor Group.
- Become a fan on our social media channels @AuthorsDoor1.

For feedback or questions, contact us at info@authorsdoor.com. We are here to support your journey from writing to successfully selling your books.

Warm regards,

L. A. Moeszinger #PubHerWorld

Contents

PART 4: TAKING ACTION

Introduction

From Dreamer to Doer: Your Empire-Building Adventure Begins Now

Welcome to the Abridged Edition of *From Idea to Empire*, a streamlined guide tailored for entrepreneurs, professionals, and students who need concise, actionable strategies for turning ideas into thriving businesses. This version delivers essential frameworks and core business principles without the additional case studies, allowing readers to focus on practical tools they can apply quickly and efficiently.

To create this Abridged Edition, 57 case studies were removed from the original version to ensure this edition offers a more concise, accessible experience. These case studies provided in-depth examples of business success across a range of industries, illustrating how real-world entrepreneurs and leaders overcame challenges, seized growth opportunities, and executed effective strategies. If you're interested in exploring these case studies, you can find them along with over 200 additional stories in the Empire Blueprint Series: Case Studies for Business Success, a three-volume set that dives into leadership, digital innovation, strategic planning, and legacy building.

This Abridged Edition emphasizes practical business planning and strategy execution, making it the perfect resource for those looking to build, grow, or optimize their ventures with a direct, no-nonsense approach. It distills the key lessons from the original into actionable frameworks—ideal for readers who want to apply insights efficiently without wading through additional narratives.

Whether you're crafting your business plan, preparing for growth, or refining an established business model, this Abridged Edition serves as a focused guide to building a strong foundation for success. And for those who seek further inspiration and context through real-world examples, we encourage you to explore the Empire Blueprint Series for the full collection of business case studies, where the stories behind success come to life.

With this edition, you'll have the roadmap to transform your ideas into reality. It's time to take the next step in your entrepreneurial journey—your empire begins here.

Why Business Planning Matters: Spoiler Alert, It's Everything
Some say that business plans are just formalities—something you put together to impress investors and then forget about. Wrong! A business plan is far more than a bunch of pretty graphs and professional jargon. It's the map that shows you how to get from where you are (which might be a notebook full of ideas and too many cups of coffee) to where you want to be (sipping champagne while your empire thrives). Without it, you're just wandering through the wilderness of entrepreneurship, hoping you'll stumble upon success by accident.

But with a business plan? You're in control. You know exactly where you're going, why you're going there, and how you're going to get there.

In "From Idea to Empire," you'll learn how to craft a business plan that doesn't just look good on paper—it works. By the end of this book, your business plan will be more than a document; it will be the north star that guides your decisions, your team, and your entire venture.

A Step-by-Step Blueprint to Empire Building
Every empire begins with a solid foundation. In Part One, we'll focus on the basics of defining your business vision and identifying key opportunities. It's not about simply following trends but about finding unmet needs and sharpening your focus

to stand out from the competition. By the end of these chapters, you'll have a crystal-clear direction for your business and the strategies needed to move forward with confidence.

In Part Two, we delve into building a solid strategy. We'll cover marketing, operations, and financial planning, providing essential frameworks to ensure your business runs like a well-oiled machine. You'll learn how to craft marketing strategies that attract customers, build an operational plan for efficiency, and develop financial projections that drive sustainable growth.

Once you've laid your foundation, Part Three will guide you through the art of communicating your business plan to the world. Writing a clear, persuasive business plan is crucial, but so is crafting executive summaries, proposals, and pitches that inspire action. We'll even cover negotiation techniques to help you secure strategic partnerships and opportunities.

Part Four focuses on execution and scaling. It's not just about starting strong but staying agile—launching your business, adjusting to challenges, and setting the stage for long-term growth. You'll learn how to manage performance, pivot when needed, and scale effectively, ensuring your business stays on track and poised for expansion.

So, Where Do We Go from Here?

You've got the vision. You've got the drive. Now, all you need is the roadmap. In the pages ahead, we're going to break down everything you need to master the art of business planning. Whether you're just starting or refining an existing business, this Abridged Edition will guide you through every stage—from the spark of an idea to building a business empire.

While this version focuses on core strategies and frameworks, the 57 real-world case studies originally interwoven have been removed for brevity. If you're looking for those detailed examples, you can find them in the Empire Blueprint Series: Case Studies for Business Success, which offers over 200 stories across its three volumes, covering everything from leadership to legacy-building.

And if you're ready for more after building your plan, don't miss the next installment in the Empire Builders Series, *Beyond the Pen: Copyright Strategies for Modern Creators*. This next book explores cutting-edge copyright strategies to help you protect the empire you're about to build.

But for now, let's roll up our sleeves and get to work. The journey from idea to empire starts right here.

Ready? Let's build.

Why I Wrote This Book

Let's be real for a second: starting a business is equal parts thrilling, terrifying, and a little like skydiving without a parachute. You stand at the edge, staring down at a vast expanse of possibilities, heart racing with excitement, and you take the leap—hoping the wind or sheer luck will carry you to success. I've been there. Spoiler alert: the freefall is exhilarating, but at some point, you need to pull the ripcord—a business plan—to ensure a safe landing.

Now, let me tell you why I'm so passionate about strategic business planning—because this isn't just another "business book," and I'm not here to dish out generic advice. From Idea to Empire is designed to give you practical tools to build something real, something lasting. I've seen too many great ideas crash and burn, not for lack of passion, but because they didn't have a plan to support them. This book exists to help you avoid those same mistakes.

When I first entered the world of entrepreneurship, I had lots of ideas, but no strategy. I was full of passion and eager to make a difference, but without a clear roadmap, I hit a lot of walls. I struggled, made mistakes, and wondered whether this whole "entrepreneur" thing was really for me. It wasn't until I discovered the power of strategic planning—after plenty of trial and error—that everything began to click.

See, having a great idea is just the tip of the iceberg. Beneath that idea lies a framework that supports it—your vision, goals, market research, financial plans, and operations. That's the structure that transforms an exciting idea into a thriving business. And that's why I wrote this book: to give you the tools, insights, and strategies I wish I had when I started out.

This Abridged Edition focuses on the core strategies needed to create that framework—without the 57 case studies from the original edition. But don't worry. Those stories, along with many others, are available in the Empire Blueprint Series: Case Studies for Business Success. If you need inspiration from real-world examples, I encourage you to explore that series to complement what you learn here.

From Idea to Empire is not about being the smartest or the most connected person in the room. It's about having a clear plan and the persistence to stick with it— especially when things get tough (and they will). I've seen far too many talented people give up, not because they lacked passion, but because they didn't have the structure to support their dreams. This book exists to ensure that doesn't happen to you.

With the right plan, the chaos of entrepreneurship becomes manageable. Instead of guessing, you'll be making informed decisions. Instead of reacting, you'll be leading with strategy and confidence. When you have a plan, you stop hoping things will work out and start knowing they will—because you've laid out the steps to get there.

Building a business isn't easy. It's not supposed to be. But with the right plan, it's infinitely more doable. A good business plan isn't set in stone—it evolves with you. It's a living, breathing document that grows, pivots, and guides you through the challenges ahead.

I wrote this book to give you more than just theory—I want to give you a blueprint that takes your idea from spark to empire. Whether you're starting fresh or scaling an existing business, this book will help you clarify your vision, set goals, understand your market, and execute your strategy.

This is for anyone ready to turn dreams into action—whether you're launching your first business or refining the next phase of your empire. You have the vision. You have the drive. And now, with this book, you have the roadmap.

So let's build something great together. The journey to your empire begins here.

What Readers Can Expect from the Book

Let's be real for a second: starting a business is equal parts thrilling, terrifying, and a little like skydiving without a parachute. You stand at the edge, staring down at a vast expanse of possibilities, heart racing with excitement, and you take the leap—hoping the wind or sheer luck will carry you to success. I've been there. Spoiler alert: the freefall is exhilarating, but at some point, you need to pull the ripcord—a business plan—to ensure a safe landing.

Now, let me tell you why I'm so passionate about strategic business planning—because this isn't just another "business book," and I'm not here to dish out generic advice. From Idea to Empire is designed to give you practical tools to build something real, something lasting. I've seen too many great ideas crash and burn, not for lack of passion, but because they didn't have a plan to support them. This book exists to help you avoid those same mistakes.

When I first entered the world of entrepreneurship, I had lots of ideas, but no strategy. I was full of passion and eager to make a difference, but without a clear roadmap, I hit a lot of walls. I struggled, made mistakes, and wondered whether this whole "entrepreneur" thing was really for me. It wasn't until I discovered the power of strategic planning—after plenty of trial and error—that everything began to click.

See, having a great idea is just the tip of the iceberg. Beneath that idea lies a framework that supports it—your vision, goals, market research, financial plans, and operations. That's the structure that transforms an exciting idea into a thriving business. And that's why I wrote this book: to give you the tools, insights, and strategies I wish I had when I started out.

This Abridged Edition focuses on the core strategies needed to create that framework—without the 57 case studies from the original edition. But don't worry. Those stories, along with many others, are available in the Empire Blueprint Series: Case Studies for Business Success. If you need inspiration from real-world examples, I encourage you to explore that series to complement what you learn here.

Introduction

From Idea to Empire is not about being the smartest or the most connected person in the room. It's about having a clear plan and the persistence to stick with it—especially when things get tough (and they will). I've seen far too many talented people give up, not because they lacked passion, but because they didn't have the structure to support their dreams. This book exists to ensure that doesn't happen to you.

With the right plan, the chaos of entrepreneurship becomes manageable. Instead of guessing, you'll be making informed decisions. Instead of reacting, you'll be leading with strategy and confidence. When you have a plan, you stop hoping things will work out and start knowing they will—because you've laid out the steps to get there.

Building a business isn't easy. It's not supposed to be. But with the right plan, it's infinitely more doable. A good business plan isn't set in stone—it evolves with you. It's a living, breathing document that grows, pivots, and guides you through the challenges ahead.

I wrote this book to give you more than just theory—I want to give you a blueprint that takes your idea from spark to empire. Whether you're starting fresh or scaling an existing business, this book will help you clarify your vision, set goals, understand your market, and execute your strategy.

This is for anyone ready to turn dreams into action—whether you're launching your first business or refining the next phase of your empire. You have the vision. You have the drive. And now, with this book, you have the roadmap.

So let's build something great together. The journey to your empire begins here.

Clarity Amidst the Chaos

Starting a business can feel like standing in the middle of a storm—ideas flying around, excitement running high, and doubts creeping in, leaving you wondering, "Where do I even start?" That's where this book steps in, providing a clear, structured roadmap to guide you through the process. You'll learn how to untangle the ideas swirling in your head and transform them into a focused, actionable business plan. By the time you finish, you'll have clarity about what you're building, why it matters, and how to get there without getting overwhelmed.

Step-by-Step Guidance, No Guesswork

This book isn't about winging it—and neither should your business be. It offers clear, step-by-step instructions to take the guesswork out of the planning process. Whether you're researching your market, defining your audience, setting goals, or building a marketing strategy, this book provides a practical framework to help you stay on track. Each chapter builds on the last, creating a seamless flow to guide you through the entrepreneurial journey with confidence and clarity.

Actionable, Not Theoretical

While theory is important, this book emphasizes practical tools and exercises you can implement immediately. As you work through the pages, you'll build your business plan alongside the chapters, ensuring your ideas turn into tangible steps toward success. This Abridged Edition offers everything you need to create a polished, functional plan—ready to execute from the moment you complete the book.

A Fun, Engaging Approach to Serious Work

Building a business is serious work, but it doesn't mean it can't be enjoyable. Expect a conversational tone and light humor to keep you engaged, even as we tackle heavy topics like financial projections and operational planning. This book will help you stay focused, strategic, and professional—without losing the passion that made you start your journey in the first place.

Case Studies Available in the Companion Series

While this Abridged Edition removes the 57 case studies included in the original, the real-world stories that inspired entrepreneurs to succeed haven't been lost. You can explore those case studies—and many more—in the Empire Blueprint Series: Case Studies for Business Success. These companion volumes provide additional insights into how businesses overcome challenges, innovate, and build lasting legacies.

A Plan That Grows With You

Your business today won't look the same five years from now—and that's a good thing! This book teaches you how to create a plan that is flexible and adaptable, allowing you to pivot as opportunities arise. Whether you're starting fresh, launching a new product, or reimagining your current business, you'll learn how to adjust your strategy without losing sight of your goals.

Equipped for the Tough Times

Entrepreneurship isn't all sunshine and rainbows. When challenges arise—and they will—this book will help you stay grounded and prepared. You'll learn how to manage risks, pivot when necessary, and turn setbacks into opportunities for growth. With the right strategies in place, you'll feel empowered to navigate challenges with resilience and optimism.

Building for the Long Game

This book isn't about chasing quick wins or overnight success. It's about playing the long game—building a business designed for sustainable growth. You'll learn how to lay a strong foundation that supports your business through every stage, from launch to legacy. The goal isn't just to succeed today but to create something that thrives for years to come.

Motivation and Empowerment at Every Step

Entrepreneurship can be tough, but it's also one of the most rewarding journeys you'll ever take. This book isn't just a guide—it's a source of motivation and empowerment to help you stay the course, even when the going gets tough. By the time you finish, you won't just have a business plan—you'll have the confidence, mindset, and strategy to build something truly extraordinary.

So buckle up. With this book as your roadmap, and your vision leading the way, the journey from idea to empire starts here. Let's build something great together.

Common Pitfalls in Business Planning: The Traps You Didn't See Coming (But Totally Should Have)

Let's face it: if building a thriving business were easy, everyone would have an empire by now. But the truth is, even the most well-crafted plans can go sideways if you don't know the traps lurking ahead. In this section, we'll explore common pitfalls that can derail even the most ambitious entrepreneurs—and more importantly, how you can avoid them.

Pitfall #1: The "I'll Wing It" Mentality

Jumping in without a plan may sound daring, but it's like building a house without a blueprint. Success requires more than improvisation; it requires a solid strategy. Solution? Don't wing it—plan it. A business plan is your roadmap and compass, keeping you on course and minimizing risks.

Pitfall #2: Analysis Paralysis

You start your plan but end up lost in endless research and second-guessing every decision. Three weeks later, you have market data—but no finished plan. Solution? Progress over perfection. A business plan is a living document that you can revise. Get the basics down, take action, and adjust as needed.

Pitfall #3: Ignoring the Numbers

Financial planning can feel overwhelming, but skipping the numbers is a rookie mistake. Without clear projections, you're flying blind. Solution? Embrace the numbers. This book will guide you through the process—even if spreadsheets aren't your thing—so you can monitor your cash flow and plan for sustainability.

Pitfall #4: The Overly Vague Vision

"I want to change the world" sounds noble, but how will you do it? Without a clear, specific vision, your plan lacks direction. Solution? Get specific. Define who your business serves, what problem it solves, and how it creates value.

Pitfall #5: The "One Size Fits All" Approach

Copy-pasting another company's business plan won't work for yours. Every business is unique, and your strategy should reflect your goals and audience. Solution? Tailor your plan to your business's strengths and vision. Learn from others, but make it your own.

Pitfall #6: Forgetting to Plan for Risks

Optimism is great, but failing to plan for challenges is a mistake. Market shifts, supply issues, and unexpected events happen. Solution? Plan for risks. Include contingency strategies in your plan to help you pivot smoothly when the unexpected arises.

Pitfall #7: Setting Unrealistic Goals

Overly ambitious goals can lead to burnout and frustration. Solution? Set SMART goals—Specific, Measurable, Achievable, Relevant, and Time-bound. Ambition is essential, but realistic milestones will keep you motivated and on track.

Pitfall #8: Neglecting Your Audience

Getting too caught up in your vision can disconnect you from your audience. Solution? Put your customers at the center of everything. Understand their needs and make sure your business plan reflects how you'll serve them effectively.

Pitfall #9: Not Leaving Room for Flexibility

Plans that are too rigid can collapse under unexpected changes. Solution? Build flexibility into your strategy. Be prepared to pivot and adapt as markets shift, technology evolves, and new competitors emerge.

Pitfall #10: Thinking the Plan is One and Done

A business plan isn't a one-time exercise. Solution? Treat your plan as a living document that evolves with your business. Revisit it regularly, make adjustments, and use it to steer your business through every stage of growth.

The Mindset of an Entrepreneur: Thinking Like a Boss (Even When You Don't Feel Like One)

Building a business requires more than just a plan—it demands a boss-level mindset. Some days you'll feel like you're on top of the world; other days, you'll question everything. The secret to success lies in how you think, react, and stay resilient through it all. This section is about adopting the mindset of a leader—one that keeps you moving forward, even when the path feels uncertain.

Entrepreneurship is filled with highs and lows. It requires more than just solving problems—it's about embracing them as part of the journey. Thinking like a boss means staying calm, making decisions under pressure, and showing up consistently, even when you're tired, overwhelmed, or unsure of the next step.

Confidence Is a Choice, Not a Feeling

Every entrepreneur faces self-doubt. The key is learning to make decisions confidently, even when doubt creeps in. Confidence isn't about having all the answers—it's about trusting that you'll figure them out along the way. Successful entrepreneurs embrace the unknown and make strategic moves, knowing that mistakes are part of growth.

Resilience in the Face of Setbacks

Failures are inevitable, but resilience separates the dreamers from the doers. You won't succeed by avoiding obstacles—you'll succeed by learning from them. This mindset keeps you moving forward when things go wrong, helping you pivot, adapt, and find new opportunities in setbacks.

Taking Responsibility for Your Success

Entrepreneurs think like CEOs from day one. That means taking ownership of wins and losses alike. A strong mindset allows you to focus on solutions instead of excuses. When you act like the leader of your venture, you create a foundation of accountability and control, empowering you to shape your business with intention.

Progress Over Perfection

Waiting for the perfect moment or the perfect product is a trap. The entrepreneurial mindset is all about taking action now. Small, consistent steps will always beat waiting for perfection. A business evolves through iteration, and so will you.

Entrepreneurship is as much a mental game as it is a business challenge. With the right mindset—one grounded in confidence, resilience, accountability, and action—you'll be able to navigate the chaos of entrepreneurship and build something truly meaningful. This Abridged Edition gives you the strategies to stay focused, think like a leader, and act like a boss, even on the toughest days.

And if you're seeking inspiration from real-world examples of entrepreneurial resilience, explore the case studies in the companion Empire Blueprint Series. These volumes dive into the successes, setbacks, and strategies of entrepreneurs who've been through the trenches—and come out on top.

With the right mindset, the impossible becomes achievable, and your business journey transforms from a dream into a sustainable reality. Let's keep moving forward—your empire awaits.

A Call to Action: Let's Stop Dreaming and Start Doing

Alright, future empire-builder, this is the moment where planning meets action. You've gathered the insights, learned from potential pitfalls, and adopted the mindset of a leader. But none of it matters unless you take the next step. It's time to move from dreamer to doer, roll up your sleeves, and start laying the foundation for your business empire.

Taking the leap can feel like standing on the edge of a cliff, but with the tools you've gained in these pages, you have a parachute: your business plan. Now it's time to jump, trust your strategy, and build something that lasts.

This Is Your Moment
Remember why you picked up this book in the first place. You have an idea that won't let go and a vision that deserves to see the light of day. This is your chance to move beyond brainstorming and bring your idea to life. Your business plan isn't just a document—it's the first step toward making your dream a reality.

Take That First Step—Right Now
Waiting for the perfect moment? It doesn't exist. Success comes from starting where you are, with what you have. Whether your next move is to write down your vision, research your audience, or sketch out financial projections—just start. Action creates momentum, and momentum builds success.

Your Empire Awaits
The road ahead won't be smooth. There will be bumps, pivots, and moments of doubt. But with every small step forward, you'll be laying the bricks of your empire. The tools and strategies in this book equip you to face challenges head-on and keep moving forward.

If you want to dive deeper into real-world examples of entrepreneurs who've taken the leap and built successful ventures, explore the Empire Blueprint Series: Case Studies for Business Success. These companion volumes capture the stories, lessons, and strategies of leaders who've navigated the same journey you're on.

What Are You Waiting For?

The world is full of great ideas that never materialized. Don't let yours be one of them. This is your call to action. Whether you're launching, refining, or scaling your business, the only thing standing between you and success is taking the next step.

So, grab your tools, revisit your business plan, and start building. Your empire is waiting, and I can't wait to see the amazing things you create.

Let's do this!

PART ONE

Breaking Ground: Blueprinting Your Empire from the Ground Up

Welcome to Part One: Breaking Ground, where your business journey begins—not with a single step, but with a blueprint and a bulldozer. Here, we'll dig deep into the bedrock of your business vision, sift through the sands to find market needs, spy on the competition with the finesse of a seasoned detective, set objectives with the precision of a Swiss watchmaker, and sketch out your business model with the creativity of a Parisian artist. Strap on your hard hat and let's start constructing your empire from the ground up—because even the tallest skyscrapers start with a solid foundation!

CHAPTER ONE

Vision Quest: Crafting Your Business Destiny

"A well-defined vision is the starting point for any successful marketing strategy. It gives your brand a voice and your actions a direction, ensuring every campaign resonates with your core mission."— PHILIP KOTLER, DISTINGUISHED PROFESSOR OF INTERNATIONAL MARKETING

Embark on the grandest adventure of all—defining the very soul of your future empire. Think of this chapter as your personal business crystal ball, helping you peer into the potential futures that await your daring venture. Crafting your business vision isn't just about setting goals; it's about dreaming big, pinning those dreams to the sky like stars, and using them to navigate the vast ocean of commerce.

What do you want to be when your business grows up? Whether it's the go-to guru of tech gadgets, the Starbucks of stationary, or the Disney of dog grooming, every mogul-to-be must start with a vision. This isn't just about scratching ideas on a napkin (although that's where some of the best ideas begin); it's about igniting a beacon that will light your way through thick and thin.

Aim to blend audacity with precision. Paint your vision with bold strokes but outline it with meticulous detail. Who are you serving? What void are you filling? How are you transforming lives? And crucially, how will your enterprise leave its mark on the world? Remember, a vision without action is just a daydream, but a vision with a strategy becomes a legacy. So let's set the compass of your entrepreneurial spirit, chart the course, and start the quest for a business destiny that not only achieves success but redefines it.

The Power of Vision: Why Every Empire Starts with a Dream

Every great empire, whether it spans across continents or is built within a single neighborhood, begins with something as simple—and as powerful—as a dream. Behind every iconic brand, revolutionary product, or transformative service lies a vision that ignited a fire in the hearts of its founders, driving them to push beyond the ordinary and into the extraordinary. But why is having a vision so critical to success? Why does every empire start with a dream?

At its essence, a business vision is more than a statement or a slogan. It's the North Star, guiding every decision, action, and strategy your business will ever make. It provides clarity in moments of confusion, purpose in times of doubt, and direction when the path ahead is unclear. Without a vision, a business is like a ship lost at sea—drifting aimlessly, subject to the whims of changing tides and the pressures of competition. A powerful vision, on the other hand, acts as a compass, keeping you anchored in your purpose while moving you toward your ultimate destination.

Take a moment to think about the most successful companies in the world. Apple didn't just sell computers; Steve Jobs had a vision that technology could change the world, that it could be beautifully designed, easy to use, and deeply integrated into our everyday lives. This wasn't merely a product goal—it was a transformative vision that changed the way people live and interact with technology. Similarly, Walt Disney didn't just create animated films. His vision was to build a magical world where people of all ages could escape reality, immerse themselves in fantasy, and where dreams would come true. Disney's empire, now spanning movies, theme parks, merchandise, and more, is rooted in that vision. It wasn't built overnight; it was shaped over decades by a relentless pursuit of a dream.

A vision is not just about making money or growing market share. It's about defining the soul of your business. It's about giving your company meaning beyond numbers on a balance sheet. Your vision becomes the foundation for the culture you build, the products or services you create, and the experiences you offer to customers. It becomes your reason for existence, and that reason is what inspires not only you but also your employees, customers, partners, and even your investors. A compelling vision connects people to something larger than themselves. It makes them feel that they are part of a meaningful journey—a journey with purpose, direction, and lasting impact.

But a vision is not just a lofty ideal that sits untouched on your company website. A true vision is living, breathing, and evolving—it is a driving force behind your daily actions and long-term decisions. In fact, it's often in moments of adversity that your vision shows its true power. When the road ahead becomes difficult and obstacles block your path, it is your vision that reminds you of why you started in the first place. It is your vision that fuels your perseverance when others might quit. It's the guiding principle that keeps you moving forward, even when the market shifts or unexpected challenges arise.

Moreover, a clear vision simplifies decision-making. In the fast-paced and ever-changing world of business, opportunities will come and go, some tempting and others distracting. Without a vision, it's easy to get sidetracked by short-term gains or pressured into decisions that don't align with your long-term goals. However, when you have a well-defined vision, every choice becomes clearer. You're not just chasing fleeting trends or immediate wins; you're building something enduring. A powerful vision acts as a filter, allowing you to discern what is essential from what is unnecessary, and what aligns with your purpose versus what pulls you off course.

The most successful leaders and entrepreneurs are those who have relentlessly pursued their vision with courage and conviction. Think of Elon Musk, whose vision for SpaceX was not merely to build rockets, but to enable the human race to become multi-planetary. This vision was audacious, seemingly impossible at the time, yet it propelled SpaceX to achieve breakthroughs that had never been done before. It's this kind of bold vision that changes industries, shapes cultures, and transforms the world. And while your own business may not be about interplanetary exploration, the principle remains the same: your vision must inspire you to reach beyond what currently exists, to create something that didn't seem possible until you dared to dream it.

So, what does this mean for you as a future business leader? How do you begin to craft a vision that will propel your business from idea to empire? First, you must recognize that this process goes far beyond simply brainstorming ideas. Your vision is not a collection of scattered thoughts or a wish list of what you hope your business will achieve. It's a deep, intentional exploration of what truly matters to you, what problems you are passionate about solving, and how your business can make a lasting difference. It's about identifying the unique mark you want to leave on the world and charting a course to make it happen.

In this section, we will explore how to harness the transformative power of your vision. You'll discover how the world's most influential companies and leaders have turned their visions into empires by staying true to their dreams. You'll also learn how to craft your own business vision that not only inspires but also drives action and results. Remember, every empire starts with a dream, but it's your commitment to that dream that will define your legacy. Today, you have the opportunity to begin that journey, and it all starts with the vision you create. Let's take the first step together.

Defining Your Future: Crafting a Vision Statement with Purpose

Now that we've explored the power of vision, it's time to distill that dream into something tangible—a vision statement. This statement serves as the compass for your business, guiding your strategies, decisions, and actions toward a common purpose. It's the essence of where you're headed and why your business exists in the first place. Crafting a meaningful vision statement is more than an exercise in words; it's about capturing the heart and soul of your future empire in a way that resonates with everyone who encounters it.

A strong vision statement isn't just for show—it should be the North Star that guides your company, motivating your team, inspiring your customers, and driving your long-term strategies. To achieve this, you need to understand that a vision statement is more than a tagline or slogan. It's a declaration of your business's purpose and potential, offering a glimpse of the future you're building. It should capture your ambition, but it also needs to be realistic enough to act as a foundation for your business's growth.

1. Why Craft a Vision Statement?

A vision statement isn't just a requirement on a business plan checklist—it's the beacon that lights your way. It defines the future you aspire to create and sets the tone for every aspect of your business, from branding to decision-making. Without a clear vision, your business risks losing focus, drifting aimlessly as it chases opportunities that don't align with your core purpose. A well-crafted vision keeps you on course, ensuring that all your efforts are directed toward fulfilling a larger mission.

Your vision statement also plays a crucial role in inspiring your team. A business is more than its products, services, or profits—it's a collective of people united by a common goal. When your employees understand and connect with your vision, they are more likely to feel motivated, engaged, and committed to bringing that vision to life. It gives them a sense of ownership and purpose, knowing that they are part of something bigger than their daily tasks.

Moreover, your vision statement can serve as a powerful marketing tool. It communicates your business's core values to customers, partners, and investors. When done right, it differentiates you from competitors by showcasing your unique identity and the long-term impact you're aiming to create. Customers want to support companies that stand for something, and a compelling vision statement helps build loyalty and trust.

2. What Makes a Vision Statement Effective?

An effective vision statement is one that not only reflects your ambition but also clearly communicates your business's direction and purpose. It should be aspirational yet grounded in reality, inspiring yet actionable. Here are the key elements of a strong vision statement:

- **Clarity**: Your vision statement must be easy to understand. It should clearly articulate your business's ultimate goal and the future you're working to create. Avoid jargon or vague language that leaves room for misinterpretation. A clear, concise statement leaves no doubt about where you're headed.

- **Inspiration**: A great vision statement should inspire and motivate. It needs to ignite passion within you, your team, and your customers. When people read your vision statement, they should feel energized and excited about the possibilities.

- **Future-Oriented**: Your vision statement is all about the future. It should describe the world or the industry as it could be once your business has achieved its goals. Paint a picture of the impact you want to make and the legacy you hope to leave behind.

- **Memorable**: A vision statement should be something that sticks. It should be short enough to remember but powerful enough to evoke emotion. Think of it as your business's battle cry—something that resonates and can be repeated easily.

- **Aligned with Values**: Your vision should align with your core values and principles. It's not just about where you want to go but also about how you want to get there. A vision rooted in values ensures that as you grow, you do so in a way that reflects your beliefs and maintains the integrity of your brand.

3. How to Craft Your Vision Statement

Creating a vision statement can feel daunting, especially if you're in the early stages of your business. But remember, this statement doesn't have to be perfect—it simply needs to encapsulate your future aspirations. Follow these steps to craft a vision statement that resonates:

- **Start with Your Why**: Ask yourself why you started this business. What problem are you solving? What change do you want to see in the world?

The answer to these questions forms the foundation of your vision. Your "why" is the emotional core of your business, and it should shine through in your statement.

- **Visualize the Future**: Imagine your business five, ten, or even twenty years from now. What does it look like? What have you accomplished? Who are you serving, and how have you impacted their lives? This exercise helps you articulate the long-term goals you're working toward.

- **Focus on Impact**: Your vision isn't just about what your business will do; it's about the difference you'll make. Consider how your products or services will change people's lives, your industry, or the world. How will your business leave a lasting legacy?

- **Keep It Simple**: Don't overcomplicate your vision. A powerful vision statement is concise and direct. Aim for a sentence or two that captures the essence of your future business, leaving room for interpretation but offering clear guidance.

- **Test It**: Once you've drafted your vision statement, share it with trusted colleagues or mentors. Get feedback to ensure that your statement resonates and inspires. Make sure it's memorable, actionable, and forward-looking.

4. Examples of Compelling Vision Statements

To help you craft your own vision statement, let's look at a few companies that have defined their futures with clarity, ambition, and purpose:

- **Tesla**: *"To create the most compelling car company of the 21st century by driving the world's transition to electric vehicles."* Tesla's vision isn't just about selling electric cars; it's about leading a global movement toward sustainable energy. The company's bold vision statement captures both its ambition and its sense of responsibility to the planet.

- **Nike**: *"Bring inspiration and innovation to every athlete in the world."* Nike's vision statement is aspirational, simple, and inclusive. By defining "every athlete" as anyone with a body, Nike positions itself as a brand for all, while also emphasizing its commitment to innovation.

- **Amazon**: *"To be Earth's most customer-centric company, where customers can find and discover anything they might want to buy online."* Amazon's vision reflects its grand ambition to be the go-to place for online shopping, while also putting customer experience at the heart of its mission.

- **IKEA**: *"To create a better everyday life for the many people."* IKEA focuses on the impact it wants to have on its customers' daily lives. Its vision is simple yet powerful, showcasing its commitment to affordable, well-designed furniture that improves living standards.

- **Patagonia**: *"We're in business to save our home planet."* Patagonia's vision transcends profit, aligning its mission with environmental activism. The simplicity and urgency of this statement convey a powerful commitment to protecting the planet while still building a successful business.

5. Bringing Your Vision to Life

Your vision statement is only the beginning. Once you've crafted it, the real work begins—integrating it into every aspect of your business. Your vision should influence your branding, your products, your marketing, and most importantly, your culture. It's not just something to hang on the wall; it's the roadmap for the journey you and your team are embarking on.

As you define your future, remember that a strong vision is both inspirational and actionable. It's the spark that sets your business in motion, but it also provides the framework that will guide you as you grow. Keep your vision front and center, and let it be the driving force behind everything you do. In the next section, we'll explore how to take that vision and turn it into concrete goals, ensuring that your dreams don't remain dreams but instead become your business's destiny.

Mapping the Market: Identifying Your Niche and Target Audience

Now that you've crafted a powerful vision for your business, it's time to zoom in and map out the terrain you'll be navigating—the market. The key to transforming your vision into a thriving business is identifying your niche and target audience. In a world of endless competition and constantly shifting consumer demands, defining these elements will set you apart and sharpen your focus.

Your niche is the specific corner of the market your business will dominate. It's the gap in the industry that your product or service fills, the unique space where your brand shines. Finding this niche helps you avoid getting lost in a crowded marketplace, allowing you to target customers who are hungry for exactly what you offer. Think of your niche as your area of expertise, where you deliver unparalleled value and stand out from the competition.

Just as important as defining your niche is identifying your target audience. These are the people who will resonate with your brand and become your loyal customers. Knowing who they are, what they need, and how your business can transform their lives is crucial to your success. Understanding your target audience isn't just about knowing demographic data—it's about understanding their desires, pain points, and behaviors so you can tailor your offerings and marketing efforts directly to them.

In this section, we'll explore how to find your niche, define your target audience, and set the foundation for a business that connects deeply with the people you're meant to serve.

1. Finding Your Niche: Carving Out Your Corner of the Market

The world of business is vast, and while it can be tempting to appeal to as many people as possible, that approach often leads to dilution and confusion. Instead, your goal is to specialize—to carve out a corner of the market where you can excel and become a go-to authority. This is your niche, and it's critical to get it right.

To find your niche, start by reflecting on your strengths, passions, and the problems you're eager to solve. What unique skills or expertise do you bring to the table? What industry gaps or underserved markets exist that align with your

11

capabilities? A niche isn't about offering everything to everyone; it's about offering something specific to a defined group of people.

Let's look at some successful niche examples:

- **Warby Parker** disrupted the eyewear industry by providing affordable, stylish glasses and focusing on a young, fashion-conscious demographic.

- **Blue Apron** carved out a niche in the meal kit delivery space by targeting busy professionals who wanted healthy, home-cooked meals without the hassle of grocery shopping.

Each of these businesses identified a specific need or desire in the market that wasn't fully addressed by the competition, and they built their offerings around that insight.

Ask yourself the following questions to narrow down your niche:

- What unmet needs exist in my industry?

- How can I leverage my unique skills or knowledge to solve these problems?

- What trends or gaps in the market can I capitalize on?

- What specific group of people or businesses would benefit most from what I offer?

Once you've honed in on your niche, you can craft your product or service to meet the precise needs of your ideal market segment. The more specialized and focused you are, the more likely you'll connect with the people who truly need what you're offering.

2. Knowing Your Audience: The Key to Your Why

Identifying your niche is only half of the equation. To succeed, you need to know exactly who your target audience is—those people who will resonate with your message, fall in love with your brand, and become loyal customers.

While some businesses make the mistake of assuming that their product will appeal to everyone, the truth is that no product or service can truly satisfy everyone's needs. Attempting to do so will only dilute your marketing efforts and confuse your brand identity. Instead, you need to focus on a specific audience that aligns with your business vision and values.

Understanding your target audience involves more than just basic demographics like age, gender, or location. It requires a deeper dive into their behaviors, needs, desires, and pain points. You need to get inside the minds of your ideal customers and understand what motivates them to make purchasing decisions.

Here are some key elements to consider when identifying your target audience:

- **Demographics**: Basic demographic information such as age, gender, income level, education, occupation, and location can help you create a broad profile of your target market. For example, if you're launching a premium fitness brand, you might focus on affluent, health-conscious individuals in urban areas.

- **Psychographics**: This goes beyond demographics to look at your audience's interests, values, lifestyle, and personality traits. For example, if your business offers sustainable fashion, you might target environmentally conscious consumers who value ethical production methods.

- **Pain Points**: What problems or challenges does your target audience face, and how can your product or service solve those problems? By identifying their pain points, you can position your business as the solution they've been looking for.

- **Behaviors**: Understanding the buying behavior of your audience can help you tailor your marketing efforts. For instance, are they impulse buyers or do they research extensively before making a purchase? Do they prefer shopping online or in person?

3. Tools and Techniques for Market Research

Now that you know the importance of identifying your niche and audience, it's time to gather the data and insights necessary to make informed decisions. Market research is the process of collecting and analyzing information about your target market and industry to understand the landscape you're entering.

Here are some effective tools and techniques for market research:

- **Surveys and Questionnaires**: Conducting surveys is a great way to gather direct feedback from potential customers. Ask questions that will help you understand their needs, preferences, and challenges.

- **Competitor Analysis**: Study your competitors to learn what's working (and what isn't) in your industry. Look at their customer reviews, product offerings, marketing strategies, and pricing models. Identify gaps where your business can excel.

- **Social Media Listening**: Pay attention to what your target audience is saying on social media. Platforms like Twitter, Facebook, and Instagram can provide insights into customer preferences, pain points, and emerging trends.

- **Focus Groups**: Bringing together a group of potential customers to discuss your product or service can offer valuable qualitative insights. You can learn what resonates with your audience and how you can refine your offerings.

- **Keyword Research**: Use tools like Google Trends or keyword planners to see what terms your target audience is searching for. This will give you a glimpse into their needs and interests, helping you shape your marketing strategy.

4. Building Customer Personas: Bringing Your Audience to Life

Once you've gathered enough data, it's time to create customer personas. These are fictional characters that represent segments of your target audience. By building detailed profiles of your ideal customers, you can better tailor your marketing messages, products, and services to meet their needs.

Each customer persona should include:

- Name, age, and occupation
- Interests, hobbies, and values
- Pain points and challenges
- Buying behavior and preferred communication channels

For example, if you're launching a meal prep service, you might create a persona like this:

Persona 1: Sarah, the Busy Professional

- Age: 35

- Occupation: Marketing Executive

- Pain Points: Struggles to find time to cook healthy meals while balancing work and family life

- Interests: Fitness, clean eating, wellness trends

- Buying Behavior: Prefers subscription-based services and convenience, often makes purchases through mobile apps

Having these personas in hand allows you to craft personalized marketing messages that speak directly to each segment of your audience. It also helps you fine-tune your offerings to better solve their problems and meet their needs.

5. Aligning Your Niche and Audience with Your Vision

Now that you've identified your niche and target audience, it's essential to ensure that they align with your overall business vision. Your vision is the big-picture future you're working toward, and your niche and audience are the stepping stones to getting there.

Ask yourself:

- Does my niche align with the goals and values outlined in my vision statement?

- Am I solving a problem or meeting a need for my target audience that reflects the impact I want to make?

- How does my product or service enhance the lives of the people I aim to serve?

By ensuring that your niche, audience, and vision are in harmony, you create a cohesive, purpose-driven business that resonates deeply with your customers and sets you up for long-term success.

6. Moving Forward: Building Strategy Around Your Audience

With a well-defined niche and a clear understanding of your target audience, you're now equipped to start building a business that truly serves the people who need it most. In the next section, we'll explore how to translate these insights into bold, actionable goals that will drive your business forward. Remember, knowing who you're serving and how you're filling a gap in the market is the foundation of any successful venture. Now, it's time to build upon that foundation and turn your vision into reality.

Setting Audacious Goals: Turning Big Dreams into Tangible Milestones

Now that you've defined your vision, mapped your market, and pinpointed your niche and target audience, it's time to take the next critical step: setting audacious goals that will guide you on your journey. Goals are the bridge between dreams and reality, transforming your lofty aspirations into actionable steps. They serve as your roadmap, marking the path from where you are now to where you ultimately want to be.

But not just any goals will do. To build a business empire, you need goals that stretch you, challenge you, and push your business beyond its comfort zone. These are *audacious goals*—big, bold, and inspiring targets that propel your business forward while keeping you aligned with your vision.

In this section, we'll explore how to set these high-reaching goals and break them down into tangible, achievable milestones. By doing so, you'll create a clear action plan that ensures your dreams don't stay in the realm of imagination but become the foundation of your business success.

1. Why Audacious Goals Matter

Setting audacious goals is about thinking big—so big, in fact, that the very thought of achieving them is both exciting and a little terrifying. These goals aren't just about incremental growth; they are about transformational change. They reflect the true scope of your vision and give you something substantial to work toward.

Why aim so high? Because audacious goals force you to rethink what's possible. They inspire creativity, innovation, and perseverance. When you set a goal that seems just out of reach, you're more likely to think outside the box, push past obstacles, and make breakthroughs that would have been impossible if you only aimed for small, safe targets.

Consider some of the most successful entrepreneurs in history—people like Elon Musk, Oprah Winfrey, and Jeff Bezos. They didn't achieve their level of success by setting modest goals. They envisioned creating global empires, transforming entire industries, and redefining what's possible in technology, entertainment, and commerce. Their audacious goals gave them the drive to keep pushing forward, even when the odds seemed stacked against them.

But big dreams alone aren't enough. To reach them, you need to break those ambitious goals down into manageable, actionable milestones. This allows you to maintain focus, track progress, and celebrate small wins along the way.

2. Crafting SMART Audacious Goals

While audacious goals are meant to be bold, they also need structure. This is where the SMART goal framework comes into play. SMART stands for:

- **Specific**: Your goal should be clear and unambiguous. What exactly do you want to achieve?

- **Measurable**: You need to track your progress. How will you know when you've achieved your goal?

- **Achievable**: While your goal should stretch your abilities, it should still be realistic. Can you reach this goal with the resources available?

- **Relevant**: Your goal should align with your broader business vision and values. Does this goal push your business in the right direction?

- **Time-bound**: Set a deadline for achieving your goal. When do you plan to accomplish it?

Let's look at an example of an audacious yet SMART goal:

- **Audacious Goal**: "Within the next five years, my business will become the leading provider of eco-friendly home products in North America, with a customer base of over 500,000 loyal buyers."

This goal is specific (targeting eco-friendly home products), measurable (500,000 loyal customers), achievable (assuming a well-crafted strategy), relevant (aligned with the vision of being a market leader), and time-bound (within five years).

By setting SMART parameters around your audacious goals, you create a structure that makes them less overwhelming and more achievable. It transforms the seemingly impossible into something you can actively work toward.

3. Breaking Big Goals into Tangible Milestones

Once you've established your audacious goals, the next step is to break them down into tangible milestones. Think of these as smaller, measurable objectives that serve as stepping stones toward your larger vision. Milestones provide clarity, making it easier to see the progress you're making, and they keep you motivated by giving you a sense of accomplishment along the way.

Let's return to our example goal—becoming the leading provider of eco-friendly home products in North America with 500,000 loyal buyers. How can we break this down?

- **Year 1 Milestone**: Build brand recognition and secure 50,000 customers by launching an aggressive digital marketing campaign and securing partnerships with eco-conscious influencers.

- **Year 2 Milestone**: Expand product lines by introducing five new sustainable products based on customer feedback and market research. Reach 100,000 customers.

- **Year 3 Milestone**: Open a distribution center to streamline fulfillment and reduce shipping costs. Reach 200,000 customers by expanding into international markets.

- **Year 4 Milestone**: Secure key retail partnerships and expand your brand presence in brick-and-mortar stores across the United States. Grow your customer base to 350,000.

- **Year 5 Milestone**: Achieve market leadership in North America with 500,000 loyal buyers, driven by both e-commerce and retail sales.

By breaking the larger goal into annual milestones, you can create a clear path forward. These smaller objectives make the larger goal seem more manageable, and they help you stay focused and organized.

4. Adapting and Adjusting Along the Way

One of the most important things to remember when setting audacious goals is that the journey will rarely be linear. Along the way, you'll face unforeseen challenges, shifts in the market, and perhaps even changes in your business vision. That's why it's crucial to remain flexible and adaptable.

As you hit each milestone, take the time to evaluate your progress. Are you on track to achieve your larger goal? Have any new opportunities or challenges emerged that require a shift in strategy? By regularly assessing your progress, you can make informed adjustments that keep you moving toward your goal without losing momentum.

It's also important to be patient with yourself. Audacious goals, by their very nature, take time to achieve. There may be periods where progress feels slow, but remember that every step forward is a step closer to realizing your dream.

5. Celebrating Small Wins and Staying Motivated

Reaching an audacious goal is an incredible accomplishment, but it's the small wins along the way that will keep you motivated and engaged. Each time you hit a milestone, take the time to celebrate and acknowledge the hard work that got you there.

Celebrating small wins helps maintain morale, keeps your team energized, and reinforces a culture of achievement. Whether it's hitting a revenue target, launching a new product, or reaching a certain number of customers, each win is a testament to the progress you're making toward your big dream.

Staying motivated during the pursuit of audacious goals is key. Surround yourself with people who believe in your vision, maintain a positive mindset, and stay focused on the bigger picture, even when the road gets tough.

6. Turning Goals into a Legacy

Audacious goals don't just lead to success—they lead to lasting impact. When you set big, bold goals and achieve them, you're not just building a business; you're creating a legacy. You're setting a new standard in your industry, improving the lives of your customers, and possibly even changing the world in your own unique way.

As you continue to set goals for your business, always keep your vision in mind. How do your goals align with the legacy you want to leave behind? How will your business continue to grow and evolve once you've achieved these major milestones? By thinking long-term and always aligning your goals with your vision, you ensure that your business doesn't just thrive—it endures.

Vision Meets Strategy: Crafting a Roadmap to Success

Now that you've defined a compelling vision, identified your niche, mapped out your audience, and set audacious goals, it's time to bring it all together into a cohesive, actionable strategy. This final step is where vision meets strategy—the point where your dream evolves from an inspiring idea into a concrete plan. A vision without strategy is little more than a daydream, but when paired with a clear roadmap, it becomes a powerful force driving you toward success.

A well-crafted strategy acts as the blueprint for building your business empire. It guides every decision, from product development to marketing campaigns, ensuring that each action you take moves you closer to your vision. The key to building a successful strategy is aligning your long-term vision with short-term actions. This means creating a roadmap that's detailed enough to guide your daily activities while flexible enough to adapt as your business grows and the market evolves.

In this section, we'll explore how to craft a strategy that turns your ambitious goals into a step-by-step plan for success. You'll learn how to prioritize initiatives, allocate resources, and measure progress to ensure that every move you make is intentional and effective.

1. Turning Vision into Strategy: The Art of Alignment

The first step in crafting a successful strategy is ensuring that everything you do aligns with your vision. Your vision is the big picture—the ultimate future you're working toward—while your strategy is the specific plan for how you'll get there. Every element of your strategy should support your long-term goals and reflect the core values outlined in your vision.

To achieve this, it's important to regularly revisit your vision and use it as a filter for decision-making. When faced with choices about product offerings, marketing approaches, or partnerships, ask yourself: *Does this move me closer to my vision?* If the answer is no, it's time to reassess and find an approach that better aligns with your overall direction.

Remember, a strategy isn't just a to-do list; it's an ongoing process that shapes every aspect of your business. It's about building a system where each department and action is working together harmoniously to achieve a common purpose. When your strategy is in sync with your vision, everything from your branding to your customer service will feel consistent, intentional, and on-brand.

2. Prioritizing Initiatives: Focusing on What Matters Most

With a bold vision in place and ambitious goals set, it can be tempting to tackle everything at once. However, the key to an effective strategy is prioritization. Not every goal or initiative needs to be pursued simultaneously. By focusing on what matters most, you can channel your resources and energy into the areas that will have the biggest impact on your business.

To prioritize your initiatives, start by identifying the activities that will move the needle the most. This often means focusing on the goals and actions that directly contribute to your revenue, market positioning, or customer growth. For example, if your goal is to reach 100,000 customers within two years, your top priority might be launching an aggressive marketing campaign and developing strategic partnerships to expand your customer base. Secondary goals, such as product diversification, may take a back seat until you've established a stronger foothold in the market.

It's also important to consider your current resources—both time and money—when prioritizing initiatives. What can you realistically achieve given your current team, budget, and timeframe? By narrowing your focus to a few high-impact initiatives, you can execute them more effectively and build momentum toward your larger goals.

3. Creating a Strategic Action Plan: From Vision to Daily Tasks

Once you've prioritized your initiatives, it's time to turn them into an actionable plan. This is where the big picture of your vision translates into specific, day-to-day activities. An action plan breaks your goals down into smaller, manageable tasks, ensuring that you make consistent progress toward your larger objectives.

Here's how to create a strategic action plan:

- **Break down your goals**: Start with your major goals and break them into smaller, achievable milestones. Each milestone should represent a significant step toward your overall goal.

- **Assign tasks**: For each milestone, assign specific tasks that need to be completed. Be as detailed as possible to ensure clarity and accountability.

- **Set deadlines**: Assign realistic deadlines for each task and milestone. These deadlines should reflect the urgency of the task and the resources available.

- **Allocate resources**: Determine who on your team will be responsible for each task, and allocate the necessary resources (budget, time, tools) to ensure successful execution.

- **Create a timeline**: Develop a visual timeline or calendar to map out when each task and milestone will be completed. This will help you stay organized and ensure that you're making steady progress.

By turning your strategy into a detailed action plan, you make it easier to stay focused, organized, and accountable. It's also a great way to keep your team aligned, ensuring that everyone is working toward the same goals with a clear understanding of their role in the process.

4. Measuring Progress and Adjusting Course

One of the most critical elements of a successful strategy is the ability to measure progress and adjust as needed. No strategy is set in stone. The business landscape is constantly evolving, and new challenges and opportunities will arise. That's why it's important to regularly assess your progress, track key performance indicators (KPIs), and make adjustments as necessary.

Set up regular checkpoints to review your progress against your goals and milestones. Are you on track to hit your targets? Are there areas where you're falling behind? These reviews will give you the data you need to make informed decisions and course-correct when needed.

When things aren't going as planned, don't be afraid to pivot. A strong strategy is flexible, allowing you to adapt to changes in the market, customer feedback, or unexpected challenges. At the same time, celebrate the milestones you achieve along the way. Recognizing progress, no matter how small, keeps you and your team motivated to keep pushing forward.

5. The Power of Consistency and Perseverance

Executing a long-term strategy takes time, patience, and perseverance. The road to success isn't always a straight line, and there will be moments of doubt or setbacks along the way. However, staying consistent and committed to your vision is what separates successful businesses from those that fall by the wayside.

Consistency doesn't mean never changing course—it means staying true to your vision while remaining flexible in your approach. Whether you're in the early stages of building your business or scaling to new heights, your strategy is what will keep you on track. Each action, each decision, and each milestone brings you one step closer to making your vision a reality.

In moments of challenge, remember why you started. Your vision is the fuel that drives your strategy, and your strategy is the engine that moves your business forward. Together, they create a powerful synergy that keeps you grounded in your purpose while propelling you toward new opportunities.

6. Vision Realized: Building a Legacy

As your strategy begins to take shape and you start hitting milestones, you'll see your vision come to life. Each goal achieved, each new customer won, and each market expanded is a testament to the power of combining vision with strategy. Ultimately, your success will be measured not only by profits and market share but by the legacy you leave behind.

A business that starts with a clear vision and follows through with a strategic plan has the potential to create lasting impact—whether that's transforming an industry, changing lives, or building a brand that stands the test of time.

As we wrap up this chapter, remember that your vision is the heart of your business, and your strategy is the roadmap that will guide you to success. Together, they create the blueprint for building an empire that not only achieves success but redefines it on your terms.

Now, let's move forward with confidence, crafting a strategy that turns your big dreams into reality, and setting the stage for your business to thrive and leave a lasting mark on the world.

Quick Tips and Recap

- **Define Your Vision**: Your vision is the guiding light of your business. It should be bold, inspiring, and aligned with your long-term goals.

- **Craft a Compelling Vision Statement**: Make it clear, concise, and purpose-driven. Your vision statement should inspire and serve as a roadmap for your future.

- **Identify Your Niche**: Focus on a specific area where your business can excel. This helps you stand out in a crowded market and connect deeply with your target audience.

- **Know Your Target Audience**: Understand who your customers are, what their pain points are, and how your product or service can solve their problems.

- **Set Audacious Goals**: Aim big. Audacious goals push you to innovate and create breakthroughs. Break them down into smaller milestones for steady progress.

- **Create a Strategic Action Plan**: Develop a detailed plan that turns your vision into actionable steps. Prioritize tasks, assign responsibilities, and set deadlines.

- **Measure Progress Regularly**: Track key performance indicators (KPIs) and adjust your strategy as necessary. Stay flexible and adapt to new challenges and opportunities.

- **Stay Consistent and Committed**: Success takes time. Stay true to your vision, follow through on your strategy, and persevere even when things get tough.

- **Celebrate Wins Along the Way**: Recognize and reward progress, no matter how small, to maintain momentum and motivation.

- **Vision + Strategy = Success**: Together, a compelling vision and a well-executed strategy will drive your business to success and help you build a lasting legacy.

This section provides a quick overview of key takeaways from the chapter, offering a practical summary for readers to reference as they move forward in crafting their business vision and strategy.

CHAPTER TWO

Unmet Needs: Tapping Into the Market's Desires

"Successful marketing is about identifying those unmet needs that people don't even know they have yet and finding innovative ways to meet them. When you truly understand your audience, you can create solutions that surprise and delight."— GARY VAYNERCHUK, CEO OF VAYNERMEDIA

Welcome to the treasure hunt of the business world—identifying unmet needs in the market. Think of it as discovering hidden gems in an overgrown jungle, except instead of machetes and maps, you're armed with market research and consumer insights. This chapter is your guide to uncovering what your future customers are silently screaming for but haven't yet found on the shelves.

Diving into the depths of consumer desire isn't for the faint of heart. It requires the curiosity of a cat and the insight of a sage. You'll need to listen—not just to what people say, but to what they don't. It's about reading between the lines of casual conversations, extracting insights from complaints, and spotting patterns where others see chaos.

Imagine yourself as a business detective, piecing together clues that lead to the holy grail of opportunities: a need so glaring that once you see it, it seems obvious. But there's a twist! Just when you think you've cracked the case, you'll need to ask, "Can I fulfill this need better than anyone else?" This isn't just about finding gaps; it's about fitting perfectly into them, like the missing piece of a puzzle that customers have been trying to solve.

So, gear up, get out your magnifying glass, and prepare to delve into the psyche of the market. Your mission is to emerge not just with observations but with a map that leads to untapped opportunities, guiding your business to be the answer to questions that haven't even been asked yet. Let's decode the whispers of the market and turn them into your business's battle cry.

Listening to the Market: The Art of Detecting Silent Demand

Now that you've defined a compelling vision, identified your niche, mapped out your audience, and set audacious goals, it's time to bring it all together into a cohesive, actionable strategy. This final step is where vision meets strategy—the point where your dream evolves from an inspiring idea into a concrete plan. A vision without strategy is little more than a daydream, but when paired with a clear roadmap, it becomes a powerful force driving you toward success.

In today's fast-paced business landscape, where every market seems saturated, the ability to detect and respond to unmet needs is a superpower. However, consumers don't always articulate their desires clearly. Often, the most significant opportunities lie in what people *aren't* saying. They're hidden in offhand comments, subtle frustrations, or routine complaints that others overlook. This is where the art of detecting silent demand comes into play.

To become an expert at identifying unmet needs, you need to sharpen your listening skills—not just in the literal sense but in how you interpret and analyze the information around you. Listening to the market isn't just about paying attention to surveys or reviews; it's about reading between the lines, understanding emotions, and interpreting behaviors. This section will teach you how to listen to the market with an open mind, attuned to the signals that reveal silent, unspoken demands.

1. The Power of Active Listening

The first step in uncovering unmet needs is mastering the art of active listening. This goes beyond simply hearing what your customers are saying. Active listening requires you to engage with the feedback, interpret underlying emotions, and pick up on subtle cues. It's about understanding the context in which customers use your products, the pain points they experience, and how they express their frustrations or desires.

Imagine you're listening to a customer complain about how long it takes to assemble a product. The obvious feedback is that the assembly process is time-consuming, but what they're *really* saying might be deeper. Perhaps they want a product that's easier to use or one that offers immediate results. The real unmet need could be simplicity, not just a faster assembly. Detecting these subtle demands requires you to peel back the layers of what's being said to discover the core problem.

2. Decoding Consumer Behavior

Consumers often reveal their needs through their actions, even if they don't say it explicitly. Behavior patterns—whether in purchasing decisions, online reviews, or how they engage with your content—can be a goldmine of insights. For instance, if you notice customers consistently using a product in a way that's different from its intended purpose, that might indicate a gap in the market. They're telling you, through their actions, that there's a need for a product or feature that doesn't yet exist.

Social media platforms, customer support interactions, and even website analytics are excellent places to observe consumer behavior. Look for patterns in the way customers talk about your products, how they use them, and where they encounter obstacles. These patterns often point to needs that aren't being met by your current offerings—or by your competitors.

3. Reading Between the Lines

Sometimes the loudest message comes from what *isn't* being said. Consumers often don't know how to articulate their unmet needs because they haven't fully recognized them themselves. That's why it's critical to pay attention to the gaps in conversation—the questions they're not asking, the features they don't mention, or the frustrations they subtly hint at but never fully express.

Take, for example, a customer who consistently buys multiple products to achieve a single goal. They may never explicitly say, "I wish there was one product that did all of this," but their purchasing behavior tells the story. Your job as a business detective is to read between the lines and recognize that there's a demand for a multi-functional product.

You can also glean insights from customer complaints. A single complaint might seem insignificant, but if you notice a recurring theme—such as a product being too expensive, hard to use, or lacking a key feature—it points to an unmet need. Listening closely to the frustrations customers share can lead you to opportunities to innovate and offer solutions they hadn't considered.

4. Harnessing Informal Feedback

While formal feedback like surveys and customer reviews is valuable, informal feedback can often provide the richest insights. This type of feedback comes from casual conversations, social media comments, and even complaints made in passing. These are the moments when customers are less guarded and more honest about their true experiences and needs.

For instance, conversations that happen organically on platforms like Twitter, Reddit, or even forums in your industry are often full of unfiltered opinions. They can reveal frustrations that formal reviews don't capture, simply because people are more candid in these informal settings. Learn to mine this informal feedback for insights and trends. What are people discussing? What do they wish they had? These conversations often hold the keys to unmet market demands.

5. Spotting Trends Before They Go Mainstream

One of the best ways to detect silent demand is by staying ahead of trends. While some trends explode onto the scene, others bubble up slowly, revealing unmet needs long before the mainstream catches on. By paying close attention to emerging trends in technology, culture, and consumer behavior, you can position yourself as a pioneer in meeting a market's desires before anyone else.

Watch how consumers adapt to new technology, what solutions they gravitate toward, and how cultural shifts influence their purchasing decisions. For example, in recent years, we've seen a growing demand for sustainable, eco-friendly products as consumers become more environmentally conscious. Companies that identified this shift early were able to tap into a massive unmet need, capturing the attention of environmentally-conscious consumers well before sustainability became a mainstream expectation.

Spotting trends requires constant observation, curiosity, and the ability to connect seemingly unrelated dots. It's about staying in tune with broader societal movements, technological advancements, and shifts in consumer behavior, and figuring out how they create new needs in your market.

6. The Business Detective's Mindset: Always Asking "What If?"

Detecting unmet needs is as much about mindset as it is about skill. You need to approach the market with curiosity, always asking, *"What if?"* What if there's a better way to solve this problem? What if consumers need something they don't even know they want yet? What if I could offer a solution that changes the game?

Adopting a business detective mindset means constantly looking for clues in everyday interactions. Whether you're chatting with a customer, reading a review, or scrolling through social media, you're on the lookout for hidden opportunities. The best business leaders are those who consistently ask the right questions and have a keen eye for spotting needs that others overlook.

By learning to listen to the market—both to what's said and unsaid—you'll gain the insights needed to uncover silent demand and position your business to meet those needs. The key is staying curious, open, and attuned to the subtle signals that point to untapped opportunities. In the next section, we'll explore how to turn these insights into actionable strategies through the power of data and market research.

Using Data to Reveal Desires: Mining Insights from Market Research

While listening to consumers and interpreting their behavior are crucial skills for uncovering unmet needs, data is the tool that brings clarity and precision to your insights. Market research allows you to take your understanding of the market to a deeper level by providing hard evidence about consumer behaviors, preferences, and pain points. With the right data, you can uncover patterns, validate assumptions, and identify new opportunities that might have otherwise remained hidden.

In this section, we'll explore how to use data effectively to mine insights, helping you tap into unmet market desires with accuracy and confidence. Whether you're using surveys, focus groups, or sophisticated analytics tools, the key to success lies in knowing how to collect, analyze, and interpret data to reveal what your customers truly want.

1. The Importance of Data-Driven Decision Making

In today's world, relying on gut feelings or anecdotal evidence isn't enough. With access to so much information, businesses that don't embrace data-driven decision-making are at a serious disadvantage. Using data allows you to cut through the noise and get an objective view of what's happening in your market. It helps you see trends, behaviors, and preferences that might not be immediately obvious and gives you the confidence to make strategic decisions based on facts rather than assumptions.

Market research provides you with insights that go beyond surface-level observations. It helps you understand what consumers are doing, why they're doing it, and how they feel about the products and services currently available to them. Armed with this information, you can better tailor your offerings to meet their unmet needs.

2. Types of Market Research: Quantitative vs. Qualitative Data

When it comes to market research, there are two primary types of data you'll be working with: quantitative and qualitative data.

- **Quantitative Data**: This type of data is all about numbers. It helps you measure behaviors, preferences, and trends in a way that can be easily analyzed and compared. Quantitative research answers questions like "How many people use this product?" or "What percentage of customers are dissatisfied with this feature?" Examples of quantitative data collection include surveys with multiple-choice questions, analytics from website traffic, and sales figures.

- **Qualitative Data**: Qualitative data provides deeper insights into the *why* behind consumer behavior. It explores motivations, emotions, and opinions, giving you a richer understanding of what drives decisions. While qualitative data is harder to measure than quantitative data, it often provides more context to the numbers. Examples of qualitative data collection include open-ended survey questions, interviews, focus groups, and customer feedback from social media or reviews.

Both types of data are valuable for uncovering unmet needs. Quantitative data helps you identify patterns and trends, while qualitative data reveals the underlying reasons for those behaviors. Together, they give you a full picture of what consumers want and why they aren't getting it from current market offerings.

3. Surveying Your Audience: Asking Smart Questions

Surveys are one of the most effective tools for collecting data about your target audience. They allow you to gather a large amount of information in a structured way, and when designed correctly, they can provide clear insights into consumer needs.

However, the key to a successful survey is asking the right questions. If your questions are too vague or poorly constructed, the data you gather will be incomplete or misleading. Here are a few tips for designing surveys that reveal unmet needs:

- **Be Specific**: Ask direct questions about your customers' pain points, desires, and behaviors. Instead of asking, "What do you think about our product?" ask, "What specific challenges do you face when using our product?"

- **Use a Mix of Open and Closed Questions**: While multiple-choice questions help quantify data, open-ended questions allow consumers to express their thoughts in their own words, revealing insights you might not have anticipated.

- **Focus on the Experience**: Instead of just asking for opinions, ask questions that dig into the user experience. For example, "How do you feel when you use this product?" or "What do you find most frustrating about the options currently available to you?"

- **Keep it Short and Focused**: Longer surveys often lead to lower response rates. Focus on the most important questions to keep your survey concise and easy to complete.

Once you've gathered responses, use quantitative data analysis tools to look for patterns and trends. Are there recurring complaints or suggestions? Does a significant percentage of respondents feel the same way about a particular feature or issue? These are indicators of unmet needs that could represent opportunities for your business.

4. Focus Groups and Interviews: Gaining Deeper Insights

While surveys provide a wide-reaching view of the market, focus groups and interviews allow you to dig deeper into consumer mindsets. These methods involve smaller groups of people and encourage open discussion, giving you richer, more nuanced insights into their needs and desires.

During focus groups, participants can discuss their experiences with a product or service in real-time, often revealing insights they wouldn't share in a survey. Focus groups also allow you to observe body language, tone, and group dynamics, giving you clues about how people truly feel about a product, even if they don't articulate it clearly.

Interviews, on the other hand, offer the opportunity to explore individual consumer perspectives in depth. Through one-on-one conversations, you can ask follow-up questions, dig deeper into pain points, and understand personal experiences in a way that broad surveys can't capture.

To make the most of focus groups and interviews, consider the following:

- **Prepare Open-Ended Questions**: Encourage participants to speak freely by asking questions like, "What frustrates you about current products in this category?" or "Can you describe your ideal experience with a product like this?"

- **Be Observant**: Pay attention to not just what people say, but how they say it. Hesitation, enthusiasm, or frustration in their tone can give you valuable clues.

- **Use Probes**: Ask follow-up questions when participants give vague answers. For example, if someone says, "It's hard to use," follow up with, "What specifically makes it difficult?"

These discussions can reveal deeper needs and desires that may not come out in structured surveys, helping you develop a more complete understanding of what your target audience truly wants.

5. Social Media Insights: Mining Unstructured Data

In today's digital age, people are constantly sharing their opinions and experiences online, whether through social media posts, product reviews, or online forums. This unstructured data—data that doesn't fit into a neat survey question—can be a goldmine for understanding unmet market needs.

Social media listening tools allow you to track mentions of your brand, products, or industry. By analyzing what people are saying in real-time, you can identify recurring themes, complaints, or desires that can lead to product improvements or new offerings.

For example, you might notice that customers on Twitter frequently mention a specific feature that's missing from products in your industry. This could be a signal that there's a widespread demand for something that's currently underdeveloped or unavailable. Similarly, reading through product reviews on platforms like Amazon can give you insights into what customers love, what they're disappointed by, and what they wish existed.

- **Look for Patterns**: Scan social media, reviews, and forums for recurring complaints, suggestions, or praises. These patterns often point to unmet needs.

- **Analyze Sentiment**: Tools like Hootsuite or Brandwatch allow you to analyze the sentiment behind mentions—whether people are talking about your industry in a positive or negative light—and give you clues about what's missing or needs improvement.

- **Join the Conversation**: Engage with your audience directly on social media or online forums. Ask questions, respond to feedback, and learn about their experiences. This informal feedback can often lead to powerful insights about unmet desires.

6. Putting Data to Work: Connecting the Dots

The ultimate goal of market research is to turn raw data into actionable insights. Once you've gathered your data, the next step is to connect the dots and extract the meaningful information that will guide your business decisions.

Here are a few steps to make the most of your data:

- **Identify Patterns and Themes**: Look for commonalities across different data sources. Are there repeated complaints, requests, or desires that show up in multiple places? These patterns often reveal significant unmet needs.

- **Prioritize Opportunities**: Not all unmet needs are created equal. Focus on the ones that align most closely with your vision, target audience, and business strengths. Determine which unmet needs present the biggest opportunities for growth or innovation.

- **Translate Insights into Action**: Take the unmet needs you've identified and start brainstorming how your business can address them. How can you refine your existing products or services to meet these needs? Are there new offerings you could develop that would better serve your target market?

By using data to reveal desires and mining insights from market research, you're not just guessing at what customers want—you're making informed decisions that position your business to meet real, unmet needs. In the next section, we'll explore how to take these insights and apply them strategically, finding gaps in competitive markets and positioning your business to fill them.

Finding the Gaps: Identifying Opportunities in Competitive Markets

In a crowded marketplace, where businesses are constantly vying for attention and customers seem to have endless options, it can feel like every need is already being met. However, even in competitive industries, gaps exist—sometimes in places no one is looking. Identifying these gaps is one of the most powerful ways to create opportunities for your business to stand out and dominate a particular niche.

Finding these opportunities requires a mix of observation, creativity, and strategic thinking. It's not just about what's missing—it's about where you can deliver something different or better than anyone else. In this section, we'll explore how to spot gaps in competitive markets and turn them into profitable opportunities that align with your business vision.

1. Understanding the Competitive Landscape

Before you can find gaps, you need a thorough understanding of the competitive landscape. This involves identifying your key competitors, analyzing their strengths and weaknesses, and understanding how they serve their customers. Competitor analysis is the foundation for uncovering untapped market potential.

Start by asking these questions:

- **Who are your main competitors?** Are they direct competitors offering similar products or services, or are they indirect competitors who satisfy the same customer need in a different way?

- **What do they excel at?** Identify what your competitors do well—whether it's pricing, customer service, innovation, or brand loyalty. This helps you understand where they are strong and where there might be an opening.

- **Where do they fall short?** Look for weaknesses or areas where competitors struggle. Are there consistent complaints about their product quality, user experience, or customer support? These gaps could represent opportunities for you to fill.

By analyzing your competitors, you can uncover where their blind spots or shortcomings leave room for a business like yours to step in and do things better.

2. Identifying Underserved Audiences

Another way to find gaps is by looking for underserved or overlooked customer segments. Even in competitive markets, businesses often focus on the same core group of consumers, leaving certain demographics or niches ignored or underappreciated.

Ask yourself:

- **Are there customer groups being overlooked?** Perhaps competitors focus on younger demographics, leaving older customers with fewer options. Or maybe they're targeting high-income earners, neglecting budget-conscious consumers.

- **What are their unmet needs?** What are these overlooked groups asking for that current market offerings don't provide? Identifying these needs can help you position your product or service as the perfect solution.

A great example of this strategy is how brands like Glossier have disrupted the beauty industry by catering specifically to younger, socially savvy consumers who value transparency and inclusivity. By focusing on a segment that was underserved by traditional beauty brands, they were able to carve out a powerful niche and build a loyal following.

3. Spotting Product and Service Gaps

Another approach to identifying gaps in competitive markets is by closely examining the products and services that are currently available. Even if the market seems crowded, there are often features, services, or entire product categories that are lacking.

Here's how to identify product or service gaps:

- **Feature Gaps**: Are there missing features that customers are asking for but competitors aren't delivering? For example, in the tech industry, early users of smartphones wanted longer battery life and better cameras—needs that weren't fully addressed until companies saw the opportunity and optimized their products.

- **Service Gaps**: Are competitors failing to deliver in areas like customer support, personalization, or convenience? Superior service, such as offering faster delivery, better user interfaces, or more personalized recommendations, can set you apart even if the core product is similar.

- **Innovation Gaps**: Many industries face stagnation when innovation slows down. By bringing fresh ideas, new technology, or unique business models to a tired market, you can find a way to differentiate. For example, Netflix wasn't the first company to rent out movies, but by innovating with a subscription model and streaming technology, they filled a gap that blockbuster video stores left wide open.

Look at what's currently available in your industry and ask yourself: *What's missing?* If consumers are left piecing together multiple products to meet their needs or are frequently complaining about limitations, there's a gap waiting to be filled.

4. Leveraging Customer Feedback to Uncover Gaps

Your own customers can be an invaluable source of insight when it comes to finding gaps in the market. The feedback they provide—whether through direct surveys, product reviews, or social media—can point you toward areas where your competitors are failing to meet expectations.

Start by listening closely to customer feedback, and look for:

- **Common Complaints**: Are customers consistently unhappy with a certain feature, product, or service in the industry? If so, this could signal an opportunity to introduce a solution that resolves these issues.

- **Requests for Customization**: If customers are asking for more customization, it means they feel existing options are too rigid. Offering more personalized services, flexible pricing plans, or customizable products can help you stand out in a market dominated by one-size-fits-all solutions.

- **Suggestions for New Features**: Sometimes customers will even tell you directly what they want. Pay attention to feature requests or suggestions in reviews, support tickets, and social media comments. These can often lead to new product innovations or service enhancements.

By staying close to your customers and actively seeking out feedback, you'll gain the insight you need to identify areas where competitors are falling short, giving you the chance to step in and fill that gap.

5. Exploring Emerging Trends and Technologies

One of the best ways to find gaps in competitive markets is by looking to the future. Emerging trends and new technologies often open up new opportunities that haven't yet been fully realized by established players. If you can identify a trend early and get ahead of the curve, you'll be in a prime position to fill gaps before your competitors catch on.

Start by tracking trends in:

- **Technology**: Are there new technologies emerging that could disrupt your industry? Think about how artificial intelligence, blockchain, or virtual reality could create new products, services, or experiences that no one else is offering.

- **Cultural Shifts**: Changes in societal values or consumer behavior can create gaps in existing markets. For example, as more consumers became concerned with sustainability, companies like Patagonia and Tesla seized the opportunity to fill the gap with eco-friendly products.

- **Regulatory Changes**: Changes in laws or regulations can also create opportunities. For instance, new regulations around privacy and data protection opened the door for companies specializing in cybersecurity and compliance services.

The key is to stay curious and remain adaptable. By keeping an eye on what's coming next, you can position your business as an innovator and tap into gaps that will soon become mainstream.

6. Differentiation: Fitting Into Gaps and Creating Your Own

Once you've identified potential gaps in the market, the next step is figuring out how to position your business to fill them. But it's not enough to simply step into a gap—you need to do it in a way that's compelling, unique, and aligned with your brand's strengths.

Here's how to differentiate yourself:

- **Offer a Superior Experience**: Whether it's through better customer service, more intuitive products, or a smoother user experience, delivering a superior experience is often the key to standing out in competitive markets.

- **Solve the Problem Better**: Even if a gap has been noticed by others, ask yourself how you can solve the problem *better* than anyone else. This could be through more efficient technology, a more user-friendly design, or a more affordable price point.

- **Build a Strong Brand Identity**: Sometimes, filling a gap is about more than the product—it's about the brand. Brands like Apple and Nike fill gaps not just because of the products they create but because they build strong, emotionally resonant brands that customers feel connected to. Focus on how your brand's identity can set you apart in a crowded market.

Remember, finding gaps isn't just about meeting a need—it's about doing it in a way that others can't or won't. The more effectively you differentiate yourself, the harder it will be for competitors to fill the same gap.

By strategically finding and filling gaps in competitive markets, you can position your business as a leader in innovation, service, or niche expertise. In the next section, we'll explore how to take these insights and use them to design customer-centric solutions that hit the mark with your audience.

Customer-Centric Innovation: Designing Solutions That Fit

Once you've identified gaps in the market and uncovered unmet needs, the next step is to design solutions that fit seamlessly into the lives of your customers. Customer-centric innovation is about putting the customer at the heart of your product or service development, ensuring that everything you create addresses their real pain points, desires, and behaviors. It's not just about creating something new; it's about creating something *better*—something that truly resonates with your target audience and improves their experience.

In this section, we'll explore how to apply customer-centric principles to your innovation process, ensuring that your solutions not only meet market demand but also deliver exceptional value that keeps customers coming back.

1. Understanding the Customer Journey

The foundation of customer-centric innovation lies in understanding your customers' journey—the full experience they have with your product or service, from discovery to purchase, to usage, and beyond. By mapping out this journey, you can identify key touchpoints where your business can step in and add value. It's not just about solving one problem; it's about designing a solution that fits naturally into every stage of the customer's interaction with your brand.

To get started, consider these steps:

- **Map the Entire Experience**: Break down the customer's journey into specific phases—awareness, consideration, purchase, usage, and post-purchase engagement. Understand what challenges or emotions they experience at each stage.

- **Identify Pain Points and Moments of Delight**: Where are customers facing friction in the current experience? What causes frustration, and what elements make the process enjoyable? These insights will guide your product development toward solutions that eliminate pain points and amplify moments of delight.

- **Focus on Simplicity and Convenience**: One of the most common desires for customers across industries is simplicity. Customers want solutions that are easy to understand, simple to use, and save them time or effort. Whether it's through intuitive design, seamless functionality, or streamlined services, simplifying the customer experience is often the key to creating a product that fits.

By understanding the entire customer journey, you can innovate in ways that enhance the overall experience, not just fix one part of it.

2. Empathy-Driven Design: Listening to the Customer

At the core of customer-centric innovation is empathy. To create solutions that fit, you need to truly understand your customers' feelings, motivations, and frustrations. This requires more than just gathering data—it's about putting yourself in the customer's shoes and designing with their needs at the forefront.

Here's how to apply empathy in your innovation process:

- **Engage in Direct Conversations**: Talking to your customers directly, whether through interviews, surveys, or focus groups, allows you to gather real insights. Ask open-ended questions to understand their experiences and pain points on a deeper level.

- **Observe Customer Behavior**: Sometimes, customers can't articulate exactly what they need, but their behavior reveals it. Watch how customers interact with your products, visit your stores, or use your website. Look for moments where they hesitate, struggle, or improvise— these are often areas ripe for innovation.

- **Co-Creation with Customers**: Invite your customers to be part of the innovation process. This could involve testing prototypes, providing feedback, or participating in beta programs. Co-creation ensures that the final product is aligned with their needs from the outset and empowers customers to feel invested in the product's success.

Empathy-driven design allows you to go beyond simply meeting a functional need and create solutions that truly resonate with customers on an emotional level.

3. Solving Real Problems, Not Hypothetical Ones

One of the biggest mistakes businesses make when innovating is designing solutions for hypothetical problems instead of real ones. It's easy to get caught up in exciting new technologies or trends, but if the solution doesn't directly address a significant pain point or desire, it won't stick. Customer-centric innovation requires that every solution you create is rooted in solving real, tangible problems that your customers are experiencing.

To ensure you're solving real problems:

- **Validate Assumptions with Data**: Before investing in new ideas, validate your assumptions through research and feedback. Are the problems you're addressing real and significant to your target audience? Use data from customer surveys, reviews, and behavior analytics to confirm that your innovation is focused on genuine needs.

- **Prioritize High-Impact Problems**: Focus on the problems that have the most significant impact on your customers' lives. Small, incremental improvements can be valuable, but breakthrough innovations often come from addressing a major pain point that no one else has solved effectively.

- **Eliminate Unnecessary Features**: Don't overcomplicate your product with features that don't address core needs. Every aspect of your solution should serve a purpose and make the customer's life easier or more enjoyable.

By focusing on real, high-impact problems, you'll ensure that your innovations are relevant, valuable, and much more likely to succeed in the market.

4. Iterative Testing: Fail Fast, Learn Faster

Creating customer-centric solutions isn't a one-time effort—it's an iterative process that involves prototyping, testing, gathering feedback, and refining your ideas. The faster you can get a working prototype in front of customers, the faster you'll learn whether it truly fits their needs.

Here's how to approach iterative prototyping:

- **Start with a Minimum Viable Product (MVP)**: Don't wait until your product is perfect to test it with customers. Develop a minimal version that addresses the core problem, and get it in front of real users as quickly as possible.

- **Gather Feedback Early and Often**: Once customers start using your MVP, gather feedback on what works, what doesn't, and what's missing. Use this feedback to guide further development, rather than relying solely on internal assumptions.

- **Embrace Failure as Part of the Process**: Not every idea will work, and that's okay. Customer-centric innovation is about learning what doesn't fit just as much as what does. Be willing to scrap features, pivot ideas, and make changes based on customer feedback. The faster you fail, the faster you'll find what truly works.

By adopting an iterative approach to innovation, you can continuously improve your solution based on real-world feedback, ensuring that the final product is truly customer-centric.

5. Personalization: Tailoring Solutions to Individual Needs

Today's customers expect personalized experiences. Whether through customized products, tailored recommendations, or flexible service options, offering personalization allows you to design solutions that feel unique and catered to each individual.

Here's how you can incorporate personalization into your innovation:

- **Offer Flexible Product Configurations**: Allow customers to tailor your product or service to fit their specific needs. This could include customizable features, add-ons, or personalized recommendations based on their preferences.

- **Leverage Data for Personalization**: Use data such as past purchases, browsing behavior, and preferences to create personalized experiences. This could mean offering personalized product suggestions, sending tailored promotions, or even customizing the customer's journey based on their behavior.

- **Focus on Personalized Support**: Customer-centric innovation doesn't stop at the product—ensure that your customer support is also personalized. Whether through chatbots that learn customer preferences or support teams trained to offer personalized solutions, creating a personalized support experience helps build long-term loyalty.

Personalization adds value to your product or service by ensuring that it fits seamlessly into each customer's unique life, increasing satisfaction and retention.

6. Designing for Future Needs: Staying Ahead of Expectations

While addressing current needs is essential, true customer-centric innovation also requires you to anticipate future needs. The best innovators think ahead, designing solutions that customers will need tomorrow—before they even realize it.

Here's how you can design for future needs:

- **Track Emerging Trends**: Keep an eye on industry trends, cultural shifts, and advancements in technology that might influence customer needs in the near future. Are there evolving behaviors or preferences that could create new gaps or desires?

- **Be Forward-Thinking in Product Design**: Design products that are adaptable, scalable, and ready to evolve as customer needs change. Future-proofing your innovation ensures that your solutions stay relevant in a rapidly changing market.

- **Incorporate Feedback Loops**: Continuously gather feedback even after launch. Listening to how customer needs evolve over time allows you to refine your offerings and stay ahead of competitors who might only be focused on present-day demands.

By innovating with the future in mind, you ensure that your business remains agile and ready to meet customers' evolving desires, keeping you at the forefront of your market.

Customer-centric innovation is about more than just creating products—it's about crafting solutions that fit perfectly into your customers' lives, addressing their real needs and anticipating future ones. In the next section, we'll explore how to validate these innovations before launching them on a broader scale, ensuring they hit the mark with your target audience.

Testing the Waters: Validating Your Idea Before Launch

After putting in the hard work to innovate and design solutions that address real customer needs, it's tempting to rush straight to market. However, even the most well-researched and thoughtfully designed product can fall short if it doesn't resonate with customers in the real world. That's where validation comes in—testing your idea with actual users before a full-scale launch. Validation helps ensure that your product is viable, desirable, and ready to succeed in the marketplace.

This final step is about gathering feedback, making adjustments, and fine-tuning your offering before committing resources to a large-scale rollout. In this section, we'll explore how to validate your idea effectively, ensuring that you're building something your customers genuinely want and will embrace.

1. Why Validation is Critical

The goal of validation is to confirm that your product or service solves the problem you set out to address and does so in a way that customers appreciate and find valuable. Skipping this step or jumping in too early can lead to costly mistakes, wasted resources, and failed launches. Validation helps you avoid these pitfalls by giving you the chance to:

- **Test assumptions**: Even with the best market research, assumptions about customer needs, behaviors, and preferences can sometimes be off. Validation allows you to test these assumptions in the real world.

- **Identify weak points**: Early feedback can reveal potential flaws in your product, such as confusing features, usability issues, or missing functionality.

- **Optimize before scaling**: It's far easier and cheaper to make adjustments before mass production, a major marketing campaign, or a full product launch. Validation gives you the insights you need to improve and fine-tune your solution.

By validating your idea, you reduce risk and increase the likelihood of a successful product launch that meets customer expectations.

2. Building a Minimum Viable Product (MVP)

One of the most effective ways to validate your idea is by building a Minimum Viable Product (MVP). An MVP is a simplified version of your product that includes only the core features necessary to solve the problem you're addressing. The goal of an MVP is to test your idea with real customers, gather feedback, and iterate based on their responses—all while minimizing time and cost investment.

Here's how to build and use an MVP:

- **Focus on Core Functionality**: Strip your product down to the essentials—what's the minimum version of your solution that solves the core problem? Don't worry about bells and whistles at this stage. Focus on delivering value with the least complexity.

- **Launch with a Small Group**: Release your MVP to a limited audience, such as early adopters or a segment of your target market. This helps you gather meaningful feedback without overexposing a potentially flawed product.

- **Gather Data**: Track how users interact with your MVP. Are they using the product as expected? Are there features they love or ignore? What feedback do they provide regarding usability, functionality, and overall experience?

The MVP process allows you to test your idea in the wild, gaining insights that will guide you toward an improved final product.

3. Pilot Programs and Beta Testing

Another valuable method for validating your product before a full launch is through pilot programs or beta testing. These approaches allow you to gather feedback from a small group of users under real-world conditions, providing insights into how your product performs and resonates with customers.

Here's how to execute a pilot program or beta test:

- **Select a Representative Audience**: Choose a group of users that closely aligns with your target audience. This ensures that the feedback you receive reflects the experiences and expectations of the people you ultimately want to serve.

- **Set Clear Expectations**: Let participants know that they are part of a pilot or beta program and that their feedback is critical to improving the final product. Encourage honest, constructive feedback and explain how their input will be used.

- **Monitor and Adjust**: Throughout the pilot or beta testing phase, actively monitor usage, track any issues that arise, and gather feedback at key intervals. Use this information to make iterative improvements before the broader launch.

Beta testing is particularly useful for identifying hidden issues or usability challenges that may not be apparent until the product is used in real-world environments.

4. Collecting and Analyzing Customer Feedback

The key to a successful validation process is gathering actionable feedback from your target audience. Feedback helps you uncover potential improvements, refine your product, and confirm whether your solution truly meets customer needs. There are several ways to collect and analyze customer feedback during validation:

- **Surveys**: After customers use your MVP or participate in a beta test, send out surveys to gather structured feedback on their experience. Use a mix of closed-ended questions (such as satisfaction ratings) and open-ended questions (allowing for more in-depth responses).

- **Interviews**: Conduct one-on-one interviews with select participants to gain deeper insights into their experience. Ask follow-up questions to understand how they felt using your product and whether it solved their problem effectively.

- **Usage Analytics**: Use data analytics tools to track how customers interact with your product. Where do they spend the most time? Which features are being used or ignored? Where do they encounter friction? Analytics provide valuable insights that aren't always expressed through direct feedback.

By analyzing both qualitative feedback and quantitative data, you can develop a comprehensive understanding of how your product is performing and where adjustments are needed.

5. Iterating Based on Feedback

Once you've collected feedback from your MVP, pilot program, or beta test, it's time to act on that information. Iterating based on feedback is essential for improving your product and ensuring it aligns with customer expectations.

Here's how to iterate effectively:

- **Prioritize Key Findings**: Review all the feedback you've gathered and identify the most critical areas for improvement. Focus first on addressing the issues that have the biggest impact on the customer experience or the product's functionality.

- **Make Incremental Changes**: Instead of overhauling the product based on initial feedback, focus on making incremental improvements. This allows you to test each change and ensure it's moving the product in the right direction.

- **Test Again**: After making adjustments, test the updated version of your product with the same group or a new set of users. This iterative process ensures continuous improvement and refinement before the full launch.

By embracing feedback and continually improving your product, you'll be better positioned to launch a solution that resonates with your audience and stands out in the market.

6. Scaling Up for Full Launch

Once your idea has been validated through MVPs, pilot programs, or beta testing, and you've iterated based on feedback, it's time to prepare for a full-scale launch. At this stage, you've refined your product and ensured that it meets customer needs, reducing the risk of failure during the broader rollout.

Here's how to scale up for launch:

- **Fine-Tune Your Marketing Strategy**: Based on the insights gathered during validation, craft a marketing message that speaks directly to the desires and pain points of your target audience. Highlight the ways your product solves the problems identified during research.

- **Prepare for Demand**: Ensure that your supply chain, production, and fulfillment processes are ready to handle a full-scale launch. If your validation process has generated strong interest, be prepared to scale quickly to meet demand.

- **Launch Strategically**: Consider launching in phases, starting with a soft launch to a specific region or audience before expanding. This allows you to monitor performance and make any last-minute adjustments before going all-in.

With validation completed and your strategy in place, you can launch your product with confidence, knowing it has been tested, refined, and built to meet real market needs.

By validating your idea before launch, you can significantly reduce risks and ensure that your product resonates with your target audience. Testing the waters with MVPs, pilot programs, and beta testing helps you gather invaluable feedback and make necessary adjustments before fully committing to the market. With a well-validated product in hand, you'll be better positioned to achieve a successful launch and turn your innovative ideas into a thriving business.

Quick Tips and Recap

- **Listen to the Market**: Pay attention to what customers aren't saying directly—read between the lines to identify silent demands and hidden needs.

- **Use Data Wisely**: Leverage both quantitative and qualitative data to reveal customer desires and market trends. Combine surveys, focus groups, and analytics to gain deeper insights.

- **Spot the Gaps**: Analyze competitors and identify underserved customer segments or missing features. Look for opportunities where competitors fall short.

- **Design for the Customer**: Focus on creating solutions that address real customer pain points. Use empathy-driven design to ensure your product fits seamlessly into their lives.

- **Test Your Ideas Early**: Build a Minimum Viable Product (MVP) or run beta tests to validate your product before a full-scale launch. Gather feedback and iterate based on customer insights.

- **Make Data-Driven Adjustments**: Use feedback and analytics to improve your product. Continuously refine and test to ensure you're addressing real needs effectively.

- **Prepare for Scale**: Once validated, plan your full launch strategically. Fine-tune your marketing message and ensure operational readiness for demand.

This summary helps you remember the core strategies for uncovering market needs, designing customer-centric solutions, and validating them effectively before launch.

CHAPTER THREE

Battle Ready: Analyzing Your Competitors

"Analyzing your competitors isn't about copying their moves, but about learning their strengths and weaknesses to find your unique edge. Success comes from seeing what they miss and delivering what the market truly wants." — SIMON SINEK, AUTHOR AND MOTIVATIONAL SPEAKER

Time to sharpen your swords and put on your armor—because in the world of business, knowing your competitors is like preparing for battle. Except, instead of a sword fight, you're up against marketing campaigns, pricing strategies, and the occasional passive-aggressive tweet. In this chapter, we'll equip you with the tools to become a master tactician, analyzing your competitors like a seasoned general surveying the battlefield.

First things first, remember that your competitors aren't villains in your story— they're more like sparring partners who help you get stronger. But that doesn't mean you shouldn't know their every move! This is where you channel your inner

Sherlock Holmes, uncovering their strengths, weaknesses, opportunities, and threats (cue the SWOT analysis). What are they doing better than you? What are they missing? And, most importantly, how can you swoop in like a business ninja and fill those gaps?

You'll want to monitor their pricing, products, customer feedback, and even how they show up on social media (yes, it's totally fair to "spy" on their Instagram). The goal here isn't just to beat them but to learn from them. Every piece of data you gather is a new weapon in your competitive arsenal.

So, get your binoculars out, do your research, and start plotting your strategy. Because in the battle of business, the best way to win isn't just by fighting harder—it's by thinking smarter. Let the games begin!

Know Thy Enemy: Identifying Your Competitors

Before you can effectively compete in the marketplace, you need to understand exactly who you're up against. It's easy to assume that your competitors are just the businesses offering similar products or services, but competition comes in many forms. To craft a winning strategy, you must first identify your *real* competitors—those who are vying for the attention, dollars, and loyalty of your target customers. In this section, we'll break down the different types of competitors and how to spot them.

1. Direct Competitors: The Obvious Rivals

Direct competitors are the most straightforward to identify. These are businesses that offer products or services that are nearly identical to yours, serving the same target audience. If a potential customer is choosing between your business and another to solve the same problem, that other business is a direct competitor.

For example, if you own a coffee shop, other coffee shops in your area are your direct competitors. You're all competing for the same customers, offering a similar experience, and likely using similar ingredients. The key to understanding your direct competitors is analyzing how their product offering compares to yours—pricing, quality, customer experience, and brand image.

2. Indirect Competitors: The Overlooked Threats

Indirect competitors might not seem like direct threats because they offer different products or services, but they still target the same customer base and fulfill a similar need. This type of competition often sneaks up on businesses because it isn't immediately obvious.

For example, that same coffee shop might see a local bakery or a convenience store as an indirect competitor. They may not specialize in coffee, but they offer alternatives like prepackaged cold brews or morning pastries that fulfill the same customer need—getting breakfast on the go. Understanding your indirect competitors helps you see the bigger picture and avoid being blindsided by businesses that could pull your customers away.

3. Potential Competitors: Tomorrow's Challenges

As the market evolves, new competitors can emerge. Potential competitors are businesses that don't yet compete directly with you but could do so in the future. This includes startups in your industry, businesses that are expanding their offerings, or companies in adjacent industries looking to diversify.

Keeping an eye on potential competitors allows you to anticipate changes in the marketplace. For example, if you own a fitness studio, a new wellness app offering virtual workout classes might not seem like a direct threat today. However, as more consumers shift toward online fitness solutions, that app could become a serious competitor in the near future. By identifying these threats early, you can adapt your strategy to stay ahead.

4. Competitors You Didn't Expect: Industry Disruptors

Sometimes competition comes from unexpected places—industries or companies you wouldn't initially consider a threat. These are the disruptors, businesses that break the rules and change the way things are done in your industry. Disruptors often use innovative technology, new business models, or fresh ideas to shake up the status quo, and they can quickly gain traction with your customer base.

For example, Uber disrupted the taxi industry, Airbnb transformed hospitality, and Amazon revolutionized retail. These disruptors weren't initially viewed as competitors by traditional players, but they changed the landscape forever. To spot potential disruptors, stay informed about technological advancements, emerging startups, and shifts in consumer behavior. If a company is solving a problem in a new, innovative way, they could become your biggest competitor—even if they don't fit the traditional mold.

5. How to Spot Your Competitors

Now that you know the different types of competitors, how do you spot them? Here are a few strategies for identifying your competitors:

- **Google Search**: A simple Google search for products or services similar to yours will reveal a lot about who you're up against. Search for keywords your customers might use, and take note of the businesses that come up in the results.

- **Customer Feedback**: Your customers can often tell you who your competitors are. Pay attention to who they mention when comparing your product or service to others. Ask them directly, "What other businesses did you consider before choosing us?"

- **Industry Research**: Look at industry reports, trade publications, and market analysis to get an overview of key players in your space. These resources often highlight major competitors as well as up-and-coming companies.

- **Social Media Monitoring**: Competitors are often active on social media. Use tools like social media listening software or simple manual searches to see which brands are engaging with your target audience online. This can give you a sense of who's competing for attention.

- **Customer Journey Mapping**: Analyze the customer journey in your industry. What options do customers have at each stage of their buying process? Mapping out the alternatives your customers might explore can reveal indirect or overlooked competitors.

6. Why Identifying Competitors Matters

Understanding your competitors—both direct and indirect—gives you critical insights into your market. It helps you recognize where you fit in and how to differentiate your business. Knowing who your competitors are also ensures that you don't operate in a vacuum. It's tempting to focus solely on what *you* offer, but without a clear view of the competition, you can miss out on opportunities to improve or areas where your business can stand out.

By knowing your competitors, you'll be better equipped to:

- Identify gaps in the market that you can fill

- Understand what customers value and how to offer something better

- Anticipate market shifts and respond proactively

- Differentiate your product or service in ways that matter to your target audience

In the next section, we'll dive deeper into how to analyze your competitors using SWOT analysis—a powerful tool for uncovering strengths, weaknesses, opportunities, and threats. This will help you craft a strategy that not only identifies your competition but also positions you to outperform them.

This section lays the groundwork for competitive analysis by helping readers identify the different types of competitors in their industry. Understanding who you're up against is the first step in creating a strategy to stand out and succeed.

SWOT Analysis: Breaking Down Strengths, Weaknesses, Opportunities, and Threats

Now that you've identified your competitors, it's time to dive deeper into understanding how they operate. The SWOT analysis—Strengths, Weaknesses, Opportunities, and Threats—is one of the most powerful tools you can use to dissect your competition. By analyzing each competitor through the SWOT framework, you can identify where they excel, where they falter, and where opportunities lie for your business to carve out its niche.

In this section, we'll break down how to conduct a competitor SWOT analysis, helping you leverage the insights you gather to refine your strategy and find your competitive edge.

1. Strengths: Understanding What Competitors Do Well

The first part of a SWOT analysis is identifying your competitors' strengths. These are the areas where they excel, the things they do better than anyone else, and the reasons why customers choose them. Understanding your competitors' strengths gives you insight into what works in the marketplace and highlights the areas where you might need to step up your game.

To identify your competitors' strengths, ask yourself:

- **What do customers love about them?** Look at reviews, testimonials, and social media mentions. Are customers raving about their product quality, customer service, or innovative features?

- **What are they known for?** Every strong competitor has a reputation. Are they known for being the affordable option, the premium brand, or the industry innovator? Understanding their brand positioning helps you recognize where they dominate.

- **How are they performing in the market?** Consider market share, revenue growth, and visibility. A competitor that is growing rapidly or has a strong foothold in the market likely has some key strengths you can learn from.

By identifying strengths, you can better understand why your competitors are successful—and whether those same strengths are areas where you can compete or if you need to differentiate in other ways.

2. Weaknesses: Pinpointing Where Competitors Fall Short

Just as important as knowing your competitors' strengths is understanding their weaknesses. Weaknesses are the areas where competitors struggle or fail to meet customer expectations. These are often the gaps where you can step in and do things better, turning their weaknesses into your opportunity.

To identify weaknesses, ask:

- **What do customers complain about?** Scan reviews and social media comments for recurring frustrations. Are customers dissatisfied with their customer service, product durability, pricing, or delivery times?

- **Where do they lack innovation?** Some competitors may be stuck in their ways or slow to adopt new technologies and trends. Is there an area where they seem outdated or resistant to change?

- **What gaps exist in their offerings?** Even successful competitors may have a limited range of products or services. Look for areas where they fail to fully meet customer needs—whether it's missing features, lack of customization, or limited availability.

Identifying weaknesses allows you to position your business as the better alternative. If a competitor consistently receives complaints about their slow delivery, for example, you could focus on fast shipping as a key selling point.

3. Opportunities: Finding Market Gaps and Growth Potential

Opportunities are external factors that your business can take advantage of to grow and gain a competitive edge. These could be emerging trends, shifts in consumer behavior, or technological advancements that your competitors haven't yet capitalized on. By identifying opportunities, you can position your business to meet needs that others are overlooking or slow to address.

To spot opportunities, consider:

- **What trends are emerging?** Stay informed about changes in consumer preferences, industry shifts, and technology advancements. Are there new trends that your competitors haven't adapted to yet, like sustainability, personalization, or digital transformation?

- **Are there underserved customer segments?** Even strong competitors may focus on a specific demographic, leaving other segments under-served. Could you target a niche market that they're ignoring, such as younger consumers, budget-conscious shoppers, or international markets?

- **Can you innovate in areas they're overlooking?** Innovation doesn't always have to be disruptive. Sometimes, small improvements can create big opportunities. If competitors are slow to improve their user experience or customer support, could you stand out by offering a smoother, more customer-friendly solution?

By identifying these opportunities, you can focus on areas where your business has the potential to grow and differentiate itself, rather than competing directly where the market is already saturated.

4. Threats: Recognizing External Risks and Challenges

Threats are external factors that could negatively impact your business or the entire market. These could include changes in regulation, new competitors entering the market, shifts in consumer behavior, or economic downturns. Recognizing threats is critical for proactively preparing your business to address potential challenges before they become significant problems.

To identify threats, ask:

- **Are there new competitors on the horizon?** Keep an eye on startups or established companies entering your industry. They may bring new ideas, innovations, or pricing strategies that could disrupt your market.

- **How is the market changing?** Pay attention to macroeconomic factors like inflation, supply chain disruptions, or changes in consumer spending habits that could pose challenges to your business or industry as a whole.

- **Are regulations or policies changing?** Government regulations, trade policies, or industry-specific laws could present hurdles. For example, new data privacy laws might require expensive updates to your tech infrastructure, or environmental regulations could lead to changes in product design or sourcing.

By recognizing these threats early, you can develop strategies to mitigate risks, such as diversifying your product offerings, expanding into new markets, or adjusting your pricing strategy to stay competitive.

5. Turning SWOT Insights into Actionable Strategy

Once you've completed a SWOT analysis of your competitors, it's time to turn those insights into a strategy that puts your business in the best possible position to compete and win. Here's how:

- **Leverage their weaknesses**: Take advantage of areas where competitors fall short by positioning your product or service as the better alternative.

For example, if your competitor has poor customer service, make exceptional service a cornerstone of your business.

- **Capitalize on market opportunities**: Focus on the opportunities your competitors haven't seized yet. This could mean targeting a niche market, embracing new technology, or developing a product that fills a gap they've missed.

- **Strengthen your defenses against threats**: Proactively address potential threats to your business by preparing for market changes or regulatory shifts. This might include diversifying your supply chain, preparing for economic downturns, or investing in innovations that future-proof your business.

- **Identify ways to differentiate**: Use the combination of your competitor's strengths, weaknesses, opportunities, and threats to identify how you can stand out in the market. Can you offer a better experience, solve problems more effectively, or innovate faster? Differentiation is key to attracting customers who are weighing their options between you and your competitors.

6. SWOT in Action: An Example

Let's take an example of a small independent bookstore competing with a larger chain. A SWOT analysis might look like this:

- **Strengths**: The larger chain has a bigger selection, brand recognition, and loyalty programs.

- **Weaknesses**: Customers complain about impersonal service and lack of local community focus.

- **Opportunities**: There's a growing trend of consumers supporting local businesses, and there's room for events and personalized recommendations that the larger chain doesn't offer.

- **Threats**: Online retailers like Amazon offer lower prices and fast shipping, which could lure customers away from both the local bookstore and the chain.

Based on this analysis, the small bookstore could focus on creating a personalized, community-driven experience that the larger chain can't replicate, such as hosting local author events, offering personalized reading recommendations, and fostering a strong local customer base through engagement and loyalty programs.

By using the SWOT analysis framework, you can break down the competitive landscape into actionable insights that allow you to find weaknesses to exploit, strengths to compete against, and opportunities to grow. In the next section, we'll take this analysis a step further and explore how to dissect your competitors' market positioning and strategy, giving you a clear understanding of how they attract customers and where you can stand out.

Dissecting Their Strategy: Understanding Their Market Positioning

Once you've completed a SWOT analysis, the next critical step in analyzing your competitors is dissecting their strategy—specifically, their market positioning. Market positioning is how a business presents itself in the minds of its target customers. It's the unique space a company occupies in the market based on its value proposition, pricing, customer experience, and branding. By understanding how your competitors position themselves, you can identify where they excel, where they're vulnerable, and how you can differentiate your own business.

In this section, we'll break down the key components of market positioning and how to analyze your competitors' strategies to find opportunities for your business to stand out.

1. Market Positioning: What It Is and Why It's Key

Market positioning is how a business defines itself relative to competitors in the eyes of its target audience. It's the reason customers choose one brand over another and reflects how a company is perceived in terms of:

- **Value Proposition**: What core value does the company promise to deliver to its customers?

- **Target Audience**: Who is the company aiming to serve? What are the demographics and psychographics of their ideal customer?

- **Differentiation**: How does the company stand out from competitors? What makes their product or service unique?

- **Customer Perception**: What emotional or practical benefits do customers associate with the brand? Is it viewed as premium, budget-friendly, innovative, reliable, etc.?

Understanding how your competitors position themselves allows you to identify areas where you can offer something different or superior, creating a competitive edge that resonates with your own target audience.

2. Analyzing Pricing Strategy: Where Do They Compete?

Pricing is one of the most visible aspects of market positioning, and it can tell you a lot about a company's strategy. Whether your competitor is positioning themselves as a low-cost leader, a premium brand, or somewhere in between, their pricing reflects their value proposition and target market.

Here's how to analyze your competitors' pricing strategies:

- **Are they focused on cost leadership?** Competitors that position themselves as the low-cost option aim to attract price-sensitive customers. Their strategy might focus on efficiency, volume sales, and minimal frills.

- **Are they positioning as premium or luxury?** Premium brands charge higher prices by offering superior quality, exclusive features, or a more personalized experience. Their target customers are less price-sensitive and value the perceived status or luxury of the product.

- **Are they somewhere in the middle?** Some competitors target the mass market with mid-range pricing, balancing affordability with decent quality and service. They may rely on a mix of scale and value to attract a broad customer base.

By analyzing your competitors' pricing, you can decide whether to compete directly on price, differentiate by offering more value for a similar price, or go premium by delivering a superior experience at a higher cost.

3. Target Audience: Who Are They Serving?

Knowing who your competitors are targeting is essential for understanding their market positioning. While many competitors may serve a broad audience, others may be focused on specific segments, such as high-income professionals, budget-conscious shoppers, or tech-savvy millennials.

To analyze their target audience, ask yourself:

- **What customer segment are they focusing on?** Are they targeting a niche market or a broad demographic? A competitor focusing on high-end professionals will position themselves differently from one targeting families or young professionals.

- **What are the key demographics and psychographics of their audience?** Are they serving younger consumers with tech-focused products? Older, more established professionals? How do they tailor their messaging and branding to resonate with these groups?

Understanding your competitors' target audience allows you to see where there may be untapped segments of the market that your business could focus on. For instance, if your competitor is focusing on a younger audience, you might be able to differentiate by targeting older professionals or families.

4. Branding and Messaging: What's Their Story?

Branding is the emotional and cultural aspect of a business's market positioning. How a company presents itself visually, the tone of its messaging, and the story it tells its customers are all part of its strategy. By analyzing your competitors' branding, you can gain valuable insights into how they connect with their audience and differentiate themselves from others.

Here's how to dissect your competitors' branding:

- **What's their brand personality?** Is their brand serious and professional, or fun and quirky? The tone and personality they use in their messaging reflect how they want to be perceived by their audience.

- **What emotions are they trying to evoke?** Strong brands connect with their customers on an emotional level. Are they trying to inspire trust, excitement, adventure, or exclusivity? The emotional appeal they use gives you insight into their brand's positioning.

- **How are they visually represented?** Look at their logos, color schemes, and design elements. How does their visual identity set them apart? Do they use clean, modern designs, or do they focus on traditional, established aesthetics?

By analyzing their branding, you can determine how they're crafting a narrative that appeals to their audience and how your own brand can stand out by offering a different story.

5. Unique Selling Proposition (USP): What Sets Them Apart?

A competitor's Unique Selling Proposition (USP) is the defining aspect of their strategy. It's what they claim makes them better, different, or more valuable than the alternatives. Their USP is the foundation of their market positioning, shaping how they attract and retain customers.

To analyze their USP, ask:

- **What do they emphasize as their key strength?** Is it product quality, price, innovation, customer service, or convenience? The USP is the main reason customers choose them over others.

- **How are they addressing customer pain points?** Competitors often position themselves by solving a specific customer problem better than anyone else. Are they known for faster delivery, superior craftsmanship, or better customer support?

- **Do they have a clear and consistent message?** Strong brands have a clear USP that's reinforced across all touchpoints—website, ads, social media, and customer interactions. Do they consistently promote the same strengths, or is their message scattered?

Once you've identified their USP, you can think about how your business can differentiate itself. Is their USP product-focused while your strength is in customer experience? Do they highlight affordability while you can offer customization or exclusivity? The key is to find a unique angle that positions your business as the superior choice for your target audience.

6. Putting It All Together: Creating Your Positioning Strategy

After dissecting your competitors' positioning strategies, it's time to apply these insights to your own business. The goal is not to copy what's already working for your competitors but to find gaps, weaknesses, or missed opportunities in their strategies that you can capitalize on.

Here's how to create your own positioning strategy based on what you've learned:

- **Differentiate where it matters**: Focus on areas where competitors fall short. If their messaging doesn't resonate with certain segments of the market, can you position your business to appeal to those overlooked customers?

- **Highlight your strengths**: Emphasize what makes your business unique and why customers should choose you over competitors. Whether it's superior service, faster delivery, or deeper expertise, make sure your value proposition is crystal clear.

- **Adapt to market trends**: If you've identified shifts in consumer behavior that competitors are slow to respond to, position your business as forward-thinking and adaptable, offering solutions that align with new trends and customer expectations.

By understanding your competitors' market positioning, you'll gain the clarity needed to carve out a distinct place in the market—one where your business offers something that no one else does quite as well.

By dissecting your competitors' strategy, you can identify key strengths and weaknesses in how they position themselves, helping you craft a competitive edge. In the next section, we'll explore how to leverage customer feedback and reviews to gain even deeper insights into your competitors' performance and what customers truly value (or dislike) about their offerings.

Learning from Their Customers: Feedback and Reviews

Your competitors' customers can be a treasure trove of insights, revealing what's working, what's not, and where opportunities lie. Customer feedback and reviews offer an unfiltered look at real experiences, opinions, and expectations. By analyzing this feedback, you can learn not only what your competitors excel at but also where they fall short—giving you the opportunity to improve upon or fill those gaps.

In this section, we'll explore how to leverage customer feedback and reviews to gain deeper insights into your competitors, helping you refine your offerings and strategy based on what customers truly want.

1. Why Customer Feedback is Invaluable

Customers are often brutally honest in their feedback, especially when they've had a poor experience. Reviews, whether positive or negative, provide a direct line into the minds of your competitors' customers, offering insights that might not be evident from simply observing your competition. Feedback sheds light on:

- **Product strengths and weaknesses**: Customers will often highlight specific features they love or criticize aspects that need improvement.

- **Customer service experience**: Feedback reveals how well your competitors manage their relationships with customers—whether it's smooth and helpful or frustrating and unresponsive.

- **Unmet expectations**: Negative reviews can reveal areas where customers feel let down. These are potential opportunities for your business to step in and do better.

By paying attention to what customers are saying about your competitors, you can uncover insights that help you shape your own customer experience, products, and services to better meet market demands.

2. Where to Find Customer Feedback and Reviews

There are several places where you can find reviews and feedback about your competitors. Monitoring these sources regularly can help you stay informed about what's happening in the market:

- **Online Review Platforms**: Websites like Google Reviews, Yelp, Trustpilot, and industry-specific review platforms are goldmines for customer opinions. These reviews often detail the entire customer journey, from product quality to service interactions.

- **Social Media**: Customers frequently share their experiences with brands on social media platforms like Twitter, Facebook, Instagram, and LinkedIn. You can track mentions, comments, and reviews to see what people are saying about your competitors.

- **E-commerce Websites**: If your competitors sell products on platforms like Amazon, Etsy, or other e-commerce sites, customer reviews and ratings provide valuable insight into how their products perform and whether they live up to customer expectations.

- **Forums and Community Platforms**: Sites like Reddit and industry-specific forums allow users to discuss their experiences with products and services more informally. These discussions can be candid and reveal pain points that more formal reviews might not capture.

By gathering feedback from multiple channels, you can form a well-rounded understanding of how customers perceive your competitors and where there are opportunities to improve.

3. What to Look for in Customer Reviews

When analyzing customer feedback, it's important to go beyond star ratings and surface-level opinions. Dive deep into the reviews to uncover actionable insights:

- **Recurring Complaints**: If you notice that multiple customers are complaining about the same issue—such as slow shipping, poor customer service, or a particular feature that doesn't work well—this points to a consistent weakness that you can address in your own offerings.

- **Positive Highlights**: Look for features or services that customers consistently rave about. This will help you identify what your competitors are doing right and where you need to step up your game. For example, if a competitor's customers love their fast, hassle-free returns process, you might consider implementing or enhancing a similar feature to match or surpass their service.

- **Suggestions and Wish Lists**: Pay attention to what customers *wish* the product or service had. These are golden opportunities for innovation. If many customers are asking for a feature your competitor doesn't offer, you can differentiate yourself by providing it.

- **Customer Sentiment**: Beyond what customers say, observe how they feel. Are they enthusiastic, loyal, and engaged, or are they frustrated and disappointed? Understanding the emotional connection (or lack thereof) customers have with your competitors helps you fine-tune your own brand messaging and customer relationships.

By extracting these insights, you can improve your own product development, customer service, and marketing strategies, ensuring you meet customer expectations more effectively than your competitors.

4. Turning Competitors' Weaknesses into Opportunities

Negative reviews are particularly valuable because they reveal where competitors are falling short. These failures represent opportunities for you to swoop in and offer a better alternative.

When analyzing negative feedback, consider:

- **What are the most common complaints?** Are customers consistently dissatisfied with customer support, product quality, or delivery times? If so, these are areas where you can improve and position your business as the better choice.

- **How severe are the issues?** Some problems are minor annoyances, while others are deal-breakers. If your competitors are losing customers due to significant issues (such as unreliable products or terrible customer service), this is a clear opportunity for you to excel in those areas.

- **Are competitors addressing these complaints?** Look at how your competitors respond to negative reviews. Are they ignoring complaints or responding in a way that fails to resolve the issue? If competitors aren't doing a good job of resolving problems, it's a chance for you to differentiate your business by offering superior customer care and responsiveness.

By addressing the gaps and weaknesses highlighted in negative reviews, you can create a competitive advantage that appeals to dissatisfied customers looking for a better alternative.

5. Learning from Competitors' Strengths: What They Do Best

While negative reviews reveal weaknesses, positive reviews provide insights into what your competitors are doing right. Understanding their strengths can help you identify best practices and benchmark your own offerings.

When analyzing positive feedback, consider:

- **What do customers consistently praise?** If there's something customers love about your competitor's product or service—whether it's quality, design, or convenience—you'll need to match or exceed that standard in your own offering to remain competitive.

- **Are they building customer loyalty?** Positive reviews often reveal why customers keep coming back. Is it because of personalized service, an easy-to-use product, or exclusive perks? If your competitors are cultivating loyalty through specific initiatives, you can adopt or improve upon similar strategies to build a loyal customer base.

- **How do they connect with their audience?** Strong customer relationships often come from a deep understanding of customer needs. Look for themes in positive reviews that point to how well your competitors connect emotionally with their audience, and use this information to enhance your own customer relationships.

Learning from what your competitors excel at can help you understand the standards customers expect and ensure you are meeting or exceeding those expectations.

6. Applying Insights: Improving Your Own Offerings

Once you've analyzed your competitors' feedback and reviews, the next step is applying those insights to improve your own business. Here's how to turn customer feedback into action:

- **Enhance Your Product or Service**: If customers frequently complain about a feature or aspect of your competitor's product, make sure your offering solves that problem. Alternatively, if they love a particular feature, see if it makes sense to integrate something similar into your product while adding your unique twist.

- **Improve Customer Experience**: Negative feedback about your competitors' customer service can be a goldmine for improving your own. If customers complain about long response times or unhelpful support, focus on creating a responsive, solution-driven support team that delights customers.

- **Refine Your Marketing and Messaging**: Customer feedback often reveals the emotional reasons behind why customers choose a brand. Use this insight to fine-tune your marketing messages. Highlight the benefits customers value most, and address any frustrations they've expressed with your competitors.

- **Capitalize on Competitor Failures**: If customers are leaving negative reviews because they feel their needs aren't being met, use this as an opportunity to attract them to your business. Position your product as the solution to their frustrations and highlight what you offer that competitors don't.

By learning from your competitors' customers, you can improve every aspect of your business—from product development to customer support—ensuring that you address the real needs of your target audience better than your competitors.

By leveraging customer feedback and reviews, you can gain deep insights into what your competitors are doing well and where they are falling short. This allows you to refine your products, services, and overall strategy to meet customer expectations more effectively. In the next section, we'll explore how to gather competitive intelligence ethically and use it to stay one step ahead in the battle for market share.

Tactical Advantage: Using Competitive Intelligence for Strategic Growth

In business, staying ahead of the competition requires more than just offering a great product or service—it demands knowing your competitors' every move. Competitive intelligence (CI) is the process of gathering, analyzing, and using information about competitors to gain a strategic advantage. When done ethically and effectively, it can provide you with the insights necessary to anticipate trends, adjust your strategy, and outperform your rivals.

In this section, we'll explore how to ethically gather competitive intelligence, leverage it for strategic growth, and stay one step ahead in the marketplace.

1. What Is Competitive Intelligence?

Competitive intelligence involves collecting and analyzing data on your competitors to better understand their strategies, strengths, weaknesses, and market positioning. The goal of CI is to make informed decisions about your own business strategy, ensuring that you're not only reacting to your competitors but also proactively positioning your business for long-term success.

CI goes beyond just knowing who your competitors are—it's about understanding their tactics, anticipating their next moves, and identifying opportunities to differentiate your brand. When used effectively, CI can help you:

- Spot market trends and shifts early
- Recognize emerging competitors or disruptive innovations
- Identify gaps in the market that your competitors aren't filling
- Fine-tune your offerings to outperform competitors

2. Ethically Gathering Competitive Intelligence

While gathering competitive intelligence is a crucial part of business strategy, it's important to do it ethically. Unethical practices like industrial espionage or hacking are not only illegal but also damaging to your reputation. Fortunately, there are plenty of legal, transparent ways to gather valuable insights about your competitors.

Here are some ethical methods to gather competitive intelligence:

- **Public Reports and Financial Data**: If your competitors are publicly traded companies, you can access their annual reports, financial filings, and earnings calls. These documents provide a wealth of information about a company's financial health, future plans, and key challenges.

- **Press Releases and News Articles**: Stay up to date on your competitors by following their news releases and media coverage. These can reveal new product launches, partnerships, or expansions. Tools like Google Alerts can help you monitor mentions of your competitors in the press.

- **Social Media Monitoring**: Social media platforms offer a window into your competitors' public-facing strategies. Observe how they engage with their audience, what content they share, and how they respond to customer inquiries. You can use social listening tools to track mentions of your competitors and analyze customer sentiment toward them.

- **Industry Conferences and Trade Shows**: Attending industry events is a great way to see what your competitors are showcasing, learn about their latest innovations, and even engage in conversations with potential customers and partners.

- **Customer Reviews and Feedback**: As discussed in the previous section, customer reviews are an invaluable source of competitive intelligence. They provide real insights into what your competitors are doing right and where they're falling short.

- **Competitor Websites and Marketing Materials**: A competitor's website can reveal a lot about their current strategy—everything from pricing structures to product offerings and branding. Sign up for their newsletters, follow their blogs, and download any free resources they offer. This will give you insights into their content strategy, messaging, and target audience.

By using these ethical approaches, you can gather actionable intelligence without crossing any legal or ethical boundaries.

3. Analyzing Competitive Intelligence: What to Look For

Once you've gathered intelligence, the next step is analyzing it. The goal is to translate raw data into strategic insights that will guide your business decisions. Here are key areas to focus on when analyzing competitive intelligence:

- **Product and Service Offerings**: How do your competitors' products or services compare to yours in terms of features, quality, and pricing? What gaps exist in their offerings, and how can you fill them?

- **Pricing Strategies**: Are your competitors offering discounts, promotions, or value-added services? Understanding their pricing strategies can help you adjust your own prices to remain competitive or position yourself as a premium option.

- **Marketing and Messaging**: What are your competitors' key marketing messages? How are they positioning themselves in the market, and what emotional or practical appeals are they using to attract customers? This analysis will help you fine-tune your own branding and messaging to stand out.

- **Customer Relationships**: How do your competitors engage with their customers? Are they fostering loyalty through rewards programs, personalized service, or community-building initiatives? Identifying gaps in customer experience can give you a competitive advantage.

By systematically analyzing these areas, you can develop a comprehensive understanding of your competitors' strategies and how you can outmaneuver them.

4. Using Competitive Intelligence to Inform Strategy

The real power of competitive intelligence lies in how you apply it. Once you've gathered and analyzed the data, it's time to use it to inform your strategic decisions. Here's how to leverage CI for growth:

- **Refine Your Value Proposition**: Use insights from your competitors to refine your unique selling proposition (USP). If a competitor excels in one area, focus on how you can differentiate by emphasizing your strengths or offering something they don't.

- **Identify New Market Opportunities**: CI can reveal untapped markets or emerging trends that your competitors are missing. Whether it's a niche customer segment or a shift in consumer preferences, seize these opportunities before your competitors do.

- **Adjust Pricing Strategies**: If you notice that your competitors are undercutting your prices, you might need to adjust your pricing or emphasize the added value you provide. Alternatively, if your competitors are positioning themselves as premium brands, you could offer a more affordable option to attract budget-conscious customers.

- **Improve Customer Experience**: By analyzing your competitors' weaknesses in customer service or support, you can enhance your own customer experience to win over dissatisfied customers. Focus on areas like faster response times, personalized interactions, or seamless purchasing experiences.

- **Anticipate Competitor Moves**: The more you understand your competitors' strategies, the better you can anticipate their next moves. If you see signs that a competitor is planning to expand into a new market or launch a new product, you can adjust your strategy to stay ahead.

By using competitive intelligence to inform these key decisions, you'll gain a tactical advantage that helps you grow strategically while staying ahead of the competition.

5. Tracking Competitors Over Time: Staying One Step Ahead

Competitive intelligence isn't a one-time task—it's an ongoing process. Markets shift, competitors evolve, and new players enter the field. To stay competitive, you need to continuously track your competitors and adjust your strategy as the landscape changes.

Here's how to maintain your competitive edge:

- **Set Up Monitoring Systems**: Use tools like Google Alerts, Mention, or Hootsuite to track your competitors' activities. These tools can notify you when a competitor makes an announcement, launches a new product, or is mentioned in the media.

- **Regularly Review Your Competitor Analysis**: Periodically revisit your competitor analysis to ensure you're up to date with their latest offerings, strategies, and market moves. Quarterly or bi-annual reviews can help you stay current.

- **Adapt Your Strategy in Real-Time**: Be prepared to pivot as new competitors emerge or existing ones shift their focus. The ability to adapt quickly to changes in the market gives you an edge in staying relevant and ahead of the competition.

By continually monitoring and analyzing your competitors, you'll remain agile and ready to adjust your strategy as needed, ensuring long-term success and sustained growth.

n this section, we've explored the power of competitive intelligence and how it can provide a tactical advantage for strategic growth. By gathering and analyzing information about your competitors, you can anticipate their moves, identify gaps in the market, and refine your own strategy to stay ahead. With this knowledge, you'll be better equipped to navigate the competitive landscape and build a business that thrives.

This concludes Chapter 3, and you are now ready to step into the next phase of sharpening your business strategy.

Quick Tips and Recap

- **Identify Your Competitors**: Understand the difference between direct, indirect, and potential competitors. Look beyond obvious rivals to find overlooked threats and emerging disruptors.

- **Use SWOT Analysis**: Break down competitors' Strengths, Weaknesses, Opportunities, and Threats to uncover gaps in their offerings and areas where you can gain an edge.

- **Analyze Market Positioning**: Study competitors' pricing, target audience, branding, and unique selling propositions (USPs) to see how they attract customers and where you can differentiate.

- **Leverage Customer Feedback**: Dive deep into reviews and feedback from competitors' customers to uncover weaknesses and opportunities for your own business to shine.

- **Apply Insights to Your Strategy**: Use competitive intelligence to refine your value proposition, identify market opportunities, improve customer experience, and anticipate competitor moves.

- **Track Competitors Regularly**: Stay vigilant and continuously monitor your competitors' strategies, market positioning, and customer feedback to maintain your competitive edge.

This summary reinforces the core concepts of competitor analysis and provides a practical, actionable framework for staying ahead of the competition.

CHAPTER FOUR

Mission Possible: Setting Clear Business Objectives

"Clear, actionable objectives are the backbone of any successful business. Without them, you're just throwing darts in the dark. Define your goals with precision, track them relentlessly, and adjust as needed to stay on course." — RAND FISHKIN, FOUNDER OF MOZ AND SPARKTORO

Cue the dramatic music—it's time to embark on your very own Mission Possible, where your task (which you'll happily accept) is to set clear, actionable business objectives that will guide your empire to greatness. Think of objectives as your roadmap, GPS, and fuel gauge all rolled into one. Without them, you're just driving in circles, hoping for a breakthrough, but with them, you're cruising straight toward success with pit stops already planned.

Now, when we say, "clear objectives," we don't mean vague ambitions like "become a billionaire" or "disrupt an industry" (though, hey, we applaud the enthusiasm). We're talking about the kind of goals that are SMART: Specific, Measurable, Achievable, Relevant, and Time-bound. Like, "increase online sales by 20% in the next quarter" or "launch three new products by the end of the year." You know, goals that are less pie-in-the-sky and more bite-sized-and-actionable.

Setting objectives is like giving your business a mission briefing—these are the targets, this is the timeline, and here's how we'll know when we've succeeded. It turns business daydreaming into a strategic, laser-focused game plan.

So, grab your notepad, chart your course, and start setting objectives that will keep your business moving forward with purpose. Because let's face it, every great mission starts with a clear plan—and your business is no exception. Now go out there and make your objectives *mission accomplished*!

The Power of Purpose: Why Setting Objectives Drives Success

In business, having a clear sense of direction is everything. Without well-defined objectives, your team might be working hard, but they'll be like a ship sailing without a destination—busy moving, but ultimately going nowhere. Setting business objectives is like plotting a course on a map. They provide a clear, actionable path to success, ensuring that everyone knows where you're headed and how to get there.

Objectives serve as the backbone of your strategy. They give your business purpose, helping you focus on what matters most. Here's why setting clear objectives is essential for driving success:

1. Focus and Alignment

Business objectives create focus. With a clear objective in place, your team knows exactly what they're working toward. This sharpens focus and ensures that all efforts, resources, and energy are aligned toward a specific goal. Without clear objectives, it's easy to get distracted by day-to-day tasks, competing priorities, or new ideas that can pull your business off track.

When your team is aligned with a shared goal, every decision becomes clearer. Objectives act as a filter for decision-making: If an action contributes to achieving the objective, it's a priority. If it doesn't, it's secondary. This alignment drives efficiency, ensuring that everyone is working toward the same outcome.

2. Measuring Progress

A key benefit of setting objectives is that they provide a way to measure your progress. Vague aspirations, like "increase sales" or "grow the business," don't give you a benchmark to track success. By setting clear, measurable objectives, such as "increase online sales by 20% in Q2," you create a target that can be tracked and evaluated.

Measurable objectives allow you to monitor performance in real-time. Are you hitting the key milestones? Are you ahead or behind schedule? With measurable goals, you can quickly identify whether your strategies are working or need adjustment. This ability to track progress keeps your business on course and helps you pivot when necessary.

3. Motivating Your Team

Objectives give your team a sense of purpose and motivation. When people know what they're working toward—and can see how their efforts contribute to the bigger picture—they're more engaged, energized, and driven to succeed. Clear objectives turn everyday tasks into meaningful actions that move the business closer to its vision.

Well-defined goals also create opportunities for celebrating wins. Reaching a key milestone or achieving a target gives your team something tangible to celebrate. This recognition boosts morale and keeps your employees motivated to tackle the next challenge.

4. Driving Accountability

Objectives create accountability by making it clear who is responsible for achieving what and by when. When everyone knows what's expected of them, it's easier to hold individuals and teams accountable for their performance. Clear objectives eliminate confusion, set expectations, and provide a roadmap for success.

Accountability also fosters a culture of ownership. When people are accountable for specific objectives, they take more responsibility for their work, knowing that their success contributes directly to the business's success. This level of ownership encourages higher performance and proactive problem-solving.

5. Turning Vision into Action

It's one thing to have a grand vision for your business, but turning that vision into reality requires actionable steps. Objectives bridge the gap between dreaming and doing. They break your big-picture vision into manageable, actionable tasks, giving you and your team a clear plan for achieving success.

By setting specific objectives, you make it easier to translate your long-term strategy into day-to-day actions. Every objective becomes a milestone on the journey toward achieving your broader goals, ensuring that you're consistently making progress and not just dreaming of a distant future.

In summary, setting clear objectives gives your business the direction, focus, and structure it needs to grow and succeed. Objectives help you measure progress, align your team, drive motivation, foster accountability, and turn your vision into actionable plans. They provide a framework that keeps your business moving forward with purpose and intention. So, as you move through this chapter, remember that each objective you set is a step toward making your business vision a reality.

Breaking Down SMART Goals: Turning Vision into Actionable Targets

Turning your business vision into reality requires more than ambition—it demands a clear plan of action. This is where SMART goals come into play. SMART goals take broad aspirations and break them down into practical, achievable steps. The SMART framework—Specific, Measurable, Achievable, Relevant, and Time-bound—ensures that your goals are actionable, realistic, and focused on measurable outcomes.

In this section, we'll break down each element of the SMART framework, giving you the tools to turn your business vision into concrete, actionable targets.

1. Specific: Clear and Well-Defined

The first element of a SMART goal is *specificity*. Vague goals, like "grow the business" or "increase revenue," don't provide clear direction or a concrete plan. A specific goal, on the other hand, defines exactly what you're aiming to achieve.

To make your goal specific, ask yourself:

- **What exactly do I want to accomplish?**
- **Who is involved?**
- **Where will this happen?**
- **Why is this goal important?**

For example, instead of saying "grow the business," a specific goal would be: "Increase online sales of Product X by 15% by improving the website's user experience and launching a targeted email campaign."

This clarity makes it easier for you and your team to focus on what needs to be done and ensures everyone is working toward the same objective.

2. Measurable: Tracking Progress and Success

A goal without measurable criteria is like trying to hit a moving target. *Measurability* allows you to track progress, evaluate success, and know when you've achieved your goal.

To make your goal measurable, ask:

- **How will I know when I've succeeded?**
- **What metrics or key performance indicators (KPIs) will I use to track progress?**

For example, if your goal is to "increase social media engagement," you could make it measurable by adding, "boost Instagram engagement by 25% over the next quarter, measured by likes, comments, and shares."

By setting clear metrics, you can easily track your progress, celebrate milestones, and adjust your approach if needed.

3. Achievable: Realistic and Attainable

While it's great to set ambitious goals, they must also be *achievable*. Unrealistic goals can demotivate your team, lead to burnout, and result in missed targets. An achievable goal is challenging yet attainable within your resources, capabilities, and constraints.

To determine if your goal is achievable, ask:

- **Do I have the resources, time, and skills to achieve this?**

- **Is this goal realistic given my current circumstances?**

For instance, instead of setting a goal to "double sales in the next month" (which may not be feasible), a more achievable goal might be, "increase sales by 20% in the next quarter by improving lead generation and expanding customer outreach."

An achievable goal keeps your team motivated and gives you confidence that success is within reach.

4. Relevant: Aligned with Broader Business Goals

Your goal should be *relevant* to your overall business objectives. A relevant goal matters to your business and aligns with your long-term vision, strategy, and values. If a goal doesn't move you closer to your big-picture mission, it might be a distraction.

To ensure relevance, ask:

- **Does this goal align with my overall business strategy?**

- **Will achieving this goal contribute to my broader objectives?**

For example, if your broader objective is to increase customer retention, setting a goal to "launch a loyalty rewards program" is highly relevant. On the other hand, focusing on an unrelated goal like "launching a new product in an untapped market" might not be the best use of your resources if customer retention is the priority.

Relevant goals keep your efforts focused on what truly matters to your business's long-term success.

5. Time-Bound: Deadlines Drive Progress

Every goal needs a sense of urgency, which is why the final element of a SMART goal is being *time-bound*. Setting a deadline creates motivation and gives your team a clear timeline for achieving the goal. It also helps you plan resources, track progress, and maintain accountability.

To make your goal time-bound, ask:

- **What's the deadline for achieving this goal?**

- **What milestones can I set along the way to track progress?**

For example, a goal like "launch three new products" becomes time-bound when you specify, "launch three new products by the end of Q3." Having this deadline ensures that the goal is a priority and that everyone is working toward a specific end date.

6. Putting SMART Goals into Action

Now that you understand the components of SMART goals, the next step is to put them into action. Here's a simple framework for creating and executing your own SMART goals:

- **Start with the big picture**: Begin by looking at your long-term vision and broader business objectives.

- **Break it down**: Break those larger goals into smaller, actionable SMART goals that you can tackle in the short term.

- **Assign ownership**: Make sure each goal has a clear owner who is responsible for driving it forward.

- **Set milestones**: For each SMART goal, establish milestones to track progress and celebrate wins along the way.

- **Review and adjust**: Regularly check in on your goals to ensure they're on track. If you're falling behind or the market conditions change, adjust your goals and timelines accordingly.

SMART goals turn your vision into an actionable roadmap. They give you a clear focus, drive accountability, and help you measure success at every step. By creating goals that are specific, measurable, achievable, relevant, and time-bound, you'll position your business for steady growth and long-term success.

This section helps readers break down their big-picture vision into specific, actionable steps using the SMART framework. With this approach, goals become clearer, progress becomes measurable, and success becomes far more achievable.

Aligning Objectives with Your Business Strategy

Setting goals is critical for driving progress, but not all goals are created equal. To ensure your efforts lead to meaningful outcomes, it's essential that your objectives align with your overall business strategy. This alignment guarantees that every goal you set moves your business closer to achieving its long-term vision, supports your core values, and fits within the competitive landscape.

In this section, we'll explore how to effectively align your objectives with your business strategy, ensuring that the goals you set are not only achievable but also strategically relevant to your growth and success.

1. Start with Your Business Mission and Vision

Your mission and vision are the cornerstones of your business strategy, outlining the purpose of your business and the direction you're heading in. Every objective you set should be a step toward fulfilling this broader mission. If your objectives don't support your mission and vision, they can lead to wasted effort or push your business in the wrong direction.

To align your objectives, ask:

- **What is my company's mission?** Does this objective directly support it?

- **What is the long-term vision for the business?** Will achieving this goal move us closer to realizing that vision?

For example, if your mission is to "deliver eco-friendly solutions for urban living," an objective to "reduce carbon emissions in manufacturing by 15% in the next year" clearly supports that mission. On the other hand, a goal like "increase market share in plastic-based products" might conflict with your mission and could hurt your brand's long-term strategy.

2. Prioritize Strategic Initiatives

Every business has a long list of things it could improve or accomplish, but resources are limited. That's why it's essential to prioritize objectives that align with your strategic initiatives—the high-impact areas that will drive growth, profitability, or market leadership.

To prioritize, consider:

- **What are the most critical areas of focus for the next year or quarter?**

- **Which goals will have the biggest impact on growth, customer satisfaction, or market position?**

For example, if expanding into new markets is a key part of your strategy, an objective like "launch two new products in international markets by the end of the year" should take priority. Objectives that don't align with your core strategic initiatives, such as exploring unrelated side projects, should be deprioritized or eliminated.

By focusing on objectives that support your key strategic initiatives, you ensure that every effort contributes directly to your business's long-term success.

3. Keep Objectives Aligned with Market Conditions

Your business doesn't operate in a vacuum. Market conditions, consumer preferences, and competitive dynamics are constantly changing. To ensure your objectives remain relevant, they need to be aligned with current market realities. Goals that made sense six months ago may no longer be as impactful in today's environment.

To align with market conditions, ask:

- **What's happening in the industry or market right now?**

- **How are competitors positioning themselves, and how does this impact my objectives?**

- **Are there emerging trends or shifts that should influence my strategic priorities?**

For instance, if a new competitor has entered your market with aggressive pricing, an objective to "improve customer loyalty by offering enhanced service" might be more effective than simply trying to match their prices. Being responsive to market conditions allows you to stay competitive and ensure your goals remain strategically sound.

4. Align Objectives Across Teams and Departments

Business strategy doesn't happen in silos. Your objectives need to align across all departments and teams to ensure everyone is working toward the same overarching goals. Misalignment can lead to inefficiencies, competing priorities, and confusion.

To ensure alignment, ask:

- **Do all team objectives align with the overall business strategy?**

- **How do individual department goals contribute to the broader company mission?**

For example, if your business strategy emphasizes customer satisfaction as a competitive advantage, both the sales and customer service teams should have objectives focused on improving the customer experience. Sales might aim to "increase customer retention by 10% in the next quarter," while customer service could set a goal to "resolve 90% of customer inquiries within 24 hours."

By aligning objectives across teams, you create synergy, ensuring that every part of the organization is working toward the same strategic outcomes.

5. Balance Short-Term Wins with Long-Term Vision

While short-term objectives are important for driving immediate progress, they should also contribute to your long-term vision. Goals that deliver quick wins but don't align with your business's future direction can create distractions or lead to short-lived successes.

To balance short- and long-term objectives, consider:

- **How does this short-term objective contribute to the long-term vision?**

- **Will this goal create lasting value or just temporary gains?**

For example, a short-term objective to "increase revenue by offering deep discounts" might deliver a quick boost in sales, but it could harm your brand's premium positioning in the long term. Instead, a more aligned goal would be to "increase revenue by expanding product offerings," which contributes both to short-term growth and long-term market leadership.

By ensuring that short-term wins support long-term goals, you maintain focus on sustainable growth and strategic progress.

6. Measure and Adjust Regularly

Even the best-aligned objectives may need to be adjusted over time. As you execute your strategy, monitor progress regularly to ensure your objectives remain aligned with the overall business direction. If market conditions change or new opportunities arise, don't hesitate to revisit and revise your goals.

To measure and adjust, ask:

- **Are our objectives still relevant in light of new data or market conditions?**

- **Do we need to pivot to stay aligned with our strategic vision?**

For instance, if your objective was to "increase market share by 5% through digital marketing" but you're seeing better results from in-person events, it may be time to adjust your strategy and shift resources to capitalize on those opportunities.

By measuring progress and remaining flexible, you ensure that your objectives continue to support your business's evolving strategy.

In summary, aligning your objectives with your overall business strategy ensures that every goal you set serves the broader purpose of driving long-term success. By focusing on relevance, prioritization, and cross-departmental alignment, you create a roadmap that keeps your business on course toward its vision. Remember, clear alignment between your goals and strategy is the key to turning ambitious objectives into tangible outcomes.

Prioritizing Goals: What to Focus on First for Maximum Impact

In business, it's easy to get overwhelmed by a long list of goals and initiatives. While it's tempting to try and tackle everything at once, spreading yourself too thin can dilute your efforts and reduce the overall impact. Prioritizing your goals ensures that you're focusing on the objectives that will drive the most value for your business and help you achieve success faster.

In this section, we'll explore how to prioritize your goals effectively, so you can focus on what matters most and ensure maximum impact for your business.

1. Assess Urgency and Importance

Not all goals are created equal. Some are critical to the immediate success of your business, while others are important but can be achieved over time. When prioritizing goals, start by assessing the *urgency* and *importance* of each objective.

To determine this, ask:

- **Is this goal time-sensitive?** (Urgency)

- **How essential is this goal to the long-term success of my business?** (Importance)

A goal that's both urgent and important should take top priority. For example, if your website is outdated and customers are abandoning their carts due to poor usability, an objective like "redesign the website for better user experience within 90 days" is both urgent and important. On the other hand, long-term goals that aren't time-sensitive, such as "launch a new product line next year," can be planned for future phases.

2. Focus on High-Impact Areas

To maximize the effectiveness of your efforts, prioritize goals that have the highest potential for impact. High-impact goals are those that will significantly move the needle for your business, whether by driving revenue, increasing customer satisfaction, or improving operational efficiency.

Ask yourself:

- **Which goals will have the biggest impact on my bottom line?**

- **Which objectives will create the most value for my customers?**

- **What goals will strengthen my market position?**

For example, if your current business strategy focuses on customer retention, setting a goal to "reduce customer churn by 15% in the next quarter" may be a high-impact objective, as it directly contributes to long-term revenue growth. High-impact goals typically align with your most critical business needs and offer the best return on investment (ROI).

3. Balance Short-Term Wins with Long-Term Objectives

While it's important to have ambitious, long-term objectives, don't neglect the power of short-term wins. Achieving smaller goals quickly can build momentum, keep your team motivated, and create early successes that contribute to larger, long-term objectives. The key is to balance short-term and long-term goals, so you're working on both immediate priorities and future growth.

To achieve this balance, ask:

- **What are the quick wins that will boost progress?**

- **How do these short-term goals contribute to my long-term vision?**

For example, if your long-term goal is to "increase market share by 10% in two years," a short-term win could be "launch a targeted social media campaign to boost brand awareness by 5% in the next quarter." This short-term goal contributes to the bigger picture while creating measurable progress along the way.

4. Evaluate Resource Availability

Every goal requires resources—whether it's time, money, personnel, or technology. When prioritizing goals, it's essential to consider the resources you have available and whether your team has the capacity to achieve multiple goals at once.

To evaluate resource availability, ask:

- **Do I have the budget, tools, and personnel to achieve this goal?**

- **Which objectives will require the most resources, and are they worth the investment?**

- **Can certain goals be deferred or delegated to different teams?**

For instance, if you're a small business with limited resources, focusing on a goal like "improve customer acquisition by 10% through cost-effective marketing strategies" may be more achievable than launching an expensive new product line. By understanding your constraints, you can prioritize goals that are realistic given your available resources.

5. Consider Dependencies and Sequencing

Some goals depend on others being completed first. When prioritizing objectives, it's important to recognize which goals are dependent on others and how they should be sequenced for maximum effectiveness.

Ask yourself:

- **Does achieving this goal rely on the completion of another goal first?**

- **Are there foundational goals that will support or unlock future objectives?**

For example, if your goal is to "launch a new e-commerce platform," but your current website infrastructure is outdated, you might first need to prioritize a goal like "upgrade website infrastructure by Q2" before proceeding with the e-commerce launch. Recognizing dependencies helps you sequence your goals logically and efficiently.

6. Align Goals with Team Strengths

When setting and prioritizing goals, consider the strengths and capabilities of your team. Goals that leverage your team's expertise and skills are more likely to be executed successfully, while goals that fall outside their core competencies may require additional training, time, or resources.

To align goals with team strengths, ask:

- **Does my team have the skills needed to achieve this goal?**

- **Which goals align with my team's existing expertise and experience?**

For example, if your team excels at digital marketing but lacks product development expertise, prioritizing a goal like "increase online sales by 20% through digital marketing campaigns" might be more achievable in the short term, compared to developing and launching a new product, which may require external resources.

7. Use a Prioritization Framework

To objectively prioritize goals, consider using a **prioritization framework** such as the **Eisenhower Matrix** or **Weighted Scoring Model**. These tools help you systematically evaluate goals based on urgency, importance, impact, and resource requirements.

- **Eisenhower Matrix**: Categorize goals into four quadrants—urgent and important, important but not urgent, urgent but not important, and neither urgent nor important. Focus on the goals in the "urgent and important" category first.

- **Weighted Scoring Model**: Assign scores to each goal based on specific criteria like impact, urgency, feasibility, and alignment with your business strategy. The goals with the highest scores should take priority.

These frameworks provide a structured way to evaluate and rank your goals, ensuring that you're focusing on what matters most.

Conclusion: Prioritize for Success

Prioritizing goals isn't about choosing which ones to tackle—it's about choosing the right ones that will drive the most impact. By focusing on urgency, importance, high-impact areas, resource availability, and dependencies, you can create a clear path to success. Remember to balance short-term wins with long-term vision, and align goals with your team's strengths to ensure consistent progress.

Effective prioritization allows you to focus your efforts, make the best use of resources, and move your business forward with purpose and clarity. By prioritizing wisely, you're setting yourself up for maximum success and impact.

Tracking Progress: How to Measure Success and Stay on Course

Once you've set your business objectives, the next crucial step is to ensure you're making steady progress toward achieving them. Tracking progress is essential for measuring success, identifying potential roadblocks, and making adjustments along the way. Without a system in place to monitor your goals, even the most well-defined objectives can drift off course.

In this section, we'll explore the best methods for tracking your progress, how to measure success, and what to do when adjustments are necessary to stay on course.

1. Set Key Performance Indicators (KPIs)

Key Performance Indicators (KPIs) are measurable values that demonstrate how effectively you're achieving your business objectives. KPIs give you a clear way to measure success and provide a real-time look at your progress.

To define your KPIs, ask:

- **What metrics will indicate that I'm making progress toward my goal?**

- **What numbers or data points can I track to measure success?**

For example, if your goal is to "increase online sales by 20% in Q1," some relevant KPIs could include:

- Website traffic

- Conversion rates

- Average order value

- Number of new customers

Each of these KPIs gives you a measurable indicator of whether you're moving toward your sales goal. Choose KPIs that are directly tied to your objectives and review them regularly to keep progress in check.

2. Establish Milestones

Milestones are smaller, intermediate goals that help you break down your larger objective into more manageable pieces. They serve as checkpoints along your journey, allowing you to celebrate small wins and gauge whether you're on track to meet the overall goal.

To set milestones, ask:

- **What smaller steps will I need to achieve on the way to my larger goal?**

- **What should I accomplish by the end of each month or quarter?**

For example, if your goal is to "launch a new product by the end of Q3," your milestones might include:

- Completing product design by the end of Q1

- Finalizing production and prototypes by the end of Q2

- Launching the marketing campaign at the start of Q3

By hitting these milestones, you'll ensure steady progress and can address any issues early on before they derail your timeline.

3. Use Progress Tracking Tools

Keeping track of multiple goals, KPIs, and milestones can get complex. That's why using digital tools and platforms designed for progress tracking is invaluable. These tools help you visualize progress, monitor KPIs, and ensure that your team stays aligned with your objectives.

Some popular progress-tracking tools include:

- **Project Management Software**: Tools like Asana, Trello, and Monday.com allow you to assign tasks, set deadlines, and track progress in real time.

- **Goal Tracking Apps**: Apps like Goalscape or Weekdone help break down objectives into smaller goals, track milestones, and provide visual representations of progress.

- **KPI Dashboards**: Software like Google Analytics, Klipfolio, or Databox offers real-time insights into your KPIs, making it easier to monitor the metrics that matter.

These tools offer a centralized place to track progress, making it easier to stay on course and quickly identify any delays or issues that need to be addressed.

4. Schedule Regular Check-Ins

Consistency is key when it comes to tracking progress. Schedule regular check-ins to review how well you're doing in relation to your objectives and KPIs. Whether it's weekly, bi-weekly, or monthly, these check-ins keep you and your team accountable and allow you to course-correct if necessary.

To conduct effective check-ins, ask:

- **Are we on track to meet our milestones?**

- **Are we hitting our KPIs?**

- **What challenges or roadblocks have emerged, and how can we address them?**

Check-ins help ensure that progress is consistently monitored and that any necessary adjustments are made quickly to avoid falling behind. Use these meetings to celebrate wins, reassign resources, or pivot strategies as needed.

5. Identify and Address Roadblocks

No matter how well you plan, unexpected obstacles may arise that hinder your progress. The key is to identify these roadblocks early and address them before they disrupt your momentum. Regularly monitoring KPIs and milestones will help you spot problems, but you'll also need to dig into the root cause of any delays or issues.

To handle roadblocks effectively, ask:

- **What is causing the delay?**

- **Are there external factors (market changes, supply chain disruptions) affecting progress?**

- **Do we need to reallocate resources or shift priorities to get back on track?**

For example, if you're behind on a goal to "increase customer acquisition by 15%," look at your KPIs to see where the problem lies. Is it a traffic issue? Low conversion rates? Identifying the exact bottleneck allows you to take corrective action, whether that means adjusting your marketing strategy, refining your messaging, or reallocating budget to underperforming areas.

6. Make Adjustments as Needed

Flexibility is crucial when tracking progress. If your goals are falling behind, or if new opportunities arise, you may need to adjust your objectives, timelines, or strategies. Pivoting doesn't mean failure; it means adapting to current realities and ensuring you stay on course for long-term success.

When considering adjustments, ask:

- **Is this goal still achievable, or do we need to revise the timeline?**

- **Are there new market conditions or business opportunities that should influence our priorities?**

- **Do we need to allocate more resources to this goal to keep it on track?**

For instance, if a new competitor enters your market and changes customer preferences, you may need to adjust your objectives to focus more on retaining existing customers rather than pursuing aggressive acquisition goals.

By remaining adaptable and willing to pivot when necessary, you'll ensure that your business stays agile and responsive to changing conditions.

7. Celebrate Milestones and Successes

Tracking progress isn't just about identifying problems—it's also about celebrating successes. Recognizing and rewarding your team when you hit key milestones or achieve your goals helps maintain motivation and engagement. These celebrations reinforce that progress is being made and keeps everyone energized to keep pushing forward.

When celebrating successes, consider:

- **Acknowledging individual contributions and team efforts**

- **Sharing progress with stakeholders to build momentum**

- **Recognizing small wins along the way, not just the final outcome**

Celebrating wins, whether big or small, helps create a positive culture of achievement and reminds your team that every step forward is valuable.

Conclusion: Stay on Track for Success

Tracking progress is vital to turning your business objectives into reality. By setting clear KPIs, establishing milestones, using tracking tools, and conducting regular check-ins, you'll stay on course and ensure steady progress. Remember, being flexible and adjusting your approach when necessary is just as important as celebrating your wins along the way. This structured approach to monitoring your goals will keep you and your team focused, motivated, and on track for long-term success.

Quick Tips and Recap

- **Set Key Performance Indicators (KPIs)**: Use measurable metrics to track progress and assess success.

- **Establish Milestones**: Break larger objectives into smaller, achievable steps to maintain momentum.

- **Use Progress Tracking Tools**: Leverage project management software, goal-tracking apps, and KPI dashboards to monitor progress effectively.

- **Schedule Regular Check-Ins**: Consistently review progress to stay on track, address challenges, and make adjustments.

- **Identify and Address Roadblocks**: Proactively identify obstacles, analyze the causes, and take corrective action to overcome them.

- **Be Flexible and Adapt**: Adjust objectives, timelines, or strategies when necessary to stay aligned with market changes and business needs.

- **Celebrate Wins**: Recognize milestones and successes to maintain motivation and team morale.

CHAPTER FIVE

Blueprints for Success: Developing Your Business Model

"Developing your business model isn't just about laying a foundation; it's about crafting a blueprint that aligns your vision with market needs and drives sustainable success." — CLAYTON CHRISTENSEN, AUTHOR AND BUSINESS CONSULTANT

Welcome to the architect's table of your business empire—where napkin sketches turn into a masterful blueprint for success! Your business model is the backbone of everything you do, the structural foundation that will either support your skyscraper dreams or leave you building sandcastles. This isn't just about figuring out how to make money (though, let's be honest, that's a big part of it); it's about creating a system that consistently delivers value to your customers while keeping the lights on in your office.

Imagine your business model as a combination of a Swiss army knife and a GPS—it needs to be flexible, useful in every situation, and always know the way forward. Whether you're selling hand-crafted dog bow ties or launching the next tech unicorn, your model should answer the big questions: Who are you serving? How are you reaching them? And most importantly, how are you going to keep the cash flowing without breaking a sweat?

As you map this out, think of yourself as both artist and engineer—balancing creativity with practicality. Be bold in your ideas, but remember, even the best dream needs a solid plan to stand tall. Whether you're embracing subscription models, one-time sales, or something wild and new, make sure it's a blueprint you're excited to build on.

So, grab your metaphorical hard hat and start developing a business model that not only works but wows. Because a strong foundation? That's the secret to constructing an empire that lasts.

Understanding the Core Elements of a Business Model

Before you dive into launching your business, you need a solid understanding of the essential building blocks that make up a successful business model. Think of these elements as the pillars that support your venture—each one contributing to a system that delivers value, keeps the cash flowing, and sustains growth over time.

In this section, we'll break down the core components of a business model, giving you a roadmap to develop a structure that is not only robust but also adaptable to changing market conditions.

1. Value Proposition: The Heart of Your Business

Your value proposition is the most crucial part of your business model—it's what makes your product or service stand out. It answers the critical question: Why should customers choose you over your competitors?

To create a strong value proposition, ask yourself:

- **What unique value do I offer?**
- **How do I solve my customers' pain points?**
- **What benefits do my products or services provide that others don't?**

For example, if you're selling eco-friendly cleaning products, your value proposition might be, "We offer safe, environmentally sustainable cleaning solutions that protect your family and the planet." A compelling value proposition will resonate with your target customers, differentiate you from competitors, and serve as the foundation of your entire business model.

2. Customer Segments: Who Are You Serving?

Understanding your customer segments is essential for designing a business model that effectively meets the needs of your target audience. Customer segments refer to the specific groups of people or businesses that your product or service is designed to serve.

To define your customer segments, consider:

- **Who are my primary customers?**
- **What are their demographics (age, income, gender, etc.) and psychographics (interests, behaviors, values)?**
- **Do I serve multiple customer segments, and how do they differ?**

For instance, if you run a fitness apparel brand, your customer segments might include athletes, fitness enthusiasts, and people looking for stylish, comfortable everyday wear. Each segment may have different needs and purchasing motivations, and your business model should address those differences.

3. Revenue Streams: How Will You Make Money?

Your revenue streams represent how your business will generate income. This is the financial engine of your business model and can take various forms depending on your product, industry, and target market.

Common revenue models include:

- **Direct sales**: Selling products or services directly to customers (e.g., e-commerce or retail).

- **Subscription services**: Charging customers a recurring fee for access to a product or service (e.g., Netflix, Spotify).

- **Freemium models**: Offering a basic version of your service for free while charging for premium features (e.g., Dropbox).

To develop your revenue streams, ask:

- **What value are customers willing to pay for?**

- **How will they pay (one-time purchase, subscription, etc.)?**

- **How many different revenue streams can I incorporate?**

A solid revenue model ensures that your business not only serves customers effectively but also sustains itself financially.

4. Key Activities: What Will You Do to Deliver Value?

The key activities of your business model are the tasks and operations you must perform to deliver on your value proposition. These are the activities that keep your business running, from product development to marketing and customer service.

To define your key activities, consider:

- **What needs to happen to deliver my product or service?**

- **What are the most important processes, resources, and tasks required to fulfill my value proposition?**

For a software company, key activities might include software development, maintaining servers, and providing technical support. For a restaurant, key activities could be sourcing ingredients, food preparation, and customer service.

Clearly identifying your key activities helps ensure that you're efficiently delivering value while maintaining operational excellence.

5. Key Resources: What Do You Need to Make It Happen?

Every business relies on key resources to operate. These include the assets, people, and tools that you'll need to deliver your product or service, manage daily operations, and grow your business.

Key resources can include:

- **Physical resources**: Equipment, inventory, facilities, or technology.

- **Human resources**: Your team, contractors, or skilled labor.

- **Intellectual resources**: Patents, proprietary software, or a strong brand.

Ask yourself:

- **What resources are critical to delivering my product or service?**

- **Do I have the necessary technology, people, and capital to achieve my objectives?**

Understanding your key resources will help you allocate them effectively and ensure that your business is set up for success from day one.

6. Cost Structure: Managing Expenses and Profitability

Every business has costs associated with delivering its product or service. The cost structure of your business model outlines the expenses involved in operating your business, from fixed costs (like rent and salaries) to variable costs (like production and marketing expenses).

To manage your cost structure, ask:

- **What are the primary costs associated with running my business?**

- **Are my costs fixed (e.g., rent, salaries) or variable (e.g., materials, shipping)?**

- **How can I optimize my costs while maintaining quality?**

For example, an e-commerce business might have fixed costs like website maintenance and employee salaries, along with variable costs like shipping and packaging materials. Balancing your cost structure with your revenue streams is essential for maintaining profitability.

Conclusion: Building a Strong Business Model

Understanding these core elements—value proposition, customer segments, revenue streams, key activities, key resources, and cost structure—is the first step to building a successful business model. Each element works together to form a cohesive structure that delivers value to your customers while ensuring your business remains profitable and sustainable.

As you start sketching out your business model, focus on creating a balance between delivering exceptional value to your customers and efficiently managing your resources and costs. A well-developed business model sets the foundation for growth, adaptability, and long-term success.

Choosing the Right Revenue Model: Subscription, One-Time Sale, or Hybrid?

One of the most critical decisions in developing your business model is determining how you will generate revenue. The right revenue model not only sustains your business but also aligns with your value proposition and customer expectations. Whether you choose a subscription-based model, one-time sales, or a hybrid approach, the goal is to create a consistent stream of income that supports your growth.

In this section, we'll explore the advantages and challenges of three common revenue models—subscription, one-time sale, and hybrid—so you can determine the best fit for your business.

1. Subscription Model: Consistent, Recurring Revenue

The subscription model involves charging customers a recurring fee—whether monthly, quarterly, or annually—in exchange for access to a product or service. This model has become increasingly popular in industries ranging from software (SaaS) to media and entertainment (like Netflix) and even physical products (such as subscription boxes).

Advantages:

- **Predictable Revenue Stream**: Subscriptions provide consistent, recurring revenue, making it easier to forecast cash flow and plan for future growth.

- **Customer Retention**: With a subscription model, you're incentivized to keep customers happy, as the ongoing relationship encourages long-term loyalty.

- **Lower Customer Acquisition Costs**: Since customers are retained over a longer period, you can spend less on constantly acquiring new buyers.

Challenges:

- **High Upfront Effort**: You need to offer continuous value to keep customers subscribed, which may require regular content, product updates, or exclusive perks.

- **Churn Risk**: Customers can cancel their subscriptions if they don't feel they're getting enough value, making it crucial to focus on retention strategies.

Is the Subscription Model Right for You?

Consider the subscription model if:

- Your product or service offers recurring value (e.g., software updates, curated product boxes, premium content).

- You want to build long-term customer relationships and generate predictable revenue.

For example, a SaaS business offering cloud storage services would be well-suited to a subscription model, as customers need continued access to storage and are likely to stay subscribed as long as they find value.

2. One-Time Sale Model: Immediate Cash Flow

The one-time sale model is the traditional approach of selling a product or service with a single transaction. Once the purchase is complete, the relationship with the customer may end unless they choose to return for another purchase.

Advantages:

- **Immediate Revenue**: One-time sales generate instant cash flow, which can be helpful for businesses needing quick capital or working with shorter sales cycles.

- **Simplicity**: It's straightforward—sell the product, receive payment, and deliver the value without the need for ongoing management.

- **Wide Customer Base**: One-time sales can attract a broader range of customers who are looking for a one-off solution rather than a recurring commitment.

Challenges:

- **Unpredictable Revenue**: Sales may fluctuate month-to-month, making it harder to predict revenue and plan long-term.

- **Constant Need for Customer Acquisition**: You'll need to continually acquire new customers to generate sales, leading to higher marketing and acquisition costs.

Is the One-Time Sale Model Right for You?

Consider the one-time sale model if:

- Your product or service is something that customers need only occasionally or as a one-off (e.g., furniture, event tickets, luxury goods).

- You prefer a simpler business model without the ongoing obligations of a subscription service.

For instance, a retailer selling custom-made furniture would likely benefit from a one-time sale model, as customers typically make a purchase and don't return until they need another piece.

3. Hybrid Model: The Best of Both Worlds

The hybrid model combines elements of both the subscription and one-time sale models, offering flexibility in how you generate revenue. This approach can be particularly effective if your business has diverse customer needs or product offerings that lend themselves to multiple pricing strategies.

Advantages:

- **Multiple Revenue Streams**: A hybrid model allows you to diversify your income, providing both predictable revenue from subscriptions and cash infusions from one-time sales.

- **Customer Flexibility**: You can cater to different types of customers—those who prefer ongoing access and those who want to make a single purchase.

- **Cross-Selling Opportunities**: You can upsell one-time customers into subscriptions or offer subscription customers one-off purchases that complement their service.

Challenges:

- **Operational Complexity**: Managing both recurring and one-time revenue streams requires more resources, as you'll need systems in place to handle both types of transactions.

- **Pricing and Value Balance**: You'll need to carefully balance pricing to ensure that neither the subscription nor the one-time purchase cannibalizes the other.

Is the Hybrid Model Right for You?

Consider the hybrid model if:

- Your business offers both recurring value and one-time products or services (e.g., a software company offering both subscription access to its platform and one-time add-ons).

- You want to diversify your revenue streams and reach a broader audience.

For example, an online education platform could use a hybrid model by offering a subscription for unlimited access to a library of courses, while also allowing one-time purchases of premium certification programs or specialized content.

4. Choosing the Best Fit for Your Business

Selecting the right revenue model depends on your product, your customers, and your long-term business goals. Here are some key questions to help you decide:

- **What type of value does my product or service offer?** If it provides continuous value over time, a subscription model may be ideal. If it's a one-time need, consider a one-time sale approach.

- **How do my customers prefer to pay?** Are they more inclined to commit to a recurring payment or make a single, upfront purchase? Customer preferences will play a significant role in determining the best model.

- **What are my financial goals?** Do you need predictable, steady revenue (subscription) or prefer flexibility and immediate cash flow (one-time sale)?

You may even choose to test multiple models. Many successful businesses start with one approach and later expand into hybrid models as they grow and gain a deeper understanding of their customer base.

Conclusion: Tailor Your Revenue Model to Your Business

Choosing the right revenue model is a foundational decision for your business, influencing not only how you make money but also how you interact with customers and deliver value. Whether you opt for the predictability of subscriptions, the simplicity of one-time sales, or the flexibility of a hybrid model, make sure your revenue strategy aligns with your value proposition and long-term vision.

By selecting a revenue model that fits your product, market, and financial goals, you'll create a sustainable income stream that supports your business's growth and success.

Identifying and Reaching Your Target Audience

One of the most critical aspects of building a successful business model is knowing exactly who you're serving. Your target audience is the group of customers who are most likely to need and want your product or service. Identifying and reaching this audience is essential because if you don't understand your customers, you could waste time and resources marketing to the wrong people or developing products that don't meet their needs.

In this section, we'll explore how to identify your target audience and craft effective strategies for reaching them, ensuring that your business model connects with the right people in meaningful ways.

1. Defining Your Ideal Customer

The first step in identifying your target audience is defining your ideal customer. This involves narrowing down the demographics, interests, behaviors, and pain points of the people most likely to buy from you. The more specific you can get, the better. Generalizing will only make it harder to reach and resonate with potential customers.

To define your ideal customer, consider:

- **Demographics**: Age, gender, location, income level, education, and occupation.

- **Psychographics**: Values, interests, lifestyles, and attitudes.

- **Behavioral Patterns**: Purchasing habits, brand loyalty, and product usage.

For example, if you're selling eco-friendly cleaning products, your ideal customer might be a 30-45-year-old environmentally-conscious homeowner with a mid-to-high income who values sustainability and healthy living. By defining these attributes, you can tailor your marketing efforts and product offerings to meet their specific needs and preferences.

2. Identifying Customer Pain Points

A key part of targeting the right audience is understanding their pain points—the problems or challenges they face that your product or service can solve. The more closely your product addresses their needs, the more likely they are to engage with your brand.

To identify customer pain points, ask:

- **What frustrations or challenges do they experience?**

- **How can my product or service provide a solution or relief?**

- **What emotional or practical needs are they seeking to fulfill?**

For example, a business offering meal kit delivery services might identify a pain point for busy professionals who struggle to find time to cook healthy meals. The service can be positioned as a solution that saves time while delivering nutritious, easy-to-prepare food. Understanding the specific pain points of your audience allows you to position your product as a must-have solution, not just a nice-to-have option.

3. Segmenting Your Audience

Not all customers are the same, even within your target market. That's where audience segmentation comes in—dividing your audience into smaller groups based on shared characteristics. Segmentation allows you to tailor your messaging, products, and marketing campaigns more effectively to meet the specific needs of each group.

Common types of segmentation include:

- **Demographic Segmentation**: Grouping customers by age, income, or occupation.

- **Behavioral Segmentation**: Categorizing based on purchasing habits or product usage.

- **Geographic Segmentation**: Targeting based on location (e.g., urban vs. rural).

- **Psychographic Segmentation**: Grouping customers by values, lifestyles, or personalities.

For instance, if you sell athletic apparel, you might segment your audience into groups such as fitness enthusiasts, professional athletes, and casual gym-goers. Each of these groups has different motivations and needs, allowing you to craft tailored messaging that speaks directly to their interests.

4. Conducting Market Research

Once you've defined your target audience and segmented them, it's time to validate your assumptions through market research. Market research helps you gather data and insights about your audience to ensure you're targeting the right people and understand their preferences.

Effective ways to conduct market research include:

- **Surveys and Polls**: Directly asking your audience questions about their preferences, challenges, and behaviors.

- **Focus Groups**: Gathering a small group of target customers to discuss their needs and opinions on your product.

- **Social Listening**: Monitoring social media platforms and online forums to see what your target audience is talking about, what they like, and what they're struggling with.

- **Competitor Analysis**: Examining your competitors' customers to understand their audience and how they're positioning their products.

Market research helps you refine your target audience definition and provides you with data-backed insights that guide your marketing and business strategies.

5. Choosing the Right Marketing Channels

Identifying your audience is just the beginning—next, you need to figure out how to reach them. Different audiences consume information and interact with brands in different ways, so it's essential to choose the right marketing channels to connect with your target customers.

To determine which channels to focus on, ask:

- **Where does my audience spend their time?** Social media? Email? Websites? In-store?

- **How do they prefer to engage with brands?** Through content, ads, newsletters, or direct sales?

- **What marketing channels are most effective for reaching similar customers?**

For example, if your audience is primarily millennials, they may be more active on social media platforms like Instagram and TikTok. On the other hand, if you're targeting business executives, LinkedIn and email marketing may be more effective.

Here are a few common marketing channels to consider:

- **Social Media**: Facebook, Instagram, Twitter, TikTok, LinkedIn.

- **Search Engine Marketing**: Google Ads, search engine optimization (SEO).

- **Email Marketing**: Newsletters, personalized email campaigns.

- **Content Marketing**: Blogs, podcasts, videos.

- **Influencer Marketing**: Partnering with influencers or thought leaders to promote your product.

Your marketing strategy should be tailored to the channels that your target audience uses most frequently. Reaching your audience where they are—whether that's on Instagram or in their inbox—will help you build stronger connections and increase your chances of converting leads into customers.

6. Crafting Messaging That Resonates

Reaching your audience isn't just about finding them on the right platform—it's about speaking to them in a way that resonates. Your messaging should reflect their values, address their pain points, and clearly communicate how your product or service improves their lives.

To craft effective messaging, consider:

- **What language, tone, and style will resonate with my audience?**

- **How can I highlight the benefits of my product in a way that speaks directly to their needs?**

- **What emotions or desires can I tap into to connect with them on a deeper level?**

For example, if your target audience is environmentally conscious, your messaging might focus on sustainability and ethical sourcing. You could use phrases like "eco-friendly," "reduce your carbon footprint," or "save the planet" to appeal to their values.

7. Building Customer Relationships

Once you've reached your target audience, the next step is to build lasting relationships. This involves not only delivering great products but also providing excellent customer service and engaging with your audience consistently. Building strong relationships turns customers into loyal brand advocates who will return to your business again and again.

Key ways to build customer relationships include:

- **Personalization**: Tailoring your interactions to individual customer preferences, such as offering product recommendations based on their past purchases.

- **Ongoing Engagement**: Keeping your audience engaged with regular communication through email marketing, social media, or exclusive offers.

- **Community Building**: Creating a community around your brand where customers can interact with each other and with your business (e.g., Facebook groups, loyalty programs).

By focusing on long-term relationships, you'll increase customer loyalty and create a foundation for sustainable growth.

Conclusion: Target Audience as the Key to Business Success

Identifying and reaching your target audience is a foundational element of building a successful business. By defining your ideal customer, understanding their pain points, segmenting your audience, and choosing the right channels to reach them, you can create a marketing strategy that effectively connects with the people who are most likely to buy from you.

Remember, your audience is the driving force behind your business. When you know who they are and how to speak their language, you can build stronger relationships, drive sales, and ultimately grow your business in meaningful and sustainable ways.

Building a Value Proposition
That Stands Out

Your value proposition is the core of your business. It's the promise you make to your customers—the reason they should choose your product or service over others. A compelling value proposition clearly explains how your offering solves a problem, delivers benefits, and provides value that your competitors don't. It's the answer to the fundamental question every customer asks: "Why should I buy from you?"

In this section, we'll break down how to build a value proposition that stands out in the market, resonates with your target audience, and clearly communicates the unique value you deliver.

1. Identify Your Customer's Problem

The first step in crafting a standout value proposition is understanding the problem your customers face. If you can pinpoint a pain point or challenge they regularly encounter, you can position your product or service as the solution. Customers are looking for something that makes their lives easier, more efficient, or more enjoyable—your value proposition should focus on addressing that need.

To identify your customer's problem, ask:

- **What specific pain point is my customer experiencing?**

- **How does my product or service solve this problem?**

- **What emotions or frustrations do they feel because of this challenge?**

For example, if you're offering an online bookkeeping service for small business owners, the problem you're solving might be the time-consuming and complicated process of managing finances. Your service can alleviate the stress of bookkeeping by simplifying and automating the process, allowing business owners to focus on growing their business.

2. Define the Benefits and Value You Deliver

Once you've identified the problem, the next step is to clearly communicate the benefits of your product or service. It's important to differentiate between features (what your product does) and benefits (how it improves the customer's life or business). Focus on the outcomes your customers will experience when they use your product.

To define the benefits, ask:

- **What specific advantages does my product or service provide?**

- **How does it improve the customer's situation?**

- **What measurable results can the customer expect?**

For example, if you're selling a project management tool, the feature might be task automation, but the benefit is that your customers will save time and reduce project delays. Clearly communicate how your product helps customers achieve their goals—whether that's saving time, reducing costs, or improving their daily life.

3. Highlight What Makes You Unique

A strong value proposition doesn't just communicate value—it also highlights what sets you apart from the competition. Your Unique Selling Proposition (USP) is the element that differentiates you from others in the market. What do you offer that no one else does? How is your approach, process, or product better than the alternatives?

To identify what makes you unique, consider:

- **What do I do better than my competitors?**
- **What features or benefits are exclusive to my product or service?**
- **How can I deliver value in a way that competitors can't?**

For example, if your competitors offer eco-friendly products but yours are also locally sourced and handcrafted, that's a unique selling point. It adds an extra layer of differentiation that makes your brand stand out to customers who value sustainability and craftsmanship.

4. Be Clear and Concise

Your value proposition needs to be clear, concise, and easy to understand at a glance. Potential customers won't spend much time deciphering a long, complicated explanation of your business. In a few sentences, you should be able to communicate the problem you solve, the benefits you offer, and what makes you different.

A great value proposition typically answers these three questions:

1. **What do you offer?**
2. **How does it make your customer's life better?**
3. **Why should they choose you over others?**

For example, here's a clear and concise value proposition for a meal delivery service:

"Healthy, chef-crafted meals delivered to your door. Save time and eat well with fresh, nutritious options customized to your diet—no cooking required."

This value proposition addresses the customer's pain point (not having time to cook), offers a benefit (eating healthy meals with no effort), and makes the business unique (chef-crafted and diet-specific options).

5. Use Language That Resonates with Your Audience

Craft your value proposition using language that resonates with your target audience. The tone, style, and wording should reflect your brand's identity while speaking directly to the customer's emotions, desires, and needs. Avoid using overly technical jargon unless your audience consists of industry experts who expect it.

To ensure your language resonates, ask:

- **What tone or style will connect with my audience (friendly, professional, casual)?**

- **How can I use the words and phrases that my audience already uses?**

- **What emotions or values can I tap into to create a stronger connection?**

For instance, if your product targets eco-conscious consumers, emphasize words like "sustainable," "organic," or "environmentally friendly." If you're selling productivity software to professionals, focus on efficiency, time-saving, and results.

6. Test and Refine Your Value Proposition

Once you've crafted your value proposition, it's important to test and refine it based on customer feedback and market response. Your initial proposition may evolve as you better understand your audience and what resonates with them. A/B testing different versions of your value proposition in marketing materials, landing pages, or emails can provide valuable insights into what messaging is most effective.

To refine your value proposition, ask:

- **Are customers responding positively to this value proposition?**

- **Does it clearly differentiate my product from competitors?**

- **Is there any confusion about what we offer or how we provide value?**

By continuously improving your value proposition, you can ensure that it stays aligned with customer needs and remains relevant as your business evolves.

7. Communicate Your Value Proposition Across All Channels

Your value proposition should be integrated across all of your marketing and communication channels—your website, social media, email campaigns, advertisements, and in-person interactions. Consistency is key to reinforcing your message and ensuring that every touchpoint with your brand clearly communicates the value you provide.

Key channels to showcase your value proposition include:

- **Homepage or landing page**: Make your value proposition front and center on your website.

- **Social media profiles**: Integrate it into your bio, posts, and advertisements.

- **Email marketing**: Reinforce your value proposition in your subject lines and content.

- **Sales pitches**: Make sure your sales team is aligned with the core value proposition when pitching to prospects.

Consistently showcasing your value proposition across all channels helps establish brand identity and makes it easier for potential customers to understand why they should choose you.

Conclusion: Crafting a Standout Value Proposition

Your value proposition is the foundation of your brand and the key to attracting the right customers. By identifying your customer's problem, defining clear benefits, highlighting your unique qualities, and keeping your message concise, you can create a value proposition that resonates and differentiates your business in a crowded market.

Remember, a strong value proposition not only drives sales—it builds lasting relationships by consistently delivering on the promises you make to your customers. Take the time to develop, refine, and communicate your value proposition effectively to set your business up for long-term success.

Testing and Refining Your Business Model

Once you've set your business objectives, the next crucial step is to ensure you're making steady progress toward achieving them. Tracking progress is essential for measuring success, identifying potential roadblocks, and making adjustments along the way. Without a system in place to monitor your goals, even the most well-defined objectives can drift off course.

Creating a business model is the first step toward building a successful venture, but it's rarely perfect from the start. Markets evolve, customer needs change, and what seemed like a solid plan may require adjustments along the way. Testing and refining your business model ensures that it's not just a theoretical framework but a practical, adaptable plan that works in the real world.

In this section, we'll explore how to test your business model through feedback, data, and real-world experimentation. We'll also discuss how to refine and adjust it to maximize efficiency, profitability, and customer satisfaction.

1. Start with a Business Model Hypothesis

Before you can test your business model, think of it as a **hypothesis**—an educated guess about how your business will create, deliver, and capture value. This hypothesis includes assumptions about your target market, value proposition, revenue streams, cost structure, and more.

To start with a hypothesis, ask:

- **Who is my target customer, and what problem am I solving?**
- **How do I deliver value to them?**
- **What are my primary revenue streams?**
- **What are my key costs, and how do I manage them?**

By framing your business model as a hypothesis, you acknowledge that it may need to be validated or adjusted based on actual market conditions. This mindset prepares you for the iterative process of testing and refining your model.

2. Test with Real Customers

Once you've established your business model hypothesis, it's time to test it with real customers. The best way to see if your business model works is by putting your product or service in front of your target audience and gathering feedback. This process helps validate whether your value proposition resonates with customers and whether they're willing to pay for what you offer.

There are several ways to test your business model:

- **Pilot programs or beta testing**: Launch a limited version of your product or service to a small group of customers. Monitor their reactions, gather feedback, and evaluate how well your value proposition solves their problems.

- **Minimum Viable Product (MVP)**: Release a simplified version of your product with just the essential features to test the core elements of your business model. This approach minimizes risk and allows you to gather insights quickly.

- **Customer interviews and surveys**: Directly engage with potential or existing customers to understand their needs, preferences, and pain points. Ask for feedback on your product, pricing, and overall experience.

The key to testing your business model is to get real-world input from the people who matter most—your customers. Their feedback will help you identify whether your assumptions are correct or if adjustments are needed.

3. Analyze Performance Metrics

Alongside customer feedback, data is your most valuable tool for refining your business model. Track key performance metrics that reveal how well your business is operating and whether it's on the right track. These metrics will give you insights into how effectively your business model is working and where improvements are needed.

Key performance metrics to track might include:

- **Customer acquisition cost (CAC)**: How much does it cost to acquire a new customer? If your acquisition costs are too high, you may need to adjust your marketing or sales strategy.

- **Customer lifetime value (CLV)**: How much revenue does each customer generate over the course of their relationship with your business? Increasing CLV can help you focus on customer retention and upselling opportunities.

- **Churn rate**: How many customers stop using your product or service within a given time frame? A high churn rate may indicate that your value proposition needs improvement or that your product isn't delivering long-term value.

- **Profit margins**: Are you generating enough profit after covering costs? If your margins are too low, you may need to optimize your pricing strategy or reduce operational expenses.

By regularly reviewing these metrics, you can identify where your business model is succeeding and where it needs refinement.

4. Identify Weak Points in Your Model

During the testing phase, you'll likely encounter areas of your business model that don't perform as expected. These weak points are opportunities to pivot or make strategic adjustments. By identifying what's not working, you can refine your approach and strengthen your business model.

To identify weak points, ask:

- **Is my value proposition resonating with customers, or are they uninterested?**

- **Are my revenue streams generating the expected income, or are there gaps?**

- **Are my costs manageable, or are they cutting into profits too much?**

- **Is my target market responding well, or do I need to explore new segments?**

For example, if customers aren't converting at the rate you anticipated, it may indicate that your value proposition needs refinement, your pricing strategy is off, or you're targeting the wrong audience. By continuously analyzing these areas, you can make the necessary changes to improve your business's performance.

5. Iterate and Refine

Testing your business model is not a one-time process; it's an ongoing effort that requires iteration. Based on customer feedback, performance data, and the insights you gain from testing, refine your business model to make it more effective and aligned with real-world demands.

Here's how to refine your business model:

- **Adjust your value proposition**: If customer feedback indicates that your product doesn't fully meet their needs, tweak your offering to better solve their pain points.

- **Optimize your cost structure**: If your costs are too high, look for ways to streamline operations, negotiate with suppliers, or eliminate unnecessary expenses.

- **Expand or adjust your revenue streams**: If one revenue stream isn't delivering as expected, consider introducing additional streams or tweaking your pricing strategy to increase profitability.

- **Explore new customer segments**: If your current target market isn't responding well, consider pivoting to a new segment that may have a stronger need for your product or service.

By iterating and refining your business model, you ensure that it stays flexible and adaptable as your business grows and market conditions evolve.

6. Monitor Market Trends and Customer Needs

Refining your business model doesn't just happen based on internal metrics or feedback; it also requires staying attuned to market trends and evolving customer needs. Industries change, new competitors emerge, and customer expectations shift over time. Keeping an eye on these external factors allows you to make proactive adjustments before problems arise.

To stay ahead of trends, consider:

- **Industry reports and market research**: Regularly review industry trends and market research to stay informed about what's happening in your space.

- **Competitor analysis**: Monitor what your competitors are doing. Are they shifting their business models, introducing new products, or targeting different customer segments?

- **Customer feedback loops**: Keep engaging with your customers to understand their changing preferences and needs. Periodic surveys or customer satisfaction reviews can provide valuable insights.

By staying adaptable and anticipating changes in the market, you'll be able to adjust your business model in ways that keep you competitive and responsive to new opportunities.

Conclusion: An Evolving Business Model for Lasting Success

Testing and refining your business model is an essential part of building a sustainable and successful venture. By treating your business model as a hypothesis, gathering real-world data and feedback, and continuously iterating based on performance, you can ensure that your business remains flexible and responsive to both internal and external changes.

Remember, a great business model is never static. It evolves as your business grows, your customers' needs change, and the market shifts. The more you test and refine, the stronger and more resilient your business will become, setting you up for long-term success.

Quick Tips and Recap

- **Start with a Business Model Hypothesis**: Frame your business model as a testable hypothesis that outlines how you plan to create, deliver, and capture value.

- **Test with Real Customers**: Use pilot programs, MVPs, and customer feedback to validate your assumptions and gather insights from your target audience.

- **Track Key Metrics**: Monitor important data like customer acquisition cost (CAC), customer lifetime value (CLV), churn rate, and profit margins to measure success and identify areas for improvement.

- **Identify Weak Points**: Look for gaps in your business model, such as ineffective value propositions, high costs, or unresponsive target markets, and address them.

- **Iterate and Refine**: Continuously improve your business model by adjusting your value proposition, revenue streams, cost structure, or customer segments based on feedback and performance.

- **Monitor Market Trends**: Stay informed about industry trends, competitor strategies, and evolving customer needs to keep your business model adaptable and relevant.

- **Embrace Flexibility**: Treat your business model as a living framework that evolves with your business, customers, and market conditions.

PART TWO

Building Your Strategy

Welcome to Part Two: Building Your Strategy, where we go from throwing spaghetti at the wall to cooking up a five-course meal with a business plan so sharp, it could slice through indecision. This is where you stop winging it and start crafting a strategy with the precision of a master chef—balancing marketing, operations, finances, and a dash of innovation to serve up a recipe for success. Whether you're fine-tuning your marketing sauce or adding a sprinkle of risk management, this is the part where you put all the ingredients together and turn your business idea into a Michelin-starred masterpiece. Bon appétit!

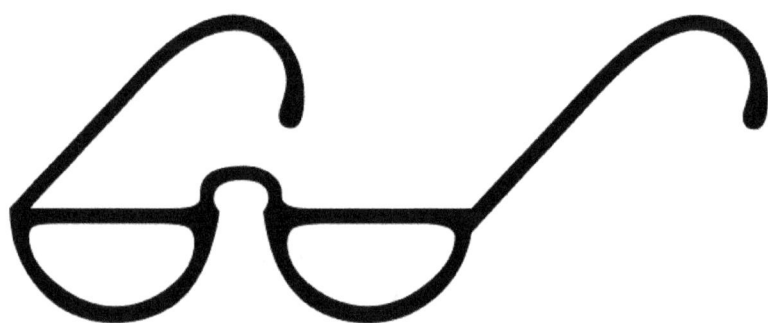

CHAPTER SIX

The Art of Attraction: Creating a Magnetic Marketing Strategy

"Great marketing isn't about pushing products; it's about pulling people in. The key is to understand your audience so well that your message feels like a personal invitation they can't resist."— SETH GODIN, MARKETING EXPERT AND BEST-SELLING AUTHOR

Welcome to the world of marketing, where your business needs to be more magnetic than a fridge covered in souvenir magnets! In this chapter, we're diving into the art of attraction, the key to drawing in customers without chasing them down like a desperate contestant on a dating show. Your marketing strategy isn't just about flashy ads or catchy slogans—it's about building a force so irresistible that customers flock to you like moths to a flame (without the burning part, of course).

The secret? It's all about knowing who your ideal customers are, speaking their language, and offering them something they can't resist. Think of your marketing as a first date with your audience—you've got to be authentic, intriguing, and maybe sprinkle in a little mystery to keep them coming back for more. Your goal is to create a brand experience that not only grabs attention but keeps it, converting curiosity into loyalty.

So, mix up your social media magic, blend in some killer content, and throw in a pinch of irresistible offers. With the right strategy, your business will have customers lining up like it's the hottest club in town. And just like that, you'll master the art of attraction and leave your competitors wondering what kind of marketing sorcery you're up to!

Understanding Your Audience: The Foundation of a Magnetic Strategy

At the heart of every successful marketing strategy is a deep understanding of your audience. Before you can attract customers, you need to know who they are, what they want, and how your product or service fits into their lives. Understanding your audience is the foundation of a magnetic marketing strategy that pulls in the right people and keeps them engaged.

In this section, we'll explore how to define your target audience, identify their needs, and craft a message that speaks directly to them.

1. Define Your Target Audience

The first step in understanding your audience is defining who they are. Your target audience isn't everyone in the world—it's a specific group of people who are most likely to benefit from and be interested in your product or service. Defining this audience helps you focus your marketing efforts, making sure you're speaking to the right people with the right message.

To define your target audience, consider:

- **Demographics**: Age, gender, income level, education, occupation, and geographic location.

- **Psychographics**: Interests, values, lifestyles, and personality traits.

- **Behavioral Patterns**: Buying habits, brand loyalty, product usage, and decision-making processes.

For example, if you're selling high-end fitness equipment, your target audience might be health-conscious professionals aged 30-50 who value quality, durability, and convenience. By narrowing your focus, you ensure that your marketing resonates with the people most likely to become loyal customers.

2. Create Buyer Personas

Once you've defined your target audience, the next step is to create buyer personas—detailed profiles that represent your ideal customers. Buyer personas help humanize your target audience, making it easier to understand their needs, motivations, and challenges. These personas guide your messaging, content, and marketing tactics, ensuring that everything you do speaks directly to your audience's desires and pain points.

When building buyer personas, ask:

- **What are their primary goals?**

- **What challenges or pain points are they facing?**

- **What factors influence their purchasing decisions?**

- **What media do they consume, and how do they engage with brands?**

For example, one of your buyer personas for a fitness brand could be "Healthy Helen," a 35-year-old mother who values convenience and wants to stay fit while balancing a busy lifestyle. Helen's pain point might be finding time for workouts, so your messaging could focus on how your product saves time and simplifies fitness routines. Creating multiple personas ensures you're reaching different segments of your target audience with tailored messaging.

3. Identify Their Needs and Desires

Understanding your audience means knowing not just who they are, but what they need and desire. Customers are looking for solutions to their problems, and your marketing strategy should position your product as the answer. The better you understand their pain points and motivations, the more effectively you can speak to them in a way that grabs their attention and addresses their needs.

To identify your audience's needs, ask:

- **What problems are they trying to solve?**

- **How does my product or service improve their life or solve these problems?**

- **What emotional or practical benefits do they want to experience?**

For example, if you're marketing a productivity app, your audience may be busy professionals who feel overwhelmed with managing tasks. Their primary need might be a simple, intuitive tool that helps them stay organized without adding complexity. By highlighting how your app streamlines task management, reduces stress, and increases productivity, you'll speak directly to their desires.

4. Understand Where They Are in the Buying Journey

Customers move through different stages of the buying journey—from awareness to consideration to decision. Knowing where your audience is in this journey helps you tailor your marketing efforts to meet them at the right point and guide them toward making a purchase.

The stages of the buying journey typically include:

- **Awareness**: The customer is just becoming aware of their problem and is looking for general information. At this stage, educational content like blog posts, infographics, or social media posts can help.

- **Consideration**: The customer is comparing options and evaluating potential solutions. Case studies, product comparisons, and testimonials can help position your brand as the best choice.

- **Decision**: The customer is ready to make a purchase and needs reassurance. Clear calls-to-action, limited-time offers, and detailed product information can help close the deal.

Tailor your marketing to each stage of the buying journey, so you're always delivering the right message at the right time.

5. Leverage Data and Research

While assumptions and personas are important, backing up your understanding of your audience with data is essential. Use data from customer surveys, focus groups, social media insights, and website analytics to gather real-world insights about your audience's behavior. This data helps you refine your strategy and ensure you're targeting the right people with the most effective messaging.

Key sources of data include:

- **Google Analytics**: Offers insights into your website visitors, including demographics, interests, and behaviors.

- **Social Media Insights**: Platforms like Facebook, Instagram, and Twitter provide analytics on audience engagement, demographics, and content performance.

- **Surveys and Polls**: Directly ask your audience about their preferences, pain points, and decision-making processes.

- **Customer Feedback**: Reviews, testimonials, and customer service interactions can provide valuable information about what your audience loves (or doesn't) about your product.

By using data to support your audience understanding, you ensure that your marketing decisions are grounded in reality rather than guesswork.

6. Tailor Your Messaging and Content

Once you have a deep understanding of your audience, the final step is to tailor your messaging and content to resonate with them. Speak their language, address their pain points, and highlight the benefits they care about most. Your marketing message should make your audience feel like you understand them and their needs, creating a personal connection that attracts and retains customers.

Key questions to guide your messaging:

- **How can I speak directly to their pain points and desires?**

- **What tone and style will resonate with my audience?**

- **How can I position my product as the perfect solution?**

For example, if your audience values sustainability, emphasize your product's eco-friendly qualities in your marketing materials. If your audience prioritizes convenience, focus on how your service saves time and simplifies their life.

Conclusion: Understanding Your Audience is the Key to Attraction
Understanding your audience is the foundation of a successful marketing strategy. By defining your target audience, creating buyer personas, identifying their needs, and tailoring your messaging to speak directly to them, you can create a magnetic pull that draws customers to your brand. Leverage data to back up your insights and continuously refine your approach to ensure you're always reaching the right people with the right message.

A deep understanding of your audience allows you to connect with them on a meaningful level, turning potential customers into loyal advocates and ensuring your marketing efforts are as magnetic as possible.

Crafting a Compelling Brand Story

Once you've set your business objectives, the next crucial step is to ensure you're making steady progress toward achieving them. Tracking progress is essential for measuring success, identifying potential roadblocks, and making adjustments along the way. Without a system in place to monitor your goals, even the most well-defined objectives can drift off course.

In today's world, where customers are bombarded with marketing messages from every direction, a compelling brand story can set you apart from the competition. Your brand story is more than just a catchy tagline or slick advertisement—it's the narrative that connects your business to your audience on an emotional level. It's the "why" behind your business, the purpose that fuels what you do, and the way you communicate your mission, values, and journey in a way that resonates with your customers.

In this section, we'll explore how to craft a brand story that engages, inspires, and turns customers into loyal advocates.

1. Understand the Power of Storytelling

Humans are hardwired to connect with stories. While facts and features can help customers make logical decisions, it's the emotional connection created by storytelling that often seals the deal. A great brand story captures attention, evokes emotions, and creates a lasting impression. It transforms your business from a faceless entity into a relatable, humanized brand that people want to support.

The power of a compelling story lies in its ability to:

- **Build trust**: Stories create authenticity and show the values behind your business.

- **Create emotional connections**: Stories resonate with people on a personal level, making your brand more memorable and relatable.

- **Differentiate your brand**: A unique story helps you stand out in a crowded market, giving customers a reason to choose you over competitors.

2. Start with Your "Why"

At the heart of every great brand story is the "why"—the reason your business exists beyond making a profit. Your "why" is the driving force behind your mission and purpose. When you share why you started your business and what motivates you, you invite customers to connect with your values and purpose on a deeper level.

To define your "why," ask yourself:

- **What inspired me to start this business?**

- **What problem am I solving for my customers?**

- **What is my business's mission or purpose beyond profits?**

For example, if you founded a sustainable clothing company, your "why" might be rooted in your passion for reducing the fashion industry's environmental impact. Sharing that personal motivation adds depth to your brand and shows customers that you're driven by more than just sales.

3. Highlight the Journey

Every brand has a story of how it came to be—the struggles, the breakthroughs, the evolution from idea to reality. Sharing the journey of your brand's growth makes your story more relatable and authentic. It helps customers see the human side of your business, showing that you faced challenges, adapted, and worked hard to create the products or services they love.

When telling your brand's journey, include:

- **The early challenges**: Share the obstacles you faced and how you overcame them. This creates a sense of resilience and perseverance.

- **Key milestones**: Highlight major turning points in your business's history—product launches, funding rounds, or key partnerships.

- **Growth and learning**: Show how your business has evolved, including lessons learned along the way. This demonstrates that your brand is constantly improving and striving to meet customer needs.

For example, if you started your business in your garage and grew it into a national brand, sharing those humble beginnings helps customers appreciate the hard work behind your success. Your journey makes your brand more relatable and authentic.

4. Connect with Your Audience's Values

A powerful brand story doesn't just focus on your business—it also speaks to the *values* of your audience. By aligning your story with what your customers care about, you create a connection that goes beyond the product. Whether your audience values sustainability, innovation, community, or creativity, your story should reflect those ideals and show how your brand embodies them.

To align your brand story with your audience's values, ask:

- **What values are most important to my target audience?**

- **How does my brand embody those values?**

- **How can I tell my story in a way that resonates with those values?**

For example, if your target audience values sustainability, your brand story might highlight your commitment to eco-friendly practices, such as sourcing ethical materials or reducing waste. By emphasizing shared values, you strengthen the emotional connection between your brand and your customers.

5. Create a Hero—Make the Customer the Star

One of the most effective storytelling techniques is to make your customer the hero of your brand story. Instead of focusing solely on your brand's achievements, position your product or service as a tool that helps your customers achieve their goals, overcome challenges, or improve their lives. This customer-centric approach shifts the spotlight from your brand to the people you serve, making your story more relatable and impactful.

To make your customer the hero, consider:

- **What problem are my customers facing?**

- **How does my product or service help them overcome that problem?**

- **What transformation or improvement do they experience as a result?**

For example, if you sell fitness products, your brand story could focus on a customer's journey from struggling with their fitness routine to feeling empowered and confident after using your product. This approach shows potential customers how your brand can help them achieve similar results, making your story more relevant and engaging.

6. Keep It Authentic

Authenticity is key to building trust and loyalty through your brand story. Customers can spot inauthenticity from a mile away, and a contrived or overly polished story may backfire. Instead, focus on being honest and transparent about your journey, mission, and values. Share your challenges as well as your successes, and don't be afraid to show the human side of your business.

To keep your brand story authentic, ask:

- **Am I being transparent about my journey and purpose?**

- **Am I sharing real stories, not just marketing hype?**

- **Do my actions as a brand align with the values I'm promoting?**

For example, if your brand is built around sustainability, make sure your business practices reflect that value. Customers appreciate brands that "walk the talk," and authenticity fosters loyalty.

7. Communicate Your Story Across Channels

Once you've crafted your brand story, it's essential to communicate it consistently across all your marketing channels. Your website, social media, email campaigns, packaging, and even customer service interactions should all reinforce the same narrative. Consistency is key to building a strong brand identity and ensuring that your story resonates with your audience wherever they encounter your business.

Key channels to share your brand story:

- **Website**: Your About Us page is a prime location for sharing your brand's origin story and mission.

- **Social media**: Use social platforms to tell shorter, engaging snippets of your brand story, share behind-the-scenes content, or highlight customer success stories.

- **Email marketing**: Weave your story into your email campaigns, especially in welcome emails or newsletters that introduce new subscribers to your brand.

- **Packaging and branding materials**: Include elements of your brand story on product packaging, labels, or promotional materials to remind customers of your mission and values.

The more consistently you communicate your story, the stronger your brand's emotional connection with customers will be.

Conclusion: Your Story Is Your Brand's Superpower

Crafting a compelling brand story is one of the most powerful ways to attract, engage, and retain customers. A well-told story builds trust, evokes emotion, and creates a lasting connection between your brand and your audience. By focusing on your "why," highlighting your journey, aligning with your audience's values, and making the customer the hero, you can create a story that resonates deeply with the people you serve.

Remember, your brand story is more than just marketing—it's the heart and soul of your business. Tell it authentically, share it consistently, and watch as your audience connects with your brand on a whole new level.

Mastering Content Marketing: Creating Value, Not Just Noise

In the digital age, content marketing has become one of the most effective ways to attract and engage your audience. However, the internet is saturated with content, and creating more of the same won't help your brand stand out. To make an impact, you need to craft content that doesn't just add to the noise but creates real *value* for your audience. When done right, content marketing builds trust, showcases your expertise, and nurtures long-term relationships with customers.

In this section, we'll explore how to create a content marketing strategy that delivers value to your audience, enhances your brand's authority, and drives measurable results.

1. Understand the Purpose of Content Marketing

Before diving into content creation, it's essential to understand the *purpose* behind content marketing. Content marketing is not about self-promotion or pushing sales—it's about offering your audience something valuable, whether that's information, education, inspiration, or entertainment. By delivering value, you position your brand as a trusted resource, making your audience more likely to engage with your business over time.

The key purposes of content marketing include:

- **Educating your audience**: Provide helpful information that solves your audience's problems or answers their questions.

- **Building brand awareness**: Use content to increase your brand's visibility and showcase your expertise.

- **Nurturing relationships**: Engage with your audience consistently to build trust and foster long-term connections.

- **Driving action**: Encourage your audience to take specific actions, whether it's subscribing to your newsletter, downloading a resource, or making a purchase.

By keeping these purposes in mind, you can ensure that every piece of content you create is designed to add value and move your audience closer to a decision, rather than simply adding noise.

2. Know Your Audience's Pain Points and Interests

Effective content marketing starts with a deep understanding of your audience's **pain points** and interests. Your content should address the challenges they face, offer solutions, and provide insights that resonate with their needs. When your content is relevant and helpful, it builds trust and positions your brand as an authority in your industry.

To identify your audience's pain points and interests, ask:

- **What common problems do my customers face?**

- **What questions are they asking?**

- **How can I create content that provides answers, guidance, or inspiration?**

For example, if your audience consists of small business owners struggling with time management, you could create blog posts, videos, or infographics offering productivity tips, time-saving tools, or organizational strategies. By delivering content that directly addresses their challenges, you build credibility and strengthen your connection with your audience.

3. Create Different Types of Content

Content marketing isn't limited to blog posts or articles. To engage a diverse audience and reach people across different platforms, you need to create a variety of content types. Offering multiple forms of content ensures that you cater to different preferences, learning styles, and stages of the customer journey.

Here are some common content types to consider:

- **Blog posts**: Written articles that provide in-depth information or answer specific questions.

- **Videos**: Engaging, visual content that can demonstrate products, explain concepts, or tell stories.

- **Infographics**: Visually appealing graphics that simplify complex information into easy-to-digest formats.

- **Podcasts**: Audio content that allows you to share interviews, discussions, or insights in a conversational format.

- **Ebooks or whitepapers**: In-depth resources that offer valuable information in exchange for email sign-ups.

- **Social media posts**: Short, engaging content designed to drive interaction and build community.

For example, a skincare brand might create blog posts on skincare routines, videos demonstrating product application, infographics on skincare ingredients, and social media posts sharing customer testimonials. This multi-format approach allows you to reach a wider audience and keep your content fresh and engaging.

4. Focus on Quality Over Quantity

In the rush to stay relevant and maintain a content schedule, many brands fall into the trap of prioritizing quantity over quality. However, producing more content doesn't necessarily mean producing better content. Quality matters far more than the volume of posts you create. One well-researched, insightful article is worth far more than multiple low-quality pieces that don't offer value to your audience.

To focus on quality, ensure that your content is:

- **Relevant**: Addresses the specific needs, questions, or interests of your audience.

- **Actionable**: Provides practical advice or steps that readers can apply immediately.

- **Well-researched**: Uses credible sources, data, and examples to back up your points.

- **Engaging**: Uses compelling storytelling, visuals, or humor to capture attention.

For instance, rather than churning out daily blog posts with generic tips, focus on creating one detailed, authoritative post per week that offers original insights, practical solutions, and real value. This will keep your audience engaged and position your brand as a credible expert.

5. Build a Consistent Content Schedule

Consistency is key when it comes to content marketing. Regularly publishing new content keeps your audience engaged, helps you stay top-of-mind, and signals to search engines that your site is active, which can improve your SEO. However, consistency doesn't mean overwhelming your audience with constant posts—it means developing a schedule that you can maintain over time.

To build a content schedule:

- **Determine your frequency**: Decide how often you'll publish content based on your capacity (e.g., weekly blog posts, daily social media updates, monthly newsletters).

- **Create a content calendar**: Plan your content topics, formats, and publishing dates ahead of time to stay organized and on track.

- **Maintain a balance**: Mix evergreen content (timeless, always-relevant topics) with timely content (seasonal trends, industry news) to keep your content strategy dynamic.

For example, a financial services company might create a monthly newsletter with investment tips, weekly blog posts on financial planning, and daily social media updates with quick money-saving tips. By sticking to a consistent schedule, the brand remains active and relevant in its audience's minds.

6. Optimize Your Content for SEO

Creating valuable content is just one piece of the puzzle—your audience also needs to be able to find it. This is where Search Engine Optimization (SEO) comes in. Optimizing your content for search engines helps ensure that your blog posts, videos, and other resources show up in search results when people are looking for information related to your industry.

Key SEO strategies include:

- **Keyword research**: Identify the terms and phrases your audience is searching for and incorporate them naturally into your content.

- **On-page SEO**: Optimize titles, meta descriptions, headers, and images to make your content more search-friendly.

- **Link building**: Encourage backlinks from reputable sites to improve your content's credibility and search ranking.

- **Mobile optimization**: Ensure that your content is mobile-friendly, as an increasing number of users access content from their smartphones.

For example, if you run a travel agency, you might write a blog post titled "Top 10 Adventure Travel Destinations in 2024" and optimize it with relevant keywords like "best adventure travel," "travel destinations," and "2024 travel trends." By optimizing your content for SEO, you increase the chances of reaching a broader audience organically.

7. Engage with Your Audience

Content marketing isn't just about publishing—it's about engagement. Interacting with your audience helps build a community around your brand, fosters trust, and keeps people coming back for more. Engaging with your audience also provides valuable feedback on what content resonates most, helping you refine your strategy.

Ways to engage with your audience include:

- **Respond to comments**: Whether on blog posts, social media, or videos, reply to comments and questions to show that you're listening and value your audience's input.

- **Encourage sharing**: Invite your audience to share your content with their networks, expanding your reach organically.

- **Ask for feedback**: Use polls, surveys, or social media prompts to get feedback on what type of content your audience wants to see more of.

For example, a home decor brand might ask its Instagram followers to share photos of how they've styled their products, using a specific hashtag. This not only engages the audience but also encourages user-generated content that promotes the brand.

Conclusion: Content That Connects and Converts

Mastering content marketing is about more than just creating content—it's about creating valuable content that resonates with your audience, solves their problems, and strengthens their connection to your brand. By understanding your audience, focusing on quality, and using a variety of content types, you can cut through the noise and offer something meaningful.

Remember, content marketing is a long-term strategy that requires consistency, engagement, and continuous improvement. When you prioritize delivering value over simply adding to the noise, you build trust, enhance your brand's reputation, and drive meaningful results for your business.

Social Media Magnetism: Building an Irresistible Presence Online

In today's digital landscape, **social media** is one of the most powerful tools for connecting with your audience, building brand awareness, and creating lasting relationships. However, standing out on social platforms requires more than just posting regularly. It's about building an irresistible presence that draws people in, engages them, and keeps them coming back for more. This is the heart of social media magnetism—the ability to make your brand so compelling online that your audience can't help but follow, like, and engage.

In this section, we'll explore how to build a magnetic social media presence that captivates your audience and strengthens your brand's digital identity.

1. Choose the Right Platforms for Your Audience

Not all social media platforms are created equal, and not every platform is right for every brand. To build an effective social media presence, it's essential to focus your efforts on the platforms where your target audience is most active. By choosing the right platforms, you'll maximize your impact and reach the people who are most likely to engage with your content.

To choose the right platforms, ask:

- **Where does my target audience spend their time online?**

- **What type of content resonates with my audience (visual, written, short-form, long-form)?**

- **Which platforms align with my brand's strengths?**

For example:

- **Instagram** is ideal for visually-driven brands such as fashion, beauty, travel, and lifestyle.

- **LinkedIn** works best for B2B companies or professional services seeking to build industry authority.

- **TikTok** attracts younger audiences with short, creative videos.

- **Facebook** appeals to a broad demographic and is ideal for building community groups and engaging diverse audiences.

By focusing on platforms where your audience is most engaged, you can avoid spreading yourself too thin and ensure that your social media efforts are strategically aligned with your business goals.

2. Create Consistent and Engaging Content

Consistency is key to building an irresistible social media presence. Your audience should know what to expect from your brand, whether it's the frequency of posts, the type of content you share, or the tone of voice you use. Creating a consistent content calendar helps you stay top-of-mind with your followers while reinforcing your brand's identity.

To create consistent and engaging content, consider:

- **Content mix**: Vary your content to keep things fresh—alternate between educational posts, entertaining content, promotions, and user-generated content.

- **Posting frequency**: Determine how often you'll post and stick to a regular schedule (e.g., daily Instagram posts, weekly LinkedIn updates, etc.).

- **Brand voice**: Develop a consistent tone of voice that reflects your brand's personality, whether it's friendly, professional, humorous, or inspirational.

For example, a fitness brand might post workout tips, healthy recipes, inspirational quotes, and customer success stories on Instagram. By keeping the content varied and relevant, they keep their audience engaged while reinforcing their brand values.

3. Leverage Visual Storytelling

Social media is a highly visual medium, and to build a magnetic presence, you need to create visually compelling content that grabs attention. Visual storytelling allows you to communicate your brand's message in a way that resonates with your audience on an emotional level. Whether through photos, videos, infographics, or graphics, visual content can convey ideas quickly and leave a lasting impression.

To use visual storytelling effectively:

- **Use high-quality images and videos**: Invest in professional photography or videography if possible, as high-quality visuals make your brand appear more polished and credible.

- **Tell a story**: Use images and videos to share your brand's journey, customer experiences, behind-the-scenes content, or product demonstrations.

- **Maintain brand consistency**: Ensure that your visuals align with your brand's colors, style, and aesthetic to create a cohesive look across your social platforms.

For example, a sustainable fashion brand might share Instagram posts showcasing the eco-friendly materials they use, behind-the-scenes footage of the production process, and customer stories about the impact of their purchases. This type of visual storytelling builds a connection between the brand and its audience while reinforcing key brand values.

4. Engage Authentically with Your Audience

Social media isn't just a one-way communication tool—it's a platform for conversation and community-building. One of the most effective ways to build a magnetic presence is by engaging authentically with your audience. People want to feel seen and heard, so responding to comments, answering questions, and engaging in discussions are crucial to building trust and loyalty.

To engage authentically:

- **Respond to comments**: Acknowledge your followers by replying to their comments and questions. Personalized responses show that you value their engagement.

- **Use interactive features**: Take advantage of interactive tools like polls, quizzes, and Q&A sessions on Instagram Stories or Facebook. These features encourage participation and make your audience feel involved.

- **Share user-generated content**: Reposting photos, reviews, or testimonials from your customers shows appreciation and builds a sense of community around your brand.

For example, a skincare brand might regularly host Instagram Q&A sessions where followers can ask questions about their skincare concerns, with the brand providing helpful advice. This direct interaction helps build trust and positions the brand as an expert in its field.

5. Collaborate with Influencers and Brand Advocates

Collaborating with influencers or brand advocates can amplify your social media reach and lend credibility to your brand. Influencers are individuals with a large, engaged following who can help introduce your brand to new audiences. When you work with influencers who align with your brand's values and target audience, their endorsement can significantly boost your brand's visibility and trust.

To collaborate with influencers effectively:

- **Choose influencers wisely**: Look for influencers whose followers align with your target audience, and who share similar values and interests with your brand.

- **Develop authentic partnerships**: Focus on building long-term relationships with influencers who genuinely believe in your product or service. Authentic partnerships come across as more credible to their followers.

- **Leverage micro-influencers**: You don't need to partner with huge influencers to make an impact. Micro-influencers (those with smaller but highly engaged audiences) can often provide better engagement rates and more targeted reach.

For example, a healthy snack brand might partner with fitness influencers who regularly post workout content and promote a healthy lifestyle. The influencer could share how the brand's snacks fit into their fitness routine, generating authentic interest from their followers.

6. Track Performance and Refine Your Strategy

To build a truly magnetic presence on social media, you need to measure your performance and refine your strategy based on what works and what doesn't. Monitoring key metrics helps you understand what content resonates with your audience, how engaged they are, and where you can improve.

Key metrics to track include:

- **Engagement rate**: The number of likes, comments, shares, and saves your posts receive relative to your follower count.

- **Follower growth**: How many new followers you gain over a specific time period.

- **Reach and impressions**: The number of unique people who see your content (reach) and the total number of times your content is viewed (impressions).

- **Click-through rate (CTR)**: The percentage of people who clicked on a link or call-to-action in your social posts.

By regularly reviewing these metrics, you can identify trends, discover what types of content perform best, and make data-driven decisions to improve your social media strategy. If certain types of posts consistently receive high engagement, for instance, you might decide to create more of that content.

7. Stay Current with Trends and Innovations

Social media is constantly evolving, with new features, platforms, and trends emerging all the time. To stay relevant and keep your social presence magnetic, it's important to stay up-to-date with these changes. Experimenting with new features or jumping on relevant trends can keep your content fresh and engaging, helping you capture your audience's attention in new ways.

To stay current:

- **Follow social media news**: Keep an eye on updates from platforms like Instagram, Facebook, TikTok, and LinkedIn to learn about new features or algorithm changes.

- **Be adaptable**: Experiment with new content formats, such as Instagram Reels, TikTok challenges, or live streaming, to see what resonates with your audience.

- **Monitor trends**: Pay attention to social media trends, hashtags, and viral content that align with your brand. Participating in trends can increase your visibility and help you stay culturally relevant.

For example, if a new TikTok trend emerges around eco-friendly living, a sustainable home goods brand could create short videos highlighting their products and how they contribute to a greener lifestyle. Staying on top of trends like this ensures that your content remains engaging and timely.

Conclusion: Building a Magnetic Social Media Presence
Social media magnetism is all about creating an online presence that is engaging, authentic, and irresistible to your audience. By focusing on the right platforms, crafting visually compelling content, engaging meaningfully with your followers,

and leveraging collaborations, you can build a social media presence that not only attracts but retains loyal customers.

Remember, the key to social media success is consistency, authenticity, and a willingness to adapt to the ever-changing digital landscape. When you combine these elements, your social media presence becomes a powerful tool for building relationships, increasing brand awareness, and driving business growth.

Converting Attraction into Action: Irresistible Offers and CTAs

Attracting attention on social media and through your marketing efforts is only half the battle. To turn that attention into meaningful action—whether it's a sale, subscription, or engagement—you need to guide your audience toward taking the next step. This is where irresistible offers and compelling calls to action (CTAs) come in. They transform casual browsers into customers, subscribers, or leads.

In this section, we'll explore how to craft offers and CTAs that are so enticing, your audience can't help but act.

1. Crafting Irresistible Offers

An irresistible offer is one that speaks directly to your audience's needs and creates a sense of urgency or excitement around your product or service. To be effective, your offer needs to deliver real value while addressing a specific problem or desire your target audience has.

To create offers that convert, consider the following strategies:

- **Solve a problem**: Ensure your offer addresses a key challenge or pain point your audience is facing. The clearer the solution you provide, the more compelling the offer.

- **Provide added value**: Offers that give more value than expected often convert better. This can include discounts, free trials, bonus content, or exclusive access.

- **Create scarcity or urgency**: Limited-time offers or scarcity (e.g., "only 10 spots left" or "sale ends in 24 hours") can motivate people to act quickly to avoid missing out.

- **Make it exclusive**: People love feeling like they're getting something special. Create offers that are exclusive to your social media followers, email subscribers, or VIP customers to make them feel valued.

For example, a skincare brand might offer a 20% discount on a popular product for 48 hours, but only to their Instagram followers. The combination of a time-sensitive discount and the exclusivity for their social media audience makes the offer irresistible, encouraging followers to act before the opportunity expires.

2. Designing Clear and Compelling CTAs

A call to action (CTA) is the prompt that tells your audience what action to take next. Without a clear and compelling CTA, even the most engaging content or attractive offer can fall flat. A great CTA not only tells people what to do but also motivates them to take action by highlighting the benefits or urgency of acting now.

Key tips for designing effective CTAs include:

- **Use action-oriented language**: Start your CTA with a strong, action-oriented verb like "Shop Now," "Download," "Join," or "Claim Your Offer."

- **Highlight the benefit**: Make it clear what the audience will get by taking action. For example, "Get Your Free Guide" or "Save 30% Today."

- **Create urgency**: Adding phrases like "Limited Time Only," "Last Chance," or "Ends Soon" can encourage quick action.

- **Keep it simple**: Your CTA should be easy to understand and straightforward. Avoid using too many words or cluttering the message. A single, focused CTA is often more effective than multiple competing ones.

For instance, a clothing brand offering a flash sale might use a CTA like: "Shop Now and Save 30%! Limited Time Only." This CTA not only tells the audience what to do (shop), but it also creates a sense of urgency and emphasizes the benefit (saving 30%).

3. Match Offers and CTAs to Each Stage of the Buyer Journey

Not everyone in your audience is ready to buy right away. Some might still be in the awareness stage, while others are ready to make a purchase. By tailoring your offers and CTAs to different stages of the buyer's journey, you can increase the likelihood of conversion.

Consider the three main stages:

- **Awareness stage**: Your audience is just discovering your brand and may not be ready to buy. In this stage, focus on offers that provide value and build trust, such as free resources, blog content, or downloadable guides. CTAs like "Learn More" or "Download Your Free Guide" work well here.

- **Consideration stage**: Your audience is comparing options and considering whether your product or service is the right fit. Offers like free trials, product demos, or case studies can help them make a decision. CTAs like "Try It Free" or "Request a Demo" can move them closer to a purchase.

- **Decision stage**: Your audience is ready to buy but may need a final push. Special promotions, discounts, or limited-time offers can drive them to act. CTAs like "Shop Now," "Claim Your Discount," or "Get Started" are effective at this stage.

For example, a SaaS company might use "Download Our Free Guide" for prospects in the awareness stage, "Schedule a Free Demo" for those in the consideration stage, and "Start Your Free Trial" for decision-stage leads.

4. Incorporate Social Proof

Adding social proof to your offers and CTAs can significantly increase conversions by showing that others have already benefited from your product or service. People are more likely to take action when they see that others have had positive experiences.

Social proof can take the form of:

- **Customer testimonials**: Highlight what real customers have said about your product or service.

- **Case studies**: Share in-depth stories of how your product solved a problem for a customer.

- **Reviews and ratings**: Display star ratings or quotes from customer reviews.

- **User-generated content**: Showcase photos, videos, or posts from customers using your product.

For example, an online course platform could use a CTA like "Join 10,000+ Students Who've Transformed Their Careers" along with a testimonial from a successful student. This combination of a clear CTA and social proof reassures potential customers that they're making a good decision.

5. A/B Test Your Offers and CTAs

Not all offers and CTAs will perform equally well, so it's essential to A/B test different versions to see which ones drive the best results. A/B testing allows you to experiment with variations of your CTAs, offers, or landing pages to determine what resonates most with your audience.

Key elements to test include:

- **Wording**: Try different phrasing for your CTAs. For example, "Get Started Today" vs. "Start Your Free Trial Now."

- **Design**: Test different button colors, sizes, or placement on the page.

- **Offers**: Experiment with different types of offers (e.g., percentage discounts vs. free shipping) to see what converts best.

- **Urgency**: Test CTAs with and without urgency elements (e.g., "Limited Time Offer" vs. no urgency).

For example, an e-commerce brand might test two CTAs—"Buy Now and Get Free Shipping" versus "Buy Now and Save 10%"—to see which one generates more sales. By analyzing the results, they can refine their approach to create the most effective CTAs.

6. Create a Seamless Path to Conversion

Finally, it's essential that the path from attraction to conversion is frictionless. If your audience clicks on your CTA but encounters a complicated or confusing checkout process, they may abandon the action altogether. To ensure a smooth conversion process, make it as easy as possible for people to follow through on your offer.

To create a seamless conversion path:

- **Simplify the user experience**: Minimize the number of steps required to complete the action (e.g., fewer form fields for lead generation or a one-click checkout option for e-commerce).

- **Ensure mobile optimization**: With more users accessing content on their phones, it's crucial that your offers and CTAs are mobile-friendly.

- **Eliminate distractions**: Keep your landing pages focused on a single offer or action. Too many competing elements can confuse the user and reduce conversions.

For example, if your CTA is "Sign Up for a Free Webinar," the landing page should have a clean design with minimal distractions and a simple form for registration. The more straightforward the process, the higher the likelihood that your audience will complete the desired action.

Conclusion: Turning Attention into Action with Irresistible Offers and CTAs
Building a magnetic online presence and attracting attention is only the beginning. To achieve real results, you need to convert that attention into meaningful action. By crafting irresistible offers that deliver value, designing clear and compelling CTAs, and optimizing the path to conversion, you can guide your audience toward taking the next step.

Whether you're driving sales, growing your email list, or building your social media following, the right combination of offers and CTAs will turn casual visitors into engaged customers. Remember to continually test and refine your approach, ensuring that your CTAs are as powerful and persuasive as your content.

Quick Tips and Recap

- **Solve a problem with your offer**: Make sure your offers directly address a key challenge or desire your audience has.

- **Provide added value**: Add incentives like discounts, free trials, or exclusive content to make your offer irresistible.

- **Use clear and action-oriented CTAs**: Start your CTAs with strong verbs like "Shop Now" or "Get Started," and keep the message simple and direct.

- **Create urgency and scarcity**: Use time-sensitive offers or limited availability to encourage quick action from your audience.

- **Tailor offers to the buyer's journey**: Adjust your offers and CTAs based on whether your audience is in the awareness, consideration, or decision stage.

- **Incorporate social proof**: Include testimonials, reviews, or user-generated content to build trust and reinforce the value of your offer.

- **A/B test your CTAs and offers**: Experiment with different variations of wording, design, and types of offers to find what resonates best.

- **Simplify the path to conversion**: Make it as easy as possible for your audience to take action by minimizing steps, ensuring mobile optimization, and reducing distractions.

- **Monitor and refine**: Continuously track performance and adjust your offers and CTAs to improve conversion rates over time.

CHAPTER SEVEN

Gears in Motion: Planning Your Operations

"Planning your operations is like setting gears in motion: the right synchronization ensures efficiency and drives your business engine forward." — TIM COOK, CEO OF APPLE INC.

Welcome to the engine room of your business, where all the gears start turning and the magic happens. Planning your operations is like fine-tuning a Swiss watch—it's all about precision, efficiency, and making sure everything ticks along without a hitch. Think of this chapter as your operations boot camp, where we transform your grand vision into a well-oiled machine that runs smoother than your morning coffee routine (well, on a good day).

From supply chains to staffing, inventory management to customer service, this is where you map out how every cog in your business works together to deliver value—and keep you from drowning in chaos. Whether you're a one-person show or leading a growing team, operations planning is your secret weapon to avoid bottlenecks, delays, and the dreaded "what went wrong?" moments.

So, grab your metaphorical wrench and start tightening the bolts on your processes. With the right operational plan in place, you'll keep everything running like clockwork—and your business humming along like a perfectly tuned engine.

Building Efficient Workflows: Streamlining Your Processes

Efficient workflows are the backbone of any successful business operation. Whether you're a solo entrepreneur or managing a growing team, creating clear, streamlined processes helps reduce bottlenecks, improve productivity, and ensure that every task is completed on time and with consistency. Building efficient workflows means designing your operations in a way that minimizes wasted effort, optimizes resources, and maximizes output.

In this section, we'll walk through how to design and implement workflows that keep your business running smoothly, from production and delivery to customer service and daily operations.

1. Map Out Your Core Processes

The first step in building efficient workflows is to map out the core processes that keep your business functioning. These are the essential activities that must be performed regularly to deliver value to your customers and keep your operations moving. By mapping out these processes, you can identify opportunities to streamline steps, eliminate redundancies, and create consistency across the board.

To start, ask yourself:

- **What are the key tasks or activities that happen daily, weekly, or monthly?**

- **What are the necessary steps involved in each task?**

- **Are there any bottlenecks or delays that frequently occur in these processes?**

For example, if you run an e-commerce business, your core processes might include receiving orders, packing and shipping products, managing inventory, and processing returns. Mapping out each of these steps—such as order fulfillment from purchase to delivery—gives you a clear overview of what's involved and where inefficiencies might be hiding.

2. Identify Bottlenecks and Redundancies

Once you've mapped out your core processes, the next step is to look for bottlenecks or redundancies that slow things down or waste resources. Bottlenecks are areas where a task gets held up, while redundancies are duplicate or unnecessary steps that add time without adding value.

To identify these, ask:

- **Where do tasks tend to pile up or slow down?**

- **Are there steps that don't contribute directly to the end result?**

- **Are there tasks being repeated unnecessarily?**

For example, if your team is frequently waiting for approval on small decisions, that approval process could be a bottleneck. Alternatively, if two team members are handling similar administrative tasks, you may find an opportunity to consolidate and streamline those responsibilities. By addressing these inefficiencies, you can free up time and energy for higher-value work.

3. Automate Where Possible

Automation is one of the most effective tools for streamlining workflows and boosting efficiency. By automating repetitive or time-consuming tasks, you free up your team (or yourself) to focus on more strategic, value-driven activities. Automation tools can handle everything from invoicing and payment processing to email marketing and inventory management, reducing the need for manual intervention.

To find automation opportunities, ask:

- **Which tasks are repetitive and time-consuming?**

- **What tools or software can handle these tasks automatically?**

- **How can automation help reduce errors or delays?**

For example, an online business might use software to automatically send confirmation emails when a customer makes a purchase or integrate an inventory management system that updates stock levels in real time as orders are placed. These automated processes cut down on manual data entry and prevent mistakes, allowing your operations to run more efficiently.

4. Create Standard Operating Procedures (SOPs)

Standard Operating Procedures (SOPs) are step-by-step guides that outline how to complete key tasks and processes. Having SOPs in place ensures consistency and quality across your operations, especially as your team grows or as new staff members are brought on board. SOPs also make it easier to scale your business because you have a documented system for replicating successful processes.

To create effective SOPs:

- **Document each step of a process**: Be clear and detailed about how each task should be performed.

- **Assign roles and responsibilities**: Specify who is responsible for each step and what tools or resources are required.

- **Make the process easy to follow**: Use plain language, checklists, or flowcharts to make the SOPs user-friendly.

For example, an SOP for a customer support team might include detailed steps for handling customer inquiries, processing refunds, and escalating issues to higher-level staff. Having these procedures in place reduces confusion and ensures that everyone is following the same process.

5. Implement Workflow Tools

Workflow management tools can be a game-changer when it comes to streamlining your processes. These tools help you visualize, track, and manage workflows, ensuring that tasks are completed on time and nothing slips through the cracks. Workflow tools allow you to assign tasks, set deadlines, track progress, and communicate with team members in one place.

Popular workflow management tools include:

- **Trello**: A project management tool that uses boards, lists, and cards to organize tasks and track progress.

- **Asana**: A robust project management tool that allows you to create workflows, assign tasks, and track deadlines.

- **Monday.com**: A highly visual tool for planning, tracking, and collaborating on projects and workflows.

These tools are especially useful if you're managing a team or multiple projects at once. They help you stay organized, ensure accountability, and provide real-time visibility into the status of ongoing work.

6. Measure and Refine Your Workflows

The final step in building efficient workflows is to continuously measure and refine them. Once you've implemented your workflows, it's important to monitor their performance and make adjustments as needed. Regularly evaluating your workflows ensures they remain effective and adapt to changing circumstances as your business grows.

To measure and refine your workflows, consider:

- **Tracking key performance indicators (KPIs)**: Monitor metrics such as task completion time, error rates, or customer satisfaction to identify areas for improvement.

- **Gathering feedback from your team**: Ask employees who are involved in daily operations for insights into what's working and where challenges arise.

- **Conducting regular reviews**: Periodically review your workflows to ensure they are still aligned with your goals and that new inefficiencies haven't developed.

For example, if you notice that order fulfillment times have increased, you might investigate whether additional steps have been added or if a bottleneck has appeared in your shipping process. Refining your workflows over time will help keep your business agile and efficient.

Conclusion: Streamlined Processes for a Well-Oiled Machine
Building efficient workflows is essential to ensuring that your business runs smoothly and consistently. By mapping out core processes, eliminating

bottlenecks, automating repetitive tasks, and implementing workflow tools, you create a system that maximizes productivity and minimizes errors. As you continuously measure and refine your workflows, you'll be better equipped to handle growth and keep your business operations running like clockwork.

Supply Chain Management: Ensuring Consistency and Reliability

Attracting attention on social media and through your marketing efforts is only half the battle. To turn that attention into meaningful action—whether it's a sale, subscription, or engagement—you need to guide your audience toward taking the next step. This is where irresistible offers and compelling calls to action (CTAs) come in. They transform casual browsers into customers, subscribers, or leads.

Supply chain management is the backbone of any product-based business. It involves the entire flow of goods and services, from sourcing raw materials to delivering the finished product to customers. An efficient and reliable supply chain ensures that you consistently meet demand, maintain quality, and avoid costly delays. Whether you're managing a local supply chain or dealing with global suppliers, optimizing your supply chain is crucial to keeping your operations running smoothly.

In this section, we'll explore how to build a strong, dependable supply chain that ensures consistency, manages risks, and supports your business's long-term success.

1. Identify Key Suppliers and Partners

The first step in building a reliable supply chain is selecting the right suppliers and partners. These are the businesses that provide you with the materials, products, or services you need to operate. Choosing reliable suppliers is essential to maintaining product quality and meeting delivery deadlines. A strong relationship with your suppliers can help you secure better terms, minimize disruptions, and foster collaboration.

To identify and vet key suppliers, consider:

- **Supplier reliability**: How consistent are they in delivering on time and meeting quality standards?

- **Product quality**: Can the supplier maintain the quality you expect? Check their certifications, past performance, and customer reviews.

- **Cost and pricing**: Are their prices competitive, and do they offer flexible pricing models as you scale?

- **Geographic location**: If you source internationally, consider the impact of shipping times, tariffs, and currency fluctuations.

- **Capacity**: Can your suppliers handle the volume of goods you require, especially if demand increases?

For example, if you're manufacturing electronics, finding a supplier that provides high-quality components, delivers on time, and scales with your business growth is essential to ensuring the success of your product line.

2. Establish Clear Communication Channels

Effective communication is key to managing a supply chain smoothly. Establishing clear communication channels with your suppliers and partners ensures that everyone is on the same page regarding expectations, timelines, and potential issues. Miscommunication can lead to delays, product shortages, or even damaged relationships with suppliers.

To foster clear communication:

- **Set clear expectations**: Communicate lead times, quality requirements, and order volumes upfront. Both you and your suppliers should understand the terms of your agreements to avoid misunderstandings.

- **Maintain regular contact**: Schedule regular check-ins to monitor progress and address any potential issues before they escalate.

- **Use technology**: Consider using supply chain management software that allows you to track orders in real time, share documents, and communicate more effectively with your partners.

For example, a fashion retailer might use a centralized platform to share design specifications, production timelines, and shipping details with their clothing manufacturers. This ensures that the manufacturers understand the retailer's needs and can deliver products as expected.

3. Plan for Supply Chain Disruptions

Even the most reliable supply chains can experience disruptions, whether due to natural disasters, political issues, shipping delays, or supplier failures. Proactively planning for disruptions helps you minimize the impact on your business and maintain customer satisfaction, even when challenges arise.

To plan for disruptions:

- **Diversify your suppliers**: Avoid relying on a single supplier for key materials or products. Having multiple suppliers reduces the risk of a major disruption if one of them experiences issues.

- **Build buffer inventory**: Keep safety stock or buffer inventory on hand to cover short-term disruptions without running out of product.

- **Create contingency plans**: Develop backup plans for critical parts of your supply chain. If a key supplier is unavailable, where can you quickly source alternatives?

- **Monitor global and local risks**: Stay informed about potential risks, such as weather conditions, labor strikes, or political changes that could impact your supply chain. This allows you to take proactive measures to mitigate their impact.

For example, an electronics company might source materials from both local and international suppliers, allowing them to quickly pivot in case of shipping delays or supply shortages. Having a contingency plan ensures business continuity during unexpected disruptions.

4. Optimize Inventory Management

Efficient inventory management is closely tied to your supply chain's success. You need to balance having enough inventory to meet customer demand without overstocking, which can lead to increased storage costs or obsolete products.

Optimizing inventory management means ensuring that the right products are in the right place at the right time, while minimizing waste and inefficiencies.

Key strategies for inventory optimization include:

- **Just-in-time (JIT) inventory**: This strategy focuses on reducing inventory levels by receiving goods only when they're needed for production or sales. JIT can reduce carrying costs but requires a highly reliable supply chain.

- **Demand forecasting**: Use historical data and market trends to predict customer demand accurately. This helps you avoid overstocking or understocking.

- **Safety stock**: Keep a buffer of extra inventory to account for unexpected demand spikes or supply chain disruptions.

- **Inventory management software**: Use technology to track stock levels, sales patterns, and reorder points in real time. Automated systems can alert you when it's time to reorder and help you manage your inventory more efficiently.

For example, a retailer might use demand forecasting software to predict peak shopping seasons, ensuring they stock up on in-demand products without overfilling their warehouse. This balance helps them meet customer needs while avoiding excess inventory costs.

5. Implement Quality Control Measures

Maintaining high standards of quality control throughout your supply chain is essential for delivering consistent products that meet customer expectations. If a product's quality falters due to poor materials or manufacturing processes, it can damage your reputation and lead to costly returns or recalls.

To implement quality control in your supply chain:

- **Set clear quality standards**: Clearly define your quality expectations and share them with your suppliers. Make sure your suppliers understand what is required and are capable of meeting these standards.

- **Conduct regular audits**: Perform regular quality checks or audits of your suppliers' facilities and processes to ensure they are complying with your standards.

- **Inspect incoming goods**: Inspect raw materials or products when they arrive at your facility to catch any defects or issues before they reach customers.

- **Develop a feedback loop**: If quality issues arise, communicate them with your suppliers and work collaboratively to resolve them and prevent future occurrences.

For instance, a food and beverage company might perform quality checks on raw ingredients as soon as they are delivered, ensuring that only high-quality ingredients are used in production. This attention to quality helps maintain the company's brand reputation and reduces waste.

6. Use Technology to Enhance Supply Chain Efficiency

Leveraging technology can significantly improve the efficiency and visibility of your supply chain. Supply chain management software, real-time tracking systems, and data analytics tools help you monitor your entire supply chain from procurement to delivery. These tools provide real-time insights, help you manage risk, and allow you to optimize the performance of your supply chain.

Technologies to consider include:

- **Supply chain management (SCM) software**: SCM platforms allow you to track shipments, monitor supplier performance, and manage orders from a single dashboard.

- **RFID and barcode scanning**: These technologies improve inventory accuracy and reduce manual errors by automating tracking processes.

- **Data analytics**: Analyzing supply chain data helps you identify inefficiencies, forecast demand, and optimize operations. You can use data to make informed decisions about supplier performance, costs, and logistics.

- **Blockchain**: For businesses that prioritize transparency, blockchain technology can provide a tamper-proof record of transactions across the supply chain, improving accountability and trust.

For example, a global retailer might use SCM software to track shipments from overseas suppliers and monitor delivery times, ensuring that products arrive on time and in good condition. This level of visibility reduces uncertainty and helps the retailer maintain reliable stock levels.

Conclusion: Building a Resilient and Reliable Supply Chain

Supply chain management is critical to ensuring your business can consistently deliver products or services to customers while maintaining quality and efficiency. By building strong relationships with reliable suppliers, planning for disruptions, optimizing inventory, and leveraging technology, you can create a supply chain that is both resilient and responsive to changes.

With a well-managed supply chain, you'll be able to meet customer demand, minimize disruptions, and keep your operations running smoothly—allowing your business to grow and succeed in the long term.

Inventory Management: Balancing Stock and Demand

Effective inventory management is crucial for running a successful business, especially if you deal with physical products. The challenge is balancing stock levels to meet customer demand without overstocking or understocking. Too much inventory ties up capital and increases storage costs, while too little inventory risks stockouts and lost sales. Mastering the art of inventory management means finding the sweet spot where you always have enough to fulfill demand, but not so much that your resources are wasted.

In this section, we'll explore how to balance inventory and demand, optimize stock levels, and streamline your inventory management process for maximum efficiency and profitability.

1. Understand Demand Patterns

The foundation of effective inventory management is understanding your demand patterns. Different products may have varying demand cycles based on seasonality, market trends, or customer preferences. By analyzing sales data and tracking demand over time, you can predict when and how much inventory you need to stock.

To understand demand patterns:

- **Analyze historical sales data**: Look at past sales performance to identify trends, such as peak periods (holidays, back-to-school season) or slow months.

- **Segment your products**: Different products may have different demand cycles. Group products into categories (e.g., seasonal, evergreen, high turnover) to manage stock levels more accurately.

- **Track industry trends**: Stay informed about broader market trends that could influence demand, such as new technology, consumer behavior shifts, or changes in purchasing power.

For example, a clothing retailer might analyze past sales data to discover that winter coats sell quickly in the fall but slowdown in the spring. Understanding this pattern allows the retailer to stock up in advance of the busy season and reduce inventory as demand drops.

2. Implement Demand Forecasting

Once you understand your demand patterns, the next step is to use demand forecasting to predict future sales. Demand forecasting helps you anticipate how much stock you'll need in the future, ensuring that you neither overstock nor understock. This process is especially important for managing seasonal fluctuations or preparing for product launches.

To implement demand forecasting:

- **Use historical data**: Analyze your previous sales data to make educated predictions about future demand.

- **Factor in market trends**: Incorporate information about upcoming market or industry trends that could influence demand, such as an expected product boom or industry shifts.

- **Account for external factors**: Include factors like economic changes, marketing campaigns, or promotional activities that could impact demand.

For instance, if you're planning a major promotional campaign, you can use demand forecasting to estimate the increase in sales and adjust your inventory levels accordingly. This ensures you're prepared for the spike in orders and can fulfill them without delay.

3. Use Inventory Management Systems

Effective inventory management requires organization and real-time visibility into your stock levels. An inventory management system (IMS) can automate tracking, streamline ordering, and give you an up-to-date view of your inventory at all times. These systems reduce manual errors and make it easier to manage stock efficiently, especially as your business grows.

Key features of inventory management systems include:

- **Real-time tracking**: Track stock levels in real time to know exactly how much inventory you have on hand at any moment.

- **Automatic reorder alerts**: Set reorder points for each product, so the system alerts you when stock reaches a predefined threshold.

- **Centralized management**: If you manage multiple warehouses or sales channels (e.g., brick-and-mortar stores and e-commerce), an IMS can help centralize stock tracking and ensure consistent inventory visibility across locations.

- **Reporting and analytics**: Get detailed reports on inventory performance, turnover rates, and slow-moving products, allowing you to make data-driven decisions.

For example, an e-commerce business that sells electronics might use an IMS to track how many units of a popular smartphone are left in stock. When the inventory reaches a certain level, the system automatically sends a notification to reorder before running out, ensuring consistent availability.

4. Optimize Reorder Points and Quantities

Another critical aspect of inventory management is setting accurate reorder points and reorder quantities. Reorder points are the stock levels at which you trigger a new order to replenish inventory, while reorder quantities determine how much you order each time. Optimizing these values helps prevent stockouts and ensures that you maintain enough inventory to meet demand.

To optimize reorder points and quantities:

- **Calculate reorder points**: Use the formula **Reorder Point = (Average Daily Sales x Lead Time) + Safety Stock**. This formula accounts for lead time (the time it takes to receive an order) and safety stock (buffer inventory for unexpected demand).

- **Determine reorder quantities**: Balance your reorder quantities based on economic order quantity (EOQ) principles, which consider ordering costs and holding costs to minimize total inventory costs.

- **Adjust based on seasonality**: If your business experiences seasonal fluctuations in demand, adjust reorder points and quantities during peak or low-demand periods.

For example, a food distributor might calculate that they sell 100 units of a particular product daily, with a 10-day lead time from the supplier and a safety stock of 500 units. Using the reorder point formula, they would reorder when stock levels reach (100 x 10) + 500 = 1,500 units. This prevents stockouts while accounting for any unexpected spikes in demand.

5. Use Just-in-Time (JIT) Inventory for Efficiency

The just-in-time (JIT) inventory strategy is a popular method for minimizing stock levels and reducing inventory holding costs. With JIT, you order and receive goods just in time to fulfill customer orders, minimizing excess inventory. This approach can be highly efficient but requires precise demand forecasting and a reliable supply chain to avoid stockouts.

To implement JIT inventory:

- **Strengthen supplier relationships**: Build strong relationships with reliable suppliers who can deliver products quickly and consistently.

- **Improve lead time accuracy**: Work closely with suppliers to understand their lead times and ensure you can receive products just in time for order fulfillment.

- **Maintain high demand visibility**: Use demand forecasting and inventory management systems to predict customer needs and place orders accordingly.

For example, a computer manufacturer using the JIT model might only order specific components after receiving a customer order. The manufacturer's suppliers deliver the parts quickly, enabling the business to assemble the computer without holding excess stock of components.

6. Manage Safety Stock for Risk Mitigation

Safety stock is extra inventory kept on hand to guard against unexpected spikes in demand or supply chain disruptions. While holding too much inventory can be costly, safety stock acts as an insurance policy to prevent stockouts and missed sales opportunities. The key is finding the right balance between having enough safety stock to cover emergencies and not tying up too much capital in unused inventory.

To manage safety stock effectively:

- **Calculate appropriate safety stock levels**: Consider factors such as demand variability, lead time uncertainty, and the criticality of the product to your operations.

- **Adjust based on risk factors**: Products with longer lead times or more volatile demand may require more safety stock, while products with predictable demand may need less.

- **Use dynamic safety stock levels**: Reevaluate safety stock levels periodically to ensure they reflect current demand patterns and supply chain conditions.

For example, a pharmaceutical distributor might keep higher safety stock levels of essential medications that are in high demand and have long lead times, ensuring that they can meet urgent customer needs even if supply chain disruptions occur.

7. Monitor and Evaluate Inventory Performance

Regularly monitoring and evaluating your inventory performance is essential to staying on top of stock levels, preventing inefficiencies, and improving your overall inventory management process. By tracking key inventory metrics, you can identify issues like slow-moving stock, high holding costs, or inaccurate demand forecasts, allowing you to make data-driven adjustments.

Key metrics to monitor include:

- **Inventory turnover rate**: This metric measures how often inventory is sold and replaced over a period. A higher turnover rate indicates efficient inventory management.

- **Stockout rate**: Track the frequency of stockouts to determine if you're underestimating demand or need to adjust reorder points.

- **Carrying costs**: Measure the cost of holding inventory, including storage, insurance, and obsolescence, to optimize stock levels.

- **Days of inventory on hand (DOH)**: This metric tells you how many days your current inventory will last based on average sales. Lower DOH indicates better efficiency.

For example, a retail store might find that its inventory turnover rate is low for a particular product category, signaling that the store is overstocking and tying up cash in unsold goods. By reducing stock levels in that category, the store can free up resources for more in-demand products.

Conclusion: Striking the Right Balance Between Stock and Demand

Inventory management is about finding the right balance between having enough stock to meet customer demand and avoiding the costs of excess inventory. By understanding demand patterns, using demand forecasting, leveraging technology, and optimizing reorder points and safety stock, you can keep your inventory lean and efficient while ensuring consistent product availability.

Effective inventory management not only boosts profitability but also improves customer satisfaction by ensuring products are always in stock and ready to ship. With the right strategies in place, you'll maintain the balance between supply and demand and keep your business running smoothly.

Team and Resource Allocation: Staffing for Efficiency

One of the most crucial aspects of running a successful business is ensuring that your team and resources are optimally allocated. Having the right people in the right roles, along with efficient use of resources, can dramatically improve productivity, reduce costs, and create a smoother workflow. Whether you're managing a small team or a large workforce, efficient staffing and resource allocation are essential for scaling your business and maintaining operational excellence.

In this section, we'll explore strategies for effective team and resource allocation to ensure that your business operates efficiently and your staff is empowered to do their best work.

1. Identify Key Roles and Responsibilities

Before you can allocate your team efficiently, it's essential to identify the key roles within your business and clarify the responsibilities of each. Every team member should have a clear understanding of what is expected of them and how their role contributes to the overall success of the business. This not only prevents overlaps and gaps in responsibilities but also helps you make better staffing decisions as your business grows.

To identify key roles:

- **Map out your organizational structure**: Identify all the necessary functions of your business, such as marketing, sales, operations, customer service, and management.

- **Define roles within each function**: For each business function, define the specific roles required. For example, within marketing, you may need a social media manager, content creator, and graphic designer.

- **Assign responsibilities**: Ensure that each role has clearly defined responsibilities and outcomes. Avoid overlaps in roles that can cause confusion or inefficiencies.

For example, a small e-commerce business might need a marketing manager to handle digital campaigns, an operations manager to oversee order fulfillment, and a customer service representative to respond to inquiries. Clearly defining each person's role ensures that everyone knows their duties and contributes to the overall workflow.

2. Hire for Skills and Cultural Fit

Effective staffing goes beyond just filling roles—it's about hiring the right people with the necessary skills and the right cultural fit for your business. Employees who align with your company's mission, values, and work culture tend to be more engaged, motivated, and productive. In addition to technical skills, look for candidates who demonstrate the soft skills that are critical to teamwork, problem-solving, and adaptability.

To hire effectively:

- **Evaluate technical skills**: Make sure candidates have the skills necessary to perform the role successfully. Conduct skills assessments or require examples of previous work (e.g., portfolios or project case studies).

- **Consider cultural fit**: Assess how well the candidate's values and work style align with your company culture. This is especially important for maintaining a positive team dynamic and ensuring long-term retention.

- **Look for growth potential**: As your business grows, it's beneficial to hire people who can evolve with your company and take on increasing responsibility.

For example, if you're hiring a project manager, look for someone with strong organizational and leadership skills who also thrives in your company's fast-paced, collaborative environment. A candidate who fits both technically and culturally will be more likely to succeed and contribute to your business's efficiency.

3. Balance Workloads and Prevent Bottlenecks

Once you've identified key roles and hired the right people, it's important to balance workloads across your team. Uneven distribution of tasks can lead to burnout for some employees while others may feel underutilized. Additionally, unbalanced workloads can create bottlenecks, slowing down operations and causing delays in project completion.

To balance workloads:

- **Assess current workloads**: Review each team member's tasks and responsibilities to ensure no one is overwhelmed or underutilized.

- **Delegate tasks effectively**: Ensure that tasks are assigned to the right people based on their strengths, skills, and capacity. Don't overload one person with too many critical tasks while others have less to do.

- **Use project management tools**: Implement project management software like Trello, Asana, or Monday.com to track tasks, deadlines, and team progress. These tools help ensure tasks are evenly distributed and projects stay on track.

For example, in a marketing team, you might notice that your graphic designer is frequently overwhelmed with requests, while your social media manager has extra capacity. You can redistribute tasks by having the social media manager take on more responsibilities for content creation, easing the designer's workload and improving efficiency.

4. Implement Cross-Training and Flexibility

Cross-training your employees is a powerful strategy for maintaining operational flexibility and preventing disruptions when key team members are unavailable. When employees are cross-trained, they can step in and perform tasks outside their usual responsibilities, ensuring that operations continue to run smoothly even when someone is on vacation, sick, or leaves the company. It also fosters collaboration and builds a more adaptable workforce.

To implement cross-training:

- **Identify key tasks**: List critical tasks or processes that are essential to your business's operations. These are the areas where cross-training is most valuable.

- **Create cross-training opportunities**: Offer training sessions where employees can learn tasks outside their usual role, or create shadowing opportunities where team members can observe colleagues in different departments.

- **Encourage skill-sharing**: Promote a culture of learning and collaboration where employees share knowledge and skills with one another.

For example, in a small business, the operations manager might be trained to handle basic customer service tasks, and the marketing manager could learn some basic logistics management. This flexibility ensures that operations continue smoothly even if a key team member is unavailable.

5. Allocate Resources Strategically

Effective resource allocation involves more than just managing your human resources—it also includes optimizing the use of tools, technology, and physical resources. Allocating these resources strategically ensures that your team has everything they need to perform their tasks efficiently without unnecessary waste.

To allocate resources effectively:

- **Assess resource needs**: Evaluate which tools, software, or equipment your team needs to perform their jobs efficiently. Ensure that every team member has access to the resources they require.

- **Monitor resource usage**: Track how resources are being used to identify underutilized or overused tools. This helps you make data-driven decisions on whether to invest in more resources or scale back on unused ones.

- **Leverage technology**: Use technology to streamline operations and make the most of your team's time. Automation tools, cloud storage, and communication platforms can improve workflow and minimize manual tasks.

For example, if your customer service team is handling a large volume of inquiries, investing in customer relationship management (CRM) software can help streamline communication and track customer interactions more effectively. This ensures the team can work more efficiently without being overwhelmed.

6. Track Performance and Adjust as Needed

Even with the best staffing plan in place, it's essential to monitor performance and make adjustments as needed. Regularly reviewing your team's productivity, workload, and overall performance helps you identify inefficiencies and areas for improvement. It also allows you to make proactive changes to your staffing or resource allocation before problems arise.

To track performance:

- **Set measurable goals**: Establish clear, measurable goals for each team member or department to track performance over time. These goals should align with your business objectives and provide a benchmark for evaluating efficiency.

- **Monitor key metrics**: Track important performance metrics such as task completion rates, customer satisfaction, or sales growth. Use these insights to identify areas where team members may need additional support or training.

- **Review regularly**: Conduct regular performance reviews or check-ins to assess how well your staffing and resource allocation are working. Be open to making adjustments based on feedback and performance data.

For example, if your sales team's performance is lower than expected, you might discover that they're spending too much time on administrative tasks rather than selling. In response, you could reallocate tasks or hire an administrative assistant to free up the sales team's time for more productive activities.

Conclusion: Efficient Team and Resource Allocation for Operational Success
Optimizing your team and resource allocation is key to running a smooth, efficient business. By clearly defining roles, hiring for both skills and cultural fit, balancing

workloads, and leveraging technology, you can create an environment where your team performs at its best. Cross-training and flexibility also ensure that operations remain uninterrupted during employee absences or peak workloads.

Regularly tracking performance and adjusting as needed will help you maintain efficiency as your business evolves, ensuring that your resources are always used in the most productive way possible.

Monitoring and Improving Operations: The Cycle of Continuous Improvement

Efficient operations don't happen by accident—they require ongoing monitoring and continuous improvement. Once you have your processes in place, the key to long-term success is regularly reviewing how well your operations are performing and making incremental adjustments to improve efficiency, quality, and overall performance. Embracing a mindset of continuous improvement helps you stay competitive, adapt to changes in the market, and ensure that your business remains efficient as it grows.

In this section, we'll explore how to monitor your operations effectively and implement a cycle of continuous improvement that drives growth and operational excellence.

1. Establish Key Performance Indicators (KPIs)

The first step in monitoring your operations is identifying the right Key Performance Indicators (KPIs). KPIs are measurable metrics that provide insight into how well your processes are functioning and whether you are meeting your business goals. By tracking these metrics, you can spot inefficiencies, identify opportunities for improvement, and ensure that your operations align with your strategic objectives.

Common KPIs to track include:

- **Production efficiency**: Measures how effectively you're using resources to produce goods or services.

- **Order fulfillment time**: Tracks how long it takes to process and fulfill customer orders, from purchase to delivery.

- **Customer satisfaction**: Measures customer feedback and satisfaction levels, often through surveys or ratings.

- **Cost per unit**: Tracks how much it costs to produce each unit of a product, including labor, materials, and overhead.

- **Employee productivity**: Measures how efficiently your team is performing their tasks, often based on output per hour or per project.

For example, if you run a manufacturing business, tracking production efficiency and cost per unit can help you identify whether there are inefficiencies in your production line that are increasing costs or slowing down output.

2. Conduct Regular Operational Audits

Regular operational audits are a critical part of maintaining efficient processes. An operational audit involves systematically reviewing your workflows, resources, and performance metrics to identify areas where you can streamline, optimize, or improve. Audits provide a comprehensive view of your business operations, uncovering issues that might not be apparent in day-to-day activities.

To conduct an operational audit:

- **Review key processes**: Examine your core workflows, such as production, order fulfillment, inventory management, and customer service, to ensure they are running as efficiently as possible.

- **Evaluate resource usage**: Assess how effectively you're using resources such as time, labor, materials, and equipment. Look for waste or underutilization.

- **Gather feedback from employees**: Ask your team for insights into what's working and where they see room for improvement. Employees who work on the front lines often have valuable perspectives on operational challenges.

For example, an e-commerce business might conduct an audit to evaluate how quickly customer orders are processed and shipped. If the audit reveals that the fulfillment process is taking longer than expected, the business can adjust its workflows or invest in faster shipping methods to improve efficiency.

3. Implement the Plan-Do-Check-Act (PDCA) Cycle

One of the most effective frameworks for continuous improvement is the Plan-Do-Check-Act (PDCA) cycle. This model emphasizes iterative improvements by systematically planning, testing, evaluating, and refining processes. The PDCA cycle is widely used in industries ranging from manufacturing to healthcare and is adaptable to any business that seeks to optimize its operations.

The steps of the PDCA cycle are:

- **Plan**: Identify an area for improvement and develop a plan to address the issue. This could involve setting new goals, redesigning a process, or implementing new technology.

- **Do**: Implement the change on a small scale. Test the new process, gather data, and monitor how well it performs.

- **Check**: Analyze the results of the test. Did the new process improve efficiency, quality, or performance? Compare the outcomes to your initial goals.

- **Act**: If the change was successful, implement it on a larger scale and integrate it into your standard operating procedures. If it wasn't, adjust the plan and test again.

For example, a retail business might use the PDCA cycle to improve inventory management. After identifying that stockouts are occurring too frequently, the company develops a plan to use demand forecasting software, tests it for a month, reviews the impact on stock levels, and then either implements the new system or makes further adjustments based on the results.

4. Leverage Data and Technology

In the modern business landscape, data and technology play a central role in monitoring and improving operations. By leveraging data analytics tools, automation software, and other technology solutions, you can gain deeper insights into your business's performance, identify trends, and make more informed decisions. Technology can also help you automate repetitive tasks, improve accuracy, and reduce manual errors.

Ways to leverage data and technology include:

- **Data analytics**: Use analytics platforms to track key metrics such as sales trends, production output, or customer satisfaction. Analyze this data to identify patterns, predict future demand, and make data-driven improvements.

- **Automation tools**: Implement automation software to streamline repetitive tasks, such as invoicing, inventory tracking, or customer communication. This frees up time for more strategic work and reduces the risk of human error.

- **Cloud-based platforms**: Use cloud-based project management and collaboration tools to monitor team performance in real time, track progress on tasks, and ensure accountability.

For instance, a manufacturing company could use data analytics software to track production output across different shifts. If the data reveals that one shift consistently underperforms, management can investigate the root cause and take corrective action, such as providing additional training or adjusting workflows.

5. Foster a Culture of Continuous Improvement

For continuous improvement to be effective, it needs to be embraced at all levels of your organization. A culture of continuous improvement encourages employees to seek out ways to enhance processes, reduce waste, and improve productivity. When everyone on the team is committed to operational excellence, small changes can compound over time, leading to significant gains in efficiency and performance.

To foster a culture of continuous improvement:

- **Encourage employee input**: Create open channels for employees to share their ideas and suggestions for improving operations. Employees are often closest to the day-to-day processes and can provide valuable insights.

- **Reward innovation**: Recognize and reward team members who contribute to process improvements, whether through cost-saving measures, time-saving initiatives, or quality enhancements.

- **Provide ongoing training**: Offer regular training and development opportunities to help employees improve their skills and stay up to date with industry best practices.

For example, a logistics company might hold monthly team meetings where employees are encouraged to suggest improvements to the shipping process. Over time, these small suggestions could lead to faster delivery times, lower shipping costs, and improved customer satisfaction.

6. Adapt to Change and Stay Flexible

The business environment is constantly changing, and your operations need to be flexible enough to adapt to new challenges and opportunities. Whether it's changes in customer preferences, technological advancements, or shifts in the competitive landscape, staying adaptable is key to maintaining operational efficiency. Regularly review your processes, stay informed about industry trends, and be willing to pivot when necessary.

To stay flexible:

- **Monitor external trends**: Keep an eye on industry trends, new technologies, and market changes that could impact your operations. This helps you stay ahead of the curve and proactively adjust your strategies.

- **Be open to experimentation**: Encourage a mindset of experimentation, where testing new processes, tools, or approaches is seen as a normal part of business. Not every experiment will succeed, but those that do can provide a competitive edge.

- **Adjust quickly when needed**: If you identify inefficiencies or changing conditions, act quickly to make adjustments. Being responsive to change allows you to maintain operational efficiency even in dynamic environments.

For example, a food delivery company might adapt to changing customer preferences by implementing contactless delivery options during a health crisis. By staying agile, the company ensures it meets customer needs while maintaining operational continuity.

Conclusion: The Cycle of Continuous Improvement for Long-Term Success
Monitoring and improving your operations is an ongoing process that requires regular attention and a commitment to excellence. By setting clear KPIs, conducting audits, leveraging technology, and fostering a culture of continuous improvement, you can ensure that your business operations remain efficient, adaptable, and responsive to change.

The cycle of continuous improvement is a powerful tool for driving growth and long-term success. When you consistently evaluate and optimize your processes, you'll not only improve efficiency and reduce costs but also position your business to thrive in an ever-changing market.

Quick Tips and Recap

- **Identify key roles and responsibilities**: Ensure each team member has clearly defined tasks and responsibilities to prevent overlap and confusion.

- **Hire for skills and cultural fit**: Look for candidates with the right skills and values that align with your company culture for long-term success.

- **Balance workloads**: Distribute tasks evenly across your team to prevent burnout and maintain high productivity levels.

- **Cross-train employees**: Implement cross-training to build flexibility within your team and ensure operations run smoothly when key members are unavailable.

- **Use technology to track tasks**: Leverage project management tools to monitor progress, assign tasks, and ensure deadlines are met efficiently.

- **Monitor and adjust team performance**: Regularly review performance metrics to identify inefficiencies and make adjustments as needed.

- **Establish KPIs**: Track performance metrics like production efficiency, customer satisfaction, and order fulfillment time to evaluate operational effectiveness.

- **Conduct regular operational audits**: Review processes and resource usage to identify areas for improvement and streamline operations.

- **Implement the PDCA cycle**: Use the Plan-Do-Check-Act framework for testing and refining new processes for continuous improvement.

- **Leverage data and technology**: Utilize data analytics and automation tools to optimize efficiency and reduce manual errors in your operations.

- **Foster a culture of continuous improvement**: Encourage your team to contribute ideas for operational enhancements and reward innovation.

- **Stay flexible**: Adapt to industry trends and changes, ensuring your business remains responsive and agile in a dynamic market.

These quick tips will help you optimize your team and operational processes, ensuring that your business remains efficient and continues to improve over time.

CHAPTER EIGHT

Numbers Game: Crafting Realistic Financial Projections

"Crafting realistic financial projections isn't just a numbers game; it's a critical exercise in forecasting the future health and potential of your business."— WARREN BUFFETT, INVESTOR AND PHILANTHROPIST

Ah, the numbers game—where spreadsheets reign supreme and dollar signs are your new best friend. Crafting financial projections might sound like a snooze-fest to some, but trust me, this is where the magic happens! Think of it as predicting the future, but instead of a crystal ball, you're armed with calculators and balance sheets. Don't worry, no need to dust off your high school algebra skills (though they might come in handy)—it's all about making informed guesses that keep your business on the road to success.

Creating realistic financial projections is like planning a cross-country road trip. You'll need to budget for gas (operating expenses), food (marketing spend), and the occasional flat tire (unexpected costs). Sure, you might hit a few bumps along the way, but having a roadmap for your finances will help you navigate the twists and turns with confidence.

Now, the trick is to dream big but stay grounded—aim for that five-star revenue but don't expect it to show up overnight. Start with small, achievable milestones and build from there. That way, when you hit those projections, it feels less like a lucky win and more like a well-executed strategy. So, buckle up, because the numbers game is about to begin, and with the right plan, you'll be rolling in green (the good kind).

Revenue Forecasting: Estimating Your Income Stream

Revenue forecasting is the backbone of your financial projections. Accurately estimating your future income allows you to plan for growth, allocate resources, and make informed business decisions. While no one has a crystal ball, you can make educated predictions based on historical data, market trends, and business goals. Think of revenue forecasting as mapping out the money that will flow into your business over a specific period, helping you prepare for the road ahead.

In this section, we'll explore how to create realistic revenue forecasts, the different methods you can use, and key factors to consider.

1. Understand the Basics of Revenue Forecasting

Revenue forecasting involves predicting how much money your business will generate over a given period—usually monthly, quarterly, or annually. This projection is critical for decision-making, budgeting, and securing investment. At its core, revenue forecasting helps you answer two key questions: How much revenue can I expect? and When can I expect it?

There are two main types of revenue forecasts:

- **Top-down forecasting**: Starts with market size and estimates what percentage of the market your business can capture. This method is more speculative and ideal for businesses with little or no historical data.

- **Bottom-up forecasting**: Starts with your current revenue, sales data, and growth rate. This approach is more precise, using real-world performance to predict future revenue.

For example, if you own an online retail store and your current monthly sales are $10,000, you would use bottom-up forecasting to project growth based on your marketing efforts, customer base, and historical sales trends.

2. Use Historical Data for Accuracy

If your business has been operating for a while, historical data is your most valuable tool for creating accurate revenue forecasts. By analyzing past performance, you can identify trends, patterns, and seasonality in your sales. This data-driven approach helps you make informed predictions about future revenue, rather than relying on guesswork.

To use historical data:

- **Analyze sales trends**: Look at your revenue over the past year or several years. Identify any patterns, such as peak sales seasons or periods of slower growth.

- **Factor in seasonality**: If your business experiences seasonal fluctuations (e.g., higher sales during the holidays), incorporate these into your projections. For example, a retail store might see a spike in revenue during December and lower sales in January.

- **Consider external factors**: Changes in the economy, market conditions, or industry trends can impact your revenue. Use historical data to adjust for external factors that might influence future performance.

For instance, if you run a coffee shop and notice that your sales consistently increase by 20% in the fall due to demand for seasonal drinks, you can project similar growth in the upcoming fall season based on past performance.

3. Factor in Market Trends and Business Goals

While historical data is essential, it's also important to account for market trends and your business goals when forecasting revenue. Your industry may be evolving, or you may be launching new products or services that could affect your revenue growth.

To factor in market trends and goals:

- **Research industry trends**: Look at market research and reports to understand where your industry is headed. Is the market expanding or contracting? Are there new competitors or innovations that could impact your business?

- **Set growth targets**: Consider your business goals, such as expanding to new locations, increasing your marketing budget, or introducing new revenue streams. These goals should be reflected in your revenue forecast.

- **Adjust for market conditions**: Consider broader economic factors like inflation, interest rates, or consumer spending patterns. Adjust your revenue forecast accordingly, especially if you expect significant market shifts.

For example, if you own a tech startup and plan to release a new app in the next quarter, you'll need to project how much revenue this launch will generate based on market demand and your marketing efforts. Similarly, if there's an economic downturn, you may want to lower your revenue expectations to reflect reduced consumer spending.

4. Consider Customer Acquisition and Retention

Revenue growth is driven by two main factors: customer acquisition (gaining new customers) and customer retention(keeping existing customers). When creating your revenue forecast, it's important to account for both. Acquiring new customers expands your revenue base, while retaining current customers ensures consistent, repeat revenue.

To factor in customer acquisition and retention:

- **Project new customer growth**: Estimate how many new customers you can realistically acquire over the forecast period. Use marketing data, lead generation trends, or customer acquisition metrics to make accurate projections.

- **Factor in customer churn**: Not all customers will stick around, so you'll need to account for customer churn (the percentage of customers you lose over time). Retaining existing customers through loyalty programs or excellent service can help stabilize revenue.

- **Calculate customer lifetime value (CLV)**: Understanding how much revenue each customer generates over their lifetime allows you to forecast the impact of both new and existing customers on your bottom line.

For example, if you run a subscription service and have a monthly churn rate of 5%, you'll want to factor this loss into your revenue forecast while also projecting how many new subscribers you'll gain from your marketing efforts.

5. Use Scenario Planning for Flexibility

Revenue forecasts are inherently uncertain, especially in unpredictable markets. To prepare for different outcomes, it's helpful to use scenario planning, where you create multiple revenue forecasts based on different scenarios: best case, worst case, and most likely case. This approach provides a more flexible, realistic view of your potential revenue.

To implement scenario planning:

- **Best-case scenario**: Assume everything goes according to plan—sales are strong, customer acquisition is high, and the market is favorable. This forecast represents your most optimistic outlook.

- **Worst-case scenario**: Plan for potential challenges, such as lower sales, higher costs, or market disruptions. This forecast helps you prepare for downturns or unexpected obstacles.

- **Most likely scenario**: Create a realistic, middle-ground forecast based on current performance, trends, and growth rates. This is typically your primary forecast and should guide your budgeting and planning decisions.

For example, a fashion retailer might project best-case revenue growth of 20% based on strong seasonal demand, a worst-case scenario of flat sales due to supply chain disruptions, and a most likely scenario of 10% growth based on historical trends.

6. Monitor and Adjust Your Forecast Regularly

Revenue forecasting is not a one-time activity. As your business grows and market conditions change, you'll need to monitor and adjust your forecasts regularly. By comparing your actual revenue to your projections, you can refine your forecasts over time, making them more accurate and actionable.

To keep your forecasts up to date:

- **Review monthly or quarterly**: Set regular intervals to review your forecasts and compare them to actual sales. If there's a significant gap, investigate why and adjust future projections accordingly.

- **Analyze discrepancies**: If your actual revenue consistently falls short of or exceeds your projections, identify the factors driving the discrepancy. Adjust your assumptions or refine your forecasting model as needed.

- **Update based on real-time data**: Incorporate new data, such as changes in customer behavior, market trends, or product performance, into your projections to keep them relevant and accurate.

For example, if a new product line is outperforming expectations, you'll want to revise your revenue forecast upward. Conversely, if a marketing campaign isn't generating the expected results, you may need to lower your projections for the coming months.

Conclusion: The Power of Informed Revenue Forecasting

Revenue forecasting is a powerful tool for managing your business's financial health and planning for growth. By analyzing historical data, factoring in market trends and customer behavior, and using scenario planning, you can create realistic and flexible revenue projections that guide your decision-making.

The key to success is staying adaptable and refining your forecasts as new data comes in. With a strong revenue forecast in hand, you'll be well-equipped to budget, allocate resources, and steer your business toward sustainable growth.

Expense Projections: Budgeting for Success

Creating accurate expense projections is just as important as forecasting your revenue. While your revenue projections give you an idea of how much money will flow into your business, your expense projections outline how much money will flow out. A clear understanding of your costs is crucial to maintaining profitability, managing cash flow, and ensuring the financial health of your business. Proper expense forecasting allows you to budget wisely, avoid surprises, and make informed decisions about where to allocate your resources.

In this section, we'll explore how to create realistic expense projections, understand the different types of expenses, and account for unexpected costs in your financial plan.

1. Identify Fixed and Variable Costs

To begin with, it's important to understand the difference between fixed costs and variable costs, as these two types of expenses behave differently over time.

- **Fixed costs** are consistent and don't change regardless of how much you sell or produce. These are ongoing expenses that must be paid regularly, such as rent, salaries, and utilities. While they provide stability, they can also be a significant drain on cash flow if not managed properly.

- **Variable costs** fluctuate depending on your sales volume or production levels. These include things like raw materials, shipping costs, and commissions. The more you sell or produce, the higher these costs will be.

To project your fixed and variable costs:

- **List all fixed costs**: Write down all the expenses you know will remain constant, such as rent, internet bills, insurance, and salaried employee wages.

- **Estimate variable costs**: Look at past sales or production data to estimate variable costs. For instance, if you know that your cost of goods sold (COGS) increases by $5 for every unit you sell, factor this into your variable expense projection.

For example, a bakery would include rent, electricity, and staff salaries as fixed costs. Flour, sugar, and packaging materials, which increase with the number of orders, would be classified as variable costs.

2. Account for One-Time and Unexpected Costs

In addition to fixed and variable costs, you should also account for one-time expenses and potential unexpected costs that could arise. One-time expenses might include things like launching a new product line, upgrading equipment, or a one-off marketing campaign. Unexpected costs can include emergency repairs, price increases from suppliers, or legal fees.

To account for these:

- **Identify one-time expenses**: Look at upcoming projects or expansions that will require one-off investments, such as new equipment, technology upgrades, or promotional events.

- **Prepare for unexpected costs**: Build a contingency fund into your expense projections. A good rule of thumb is to allocate a small percentage (typically 5-10%) of your projected expenses to cover unanticipated costs.

For instance, a tech company planning to launch a new software product might need to budget for a one-time marketing campaign, as well as unexpected costs like hiring freelance developers to meet deadlines.

3. Project Costs for Key Business Functions

A detailed expense projection should cover all key business functions, including operations, marketing, personnel, and research and development (R&D). Understanding how each area contributes to your overall costs will help you create a more precise budget and ensure that you allocate resources effectively.

Here's how to break down expenses for each key function:

- **Operations**: These costs include production, inventory, shipping, and logistics. If you're running a product-based business, operations might be one of your largest expense categories.

- **Marketing**: Advertising, promotional campaigns, social media management, and customer acquisition efforts fall under marketing expenses. If your business relies on growth through marketing efforts, make sure to allocate a realistic portion of your budget to this area.

- **Personnel**: Salaries, wages, benefits, and payroll taxes are the primary personnel costs. If you're planning to expand your team, project the costs of hiring new employees or offering raises.

- **Research and Development (R&D)**: If your business involves innovation or new product development, R&D costs such as research, product testing, and prototyping should be factored in.

For example, a retail business would project operational expenses like stocking inventory and shipping costs, while also budgeting for marketing campaigns such as email newsletters and social media ads.

4. Consider Seasonality and Growth

When projecting expenses, it's important to take into account seasonal fluctuations and business growth. Certain times of the year may have higher expenses, particularly if your business is seasonal, or if you anticipate significant growth that will require additional resources.

To account for seasonality and growth:

- **Anticipate seasonal changes**: If your business experiences increased sales during specific months (e.g., a clothing store during the holiday season), plan for higher marketing costs, temporary staffing, or increased inventory.

- **Plan for growth**: If you expect rapid growth in the coming months, you may need to scale up operations. This might mean investing in more inventory, hiring new staff, or increasing your marketing spend. Make sure your expense projections reflect these growth-related costs.

For instance, a landscaping company might plan for higher expenses in the spring and summer, when they hire more seasonal workers and increase their marketing efforts to capitalize on peak demand.

5. Use Benchmarks and Industry Data

If you're unsure about certain expense projections, industry benchmarks and comparable data can be a valuable resource. Industry averages can give you an idea of how much similar businesses spend on operations, marketing, or personnel, allowing you to create more informed projections.

To use benchmarks effectively:

- **Research industry averages**: Look for data on typical expense ratios in your industry. For example, businesses in the restaurant industry typically spend 25-30% of their revenue on food costs and 30-35% on labor.

- **Adjust based on your business**: Use benchmarks as a starting point, but adjust for your unique business situation. For example, a startup may need to allocate more funds to marketing to build brand awareness, compared to an established company.

- **Consult with industry experts**: If you're unsure about certain costs, consult with industry professionals or financial advisors who have experience in your field. They can provide insights on expenses that might be difficult to project on your own.

For instance, a SaaS company might find that similar businesses allocate around 40% of their budget to personnel and 15% to marketing, helping them plan their own expenses more accurately.

6. Monitor and Adjust Your Expense Projections

Expense projections are not static; they should be monitored and adjusted regularly as your business grows and market conditions change. By comparing your actual expenses to your projected expenses, you can refine your forecasts and ensure that your budgeting remains accurate over time.

To monitor and adjust your expense projections:

- **Review monthly or quarterly**: Set regular intervals to review your expense projections and compare them to actual spending. Identify any discrepancies and adjust future projections accordingly.

- **Analyze cost variances**: If certain costs consistently exceed your projections (e.g., higher-than-expected shipping fees or marketing costs), investigate why and adjust your budget to reflect the reality.

- **Refine based on business changes**: If your business undergoes significant changes—such as launching a new product, expanding to a new location, or experiencing rapid growth—revisit your expense projections to account for new costs.

For example, a retail store might realize after a few months that they've been underestimating shipping costs due to increased online orders. By revising their projections, they can better allocate resources to manage these expenses.

Conclusion: Budgeting for Financial Success
Expense projections are an essential part of managing your business's financial health. By identifying fixed and variable costs, accounting for one-time and unexpected expenses, and breaking down costs across key business functions, you can create a realistic budget that supports your goals. Factoring in seasonality, growth, and industry benchmarks will help you stay on track, while regular monitoring and adjustments ensure that your expense projections remain accurate as your business evolves.

A well-crafted expense projection gives you the financial clarity you need to operate efficiently, avoid costly surprises, and ultimately achieve long-term success.

Cash Flow Management: Ensuring Liquidity and Stability

Cash flow management is the lifeblood of any business. While revenue and expense projections are critical for planning, cash flow tells you how much money is actually available to keep your operations running day to day. Managing cash flow effectively ensures that your business remains liquid (able to pay bills and expenses) and stable during both predictable cycles and unexpected challenges.

In this section, we'll explore how to create accurate cash flow projections, strategies to improve liquidity, and tools to help manage your cash flow for long-term success.

1. Understand the Basics of Cash Flow

Cash flow refers to the movement of money into and out of your business over a specific period. Positive cash flow occurs when more money is coming into your business than going out, while negative cash flow happens when outgoing payments exceed incoming cash.

There are two key components to cash flow:

- **Cash inflows**: These are the funds coming into your business, including sales revenue, loans, and investments. Cash inflows may come from customers paying for products or services, investors contributing capital, or receiving a loan or grant.

- **Cash outflows**: These are the expenses and payments your business must make, such as rent, salaries, inventory purchases, loan repayments, and utilities.

While generating revenue is essential, businesses can still struggle if they don't have enough cash on hand to meet their immediate obligations. That's why managing cash flow is crucial for maintaining liquidity and avoiding cash shortages.

2. Create a Cash Flow Projection

A cash flow projection estimates how much money will flow into and out of your business over a specific period (monthly, quarterly, or annually). This allows you to predict when you may experience cash surpluses or shortfalls and plan accordingly.

To create a cash flow projection:

- **Estimate cash inflows**: Start by forecasting your expected revenue for the period. Include all sources of cash inflows, such as sales revenue, loan proceeds, or new investments.

- **Estimate cash outflows**: List all anticipated expenses, including rent, salaries, utilities, loan repayments, taxes, and inventory purchases.

- **Calculate net cash flow**: Subtract total cash outflows from total cash inflows to determine your **net cash flow**. If this number is positive, you'll have surplus cash for the period. If it's negative, you'll need to find ways to cover the shortfall.

For example, if your expected cash inflows for the month are $20,000 and your cash outflows are $18,000, your net cash flow would be +$2,000, indicating a cash surplus. On the other hand, if your inflows are $15,000 and your outflows are $18,000, you'd have a shortfall of -$3,000, meaning you'll need to find additional funds to cover your expenses.

3. Track and Improve Cash Flow Regularly

Managing cash flow isn't a one-time activity. It requires regular tracking and adjustments to ensure you maintain sufficient liquidity. By monitoring cash flow closely, you can spot potential issues early and take corrective action before they become critical.

To track and improve cash flow:

- **Monitor cash flow daily or weekly**: Regularly review your cash flow to ensure that you have enough cash on hand to cover your short-term obligations. Use accounting software to automate tracking and generate reports.

- **Speed up receivables**: Encourage customers to pay their invoices faster by offering early payment discounts or reducing payment terms (e.g., from 30 days to 15 days). This speeds up your cash inflows and reduces the risk of late payments.

- **Delay payables**: Where possible, negotiate longer payment terms with suppliers (e.g., from 30 days to 45 days) to slow down cash outflows. This can give you more time to pay your bills without straining cash reserves.

- **Cut unnecessary expenses**: Regularly review your expenses and cut any non-essential costs to reduce cash outflows. Consider delaying non-urgent purchases or scaling back on discretionary spending.

For instance, a service-based business might offer a 2% discount to clients who pay their invoices within 10 days rather than the standard 30 days. This speeds up cash collection, ensuring they have enough liquidity to cover operational expenses.

4. Plan for Seasonal Cash Flow Fluctuations

Many businesses experience seasonal fluctuations in cash flow, with peak periods of sales followed by slower months. Planning for these fluctuations is essential to ensuring liquidity throughout the year, especially during lean periods when sales may drop but expenses remain constant.

To manage seasonal cash flow fluctuations:

- **Build a cash reserve**: Set aside cash during peak sales periods to cover expenses during slower months. A cash reserve acts as a buffer to prevent cash shortages when sales slowdown.

- **Adjust expenses in off-seasons**: During low-revenue periods, reduce variable expenses where possible. For example, cut back on inventory purchases or temporary staff to minimize cash outflows.

- **Consider financing options**: If you expect a short-term cash flow gap, consider using a business line of credit or short-term loan to cover expenses until sales pick up again. Be sure to account for interest and fees when using financing.

For example, a retail store that experiences peak sales during the holiday season might set aside some of its holiday profits to cover rent and payroll during slower months like February and March.

5. Use Cash Flow Management Tools

There are many tools available to help you manage cash flow more effectively. These tools automate the tracking of cash inflows and outflows, generate cash flow reports, and provide real-time visibility into your liquidity position. By using cash flow management software, you can stay on top of your finances and make proactive decisions to maintain stability.

Popular cash flow management tools include:

- **QuickBooks**: This accounting software offers real-time cash flow tracking, invoice management, and cash flow forecasting, making it ideal for small businesses.

- **Xero**: Xero provides cash flow reporting and forecasting tools, as well as integrations with invoicing and payment platforms to improve cash collection.

- **Float**: This cash flow forecasting software integrates with accounting platforms to provide detailed cash flow projections, helping businesses predict future cash positions and identify potential shortfalls.

For instance, a small business using QuickBooks can track its daily cash inflows and outflows, create automatic invoices, and receive alerts if cash reserves fall below a certain threshold, ensuring that cash flow remains stable.

6. Maintain a Cash Flow Cushion

Even with careful planning, cash flow can sometimes be unpredictable. To protect your business from unexpected cash shortfalls, it's important to maintain a cash flow cushion—an extra buffer of cash reserves that can cover unforeseen expenses or periods of low revenue. This cushion provides peace of mind and allows you to weather financial storms without jeopardizing your business's stability.

To build a cash flow cushion:

- **Set aside a percentage of profits**: Each month, allocate a portion of your profits to a cash reserve account. Aim to build a cushion that covers 3-6 months of operating expenses.

- **Reinvest excess cash**: During periods of strong cash flow, consider reinvesting excess cash into your cushion rather than immediately spending it on new projects or expenses.

- **Be disciplined**: Only dip into your cash flow cushion for emergencies or unexpected cash shortfalls. Avoid using it for discretionary spending or unnecessary investments.

For example, a tech startup might set aside 10% of its monthly profits into a cash reserve fund, building a cushion that can cover 6 months of operating expenses in case of unexpected market downturns or delays in product launches.

Conclusion: Maintaining Liquidity and Stability Through Cash Flow
Effective cash flow management is essential to the financial health and stability of your business. By creating accurate cash flow projections, tracking inflows and outflows regularly, and implementing strategies to improve liquidity, you can ensure that your business remains well-funded and capable of covering its expenses. Planning for seasonal fluctuations, using cash flow management tools, and building a cash flow cushion further safeguard your business against financial disruptions.

A strong cash flow strategy allows you to navigate short-term challenges, take advantage of growth opportunities, and keep your business on solid financial footing for the long term.

Profit and Loss Statements: Visualizing the Bottom Line

A Profit and Loss Statement (P&L)—also known as an Income Statement—is one of the most critical financial documents for any business. It provides a snapshot of your company's financial performance over a specific period, showing whether your business is generating a profit or running at a loss. By outlining your revenue, expenses, and net profit (or loss), the P&L statement gives you a clear picture of your bottom line and helps you make informed financial decisions.

In this section, we'll break down the components of a P&L statement, explain how to interpret the results, and discuss how this tool can guide your business's financial strategy.

1. Understanding the Components of a P&L Statement

A P&L statement is composed of several key sections that give you a comprehensive view of your business's income and expenses. Understanding these components is essential to reading and using your P&L effectively.

The main sections include:

- **Revenue (Sales)**: This is the total income generated from selling your products or services during the specified period. It's the starting point for your P&L.

- **Cost of Goods Sold (COGS)**: These are the direct costs associated with producing the goods or services your business sells. COGS includes materials, labor, and other expenses directly tied to production. Subtracting COGS from revenue gives you your gross profit.

- **Gross Profit**: Gross profit is the amount of money left after subtracting COGS from your revenue. It shows how efficiently you're producing your products or services.

Formula: **Gross Profit = Revenue – COGS**

- **Operating Expenses**: These are the indirect costs of running your business, such as rent, utilities, marketing, and administrative salaries. Operating expenses are necessary to keep the business running but are not tied directly to production.

- **Operating Income**: Also known as **Operating Profit**, this is your gross profit minus your operating expenses. It represents the profit your business generates from its core operations before taxes and interest.

Formula: **Operating Income = Gross Profit – Operating Expenses**

- **Other Income and Expenses**: This section includes any additional revenue or expenses not related to your core business activities, such as interest income, investment gains, or loan interest.

- **Net Profit (Net Income)**: Finally, net profit is the total amount of profit (or loss) after all expenses—including taxes, interest, and non-operating costs—have been deducted from revenue. This is your bottom line, showing whether your business is profitable or not during the period.

Formula: **Net Profit = Operating Income – Taxes – Interest + Other Income**

For example, if your business generated $100,000 in sales, spent $30,000 on COGS, and had $40,000 in operating expenses, your operating income would be $30,000. After accounting for taxes and interest, your net profit might be $25,000, reflecting your overall profitability.

2. Interpreting the Results

A P&L statement provides valuable insights into your business's financial health, but understanding how to interpret the numbers is key to making informed decisions. By carefully reviewing the different sections, you can identify trends, spot inefficiencies, and plan for the future.

Here's how to interpret the key areas:

- **Gross profit margin**: This metric measures how efficiently your business is turning revenue into profit before operating expenses are deducted. A high gross profit margin indicates efficient production, while a low margin suggests that your costs of production might be too high.

Formula: **Gross Profit Margin (%) = (Gross Profit / Revenue) x 100**

For example, if your gross profit is $70,000 from $100,000 in sales, your gross profit margin is 70%. This indicates that you're retaining 70% of your revenue after covering production costs.

- **Operating profit margin**: This metric shows how much of your revenue is left after operating expenses. It's a good indicator of how well you manage the day-to-day running of your business.

Formula: **Operating Profit Margin (%) = (Operating Income / Revenue) x 100**

For example, if your operating income is $30,000 from $100,000 in sales, your operating profit margin is 30%. This means 30% of your revenue is profit after deducting operational expenses.

- **Net profit margin**: The net profit margin reveals how much of each dollar in revenue is actually profit after all expenses, including taxes and interest. It's the ultimate measure of your business's profitability.

Formula: **Net Profit Margin (%) = (Net Profit / Revenue) x 100**

For example, if your net profit is $25,000 from $100,000 in revenue, your net profit margin is 25%, meaning that for every dollar in sales, $0.25 is pure profit.

By comparing your gross profit, operating profit, and net profit margins, you can determine where your business is most efficient and where it needs improvement. For instance, a high gross profit margin but a low net profit margin may indicate high operating costs or other inefficiencies in your non-production-related expenses.

3. Using P&L Statements to Make Strategic Decisions

A P&L statement is more than just a financial summary—it's a powerful tool for making strategic decisions. By reviewing your P&L statement regularly (monthly, quarterly, or annually), you can track your progress, adjust your budget, and make informed choices about how to allocate resources.

Here's how to use your P&L for decision-making:

- **Identify cost-saving opportunities**: If your operating expenses are consistently high, look for areas where you can cut costs, such as renegotiating vendor contracts or reducing discretionary spending.

- **Focus on revenue growth**: Analyze which products or services are driving the most revenue and profitability. This can guide your marketing efforts or product development strategies.

- **Set performance benchmarks**: Use your P&L to establish performance benchmarks and track key metrics like gross profit margin, operating profit margin, and net profit margin over time. Compare these metrics to industry averages to see how your business stacks up against competitors.

- **Plan for taxes and reinvestment**: Net profit gives you a clear view of your available funds for tax payments, reinvestments, or growth initiatives. Knowing your bottom line helps you decide how much you can reinvest in the business or pay out to stakeholders.

For example, if you notice that your operating expenses have been increasing steadily, you might decide to hold off on hiring new staff or scale back marketing spending until you can better control these costs.

4. Review P&L Statements Regularly

Regularly reviewing your P&L statements is critical for tracking progress and staying on top of your business's financial performance. Depending on your business size and complexity, you may want to review P&L statements monthly (for fast-growing businesses) or quarterly (for more stable operations).

During these reviews, ask yourself:

- **Are we meeting our revenue targets?** If not, what's causing the shortfall, and how can we adjust our strategy?

- **Are expenses in line with projections?** If expenses are higher than expected, where can we reduce costs without sacrificing quality or service?

- **How does this period compare to the previous one?** Look for trends, such as improving gross profit margins or rising net income, and use them to guide future decisions.

- **Is the business still profitable?** If your net profit is consistently negative, you may need to rethink your business model, cut expenses, or find ways to boost revenue.

By consistently reviewing your P&L, you'll have a more accurate picture of your financial health and be able to make proactive decisions to keep your business on track.

5. Understand the Limitations of P&L Statements

While P&L statements are invaluable, they do have limitations. For one, they don't reflect cash flow, which is why you should also use cash flow statements to ensure liquidity. Additionally, P&L statements don't account for assets and liabilities—those are tracked in your balance sheet. As such, P&L statements should be used in conjunction with other financial documents to get a complete picture of your business's financial health.

For example, while your P&L might show a net profit, a cash flow statement could reveal that you're low on cash due to outstanding receivables. By using both together, you can avoid potential cash flow shortages while maintaining profitability.

Conclusion: Visualizing Profitability with P&L Statements

Profit and Loss Statements provide a powerful snapshot of your business's profitability, helping you visualize your revenue, costs, and net profit. By understanding the key components—revenue, COGS, operating expenses, and net profit—you can get a clear view of your financial health and make informed strategic decisions.

Regularly reviewing and interpreting your P&L allows you to spot trends, identify areas for improvement, and optimize your business operations for long-term success. With this tool, you'll be better equipped to visualize your bottom line, manage your finances wisely, and keep your business on the path to profitability.

Adjusting Projections: Revisiting and Refining as You Grow

As your business grows, your initial financial projections will likely need to be revisited and refined to reflect new realities. Growth brings change—whether it's expanding into new markets, launching new products, or responding to shifting customer demands. Adjusting your financial projections ensures that your business remains on track, allowing you to stay agile and make informed decisions that support sustainable growth.

In this section, we'll explore why and how you should revisit and adjust your financial projections regularly, the key factors to consider, and how to integrate new data into your updated forecasts.

1. Why Adjusting Financial Projections is Essential

When you first create financial projections, they are based on assumptions about revenue, expenses, and growth. However, as your business evolves, these assumptions may no longer hold true. Adjusting projections ensures that you're always working with the most accurate financial data, helping you avoid shortfalls, plan for investments, and manage cash flow effectively.

Key reasons to adjust financial projections include:

- **Business growth**: Expanding into new markets, hiring additional staff, or increasing production capacity can alter both your revenue and expense forecasts.

- **Changes in market conditions**: Shifts in the economy, industry trends, or competitive landscape can affect your revenue potential and cost structure.

- **Operational changes**: Launching new products, services, or marketing campaigns may impact your cash flow and profitability.

- **Unexpected events**: External factors, such as supply chain disruptions, regulatory changes, or global events, can significantly impact your financial performance.

For example, a retail business may need to adjust its projections after opening new locations, as both sales and operating expenses will increase.

2. Set Regular Review Intervals

To keep your projections aligned with your business's reality, it's important to schedule regular reviews of your financial forecasts. By comparing your actual performance against your projected revenue and expenses, you can identify any discrepancies early and make adjustments before small issues turn into larger problems.

Recommended review intervals:

- **Monthly**: For fast-growing businesses or those with rapidly changing circumstances, monthly reviews are essential to keep forecasts accurate.

- **Quarterly**: For more stable businesses, quarterly reviews offer a balance between staying on top of performance and avoiding over-analysis.

- **Annually**: Conduct an annual review to make major adjustments and plan for long-term growth. This is particularly important when setting budgets or making strategic decisions for the upcoming year.

For instance, if a software company is rapidly onboarding new clients, it should review its revenue and cash flow projections monthly to ensure it can scale without running into cash flow problems.

3. Incorporate New Data and Trends

Financial projections should be grounded in real-time data and emerging trends. Each time you revisit your projections, update them with the most current information available. This includes not only actual sales and expenses but also broader market trends and industry insights.

How to incorporate new data:

- **Use actual sales and expense data**: Compare your projected revenue and expenses to actual numbers. If there's a significant gap, reassess your assumptions. For example, if actual sales are lower than expected, you may need to lower your future revenue projections.

- **Monitor market trends**: Stay informed about economic changes, consumer behavior shifts, and new competitors. If the market is growing faster or slower than anticipated, adjust your projections accordingly.

- **Track internal performance metrics**: Monitor KPIs such as customer acquisition rates, conversion rates, and operating efficiency. Use these metrics to refine your forecasts based on actual performance.

For example, if a direct-to-consumer business sees a spike in online sales due to an industry trend favoring e-commerce, it may need to increase its revenue projections while adjusting for higher shipping and customer service costs.

4. Adjust for Growth Opportunities and Challenges

Growth creates opportunities, but it also introduces new challenges. As your business scales, you'll need to account for additional costs, more complex operations, and potential bottlenecks. On the other hand, new opportunities—such as entering new markets or launching products—may require additional investment but could also lead to higher revenue projections.

Key areas to adjust for growth:

- **Hiring and staffing costs**: As you grow, you may need to hire more employees or increase payroll. Adjust your expense projections to include salary, benefits, and training costs for new hires.

- **Operational scalability**: Expansion often means higher production or service delivery costs. If you're manufacturing more products or handling more customers, factor in increased supply chain or operational costs.

- **Marketing and customer acquisition**: Growth often requires more aggressive marketing and customer acquisition strategies. Project higher marketing expenses as you work to capture more market share.

For example, a SaaS company expanding into international markets may need to adjust its projections for increased marketing expenses, legal fees for compliance, and additional customer support teams in new regions.

5. Scenario Planning for Future Adjustments

As you grow, one of the best ways to manage uncertainty is by using scenario planning—creating multiple financial projections based on different potential outcomes. Scenario planning helps you prepare for various possibilities, ensuring that you're ready for both best-case and worst-case scenarios.

How to use scenario planning:

- **Best-case scenario**: Assume rapid growth, high sales, and favorable market conditions. What would your revenue, expenses, and profits look like if everything went as planned?

- **Worst-case scenario**: Account for challenges such as a downturn in sales, increased costs, or a sudden market disruption. How would your business handle this, and what measures could you take to mitigate the impact?

- **Most likely scenario**: Create a projection based on current performance, historical trends, and reasonable growth assumptions. This should be your baseline forecast.

For example, a manufacturing company might create a worst-case scenario that accounts for supply chain disruptions, increased material costs, or lower-than-expected sales. This would allow them to plan contingency measures, such as sourcing alternative suppliers or cutting non-essential expenses.

6. Maintain Flexibility and Stay Agile

The key to successfully adjusting projections as you grow is flexibility. Business conditions change constantly, and maintaining an agile mindset will help you adapt quickly. Projections are not set in stone—they are a tool to guide decision-making and should be revised as new information becomes available.

Ways to stay flexible:

- **Embrace change**: Be open to revising your projections regularly. Don't be afraid to adjust when things don't go according to plan—adapt your forecasts based on new data.

- **Prioritize resources**: If your projections reveal a cash shortfall or lower profitability, be prepared to cut non-essential expenses or delay large investments until your financial outlook improves.

- **Prepare for new opportunities**: Stay nimble so you can take advantage of new opportunities that arise, whether it's launching a new product, entering a new market, or scaling operations.

For instance, a retail business that suddenly sees an increase in demand due to a viral marketing campaign should quickly adjust its projections to allocate more resources to inventory, staffing, and customer service to meet the new demand.

Conclusion: Revisiting and Refining Projections for Sustained Growth

As your business grows and changes, your financial projections should grow and change with it. Regularly reviewing and adjusting your revenue, expense, and cash flow projections ensures that you're working with up-to-date financial data, allowing you to plan effectively and maintain profitability. By incorporating real-time data, accounting for growth opportunities and challenges, and using scenario planning, you'll be well-prepared to adapt to whatever the future brings.

The ability to refine your projections as you go is a powerful tool for keeping your business on track for sustainable growth, ensuring that your financial strategy evolves alongside your expanding business.

Quick Tips and Recap

- **Regularly review your financial projections**: Schedule monthly, quarterly, or annual reviews to ensure your projections remain accurate as your business grows.

- **Incorporate real-time data**: Use actual sales and expense figures to adjust your forecasts, ensuring they reflect current performance and trends.

- **Monitor market and industry changes**: Stay informed about market conditions, consumer behavior shifts, and competitor activity to update your projections accordingly.

- **Account for growth-related costs**: Adjust projections for additional staffing, operational expenses, and marketing efforts as your business scales.

- **Use scenario planning**: Create multiple projections (best-case, worst-case, and most likely) to prepare for different outcomes and stay flexible.

- **Plan for unexpected events**: Build contingency plans into your projections to cover potential disruptions, such as supply chain issues or economic downturns.

- **Stay flexible and agile**: Be ready to revise your projections regularly and adapt to changes in your business environment.

- **Focus on cash flow**: Always keep an eye on cash flow and ensure your projections maintain liquidity, even as your business expands.

- **Utilize technology**: Leverage financial management tools to automate data collection and analysis, making it easier to adjust projections quickly.

By regularly refining your financial projections, you'll stay prepared for the future, manage growth effectively, and ensure the long-term financial health of your business.

CHAPTER NINE

Safety Nets: Strategies for Risk Management

"Risk management is like having a business safety net—it's not about dodging every challenge but about preparing to tackle them with agility. The real power comes from anticipating potential issues and having strategies that keep your business resilient and ready to thrive."

— JOANNA WIEBE, FOUNDER OF COPYHACKERS

Welcome to the high-flying world of risk management, where your job is to keep your business soaring without plummeting into the abyss of unforeseen disasters. Think of risk management as your trusty parachute—it's not about avoiding turbulence but ensuring that you're prepared for the occasional free-fall. The goal is to identify potential pitfalls before they send you crashing, so you can glide gracefully over any obstacles that come your way.

In this chapter, we'll tackle how to build a safety net that's less about worrying and more about smart planning. From insurance policies that cover you like a warm safety blanket to contingency plans that are your emergency exit signs, risk management is all about being proactive rather than reactive. It's like having a backup plan for your backup plan. Because let's face it, in the business world, things don't always go according to plan—and that's where your risk strategies come in to save the day.

So, get ready to embrace your inner risk manager. We'll cover everything from spotting potential hazards to crafting strategies that keep your business as safe as houses (or at least as safe as a heavily fortified bunker). After all, the best way to avoid disaster is to plan for it—and with the right strategies in place, you'll be navigating the wild business landscape with the grace of a trapeze artist.

Identifying Risks: Spotting Hazards Before They Happen

The first step in effective risk management is identifying potential risks before they can impact your business. Every business, regardless of size or industry, faces risks that can disrupt operations, damage reputations, or hurt financial performance. By recognizing these hazards early, you can put strategies in place to prevent or mitigate their impact. Identifying risks involves a combination of foresight, analysis, and vigilance, helping you anticipate the challenges that could derail your business plans.

In this section, we'll explore the different types of risks your business might face and provide practical methods for spotting these hazards before they happen.

1. Types of Risks Your Business Might Face

Risks can arise from various areas of your business, and it's essential to understand the different types so you can address them effectively. Here are some common categories of risks to consider:

- **Operational Risks**: These are risks related to your day-to-day operations. They include equipment failures, supply chain disruptions, staff shortages, and process inefficiencies. Operational risks can cause delays, increase costs, and reduce productivity.

- **Financial Risks**: Financial risks affect your company's bottom line. These include cash flow issues, rising costs, debt management challenges, and fluctuating interest rates. Financial risks also involve market risks, such as changes in customer demand or economic downturns that could affect your revenue.

- **Strategic Risks**: These are risks related to your long-term business strategy and decisions. Launching a new product, expanding into a new market, or pivoting your business model are all strategic risks that could either pay off or result in losses if not carefully planned.

- **Legal and Compliance Risks**: These risks involve potential legal issues and regulatory compliance. This could include lawsuits, data privacy violations, breaches of contract, or failing to meet industry-specific regulations. Fines, legal battles, or damage to your reputation can arise from these risks.

- **External Risks**: These are risks that stem from outside your business and are often beyond your control. Examples include natural disasters, political instability, economic recessions, changes in market conditions, or industry disruption caused by new technology or competitors.

For example, if your business relies on an international supplier for key materials, external risks such as trade restrictions, currency fluctuations, or geopolitical events could significantly disrupt your supply chain.

2. Conducting a Risk Assessment

To spot potential hazards before they happen, it's important to conduct a risk assessment. This involves identifying all possible risks, assessing their likelihood and potential impact, and determining how they can be managed. A thorough risk assessment will give you a comprehensive view of the vulnerabilities within your business.

Steps to conduct a risk assessment:

- **Identify key areas of risk**: Break down your business into its core functions—such as operations, finance, marketing, and HR—and list potential risks for each area. Consider what could go wrong and the consequences if it does.

- **Assess the likelihood and impact**: For each risk, evaluate how likely it is to occur and what the potential impact would be on your business. Use a simple scale (e.g., low, medium, high) to categorize the likelihood and severity. For example, a minor operational disruption might be low risk, but a cybersecurity breach could be high risk with severe consequences.

- **Prioritize risks**: Once you've assessed all potential risks, prioritize them based on their likelihood and impact. Focus on addressing high-probability, high-impact risks first, as these are the most likely to threaten your business.

For example, a restaurant might assess the risk of food safety violations (a high-impact, high-probability risk) as more critical than the risk of a seasonal dip in sales (a low-impact, medium-probability risk).

3. Tools for Spotting Risks

Identifying risks isn't a one-time process—it requires ongoing monitoring and evaluation to stay ahead of potential threats. Fortunately, there are several tools and methods you can use to consistently spot hazards in your business environment:

- **SWOT Analysis**: A **SWOT analysis** (Strengths, Weaknesses, Opportunities, and Threats) is a simple but effective tool for identifying both internal and external risks. It helps you evaluate your business's weaknesses and external threats, making it easier to anticipate potential problems.

- **Risk Registers**: A **risk register** is a living document that lists all potential risks, along with their likelihood, impact, and mitigation strategies. This tool allows you to track and update risks as your business evolves, helping you stay organized and proactive.

- **Scenario Planning**: **Scenario planning** involves creating hypothetical situations based on potential risks and determining how your business would respond. For instance, what would happen if your largest supplier went out of business? By preparing for these scenarios in advance, you're better equipped to handle them if they happen.

- **Consult Experts**: Working with industry experts, consultants, or legal professionals can help you spot risks that may not be immediately obvious. These professionals can provide insights into industry-specific risks or emerging regulatory changes.

For example, a retail store might conduct regular SWOT analyses to identify risks associated with customer trends, supply chain vulnerabilities, and competitive threats. They might also maintain a risk register to track inventory management risks and employee turnover.

4. Involving Your Team in Risk Identification

Risk identification shouldn't just be the responsibility of business owners or executives—your entire team can help spot risks in their respective areas of expertise. Employees who are on the front lines often have valuable insights into potential operational, financial, or customer-related risks that you may not see.

Ways to involve your team:

- **Encourage open communication**: Create a culture where employees feel comfortable reporting concerns or potential risks without fear of repercussions. Make it clear that risk management is everyone's responsibility.

- **Hold regular risk review meetings**: Set up monthly or quarterly meetings to discuss potential risks with your team. Ask for feedback on issues they've encountered or noticed in their daily work.

- **Use suggestion boxes**: Implement anonymous suggestion boxes (physical or digital) where employees can report risks or suggest improvements to mitigate potential hazards.

For instance, a warehouse team might report inefficiencies or safety hazards in the storage process, which could reduce the risk of accidents or lost inventory. By involving them in risk identification, you get a clearer picture of operational risks.

5. Stay Informed and Proactive

Risk identification is an ongoing process, so it's important to stay informed about changes in your industry, market, and regulatory environment. Being proactive and keeping up with industry news, emerging technologies, and shifts in consumer behavior can help you anticipate potential risks before they become major problems.

Here's how to stay informed:

- **Monitor industry trends**: Subscribe to industry publications, follow relevant blogs, and attend industry conferences to stay updated on changes that could affect your business.

- **Keep an eye on regulations**: Ensure your business complies with the latest laws and regulations, especially if you operate in highly regulated industries like healthcare, finance, or food service.

- **Use technology**: Leverage data analytics, monitoring tools, and automation to track performance metrics and spot anomalies that could indicate underlying risks (e.g., financial irregularities or customer churn).

For example, a software company could monitor emerging cybersecurity threats through industry reports and regularly update their systems to protect against potential data breaches.

Conclusion: The Importance of Spotting Risks Early

Identifying risks before they become major problems is one of the most important steps in managing and protecting your business. By understanding the different types of risks, conducting thorough risk assessments, using appropriate tools, and involving your team, you'll be better equipped to spot hazards and take proactive steps to mitigate them.

Staying informed and continually monitoring for risks is key to long-term business success. The earlier you identify potential threats, the better prepared you'll be to navigate challenges, prevent disruptions, and maintain a stable, thriving business.

Mitigation Strategies: Reducing the Impact of Risk

Once you've identified the risks that could affect your business, the next crucial step is to develop mitigation strategies—plans to reduce the likelihood or impact of those risks. Risk mitigation is about preparing for potential problems so they don't derail your operations or damage your reputation. While it's impossible to eliminate all risks, you can significantly reduce their impact by being proactive, implementing strong controls, and developing contingency plans.

In this section, we'll explore various risk mitigation strategies that can help protect your business, from strengthening internal processes to diversifying income streams and using technology to safeguard operations.

1. Diversify Revenue Streams

One of the most effective ways to mitigate financial risk is to diversify your revenue streams. Relying too heavily on a single product, market, or customer base can make your business vulnerable to disruptions. By broadening your sources of income, you reduce the risk of a sudden drop in revenue if one area underperforms.

Steps to diversify revenue:

- **Expand product or service offerings**: Consider adding new products or services that complement your existing ones. For example, a bakery could start offering catering services or selling baking kits online to reach a broader audience.

- **Target new customer segments**: Identify untapped markets or demographics that could benefit from your offerings. Expanding into new markets can reduce reliance on a single customer base.

- **Develop partnerships or collaborations**: Partnering with other businesses or influencers can help you reach new customers and create additional revenue streams through joint ventures or cross-promotions.

For instance, a software company that primarily sells to small businesses could diversify by developing an enterprise version of its product for larger corporations, reducing the risk of market saturation in its original segment.

2. Strengthen Internal Controls and Processes

Operational risks often arise from inefficiencies, mismanagement, or lack of oversight. By strengthening your internal controls and processes, you can reduce the likelihood of these risks materializing. This includes implementing checks and balances, automating tasks, and creating clear guidelines for your team to follow.

Ways to improve internal processes:

- **Standardize workflows**: Create standard operating procedures (SOPs) for critical tasks, ensuring that everyone follows the same steps and maintains consistency. This minimizes errors and increases efficiency.

- **Implement quality control**: Establish a system for regularly monitoring and testing the quality of your products or services. This can help catch problems early, reducing the likelihood of defects or customer complaints.

- **Automate repetitive tasks**: Use technology to automate time-consuming tasks, such as data entry, billing, or inventory management. Automation reduces human error and frees up your team to focus on more strategic activities.

For example, a manufacturing business could implement a quality control system that checks for defects at multiple stages of production, ensuring that issues are caught before products reach customers.

3. Build Strong Relationships with Suppliers

Supply chain disruptions can be a significant risk for businesses, especially those that rely on specific suppliers for critical materials or products. To mitigate this risk, it's essential to build strong, collaborative relationships with your suppliers. By fostering open communication and creating contingency plans, you'll be better prepared to navigate disruptions and maintain business continuity.

Strategies to mitigate supply chain risk:

- **Diversify suppliers**: Avoid relying on a single supplier for essential goods. By establishing relationships with multiple suppliers, you create backup options if one experiences delays or shortages.

- **Negotiate flexible terms**: Work with suppliers to secure flexible payment or delivery terms that accommodate your needs during times of uncertainty. This can give you more breathing room when managing cash flow or inventory.

- **Maintain buffer inventory**: Keep a safety stock or buffer inventory of essential materials to cover any short-term disruptions. While this ties up some capital, it helps ensure you can continue operating if a supplier is temporarily unable to deliver.

For instance, a clothing retailer that relies on overseas suppliers might establish relationships with both international and local suppliers to mitigate risks related to shipping delays, customs issues, or political instability.

4. Implement Cybersecurity Measures

As businesses become more reliant on digital technology, cybersecurity risks have become increasingly prevalent. Data breaches, hacking, and phishing attacks can not only lead to financial losses but also damage your reputation and customer trust. Mitigating cybersecurity risks is critical, especially if your business handles sensitive customer data, financial information, or proprietary technology.

Cybersecurity strategies include:

- **Use strong passwords and two-factor authentication**: Ensure that all company accounts, especially those with sensitive data access, are protected by strong, unique passwords. Implement two-factor authentication (2FA) for an additional layer of security.

- **Regularly update software and systems**: Keep all software, including antivirus programs and operating systems, up to date. Patches and updates often fix vulnerabilities that hackers could exploit.

- **Train employees on cybersecurity best practices**: Conduct regular training sessions to educate your team on identifying phishing scams, avoiding malware, and following data security protocols.

- **Backup data**: Regularly back up critical business data to a secure location, such as a cloud-based storage system. In the event of a data breach or system failure, having backups ensures you can recover quickly.

For example, an e-commerce business might invest in an encrypted payment gateway, implement 2FA for staff accounts, and run regular cybersecurity training for employees to mitigate the risk of a data breach.

5. Use Insurance as a Financial Safety Net

Insurance is one of the most fundamental risk mitigation tools available to businesses. By transferring the financial burden of specific risks to an insurance provider, you can protect your business from significant losses caused by events like property damage, liability claims, or employee injuries.

Common types of business insurance include:

- **General liability insurance**: Covers legal fees and damages if your business is sued for property damage, bodily injury, or advertising injuries.

- **Property insurance**: Protects your physical assets—such as your building, equipment, and inventory—against damage caused by events like fire, theft, or vandalism.

- **Workers' compensation insurance**: Required in most regions, this insurance covers medical expenses and lost wages for employees who are injured on the job.

- **Cyber liability insurance**: Covers costs related to data breaches, including customer notification, credit monitoring, and legal fees.

For example, a restaurant might carry general liability insurance to protect against slip-and-fall claims from customers, as well as property insurance to cover equipment damage in the event of a kitchen fire.

6. Create a Crisis Management Plan

A crisis management plan outlines how your business will respond to emergencies, such as natural disasters, public relations crises, or financial setbacks. Having a well-developed plan ensures that you can act quickly and effectively to minimize the impact of the crisis on your operations, finances, and reputation.

Elements of a crisis management plan include:

- **Emergency communication protocols**: Establish a clear communication plan for internal staff, customers, suppliers, and stakeholders during a crisis. Ensure that everyone knows who to contact and how to respond.

- **Designate a crisis response team**: Assign specific roles and responsibilities to key team members, such as a crisis manager, media spokesperson, or financial lead.

- **Develop recovery procedures**: Outline the steps you'll take to recover from the crisis, whether that means finding new suppliers, addressing customer complaints, or rebuilding damaged infrastructure.

For example, a software company might develop a crisis management plan that includes protocols for handling a major data breach, such as notifying customers, investigating the cause, and working with legal and IT teams to mitigate the damage.

Conclusion: Proactively Reducing Risk Impact

Mitigating risks is about being proactive rather than reactive. By diversifying revenue streams, strengthening internal processes, building relationships with suppliers, and implementing cybersecurity measures, you can reduce the likelihood and impact of potential threats to your business. Additionally, using insurance as a financial safety net and having a robust crisis management plan in place ensures that your business is well-prepared to handle unexpected challenges.

Taking the time to develop comprehensive mitigation strategies will not only protect your business but also give you the confidence to navigate the inevitable risks of entrepreneurship with greater resilience and preparedness.

Building a Contingency Plan: Preparing for the Unexpected

In business, no matter how well you plan, unexpected events can and will happen. Whether it's a sudden supply chain disruption, a major financial shortfall, or an external crisis like a natural disaster, being prepared is essential to minimizing the impact of unforeseen events. A contingency plan is your business's safety net—designed to provide clear actions and alternatives when things go wrong.

Creating a robust contingency plan ensures you're not scrambling in the heat of the moment but instead have a well-thought-out strategy to keep your operations running and minimize potential damage. In this section, we'll explore how to build an effective contingency plan that keeps your business prepared for any emergency.

1. Identify Critical Areas of Vulnerability

The first step in building a contingency plan is to identify the critical areas of your business that would be most affected by unexpected events. These are the areas that, if disrupted, could halt operations or significantly impact your bottom line.

Focus on these key areas:

- **Core operations**: What processes or resources are essential to your day-to-day operations? This might include production lines, key suppliers, or service delivery systems.

- **Supply chain**: Consider the suppliers and partners you depend on for materials, goods, or services. A disruption here could halt production or delay delivery to customers.

- **Personnel**: Identify key personnel whose absence would disrupt operations, such as managers, specialized staff, or technical experts.

- **Technology**: Evaluate your business's dependence on technology, including software systems, data storage, and IT infrastructure. How would a systems failure or data breach affect your ability to function?

- **Cash flow and finances**: Assess your financial health and cash flow. Would an unexpected expense or sudden drop in revenue put you at risk of not being able to cover expenses or payroll?

For example, a restaurant's core vulnerability might be its supply chain, since running out of key ingredients would halt service. A tech startup might focus on its IT infrastructure, where a server crash could prevent users from accessing their product.

2. Develop Actionable Response Plans

Once you've identified the critical areas of vulnerability, the next step is to create actionable response plans for each potential risk. These plans should provide step-by-step guidance on what to do if a specific crisis occurs, who is responsible for managing the response, and what resources or alternatives can be deployed.

Key elements of an actionable response plan include:

- **Trigger events**: Clearly define the events or circumstances that would trigger the contingency plan. For example, the loss of a key supplier, a system outage, or a 20% drop in revenue.

- **Response actions**: Outline the specific actions that need to be taken. For example, if a supplier cannot deliver materials, you may need to activate secondary suppliers or switch to alternative materials.

- **Assigned roles**: Designate who is responsible for executing each part of the plan. Identify decision-makers, communications leads, and operational managers who will coordinate the response.

- **Resource allocation**: Determine what resources will be needed and where they will come from. This could include backup equipment, temporary staff, or additional funds.

For instance, if a manufacturer faces a supply chain disruption, their response plan might include contacting backup suppliers, reallocating inventory to priority customers, and reassigning staff to maintain production.

3. Create a Communication Plan

Clear communication is critical during any crisis. Your contingency plan should include a detailed **communication plan** that outlines how information will be shared with your team, customers, suppliers, and other stakeholders. During a crisis, timely and transparent communication helps maintain trust and keeps everyone on the same page.

Key elements of a communication plan:

- **Internal communication**: Establish a clear protocol for informing employees about the situation. Specify how they will receive updates (e.g., email, phone calls, or internal messaging systems) and who will communicate these updates.

- **Customer communication**: Plan how you will inform customers if your operations are affected. This could involve sending out email alerts, posting updates on your website, or reaching out through social media.

- **External partners**: Identify which external partners (e.g., suppliers, service providers, investors) need to be informed, and assign team members to manage these communications.

- **Crisis spokesperson**: Designate a spokesperson to handle all public-facing communications, particularly if the crisis could attract media attention. This ensures consistent messaging and avoids misinformation.

For example, if an e-commerce company experiences a website outage, they could send a proactive email to customers explaining the issue, provide an estimated resolution time, and update their social media channels with regular progress reports.

4. Plan for Financial Flexibility

A sudden crisis can place a heavy strain on your business's finances, so part of your contingency plan should include provisions for financial flexibility. This could involve setting aside an emergency fund, securing a line of credit, or planning for cost-cutting measures that can be implemented quickly if necessary.

Ways to ensure financial flexibility:

- **Build an emergency fund**: Set aside cash reserves that can cover essential expenses (e.g., rent, payroll, utilities) for at least three to six months. This provides a cushion during periods of reduced revenue or unexpected costs.

- **Maintain access to credit**: Secure a business line of credit or establish relationships with lenders in advance. Having quick access to credit can help bridge cash flow gaps during a crisis.

- **Identify non-essential expenses**: Regularly review your expenses and identify areas where you can cut back in the event of financial hardship. For example, scaling back marketing campaigns or deferring non-essential investments.

- **Renegotiate terms with suppliers**: If your cash flow is tight, communicate with suppliers to negotiate extended payment terms or discounts.

For instance, a retail business might have a line of credit in place to cover operational expenses during a seasonal sales slump or unexpected supply chain delays.

5. Test and Update Your Plan Regularly

A contingency plan is only useful if it's tested and updated regularly to reflect changes in your business or industry. Conduct simulations or drills to test your plan's effectiveness and make adjustments based on the results. Regular testing ensures that everyone knows their role and that the plan can be implemented smoothly during a real crisis.

Steps to test and update your plan:

- **Run simulations**: Conduct mock scenarios where your team responds to a hypothetical crisis. Evaluate how well the plan works and identify areas where improvements are needed.

- **Review and update annually**: Review your contingency plan at least once a year, or more frequently if your business undergoes significant changes (e.g., new product launches, major growth, or new regulations). Update the plan to reflect any new risks or vulnerabilities.

- **Incorporate feedback**: After testing or a real-life crisis, gather feedback from your team about what worked well and what didn't. Use this input to fine-tune your contingency plan.

For example, a small business might run a quarterly simulation where they test their response to a supply chain disruption, updating the plan as necessary based on how effectively their team handles the situation.

6. Document and Share Your Contingency Plan

Finally, ensure that your contingency plan is well-documented and easily accessible to key team members. Keep digital and physical copies in secure but easily accessible locations. Additionally, provide training to your employees so they understand the plan and their roles during an emergency.

Key documentation steps:

- **Create a detailed written plan**: Include all action steps, assigned roles, and contact information in a written document. This should cover every identified risk and the corresponding response plan.

- **Store in multiple locations**: Store the plan in both physical and digital formats, ensuring that it can be accessed during a crisis. For digital copies, use cloud storage for remote access in case of physical damage to your office.

- **Train employees**: Regularly train employees on the contingency plan, including their specific roles and responsibilities. Make sure they know where to access the plan in an emergency.

For instance, a logistics company could store their contingency plan both in the cloud and on-site, ensuring that their managers can access it even if one system fails.

Insurance and Financial Safeguards: Protecting Your Business Assets

In the world of risk management, insurance and financial safeguards are your safety nets, providing protection against unexpected financial losses and helping you recover from crises without jeopardizing the future of your business. Whether it's property damage, liability claims, or a sudden halt in operations, insurance policies and financial planning can provide the stability you need to weather disruptions. Implementing these safeguards is crucial for minimizing the financial impact of unforeseen events, ensuring that your business can continue to operate even when the unexpected occurs.

In this section, we'll explore the different types of business insurance and financial protections available, along with how to choose the right safeguards to protect your assets.

1. Types of Business Insurance

Business insurance is an essential component of your risk management strategy. Different types of insurance cover different aspects of your business, from physical property to legal liabilities. The right mix of policies depends on your industry, the size of your business, and the specific risks you face.

Here are the most common types of business insurance you should consider:

- **General Liability Insurance**: This is the most basic form of insurance for businesses and covers claims related to bodily injury, property damage, and personal injury (e.g., defamation). If a customer slips and falls at your business, general liability insurance would cover the medical costs and legal fees.

- **Property Insurance**: Property insurance covers damage or loss of physical assets, such as buildings, equipment, inventory, and furniture. Events like fire, theft, or vandalism are typically covered. Property insurance is crucial if your business relies heavily on physical locations or expensive equipment.

- **Business Interruption Insurance**: Also known as business income insurance, this policy covers the loss of income that occurs if your business operations are temporarily halted due to an event like a fire or natural disaster. It can help you cover ongoing expenses, such as rent and employee wages, while you recover from the interruption.

- **Professional Liability Insurance**: This type of insurance, sometimes called errors and omissions (E&O) insurance, covers businesses that provide professional services (e.g., consultants, lawyers, or accountants). It protects against claims of negligence or mistakes made in the course of providing services.

- **Workers' Compensation Insurance**: If you have employees, workers' compensation insurance is typically required by law. It covers medical expenses and lost wages for employees who are injured on the job, helping to protect your business from lawsuits related to workplace injuries.

- **Cyber Liability Insurance**: In an increasingly digital world, cyber liability insurance protects businesses from the financial fallout of data breaches, cyberattacks, and other digital threats. It can cover the costs of notifying affected customers, recovering compromised data, and addressing legal fees.

For example, a retail store might invest in general liability insurance to cover customer accidents, property insurance to protect against damage to the building, and business interruption insurance to cover lost income in case of a fire that temporarily shuts down the store.

2. Choosing the Right Insurance Policies

Not every business needs every type of insurance, so it's important to assess your specific risks and choose the policies that best align with your needs. This involves evaluating the size of your business, the industry you're in, and the potential financial impact of different risks.

To choose the right insurance policies:

- **Conduct a risk assessment**: Identify the most significant risks your business faces. Are you more vulnerable to property damage, legal liabilities, or operational disruptions? Use this assessment to prioritize which types of insurance to invest in.

- **Consult with an insurance broker**: An experienced insurance broker can help you assess your needs and find the best policies to cover your specific risks. They can also help you navigate the complexities of policy terms and premiums.

- **Consider the size of your business**: Smaller businesses with fewer employees may need less coverage than larger, more complex businesses. However, if you have valuable assets or work in a high-risk industry, more comprehensive coverage might be necessary.

- **Review policy limits and deductibles**: Ensure that the coverage limits of your policies are high enough to protect your business in the event of a major loss. Balance this with the affordability of the deductible, which is the amount you'll need to pay out of pocket before the insurance kicks in.

For instance, a software development company might prioritize professional liability insurance to protect against client claims of project errors, while a construction company would need robust workers' compensation and property insurance due to the physical nature of their work.

3. Financial Safeguards: Emergency Funds and Credit Access

In addition to insurance, financial safeguards such as emergency funds and access to credit provide a crucial safety net when unexpected expenses arise or income is disrupted. These measures ensure that your business has the liquidity needed to weather short-term financial challenges without facing a cash flow crisis.

Here are two key financial safeguards to implement:

- **Emergency Fund**: An emergency fund is a reserve of cash set aside to cover unexpected expenses, such as equipment repairs, sudden drops in sales, or temporary closures. Having an emergency fund allows you to maintain operations without needing to take on high-interest debt or cut essential costs.

- How much to save: Aim to save enough to cover at least 3 to 6 months of operating expenses. This includes rent, payroll, utilities, and other fixed costs that will continue even during a disruption.

- Where to keep it: Store your emergency fund in an easily accessible, low-risk account, such as a business savings account, so you can access the cash quickly when needed.

For example, a restaurant might keep an emergency fund to cover costs if it needs to close for a few weeks due to a kitchen renovation or unexpected repairs.

- **Business Line of Credit**: A business line of credit provides flexible access to funds that can be drawn on when needed, similar to a credit card. Unlike a loan, which provides a lump sum upfront, a line of credit allows you to borrow only what you need, when you need it, and pay interest only on the amount borrowed.

- When to use it: A line of credit is useful for covering short-term cash flow gaps, such as paying suppliers while waiting for customer payments or covering unexpected expenses during a slow sales period.

- **Establishing a line of credit**: Set up a line of credit before you need it, so it's available as a safety net in times of financial uncertainty. Work with your bank or financial institution to determine the credit limit and interest rates.

For instance, a seasonal business like a landscaping company might use a line of credit to cover expenses during the off-season when revenue is low but operating costs continue.

4. Review and Update Insurance and Financial Plans Regularly

Your business's insurance and financial safeguards should be reviewed and updated regularly to ensure they continue to meet your needs as your business grows and evolves. Changes in the size of your business, new products or services, or shifts in the industry can all affect your risk profile, and your coverage should reflect these changes.

Steps to review and update your safeguards:

- **Annual insurance review**: At least once a year, review your existing insurance policies to ensure they provide adequate coverage. Update policies to reflect changes in assets, employees, or business operations. For example, if you've purchased new equipment or expanded your physical space, you may need to increase your property insurance coverage.

- **Monitor your emergency fund**: As your business grows, your expenses will increase, which means your emergency fund should also grow. Periodically reassess how much you've saved to ensure your fund can still cover 3 to 6 months of expenses.

- **Reevaluate your line of credit**: If your business experiences rapid growth or changes in cash flow needs, you may need to increase your line of credit. Regularly check the terms of your credit agreements to ensure they remain favorable and aligned with your financial strategy.

For example, a retail business that expands to multiple locations should reassess its property insurance to cover new spaces and review its line of credit to ensure it can manage the increased inventory needs of multiple stores.

5. Benefits of Having Strong Financial Safeguards

The combination of insurance and financial safeguards provides a solid foundation for business resilience. Some of the key benefits include:

- **Peace of mind**: Knowing that you have coverage in place for major risks and financial safeguards for emergencies allows you to focus on growth without constantly worrying about potential setbacks.

- **Business continuity**: Insurance and financial safeguards help keep your business running smoothly, even in the face of disruptions. You'll have the resources to recover quickly from property damage, legal claims, or operational downtime.

- **Financial stability**: With an emergency fund and access to credit, your business can maintain stable cash flow even when facing unexpected expenses or temporary declines in revenue.

- **Customer and stakeholder confidence**: When your business is well-protected, customers, investors, and employees can have confidence in your ability to manage risks and navigate challenges effectively.

For example, a tech startup that faces a data breach can use its cyber liability insurance to cover the costs of recovery and its emergency fund to manage operational expenses during the crisis, ensuring minimal disruption to its services.

Conclusion: Securing Your Business with Insurance and Safeguards

Insurance and financial safeguards form the backbone of your business's risk management strategy, providing protection against a wide range of potential hazards. By carefully selecting the right insurance policies, building an emergency fund, and maintaining access to credit, you can protect your business from financial harm and ensure continuity in the face of unexpected challenges.

With these safeguards in place, you'll be better equipped to handle disruptions and maintain the stability of your business, allowing you to focus on growth with greater confidence and security.

Monitoring and Revisiting Your Risk Management Plan: Staying Prepared

Risk management is not a one-time effort—it's a continuous process. As your business grows and the landscape changes, new risks can emerge, and old risks can evolve. Monitoring and revisiting your risk management plan ensures that your strategies remain relevant and effective over time. Staying prepared means regularly assessing the state of your business, identifying new vulnerabilities, and updating your risk mitigation strategies accordingly.

In this section, we'll explore how to continuously monitor risks, the importance of revisiting your plan regularly, and how to stay ahead of emerging threats.

1. Regularly Assess and Identify New Risks

The business environment is constantly changing, and new risks can arise due to market shifts, technological advancements, regulatory changes, or internal growth. By regularly assessing your business operations and the external environment, you can spot emerging risks early and address them before they become significant threats.

Here's how to stay on top of new risks:

- **Conduct regular risk assessments**: Set a schedule to review your risk management plan—whether quarterly, bi-annually, or annually—depending on the complexity of your business. Identify any new risks that have emerged since the last assessment, and reassess the likelihood and impact of existing risks.

- **Monitor industry trends and external factors**: Stay informed about industry changes, economic conditions, and market trends that could introduce new risks. For example, new government regulations, shifts in consumer behavior, or advancements in technology can all create new challenges.

- **Track internal changes**: As your business grows and evolves, so do its risks. Expansion into new markets, the launch of new products, or changes in staffing can introduce new vulnerabilities. Ensure your risk management plan adapts to these internal shifts.

For instance, if your business adopts new technology or moves into a different geographic market, these changes may introduce data security risks or expose you to new compliance requirements, making it necessary to update your risk management plan.

2. Track the Effectiveness of Existing Strategies

It's not enough to simply implement a risk management plan—you need to ensure that the strategies you've put in place are working as intended. Regularly tracking the performance of your risk mitigation efforts helps you identify which strategies are effective and where improvements are needed.

Steps to track effectiveness:

- **Monitor risk indicators**: Set up key risk indicators (KRIs) to track the performance of your risk management strategies. These indicators act as early warning signs, signaling when a particular risk is escalating or when your strategies are not working as expected. For example, tracking customer complaints might alert you to a product quality issue before it becomes a larger problem.

- **Review incident reports**: Examine any risk-related incidents that have occurred, even if they didn't result in major damage. Were the mitigation strategies you had in place effective? If not, what could have been done differently to reduce the impact or prevent the issue altogether?

- **Assess response times and execution**: Evaluate how quickly and efficiently your team responded to risks that arose. If there were delays or miscommunication, consider how you can improve the execution of your risk management plan.

For example, if a retail business experiences a supply chain disruption but resolves the issue quickly by activating its contingency plan, this shows that the mitigation strategy is effective. However, if there were delays in activating backup suppliers, the plan might need refinement.

3. Adapt to Changes in the Business Environment

The business environment is fluid, and your risk management plan needs to be flexible enough to adapt. New competitors, evolving customer preferences, and shifts in regulations are just a few of the factors that can introduce new risks or change the nature of existing ones. Your ability to stay agile and adapt your plan to these changes is critical to staying prepared.

Key factors to watch for:

- **Regulatory changes**: Keep an eye on new laws or regulations that might affect your industry, such as changes in labor laws, environmental policies, or data privacy regulations. Staying compliant is essential to avoiding fines and legal issues.

- **Technological advancements**: As technology evolves, so do the risks associated with it. For example, adopting new software or using cloud storage solutions might introduce new cybersecurity threats. Regularly reassess the technological risks your business faces.

- **Economic shifts**: Economic downturns, inflation, or changes in consumer spending habits can all introduce financial risks. Be prepared to adjust your financial strategies, such as cutting unnecessary expenses or seeking new revenue streams, to mitigate the impact.

For instance, a healthcare business might face new compliance risks as data privacy regulations evolve. They would need to update their risk management plan to include more robust data protection measures and regular audits to stay compliant.

4. Regularly Update and Improve Your Risk Management Plan

As you identify new risks and assess the effectiveness of your strategies, it's important to update and improve your risk management plan regularly. Sticking to the same plan year after year without adjustments leaves your business vulnerable to emerging threats. By continuously refining your plan, you stay ahead of potential risks and maintain the flexibility to handle challenges as they arise.

Steps to update your plan:

- **Incorporate feedback**: Gather feedback from employees, managers, and other stakeholders involved in executing your risk management plan. Learn from their experiences to identify what's working and where improvements are needed.

- **Update risk mitigation strategies**: If certain risks are no longer relevant, remove them from the plan. If new risks have emerged, create specific strategies to mitigate them. Reassess the priority level of each risk as business conditions change.

- **Test and simulate**: Conduct regular testing of your updated risk management plan. Simulate different risk scenarios and evaluate how your team responds. Testing your plan in a controlled environment allows you to identify weak points and improve execution before a real crisis occurs.

For example, a logistics company that regularly handles large shipments might simulate a scenario in which its main transportation route is blocked. Testing its contingency plan helps identify any delays or gaps in the response process and allows the company to make necessary adjustments.

5. Foster a Risk-Aware Culture

The most successful risk management strategies involve the entire organization, not just leadership or risk managers. Fostering a risk-aware culture ensures that everyone in your business is actively looking for potential risks and understands their role in mitigating them. When all employees are engaged in the risk management process, it becomes easier to spot vulnerabilities early and respond quickly when challenges arise.

Steps to create a risk-aware culture:

- **Communicate the importance of risk management**: Make risk management a regular part of team meetings, training sessions, and internal communications. Ensure that employees understand how risk impacts the business and their role in mitigating it.

- **Encourage open communication**: Create a culture where employees feel comfortable reporting potential risks, whether it's a security issue, operational inefficiency, or customer concern. Empower them to speak up without fear of repercussions.

- **Provide training and resources**: Offer ongoing training on risk management practices, particularly in areas like cybersecurity, compliance, and safety. Equip your team with the tools and knowledge they need to identify and manage risks.

For instance, a software development company could train its employees on recognizing phishing scams or handling data breaches. By making risk awareness part of the company's culture, they can proactively prevent cyberattacks before they escalate.

234

Conclusion: Staying Prepared Through Ongoing Monitoring and Updates

Monitoring and revisiting your risk management plan is essential to staying prepared for new and evolving challenges. By regularly assessing your risks, tracking the effectiveness of your strategies, and adapting to changes in the business environment, you can ensure that your plan remains relevant and effective over time. Engaging your entire team in the risk management process and fostering a risk-aware culture further strengthens your ability to navigate uncertainties with confidence.

A dynamic risk management plan not only protects your business from unforeseen disruptions but also positions you to respond proactively to emerging threats, ensuring long-term stability and resilience in an ever-changing business landscape.

Quick Tips and Recap

- **Conduct regular risk assessments**: Review your business's vulnerabilities quarterly or annually to identify new risks and adjust for changing conditions.

- **Monitor key risk indicators (KRIs)**: Set up KRIs to track early warning signs of escalating risks, helping you take action before problems worsen.

- **Evaluate the effectiveness of your strategies**: Regularly review how well your risk mitigation strategies are working by tracking incidents and assessing response times.

- **Stay agile and adaptable**: Update your risk management plan as your business grows, new technologies emerge, or market conditions change.

- **Test your contingency plans**: Run simulations or mock scenarios to ensure your team knows how to respond quickly and effectively during a crisis.

- **Engage your entire team**: Foster a risk-aware culture where employees understand their role in spotting and addressing risks.

- **Monitor external factors**: Stay informed about regulatory changes, industry trends, and economic shifts that could introduce new risks to your business.

- **Incorporate feedback for improvement**: After each risk-related incident or test, gather feedback to improve your risk management strategies and ensure continual refinement.

- **Keep your risk management plan dynamic**: Regularly update your plan to stay relevant and protect your business from evolving threats.

By implementing these quick tips, you can ensure that your business remains prepared, resilient, and capable of navigating the uncertainties ahead.

CHAPTER TEN

Future Proof: Innovating
with Technology

"To stay ahead in business, you need to embrace technology like it's your new best friend. Innovation isn't just about using the latest tools; it's about integrating them in ways that propel your business forward and keep you at the cutting edge. The right tech can turn today's trends into tomorrow's advantages." — BRIAN SOLIS,
DIGITAL ANALYST AND AUTHOR

Welcome to the future, where technology is your crystal ball and innovation is the magic wand that keeps your business ahead of the curve. In this chapter, we're diving headfirst into the tech realm, where staying relevant means keeping up with the latest gadgets, apps, and digital wizardry. Think of it as your personal upgrade to a business model 2.0—where cutting-edge tools and futuristic thinking transform your enterprise from a dinosaur into a sleek, agile unicorn.

Innovation isn't just about jumping on the latest tech bandwagon; it's about integrating new solutions in ways that make sense for your business. From AI that predicts your next big move to automation that handles the grunt work, the right technology can turn your business from a mere player into a game-changer. So, strap on your virtual reality headset and get ready to explore the latest in tech trends and digital strategies.

Remember, the future doesn't wait, and neither should you. Embrace the tech tide, ride the waves of innovation, and future-proof your business with tools that make you look like a genius today and a visionary tomorrow. Because in the ever-evolving world of technology, staying ahead is the only way to avoid becoming a relic of the past.

Leveraging AI and Machine Learning: Transforming Data into Strategy

In today's fast-paced business world, artificial intelligence (AI) and machine learning (ML) are more than just buzzwords—they are transformative tools that can help businesses gain a competitive edge by turning data into actionable strategies. AI and ML allow companies to automate processes, improve decision-making, and enhance customer experiences by analyzing vast amounts of data more quickly and accurately than any human team could manage.

In this section, we'll explore how AI and ML can be leveraged to transform your data into strategic insights that propel your business forward. From predictive analytics to personalized customer interactions, AI is a game-changer that makes your business smarter, more efficient, and more responsive to market demands.

1. Understanding AI and Machine Learning

Before diving into applications, it's essential to understand what AI and ML are and how they function:

- **Artificial Intelligence (AI)**: AI refers to the simulation of human intelligence in machines. AI systems can perform tasks like decision-making, language understanding, and problem-solving, often mimicking human behaviors but at much faster speeds.

- **Machine Learning (ML)**: A subset of AI, ML focuses on algorithms that allow machines to learn from and make predictions based on data. With machine learning, the more data you feed into a system, the better it becomes at making predictions or recognizing patterns without being explicitly programmed.

In simple terms, AI can "think," while ML allows it to "learn." By analyzing massive amounts of data, AI and ML can detect trends, make recommendations, and even automate actions that would take humans much longer to perform.

2. Predictive Analytics: Forecasting Trends

One of the most powerful applications of AI and ML in business is predictive analytics—the ability to forecast future trends, customer behaviors, and market shifts based on historical data. AI-driven analytics tools can help your business predict everything from customer purchasing behavior to supply chain disruptions, allowing you to make proactive decisions rather than reactive ones.

Key benefits of predictive analytics:

- **Demand forecasting**: Predict when your customers are most likely to make a purchase, and ensure you have the right inventory or services in place to meet that demand.

- **Customer behavior analysis**: Analyze data on customer behavior to predict future actions, such as which products are most likely to be bought next, or when a customer might be at risk of leaving.

- **Market trend identification**: Stay ahead of your competitors by identifying shifts in market trends early and adjusting your strategies accordingly.

For example, a retail company might use predictive analytics to determine which products will be in high demand during the holiday season based on previous sales data, allowing them to stock the right inventory at the right time.

3. Personalized Customer Experiences: Elevating Engagement

AI and machine learning can be powerful tools for creating personalized customer experiences, a critical factor in today's customer-centric marketplace. Consumers expect tailored interactions, and AI makes it easier than ever to deliver on these expectations. With AI, you can analyze customer data to provide personalized recommendations, offers, and communications that make each customer feel valued and understood.

How AI enhances personalization:

- **Recommendation engines**: AI-powered recommendation systems, like those used by Amazon or Netflix, analyze past behaviors to suggest products, services, or content that align with a customer's preferences. This increases engagement and boosts sales.

- **Chatbots and virtual assistants**: AI-driven chatbots can provide personalized, real-time customer service, answering questions or resolving issues based on a customer's previous interactions with your business.

- **Dynamic pricing and offers**: AI algorithms can adjust pricing, promotions, and offers based on customer behavior, demographics, or market conditions, creating a personalized shopping experience that maximizes conversions.

For example, an e-commerce site could use AI to recommend products based on a customer's browsing history, sending them personalized email offers for items they are most likely to purchase.

4. Automating Processes: Increasing Efficiency, Cutting Costs

AI and machine learning aren't just about data—they can also automate a wide range of business processes, allowing your company to operate more efficiently and reduce costs. From automating customer service interactions to streamlining back-office functions, AI can free up valuable time for your team to focus on more strategic activities.

Common areas of AI-driven automation:

- **Customer service**: Chatbots and AI-driven customer support systems can handle common customer inquiries 24/7, reducing the need for live agents and improving response times.

- **Inventory management**: AI can predict stock levels based on demand, ensuring that you never run out of popular products while minimizing overstock.

- **Marketing automation**: Machine learning algorithms can optimize email marketing campaigns, social media ads, and content marketing strategies by predicting which messages will resonate most with your target audience.

For instance, a company that uses AI to automate customer service inquiries can handle a higher volume of customer interactions while lowering labor costs and improving customer satisfaction with faster response times.

5. AI-Powered Decision Making: Data-Driven Strategies

The power of AI lies in its ability to process vast amounts of data and extract insights that inform better decision-making. By integrating AI into your decision-making process, you can make smarter, data-driven decisions that are based on real-time information and predictive models rather than guesswork or intuition.

AI-powered decision-making applications:

- **Sales and marketing strategy**: AI can analyze customer and sales data to recommend marketing strategies, pricing models, or new customer segments to target.

- **Operational efficiency**: Use AI to optimize supply chains, reduce waste, and improve production efficiency by analyzing data across multiple touchpoints.

- **Financial forecasting**: AI can help predict revenue, manage cash flow, and identify areas where costs can be reduced, ensuring long-term financial stability.

For example, a manufacturing company might use AI to analyze production data and identify inefficiencies in its supply chain, helping it reduce costs and improve delivery times.

6. Implementing AI in Your Business: Getting Started

While AI and machine learning offer immense potential, implementing these technologies requires careful planning and the right tools. Here are some steps to help you get started:

- **Identify the right use cases**: Look at areas of your business where AI could have the most impact, such as customer service, marketing, or operations. Start with a single project that addresses a specific business challenge.

- **Invest in the right tools**: There are many AI and machine learning platforms available, from cloud-based solutions to custom-built systems. Choose tools that integrate well with your existing software and can scale as your business grows.

- **Start small and scale up**: Don't feel like you need to automate your entire business overnight. Start with a pilot project, measure its success, and expand AI applications gradually as you see results.

- **Upskill your team**: While AI will automate many tasks, it also requires people who can manage and interpret the results. Ensure your team has the training and knowledge to work effectively with AI-powered tools.

For example, a retail company might start by implementing an AI-powered chatbot to handle customer service inquiries, and then gradually integrate AI-driven recommendation engines to personalize shopping experiences.

Conclusion: Transforming Data into a Strategic Advantage

Leveraging AI and machine learning allows businesses to transform data into actionable insights, automate processes, and deliver personalized customer experiences at scale. By incorporating AI into your business strategy, you can stay ahead of market trends, optimize operations, and create lasting customer relationships that drive growth.

As AI and machine learning continue to evolve, they will become even more integral to business success. By embracing these technologies now, you'll not only future-proof your business but also unlock new levels of efficiency, creativity, and innovation.

Automation: Streamlining Operations for Maximum Efficiency

In a world where speed, accuracy, and efficiency are crucial for business success, automation has become a vital tool for staying competitive. Automating routine and repetitive tasks frees up valuable time and resources, allowing businesses to focus on higher-value activities like strategy, innovation, and customer engagement. Whether you're running a small startup or a large enterprise, automation can streamline operations, reduce human error, cut costs, and improve overall productivity.

In this section, we'll explore how automation can help your business operate more efficiently and strategically, covering everything from automating administrative tasks to optimizing complex workflows.

1. The Benefits of Automation

Automation brings a range of benefits to businesses of all sizes, enhancing efficiency and enabling companies to achieve more with fewer resources. Key advantages include:

- **Increased productivity**: By automating repetitive tasks, employees can focus on more strategic work that requires creativity, problem-solving, and decision-making. This leads to higher output without the need for additional staff.

- **Reduced errors**: Manual processes are prone to human error, especially when dealing with large volumes of data. Automation ensures tasks are completed with precision and consistency, reducing costly mistakes.

- **Cost savings**: Automating labor-intensive tasks can significantly reduce operational costs by lowering the need for manual labor. Automation also helps prevent expensive errors, such as data entry mistakes or missed deadlines.

- **Scalability**: Automation allows businesses to scale more easily. As your company grows, automated systems can handle increasing workloads without the need for proportional increases in personnel.

For example, a company that automates its invoice processing system can eliminate manual data entry, ensuring that invoices are processed faster, more accurately, and at a lower cost than before.

2. Automating Administrative Tasks: Freeing Up Time

One of the most common uses of automation is in administrative tasks—the repetitive, time-consuming activities that keep the business running but don't necessarily contribute to growth. By automating these tasks, businesses can streamline processes, reduce errors, and save valuable employee hours.

Here are some common administrative tasks that can be automated:

- **Invoicing and billing**: Automation tools can generate, send, and track invoices, ensuring timely payments and reducing the need for manual follow-up. This helps improve cash flow and reduces administrative overhead.

- **Data entry**: Automating data entry from customer forms, invoices, or contracts minimizes the risk of human error and ensures data is captured accurately and consistently.

- **Scheduling**: Automate appointment scheduling, meeting coordination, and employee shift planning using tools that sync with calendars and send reminders. This reduces the back-and-forth communication required for manual scheduling.

- **Email management**: Automation can sort, categorize, and prioritize emails, responding to simple inquiries automatically while flagging more important messages for personal attention.

For instance, a service-based company might use automation to handle client invoicing, reducing the time spent on administrative work and ensuring that payments are processed promptly.

3. Automating Customer Service: Enhancing Responsiveness

Customer service is another area where automation can significantly improve efficiency and customer satisfaction. With the rise of chatbots, AI-driven virtual assistants, and automated customer support systems, businesses can provide fast, accurate responses to customer inquiries at any time of day.

Benefits of automating customer service:

- **24/7 availability**: Automated systems, such as chatbots, can handle customer inquiries outside of business hours, providing answers to common questions and reducing wait times for customers.

- **Instant responses**: Automation allows for instant responses to customer inquiries, improving customer satisfaction and minimizing frustration caused by long wait times.

- **Seamless handoff**: When automation can't solve a problem, it can smoothly transfer customers to a live representative, providing the agent with the context they need to resolve the issue quickly.

For example, an e-commerce company could use a chatbot to handle inquiries about order status, product availability, or return policies. This allows customers to get answers instantly without having to wait for a customer service agent.

4. Optimizing Marketing and Sales Automation

Automation can also be a game-changer in the areas of marketing and sales, helping businesses engage with potential customers more efficiently, nurture leads, and close deals faster. Marketing and sales automation tools use data and customer behavior to personalize interactions, trigger automated campaigns, and streamline the sales process.

Key areas of marketing and sales automation:

- **Email marketing**: Automation tools can send personalized email campaigns based on customer actions or preferences, such as follow-up emails after a purchase or reminders for abandoned shopping carts.

- **Lead nurturing**: Automation allows businesses to engage with leads at different stages of the sales funnel with tailored content and offers, helping move prospects closer to a purchase decision without requiring manual follow-up.

- **Social media management**: Automate the scheduling and posting of content across social media platforms, ensuring consistent engagement with followers without the need for manual updates.

- **Customer relationship management (CRM)**: Automated CRM tools track customer interactions, manage leads, and streamline the sales process, allowing sales teams to focus on high-priority tasks like closing deals.

For example, a software company might use marketing automation to send a series of onboarding emails to new customers, guiding them through the setup process and offering tips for success—all without manual intervention.

5. Supply Chain and Inventory Management Automation

Automation can transform supply chain and inventory management, reducing inefficiencies and ensuring that businesses have the right products available when they're needed. Automated systems can monitor inventory levels, track shipments, and reorder stock automatically, minimizing the risk of stockouts or overstocking.

Automation in supply chain and inventory management includes:

- **Inventory tracking**: Automated systems monitor inventory in real-time, tracking stock levels and automatically reordering items when they reach predefined thresholds.

- **Supplier management**: Automation can streamline communication with suppliers, track shipments, and manage purchase orders, ensuring that supplies arrive on time without manual intervention.

- **Order fulfillment**: Automated systems can route orders to the appropriate warehouse or fulfillment center, optimizing shipping routes and reducing delivery times.

For example, a retail business might use an automated inventory management system that alerts the purchasing department when stock levels fall below a certain point, automatically placing orders with suppliers to replenish key products.

6. Getting Started with Automation: Steps for Implementation

Implementing automation requires thoughtful planning and a step-by-step approach to ensure that your business reaps the full benefits. Here are some steps to help you get started:

- **Identify repetitive tasks**: Start by identifying which processes in your business are repetitive, time-consuming, and prone to error. These are the best candidates for automation.

- **Choose the right tools**: There are numerous automation tools available, from simple task automation software to comprehensive enterprise automation platforms. Select tools that align with your business needs and can scale as you grow.

- **Test and optimize**: Start small by automating a single task or process, and measure the results. Monitor efficiency gains, error reduction, and employee feedback to determine whether the automation is effective.

- **Train your team**: Ensure that your employees understand how to use the new automation tools and how their roles will evolve as a result. Automation should complement human work, not replace it entirely.

For example, a small business could start by automating its email marketing campaigns, using a tool like Mailchimp or HubSpot to send targeted messages to customers based on their behavior.

Conclusion: Maximizing Efficiency with Automation

Automation is a powerful tool for streamlining operations, improving productivity, and reducing costs. By automating repetitive tasks, customer service, marketing, sales, and inventory management, businesses can free up valuable time and resources to focus on strategic growth and innovation. Whether you're just starting out with simple automations or implementing more advanced workflows, automation has the potential to revolutionize the way your business operates.

As technology continues to evolve, automation will only become more integral to business success. By embracing it now, you'll ensure that your operations remain efficient, scalable, and future-proofed in an increasingly competitive landscape.

Cloud Computing: Flexibility, Scalability, and Collaboration

As businesses evolve, the need for adaptable, efficient, and collaborative solutions becomes more pressing. Cloud computing provides the foundation for this transformation, offering businesses the ability to store, manage, and access data and applications over the internet rather than relying on physical servers or hardware. This shift to the cloud brings unprecedented flexibility, scalability, and collaboration opportunities, making it a cornerstone of modern business operations.

In this section, we'll explore how cloud computing can empower your business to operate with greater agility, enhance collaboration among teams, and scale seamlessly as your business grows.

1. What Is Cloud Computing?

At its core, cloud computing is the delivery of computing services—including storage, processing power, databases, networking, software, and analytics—over the internet (the cloud). Instead of relying on local servers or personal computers to store and manage data, businesses can access these resources from anywhere with an internet connection.

Cloud computing comes in three main forms:

- **Infrastructure as a Service (IaaS)**: This model provides virtualized computing resources over the internet, such as servers, storage, and networking. It's ideal for businesses that want control over their IT infrastructure without the hassle of managing physical servers.

- **Platform as a Service (PaaS)**: PaaS provides a platform allowing businesses to develop, run, and manage applications without worrying about the underlying infrastructure.

- **Software as a Service (SaaS)**: SaaS delivers fully functional software applications over the internet. Businesses can use these applications on a subscription basis, without needing to install or maintain the software on their own devices.

Examples of cloud computing include services like Amazon Web Services (AWS) for IaaS, Microsoft Azure for PaaS, and popular SaaS tools like Google Workspace or Salesforce.

2. Flexibility: Working from Anywhere

One of the most significant advantages of cloud computing is its flexibility. With cloud-based solutions, employees can access data and applications from any location, on any device, as long as they have an internet connection. This flexibility makes it easier for businesses to support remote work, enable on-the-go productivity, and adapt to changing work environments.

Benefits of cloud flexibility:

- **Remote access**: Employees can access files, documents, and tools from anywhere in the world, fostering a more adaptable work environment. Whether employees are traveling, working from home, or in the office, they have seamless access to the resources they need.

- **Business continuity**: In the event of a disaster, like a power outage or a natural disaster, cloud computing ensures that critical data and applications remain accessible, allowing your business to continue operating without major disruptions.

- **Device independence**: Cloud services work across various devices, including laptops, smartphones, and tablets. This device independence means employees can use the tools they are most comfortable with while staying connected to the company's systems.

For instance, a company with remote employees can use cloud platforms like Google Drive or Microsoft OneDrive to store and share documents in real time, enabling seamless collaboration across time zones.

3. Scalability: Growing with Your Business

Cloud computing's scalability is another major advantage, enabling businesses to adjust their computing resources based on current needs. As your business grows, the cloud allows you to easily scale up (or down) without the need for costly hardware upgrades or complex infrastructure changes.

How cloud scalability works:

- **On-demand resources**: Cloud providers allow businesses to add more storage, processing power, or software licenses with just a few clicks. You only pay for the resources you use, so there's no need to overinvest in physical servers or IT infrastructure upfront.

- **Automatic scaling**: Some cloud services automatically adjust resources based on real-time demand. For example, during peak times, a cloud-based e-commerce platform might increase its server capacity to handle more traffic, then scale back down during off-peak hours.

- **Global reach**: Cloud platforms often have data centers worldwide, allowing businesses to expand their operations into new regions without worrying about physical infrastructure. This ensures consistent performance and low latency for customers across the globe.

For example, a growing startup using cloud computing for its website hosting could start with minimal resources and quickly scale up as traffic increases, without needing to invest in new servers or additional IT personnel.

4. Collaboration: Empowering Teams to Work Together

Cloud computing also enhances **collaboration** by making it easier for teams to work together in real time, regardless of location. Cloud-based tools facilitate seamless sharing of documents, communication, and project management, ensuring that everyone stays on the same page.

Ways the cloud improves collaboration:

- **Real-time document sharing**: Cloud-based platforms like Google Workspace, Microsoft 365, or Dropbox allow multiple users to work on the same document simultaneously. Teams can collaborate in real time, make updates, leave comments, and see changes as they happen.

- **Unified communication**: Cloud solutions often integrate with communication tools like Slack, Zoom, or Microsoft Teams, allowing teams to communicate, share files, and manage projects from a single platform.

- **Project management**: Cloud-based project management tools, such as Trello, Asana, or Monday.com, allow teams to organize tasks, assign responsibilities, and track progress. These tools ensure that projects stay on schedule and that everyone has access to the latest information.

- **Version control**: With cloud computing, files are always saved and updated in real-time, ensuring that everyone is working on the most recent version of a document. Version control features allow you to revert to previous versions if needed, providing an added layer of security.

For example, a marketing team working on a campaign can use Google Docs to draft content, share feedback in real-time, and update documents from any location—allowing for more efficient collaboration.

5. Cloud Security: Protecting Your Data

As businesses move more operations to the cloud, data security becomes a top priority. Cloud providers invest heavily in security measures to protect your data, offering advanced encryption, authentication protocols, and continuous monitoring to prevent unauthorized access or breaches.

Cloud security benefits:

- **Encryption**: Data stored in the cloud is typically encrypted, both at rest and in transit, ensuring that sensitive information is protected from hackers or unauthorized access.

- **Access control**: Cloud platforms offer detailed access controls, allowing you to specify who can access specific files or systems. Multi-factor authentication (MFA) adds an extra layer of protection.

- **Data backups**: Cloud services automatically back up data to ensure it can be recovered quickly in the event of accidental deletion or a security breach.

- **Compliance**: Cloud providers often comply with industry-specific regulations, such as GDPR or HIPAA, ensuring that your business remains compliant with legal standards for data protection.

For example, a healthcare company using cloud services like AWS can take advantage of built-in HIPAA-compliant features to securely store patient data while ensuring privacy and regulatory compliance.

6. Choosing the Right Cloud Solutions for Your Business

With so many cloud services available, selecting the right solutions for your business depends on your specific needs, budget, and goals. Here's how to choose the best cloud computing options:

- **Identify your needs**: Determine which areas of your business could benefit most from cloud services. Do you need flexible storage, improved collaboration, or enhanced scalability? Understanding your goals will help you select the right tools.

- **Assess security requirements**: Ensure that the cloud provider offers the necessary security measures to protect your data, especially if your business deals with sensitive or regulated information.

- **Choose scalable solutions**: Opt for cloud services that can grow with your business. Look for platforms that allow you to easily scale resources up or down as your needs change.

- **Consider integration**: Choose cloud platforms that integrate with the tools and software you already use. Seamless integration will streamline workflows and minimize disruption during the transition to the cloud.

For instance, a business looking to enhance collaboration across its global workforce might choose Google Workspace for its suite of cloud-based productivity tools, while also using AWS for scalable infrastructure solutions.

Conclusion: Leveraging Cloud Computing for a Flexible, Scalable Future
Cloud computing offers businesses the flexibility, scalability, and collaboration tools they need to thrive in today's fast-paced environment. By leveraging cloud solutions, you can provide your team with access to critical data and applications from anywhere, scale your resources to meet growing demands, and enhance collaboration across your organization.

As businesses continue to embrace remote work and digital transformation, the cloud will play an increasingly important role in ensuring operational efficiency and resilience. By integrating the right cloud solutions, you'll be well-positioned to adapt to changes, grow your business, and maintain a competitive edge in the digital era.

The Internet of Things (IoT): Connecting Devices for Smarter Business

In the era of digital transformation, the Internet of Things (IoT) is revolutionizing the way businesses operate by creating a network of interconnected devices that can communicate and share data in real-time. This web of smart devices—ranging from sensors and machinery to everyday office tools—gives businesses the power to monitor, automate, and optimize their operations like never before. By leveraging IoT technology, businesses can make more informed decisions, improve efficiency, and create new opportunities for innovation.

In this section, we'll explore how IoT works, its practical applications in different industries, and how integrating connected devices can transform your business for the better.

1. What Is the Internet of Things (IoT)?

The Internet of Things (IoT) refers to the growing network of physical devices embedded with sensors, software, and other technologies that enable them to collect and exchange data over the internet. These devices can range from simple sensors to complex machines, allowing them to communicate with each other and with centralized systems, creating a seamless flow of real-time information.

How IoT works:

- **Sensors and devices**: Devices are equipped with sensors that monitor specific conditions—such as temperature, location, or energy consumption—and send that data to other devices or systems.

- **Connectivity**: Through internet connections, IoT devices share the collected data with cloud-based platforms or control systems, where it can be analyzed or used to trigger automated actions.

- **Data processing**: The data collected by IoT devices is processed and analyzed to generate insights, predict trends, or activate automated responses.

For example, a smart thermostat in a warehouse can collect temperature data and automatically adjust heating or cooling systems to maintain optimal conditions, all without human intervention.

2. IoT in Business: Practical Applications Across Industries

The power of IoT lies in its versatility—it can be applied across a wide range of industries to improve operations, reduce costs, and create new value for customers. Let's take a look at how IoT is being used in different sectors:

- **Manufacturing**: In manufacturing, IoT devices can monitor machinery in real-time, detecting potential malfunctions or inefficiencies before they lead to costly downtime. This predictive maintenance reduces repair costs, improves productivity, and ensures equipment is operating at peak efficiency. IoT-connected systems can also optimize the supply chain by tracking inventory, managing logistics, and monitoring production levels.

Example: A car manufacturer uses IoT sensors on production lines to monitor equipment performance and alert maintenance teams if a machine shows signs of wear, preventing unexpected breakdowns.

- **Retail**: Retail businesses use IoT to improve inventory management, enhance customer experiences, and optimize energy consumption. Smart shelves can monitor product stock levels and automatically reorder items when inventory runs low. Retailers can also use IoT devices to analyze customer behavior in stores, such as foot traffic patterns, and adjust store layouts accordingly to increase sales.

Example: A supermarket chain uses IoT sensors in refrigerators to monitor temperature and ensure food safety while minimizing energy consumption. If temperatures exceed acceptable ranges, the system sends automatic alerts to store managers.

- **Logistics and transportation**: IoT-enabled tracking devices allow logistics companies to monitor shipments in real-time, improving delivery accuracy and reducing delays. By connecting vehicles, goods, and warehouses through IoT, companies can optimize routes, improve fuel efficiency, and track the condition of shipments throughout transit.

Example: A shipping company uses IoT-enabled GPS trackers to provide real-time location data on deliveries, allowing customers to track their packages and ensuring that logistics managers can reroute vehicles as needed to avoid traffic congestion.

- **Healthcare**: IoT devices in healthcare—such as wearables, remote monitors, and smart medical equipment—help medical professionals collect real-time patient data and provide more accurate diagnoses. This technology also enables remote monitoring of patients, improving care quality and reducing hospital visits.

Example: A hospital uses IoT devices to monitor patients' vital signs, sending alerts to medical staff if a patient's condition changes, allowing for faster response times and better care.

- **Agriculture**: IoT can help farmers monitor soil conditions, weather patterns, and crop health in real-time. Sensors placed in fields can collect data on moisture levels and send alerts when crops need watering. This leads to more efficient water usage, better crop yields, and reduced waste.

Example: A farm uses IoT soil sensors to track moisture levels and automatically activate irrigation systems only when necessary, saving water and improving crop growth.

3. Improving Efficiency and Reducing Costs with IoT

By connecting devices and systems through IoT, businesses can streamline operations, reduce waste, and cut costs across various areas of their operations. Here's how IoT enhances efficiency and lowers costs:

- **Predictive maintenance**: IoT devices can monitor equipment performance and predict when maintenance is needed, reducing the likelihood of unexpected breakdowns and minimizing downtime. This leads to lower maintenance costs and longer equipment lifespans.

Example: A factory using IoT sensors on its machinery can detect minor issues early, scheduling maintenance before major repairs or costly downtime are needed.

- **Energy management**: Smart devices can monitor and control energy usage in real time, helping businesses optimize their energy consumption and reduce utility costs. Automated systems can adjust lighting, heating, cooling, and other energy-intensive processes based on real-time data.

Example: An office building uses IoT-connected thermostats and lighting systems to automatically adjust energy use based on occupancy, saving on energy costs and reducing environmental impact.

- **Inventory optimization**: IoT sensors and systems can track inventory levels in real-time, preventing overstocking or stockouts. Automated reordering and inventory management reduce waste and ensure that the right products are always available when needed.

Example: A retail store uses IoT-enabled shelves to track product levels, ensuring that popular items are automatically reordered when stock is low, preventing lost sales due to out-of-stock items.

- **Process automation**: IoT enables businesses to automate manual processes, from adjusting equipment settings to managing logistics workflows. Automation reduces the need for manual intervention, speeds up operations, and reduces the risk of human error.

Example: A warehouse uses IoT-connected robotic systems to automate picking and packing processes, improving order accuracy and reducing labor costs.

4. IoT and Data-Driven Insights: Making Smarter Decisions

The real power of IoT lies in the **data** it generates. By collecting and analyzing vast amounts of data from connected devices, businesses can gain actionable insights into their operations, customers, and market trends. These insights enable smarter decision-making and more targeted strategies.

How IoT data drives business decisions:

- **Real-time monitoring**: IoT devices provide continuous, real-time data, enabling businesses to monitor performance and make adjustments on the fly.

- **Predictive analytics**: By analyzing historical data from IoT devices, businesses can predict future trends, such as customer demand, equipment failures, or supply chain disruptions. This allows for proactive planning and resource allocation.

- **Operational efficiency**: IoT data can reveal inefficiencies in workflows, helping businesses identify areas for improvement and optimize operations to reduce waste and increase productivity.

For example, a retail business using IoT sensors to track customer foot traffic can analyze the data to optimize store layouts, ensuring high-traffic areas are stocked with high-demand products.

5. Security Considerations in IoT

While IoT offers significant benefits, it also introduces new **security risks**. Connected devices can be vulnerable to hacking, data breaches, and other cyber threats, making it essential for businesses to implement robust security measures to protect their IoT networks and data.

Key IoT security best practices:

- **Encryption**: Encrypt data both in transit and at rest to protect sensitive information from unauthorized access.

- **Authentication**: Implement strong authentication protocols, such as multi-factor authentication, to ensure that only authorized users can access IoT devices and systems.

- **Regular updates**: Keep IoT devices and systems updated with the latest security patches and firmware to protect against vulnerabilities.

- **Network segmentation**: Use network segmentation to isolate IoT devices from other critical systems, reducing the risk of a breach spreading across your entire network.

For example, a company using IoT sensors to monitor sensitive data, such as healthcare records or financial transactions, must implement encryption and authentication measures to ensure data privacy and security.

Conclusion: Unlocking the Power of IoT for a Smarter Business

The Internet of Things (IoT) is transforming industries by connecting devices, automating processes, and providing real-time insights that enable smarter decision-making. From manufacturing to healthcare, retail to agriculture, IoT can improve operational efficiency, reduce costs, and create new value for businesses of all sizes.

By embracing IoT, your business can gain a competitive advantage in today's data-driven world. However, it's essential to implement robust security measures to protect your IoT network and ensure that the benefits of connected devices outweigh the potential risks.

As IoT continues to evolve, it will play an increasingly central role in shaping the future of business. By integrating IoT into your operations, you'll be better equipped to innovate, optimize, and succeed in the ever-connected world of tomorrow.

Cybersecurity: Safeguarding Your Digital Future

As businesses increasingly rely on digital tools and technologies, cybersecurity has become more crucial than ever. While innovations like cloud computing, the Internet of Things (IoT), and artificial intelligence offer tremendous benefits, they also open up new vulnerabilities that cybercriminals are eager to exploit. A successful cyberattack can result in significant financial loss, reputational damage, and legal consequences for businesses. This makes safeguarding your digital infrastructure essential to protect your data, customers, and operations.

In this section, we'll cover the key elements of cybersecurity, from identifying potential threats to implementing effective security measures, and why taking a proactive approach to digital security is critical for future-proofing your business.

1. The Growing Importance of Cybersecurity

With cyberattacks becoming more sophisticated and widespread, businesses of all sizes are at risk. Hackers target everything from small businesses with weak defenses to large enterprises with massive data reserves. The fallout from a successful attack can be devastating, from exposing sensitive customer information to shutting down operations altogether.

Key statistics highlighting the importance of cybersecurity:

- **Ransomware attacks**: Cybercriminals use ransomware to lock businesses out of their own systems, demanding a ransom to restore access. The average ransom paid by companies has increased dramatically in recent years.

- **Data breaches**: Breaches that expose customer data can lead to significant fines, especially with regulations like the General Data Protection Regulation (GDPR) and the California Consumer Privacy Act (CCPA) in place.

- **Financial and reputational damage**: Beyond the direct financial losses, data breaches can harm a company's reputation, erode customer trust, and lead to legal consequences.

For example, a retail business that suffers a data breach exposing customer credit card information may not only face hefty fines but could also lose customer trust, leading to a significant drop in sales.

2. Common Cybersecurity Threats

Cybersecurity threats come in many forms, and staying informed about the most common types of attacks is essential for effective protection.

Some of the most prevalent threats include:

- **Phishing attacks**: Phishing is a technique used by hackers to trick individuals into providing sensitive information (such as passwords or financial details) by pretending to be a trusted source. Phishing emails are often disguised as legitimate communications from companies or financial institutions.

- **Ransomware**: Ransomware attacks encrypt a business's data, making it inaccessible until a ransom is paid. Even when the ransom is paid, there's no guarantee the data will be restored.

- **Malware**: Malware (malicious software) can infect your systems and steal data, disrupt operations, or even take control of your network. It often enters systems through compromised downloads or emails.

- **DDoS attacks**: Distributed Denial of Service (DDoS) attacks overwhelm a business's network or website with a flood of traffic, causing it to crash and become unavailable to customers or employees.

- **Insider threats**: Not all cybersecurity threats come from external hackers. Sometimes, employees or contractors with access to sensitive systems can unintentionally (or intentionally) compromise your security.

For instance, a small business may be targeted by a phishing email that tricks an employee into revealing their login credentials, allowing hackers to gain access to the company's systems and steal sensitive data.

3. Essential Cybersecurity Measures

To protect your business from these evolving threats, it's important to implement a comprehensive cybersecurity strategy. Here are the essential measures every business should take to safeguard its digital infrastructure:

- **Firewalls**: A firewall acts as a barrier between your internal network and external threats, monitoring and controlling incoming and outgoing network traffic based on security rules. Firewalls prevent unauthorized access to your network while allowing safe, legitimate communications to pass through.

- **Encryption**: Encrypting your data ensures that even if it's intercepted or stolen, it remains unreadable to unauthorized users. Data should be encrypted both in transit (as it's sent over the internet) and at rest (when stored on servers or in the cloud).

- **Multi-factor authentication (MFA)**: MFA requires users to provide two or more forms of identification (such as a password and a verification code sent to their phone) before gaining access to sensitive systems or data. This adds an extra layer of protection, making it harder for hackers to gain access with stolen passwords alone.

- **Regular software updates**: Many cyberattacks exploit known vulnerabilities in outdated software. Ensure that all software, operating systems, and applications are updated regularly with the latest security patches.

- **Backup and recovery systems**: Regularly backing up your data ensures that even if it's lost or compromised, you can recover it quickly and minimize downtime. Store backups securely, ideally both on-site and in the cloud, to protect against ransomware attacks and hardware failures.

- **Employee training**: Human error is one of the leading causes of cybersecurity breaches. Providing employees with regular training on how to identify phishing attempts, avoid malware, and follow safe online practices can significantly reduce the risk of an attack.

For example, a healthcare company could use encryption to protect patient data and multi-factor authentication to secure access to medical records, ensuring compliance with privacy regulations like HIPAA while protecting sensitive information from cyber threats.

4. Proactive Monitoring and Incident Response

Even with strong defenses in place, no business is entirely immune to cyberattacks. That's why it's crucial to have a proactive monitoring system and an incident response plan to quickly detect and address potential security breaches.

Key components of proactive monitoring and incident response include:

- **Real-time threat detection**: Use security software that provides real-time monitoring and alerts for suspicious activity. This allows you to respond to potential threats before they cause significant damage.

- **Incident response plan**: Develop a comprehensive incident response plan that outlines the steps to take if a breach occurs. This should include identifying the source of the breach, containing the threat, notifying affected stakeholders, and restoring normal operations.

- **Regular security audits**: Conduct routine security audits to evaluate your systems for vulnerabilities and ensure that security protocols are being followed. Audits can help identify weak points before they're exploited by cybercriminals.

- **Penetration testing**: Hire cybersecurity experts to perform penetration testing—simulated cyberattacks on your systems to identify vulnerabilities that hackers could exploit. This proactive approach helps you fix weak points before a real attack occurs.

For instance, a financial services firm could implement real-time threat detection systems that alert their IT team to unusual login attempts, enabling them to act swiftly and prevent unauthorized access to sensitive financial data.

5. Cybersecurity in the Cloud

As businesses increasingly move their operations to the cloud, ensuring the security of cloud environments becomes a top priority. Cloud providers often implement their own security measures, but it's up to businesses to ensure that they're using those tools effectively.

Best practices for securing your cloud environment:

- **Choose reputable cloud providers**: Ensure that your cloud provider complies with industry security standards, such as ISO/IEC 27001, and offers robust security features like encryption, access controls, and regular backups.

- **Manage access**: Control who has access to your cloud systems and data by using strong passwords, MFA, and role-based access control (RBAC) to limit access to only those who need it.

- **Secure API integrations**: Many businesses use APIs (application programming interfaces) to connect different cloud applications and services. Ensure that these APIs are securely configured and regularly monitored to prevent unauthorized access.

- **Monitor cloud usage**: Use cloud security tools to monitor who is accessing your cloud infrastructure, what they're doing, and whether they're following security protocols.

For example, a company using a cloud-based customer relationship management (CRM) system can enable MFA and restrict access based on employee roles to ensure that only authorized personnel can view or edit sensitive customer data.

Conclusion: Securing Your Business's Digital Future
Cybersecurity is an essential aspect of any modern business strategy, especially as more operations move online and more sensitive data is stored digitally. By taking proactive steps—such as implementing strong security measures, training employees, and developing an incident response plan—you can significantly reduce the risk of a cyberattack and protect your business from the devastating consequences of a breach.

As technology evolves and cyber threats become more sophisticated, maintaining a robust cybersecurity posture will help future-proof your business. Investing in the right tools, training, and monitoring systems today will safeguard your digital future, ensuring that your business can continue to thrive in an increasingly interconnected world.

Quick Tips and Recap

- **Implement multi-factor authentication (MFA)**: Strengthen account security by requiring two or more forms of verification to access systems.

- **Use encryption for sensitive data**: Protect your data both in transit and at rest with encryption to prevent unauthorized access.

- **Install firewalls**: Set up firewalls to monitor and control incoming and outgoing traffic, acting as a barrier against potential threats.

- **Regularly update software and systems**: Ensure all software, operating systems, and applications are kept up to date with the latest security patches.

- **Train employees on cybersecurity best practices**: Regularly educate your team on how to spot phishing attacks, avoid malware, and practice safe online behavior.

- **Backup data frequently**: Regularly back up your data to secure locations to ensure recovery in the event of a cyberattack or system failure.

- **Monitor for real-time threats**: Use proactive monitoring tools to detect and respond to cyber threats in real-time.

- **Create an incident response plan**: Develop a clear, actionable plan for responding to cybersecurity breaches to minimize damage and recover quickly.

- **Conduct regular security audits**: Periodically review your systems and protocols to identify vulnerabilities and improve your cybersecurity defenses.

- **Choose secure cloud providers**: Ensure your cloud provider offers robust security features and that your business is using them effectively to protect your data in the cloud.

By following these tips, your business will be better equipped to protect its digital infrastructure, prevent cyberattacks, and respond effectively to any threats that arise.

PART THREE

Communicating Your Vision

Welcome to the art of communication, where your vision goes from a scribbled note on a napkin to a full-blown blockbuster hit. In this chapter, we'll explore how to take your grand ideas and transform them into compelling narratives that captivate your audience, inspire your team, and make stakeholders sit up and take notice. Think of it as your chance to become a business storyteller extraordinaire, turning your vision into a story so engaging that even your cat would pause its nap to listen. With the right words, a dash of charisma, and a sprinkle of strategic flair, you'll craft messages that don't just inform but excite, persuade, and rally everyone around your cause. So, get ready to polish your narrative skills and broadcast your vision with the flair of a Broadway show and the precision of a maestro!

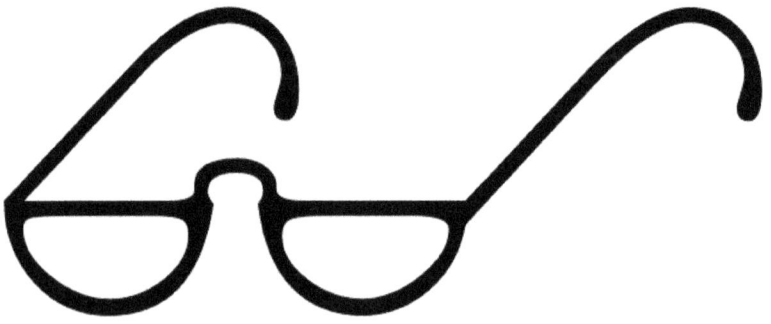

CHAPTER ELEVEN

The Master Plan: Writing a Compelling Business Plan

"A business plan should be more than a set of figures and forecasts—it should tell a compelling story. Make it engaging and insightful, so it not only informs but excites your readers about your vision and potential." — NEIL PATEL, MARKETING EXPERT AND ENTREPRENEUR

Welcome to the thrilling world of business plans, where your visionary dreams are transformed into a blueprint that even your most skeptical investor can't ignore. Writing a compelling business plan is a bit like crafting a high-stakes novel—except instead of fictional dragons and heroic quests, you're dealing with market trends, financial forecasts, and strategic goals. But fear not! With the right approach, you'll turn this essential document into a gripping narrative that captures attention and commands respect.

Picture this: your business plan isn't just a dry collection of data and projections; it's the ultimate storytelling tool that transforms your grand vision into a reality that leaps off the page. Start with a bang by outlining your business's mission with such passion and clarity that even the most jaded reader will be inspired. Follow up with a market analysis so sharp and insightful that it feels like you've read the future. Then, dive into your strategy section like a maestro conducting an orchestra, showing how each element of your plan harmonizes to create a symphony of success.

But here's the secret sauce: make your business plan as engaging as it is informative. Infuse it with personality and flair. Use real-world examples and anecdotes to bring your data to life, and don't shy away from showcasing your enthusiasm. Your goal is to make readers feel like they're on this journey with you, eager to see what happens next.

In the financial projections section, avoid the dry, jargon-filled narrative. Instead, explain your numbers with the same clarity and excitement you'd use to describe your favorite hobby. After all, if you can't get excited about your own business, why should anyone else?

End with a strong, inspiring conclusion that ties everything together, leaving your audience not just convinced but excited about the road ahead. A compelling business plan isn't just a roadmap; it's a reflection of your dedication, creativity, and strategic acumen. So, roll up your sleeves, get ready to channel your inner storyteller, and craft a business plan that's not just a document but a powerful manifesto for your future success.

Crafting Your Mission Statement: Defining Your Purpose and Vision

A compelling business plan begins with a **mission statement**—the heart and soul of your business. This short but powerful statement defines your company's purpose, vision, and core values, offering a clear answer to the question: "Why does your business exist?" It sets the stage for everything that follows, providing direction not only for the business itself but also for investors, employees, and partners.

Crafting a mission statement requires reflection on what truly drives your business and what you aim to achieve in the long run. It's more than just words on paper— it's the guiding principle that informs your decisions, shapes your culture, and communicates your brand's identity to the world.

1. Purpose: Why Does Your Business Exist?

The first element of a mission statement is defining the purpose of your business. What problem are you solving? What need are you fulfilling? This is where you explain the reason your business exists in the market and why it matters. The clearer you are about your purpose, the more compelling your mission statement will be.

- **Questions to ask**:
    - What problem are we solving for our customers?
    - What needs are we fulfilling?
    - Why did we create this business in the first place?

For example, if you're starting a company that makes eco-friendly packaging, your purpose might be to reduce plastic waste and help businesses adopt more sustainable packaging solutions. Your mission statement could read: *"Our mission is to create innovative, sustainable packaging solutions that help businesses reduce their environmental footprint while enhancing product value."*

2. Vision: Where Do You Want to Go?

Your mission statement should also reflect your vision—a forward-looking statement about the future of your business. The vision outlines your long-term goals and what success looks like as you grow. It's the "big picture" of what your business can achieve, whether that's becoming a market leader, revolutionizing an industry, or expanding into new territories.

- **Questions to ask**:
    - What is the ultimate goal of our business?
    - How will the world be different because of our business?
    - What do we want to achieve in the next five to ten years?

Using the eco-friendly packaging company as an example, your vision might be: *"We envision a world where all businesses choose sustainable packaging, drastically reducing the impact of plastic waste on our planet."*

This gives your mission statement both a practical purpose and an aspirational future to strive toward.

3. Core Values: What Principles Guide Your Business?

A strong mission statement is rooted in core values—the beliefs and principles that guide your business decisions and interactions. Core values shape the culture of your company and influence how you treat your customers, employees, and partners. They help stakeholders understand what you stand for and what they can expect from working with or buying from your company.

- **Questions to ask:**
    - What values are most important to us?
    - How do we want to be known in the market?
    - What principles will guide our decisions and actions?

For example, your core values might include sustainability, innovation, and integrity. When woven into your mission statement, these values not only define your business ethos but also help differentiate you from competitors.

"Our mission is to create innovative, sustainable packaging solutions that help businesses reduce their environmental footprint while enhancing product value. We are committed to integrity, innovation, and sustainability in everything we do, envisioning a future where businesses prioritize the planet."

4. Keeping It Simple and Impactful

A mission statement should be concise, clear, and **easy to understand**. You want it to inspire both your internal team and external audiences without getting bogged down in jargon or overly complex language. Aim for no more than two to three sentences that clearly communicate your purpose, vision, and values.

- **Tips for writing a strong mission statement:**
    - Keep it short and focused.

o   Avoid buzzwords or complicated phrases.

o   Make sure it resonates emotionally as well as logically.

o   Write with passion—your mission statement should inspire others.

Remember, the mission statement isn't just a formality; it's a tool that communicates who you are as a business and what drives you toward success.

5. Examples of Strong Mission Statements

Let's look at a few examples of well-crafted mission statements from successful companies:

- **Tesla**: "To accelerate the world's transition to sustainable energy." This mission statement is clear and ambitious. It defines the company's purpose and vision in one simple sentence, capturing Tesla's drive to make a global impact.

- **Patagonia**: "We're in business to save our home planet." Patagonia's mission statement reflects the company's deep commitment to environmental sustainability and social responsibility. It's short, powerful, and packed with meaning.

- **Google**: "To organize the world's information and make it universally accessible and useful." Google's mission is straightforward and purpose-driven, emphasizing both the "what" and the "why" behind the company's existence.

Conclusion: Crafting Your Mission Statement for Success

Your mission statement is the foundation of your business plan. It's the "why" behind everything you do, and it sets the tone for how you'll execute your vision. By clearly defining your purpose, articulating a long-term vision, and embedding your core values, you'll craft a mission statement that not only inspires your team but also captures the interest of potential investors, partners, and customers.

Take the time to make your mission statement memorable, impactful, and aligned with the goals of your business. The clarity and passion you put into it will ripple through every part of your business, guiding you on your journey toward success.

▶ Our model publishing house business plan: The Ridge Publishing Group 2021–2025 Business Plan can be found in the **Appendix**. If you are interested in receiving an electronic copy of this document, email us at documents@AuthorsDoor.com with the subject line "Request for The Ridge Publishing Group 2021–2025 Business Plan." Upon receiving your email, we will promptly send you a Microsoft Word copy of the document. **Disclaimer:** Please note that all agreements are provided for informational purposes only and should not be construed as legal advice. We recommend consulting with a qualified attorney to ensure that any legal documents or decisions are tailored to your specific circumstances.

Market Analysis: Understanding the Landscape

A thorough market analysis is one of the most critical sections of your business plan, as it demonstrates your deep understanding of the environment in which your business operates. Investors, lenders, and stakeholders want to know that you've done your homework. By showing a clear picture of the industry, target market, competitors, and potential opportunities, you establish yourself as a business owner with both vision and insight.

In this section, we'll break down how to conduct an effective market analysis, covering the key elements that will help you understand the landscape, uncover opportunities, and set your business up for success.

1. Industry Overview: Where Does Your Business Fit?

Start your market analysis with a broad overview of the industry you're entering. This helps contextualize your business and show that you understand the big picture. Discuss the size of the industry, its current state, growth trends, and any emerging developments that could impact your business.

- **Questions to ask:**
    - How large is the industry in terms of revenue or market size?

- o   Is the industry growing, shrinking, or stable? What are the growth projections?

- o   Are there emerging trends or technologies that could impact the industry?

- o   What external factors (e.g., economic, regulatory, technological) are influencing the industry?

For example, if you're starting an eco-friendly packaging company, you might discuss the global shift toward sustainability and the growing demand for environmentally conscious solutions. You could also highlight how government regulations, such as bans on single-use plastics, are shaping the industry and creating opportunities for growth.

Example: *"The global packaging industry is projected to reach $1 trillion by 2025, driven largely by the demand for sustainable solutions. The shift towards eco-friendly packaging, accelerated by consumer demand and government regulations, presents a prime opportunity for companies offering biodegradable and recyclable materials."*

2. Target Market: Identifying Your Ideal Customers

After providing an overview of the industry, **zero in on your target market—** the specific group of customers your business will serve. Understanding your target audience is crucial for crafting effective marketing strategies and positioning your products or services. Provide a detailed analysis of who your customers are, what they need, and how your business will meet those needs.

- **Key elements to include**:
    - o   **Demographics**: Define your target market by age, gender, income level, education, location, and other relevant factors.

    - o   **Psychographics**: Go beyond demographics by examining the attitudes, interests, and behaviors of your target customers. What motivates them? What challenges do they face?

- o **Customer needs and pain points**: Identify the specific needs or problems your target audience faces and how your business provides solutions.

- o **Market size and potential**: Estimate the size of your target market and its growth potential. How many potential customers are there, and what percentage of the market can you realistically capture?

For example, if your eco-friendly packaging company targets small to mid-sized businesses in the food and beverage industry, describe those businesses in detail. Explain why they would benefit from your product and how your solution solves their problems, such as reducing environmental impact and complying with regulations.

Example: *"Our target market consists of small to mid-sized businesses in the food and beverage industry that are seeking sustainable packaging solutions. These businesses are increasingly focused on reducing their environmental footprint to meet both regulatory requirements and growing consumer demand for eco-friendly products. The U.S. market for sustainable packaging solutions is expected to grow at a compound annual growth rate (CAGR) of 7.5%, representing a significant opportunity for growth."*

3. Competitive Analysis: Knowing Your Rivals

Understanding your **competition** is critical for differentiating your business in the marketplace. A thorough competitive analysis shows that you know who your competitors are, what they offer, and how your business will stand out. This section highlights the strengths and weaknesses of competitors and helps you position your business to capture market share.

- • **Questions to ask**:

  - o Who are your direct competitors (those offering similar products/services)?

  - o Who are your indirect competitors (those solving the same problem in a different way)?

  - o What are your competitors' strengths and weaknesses?

o What is their pricing, marketing, and distribution strategy?

o How will your business differentiate itself from competitors?

Your competitive analysis should also address barriers to entry in the market. Are there high costs, regulatory challenges, or technological hurdles that make it difficult for new competitors to enter the market? Addressing these factors helps illustrate the viability of your business.

For instance, if your eco-friendly packaging company faces competition from larger, established packaging companies, you might differentiate your business by offering more affordable, customizable solutions for small businesses.

Example: *"Our primary competitors include established packaging companies like XYZ Packaging and GreenWrap, both of which offer sustainable solutions but cater primarily to large corporations. While these companies dominate the large-scale packaging sector, they often overlook the needs of smaller businesses seeking cost-effective, customizable options. Our competitive advantage lies in offering flexible, affordable packaging tailored to the unique requirements of small and mid-sized businesses."*

4. Market Trends and Opportunities: Spotting the Gaps

Finally, your market analysis should highlight current trends and opportunities that your business can capitalize on. These could be changes in consumer behavior, emerging technologies, or shifts in regulatory policies. By identifying gaps in the market, you position your business as a solution to unmet needs.

- **Questions to consider:**

    o What trends are shaping the market (e.g., digital transformation, sustainability, personalized experiences)?

    o What opportunities exist that competitors aren't addressing?

    o Are there specific segments of the market that are underserved or ignored?

    o What emerging technologies or innovations could give your business a competitive edge?

For example, a growing trend toward sustainability and eco-conscious consumerism might be an opportunity for your eco-friendly packaging company to fill a gap by offering innovative, biodegradable materials that larger companies have yet to adopt.

Example: *"The rise of eco-conscious consumerism presents a significant opportunity for growth in the sustainable packaging market. While many large companies have embraced recyclable materials, there is a growing demand for biodegradable options that minimize environmental impact further. Our company is uniquely positioned to meet this demand by offering innovative packaging solutions made from plant-based, biodegradable materials that appeal to businesses seeking more sustainable alternatives."*

5. Conclusion: Presenting a Clear Picture

A well-executed market analysis demonstrates your deep understanding of the industry, your target customers, and your competition. It paints a clear picture of the landscape your business will navigate and provides a strong foundation for your strategies. By thoroughly analyzing your market, you build credibility and confidence in your business plan.

- **Recap the key points**:
    - Clearly define the industry you operate in and its growth potential.
    - Identify your target audience and show how your business will meet their needs.
    - Analyze your competitors and highlight your unique selling proposition (USP).
    - Showcase market trends and opportunities that your business can leverage.

The more detailed and insightful your market analysis, the more compelling your business plan will be, positioning you as a well-informed entrepreneur with a clear path to success.

Conclusion: Understanding the Market Landscape

Market analysis is more than just a deep dive into facts and figures; it's your opportunity to show how your business fits into the larger ecosystem. By understanding the landscape—industry trends, competitors, and customer needs—you'll be able to identify gaps in the market and leverage them to position your business for growth. With a thorough market analysis, you not only demonstrate your expertise but also build a strong case for why your business is poised for success.

Business Strategy: The Blueprint for Success

Your business strategy is the roadmap that guides your company from its current state to the future you envision. While the mission statement defines your purpose, and the market analysis helps you understand the landscape, the business strategy outlines how you're going to achieve your goals. It is your detailed plan for building a successful, sustainable business by leveraging opportunities, overcoming challenges, and differentiating yourself from competitors.

In this section, we will explore how to develop a clear, actionable strategy that covers your goals, business model, marketing approach, operational plans, and growth tactics. A well-thought-out strategy serves as the foundation for making decisions, allocating resources, and executing your business plan effectively.

1. Setting SMART Goals: Turning Vision into Action

At the core of your business strategy are your **goals**—the specific, measurable objectives that will guide your actions. To ensure that your goals are effective, they should follow the SMART framework:

- **Specific**: Clearly define what you want to achieve.

- **Measurable**: Establish criteria to measure your progress.

- **Achievable**: Make sure your goals are realistic given your resources.

- **Relevant**: Ensure that your goals align with your overall business vision.

- **Time-bound**: Set a deadline for achieving your objectives.

Start by breaking your long-term vision into smaller, actionable steps. These goals should cover key areas like sales growth, customer acquisition, product development, and brand awareness.

- **Example**: "Increase online sales by 25% over the next 12 months by launching a targeted digital marketing campaign and expanding product offerings to meet customer demand."

Your SMART goals act as the driving force behind your strategy, helping you stay focused on what matters most and measuring your success along the way.

2. Defining Your Business Model: How Will You Make Money?

A crucial element of any business strategy is your business model—the way your company creates, delivers, and captures value. This defines how your business will make money and outlines the products or services you offer, your pricing strategy, and how you'll generate revenue.

- **Types of business models**:
    - **Product sales**: You sell a tangible product directly to customers.
    - **Service-based**: You offer services (e.g., consulting, coaching, repairs) in exchange for payment.
    - **Subscription model**: Customers pay a recurring fee (monthly, annually) for access to your products or services.
    - **Freemium**: You offer basic services for free while charging for premium features or add-ons.
    - **Marketplace model**: You act as an intermediary between buyers and sellers, often taking a commission on each transaction.

For instance, if your eco-friendly packaging company follows a B2B model, you might sell biodegradable packaging products directly to small and mid-sized businesses, with a focus on long-term contracts and bulk orders. Additionally, you may incorporate a subscription model, where clients receive regular shipments of packaging materials on a recurring basis.

- **Example**: "Our business model combines direct B2B sales with a subscription service that allows small and mid-sized businesses to receive monthly shipments of customizable, eco-friendly packaging solutions."

By clearly defining how your business will generate revenue, you create a solid foundation for your financial projections and growth strategies.

3. Marketing Strategy: How Will You Reach Your Customers?

Once you know what you're selling and how your business will generate revenue, the next step is to figure out how to reach your customers effectively. Your marketing strategy is the bridge between your products or services and the customers who need them. It outlines how you will create awareness, attract leads, and convert them into loyal customers.

Key elements of your marketing strategy include:

- **Target audience**: Who are your ideal customers? Refer back to your market analysis for a detailed understanding of your target audience's demographics, needs, and preferences.

- **Value proposition**: What unique benefit or solution does your business offer that differentiates you from competitors?

- **Marketing channels**: Which channels will you use to reach your audience? Common channels include social media, search engine optimization (SEO), email marketing, paid advertising (Google Ads, Facebook Ads), content marketing (blogging, video), and influencer marketing.

- **Brand messaging**: What tone, language, and visual identity will you use to communicate with your audience? Your messaging should reflect your brand values and resonate with your target market.

- **Example**: "Our marketing strategy will focus on building brand awareness through digital channels, including a targeted social media campaign highlighting the sustainability of our products, an SEO-optimized blog to educate businesses about eco-friendly packaging, and email marketing to nurture leads and convert them into subscribers."

By developing a clear marketing strategy, you ensure that your business reaches the right customers and builds lasting relationships with them.

4. Operational Plan: Turning Strategy into Execution

A brilliant strategy is useless without the ability to execute it. Your operational plan details how your business will function on a day-to-day basis to achieve your goals. This includes everything from sourcing materials and managing inventory to delivering your products or services and providing customer support.

- **Key elements of an operational plan**:
    - o **Suppliers and partners**: Identify the suppliers or vendors you'll work with and any strategic partnerships that are critical to your operations.
    - o **Production process**: Outline how you'll create your products or deliver services. What are the steps involved? How will you ensure quality control?
    - o **Logistics and delivery**: How will you get your products to customers? Will you ship directly, partner with third-party logistics providers, or operate a physical storefront?
    - o **Customer service**: What systems will you put in place to handle customer inquiries, returns, or complaints?

For example, your eco-friendly packaging company might source biodegradable materials from certified suppliers, manufacture the packaging in-house or through a contracted facility, and deliver products to clients via a third-party logistics provider.

- **Example**: "Our operational plan involves sourcing biodegradable materials from local suppliers to reduce our carbon footprint. We will manage production in-house to ensure quality control and use third-party logistics providers to deliver products nationwide."

Your operational plan ensures that your strategy is feasible and outlines the steps you'll take to turn your goals into reality.

5. Growth and Scaling Strategy: How Will You Expand?

A strong business strategy also considers the future. As your business gains traction, you'll need to plan for growth and scaling. This section outlines how you'll expand your customer base, increase sales, and grow your operations over time.

- **Questions to consider**:
    - How will you expand your market reach? Will you enter new markets, launch new products, or open additional locations?
    - How will you scale your operations? Will you hire more employees, increase production capacity, or invest in new technology?
    - What metrics will you use to measure growth? Revenue, profit margins, customer acquisition rates, and market share are common growth metrics.

For instance, your eco-friendly packaging company might initially focus on U.S.-based clients, but plan to expand into international markets within five years. You could also diversify your product line by offering additional eco-friendly solutions, such as reusable packaging materials.

- **Example**: "Over the next five years, we plan to expand our product offerings to include reusable packaging materials and enter international markets in Europe and Canada. We will also invest in automated production systems to scale operations efficiently as demand increases."

By planning for growth, you position your business for long-term success and demonstrate your commitment to continuous improvement and innovation.

Conclusion: Building a Blueprint for Success

Your business strategy is the blueprint for achieving your vision and turning your business plan into reality. By setting clear goals, defining a sustainable business model, outlining your marketing approach, detailing your operational plans, and preparing for growth, you create a comprehensive roadmap that guides your company's success. A well-crafted strategy not only aligns your team but also instills confidence in investors and stakeholders, showing that you're prepared for both the challenges and opportunities ahead.

With your strategy in place, your business has a solid foundation to move forward and scale effectively, ensuring that your entrepreneurial vision becomes a thriving reality.

▶ Our strategic growth business plan—hybrid: publishing, e-commerce, and fashion: LA Survival Gear and Prep Writer 2018–2022 Business Plan can be found in the **Appendix**. If you are interested in receiving an electronic copy of this document, please email us at documents@AuthorsDoor.com with the subject line "Request for LA Survival Gear and Prep Writer 2018–2022 Business Plan." Upon receiving your email, we will promptly send you a Microsoft Word copy of the document. **Disclaimer:** Please note that all agreements are provided for informational purposes only and should not be construed as legal advice. We recommend consulting with a qualified attorney to ensure that any legal documents or decisions are tailored to your specific circumstances.

Financial Projections: Turning Vision into Numbers

The financial projections section of your business plan is where your visionary ideas and strategic planning translate into hard numbers. Investors, lenders, and stakeholders rely heavily on these figures to evaluate the viability and profitability of your business. This section paints a clear picture of your company's financial future, offering insight into expected revenue, expenses, and profitability. Done right, your financial projections demonstrate that your business is not only innovative but also capable of generating sustainable profits.

In this section, we'll explore how to develop realistic and compelling financial projections, covering key components like income statements, balance sheets, cash flow forecasts, and funding needs.

1. Income Statement: Projecting Revenue and Profit

The income statement, also known as the profit and loss (P&L) statement, is a financial report that shows your projected revenue, expenses, and profit over a specific period (usually monthly, quarterly, and annually). It answers the fundamental question: Is your business going to make money?

To create your income statement, you'll need to project the following:

- **Revenue**: Estimate how much money your business will bring in from sales. This should be based on your sales forecast and market research, accounting for growth over time.
  - o **Example**: If you plan to sell eco-friendly packaging to small businesses, your revenue forecast should be based on expected sales volume, pricing strategy, and customer acquisition. Be realistic—investors want to see projections grounded in data, not wishful thinking.

- **Cost of Goods Sold (COGS)**: This represents the direct costs associated with producing your products or delivering your services, such as materials, labor, and manufacturing expenses.
  - o **Example**: In an eco-friendly packaging business, COGS might include the cost of biodegradable materials, manufacturing, and shipping.

- **Operating Expenses**: These are the costs required to run your business, including rent, utilities, employee salaries, marketing, and administrative costs.

- **Gross Profit**: Subtract COGS from revenue to calculate your gross profit—the amount of money left after covering the costs of producing your goods or services.

- **Net Profit**: Finally, subtract operating expenses from gross profit to determine your net profit—the amount your business will earn after all expenses have been paid.

Example of a simplified income statement projection:

Year 1	Year 2	Year 3
Revenue	$500,000	$750,000
Cost of Goods Sold (COGS)	$200,000	$300,000
Gross Profit	$300,000	$450,000
Operating Expenses	$250,000	$300,000
Net Profit	$50,000	$150,000

This simple breakdown shows potential investors that you understand the financial mechanics of your business and how it will grow over time.

2. Cash Flow Forecast: Ensuring Liquidity

While the income statement shows profitability, the cash flow forecast focuses on cash management—how much cash will flow in and out of your business. This is critical because even a profitable business can run into trouble if it doesn't have enough cash on hand to meet its obligations, such as paying employees or suppliers.

The cash flow forecast breaks down the following:

- **Cash inflows**: This includes all cash that enters your business, typically from sales, loans, or investments.

    o **Example**: In your eco-friendly packaging business, your cash inflows might come from direct sales to customers and any initial funding or investments you've secured.

- **Cash outflows**: These are all the expenses that require cash payments, including rent, salaries, supplier payments, marketing, and loan repayments.

- **Net cash flow**: Subtract cash outflows from cash inflows to determine your **net cash flow**—the amount of cash available at the end of each period. Positive cash flow means your business is generating more cash than its spending, while negative cash flow signals that your expenses are outpacing revenue.

Investors pay close attention to your cash flow projections to ensure that your business can maintain liquidity and avoid cash shortages, especially during the startup phase.

Example of a cash flow forecast (monthly breakdown for Year 1):

Month	Cash Inflows	Cash Outflows	Net Cash Flow
January	$50,000	$60,000	-$10,000
February	$60,000	$55,000	$5,000
March	$70,000	$60,000	$10,000

This example shows that while the business may experience some negative cash flow in the beginning (common for new businesses), it quickly stabilizes and begins generating positive cash flow.

3. Balance Sheet: Showing Financial Health

The balance sheet provides a snapshot of your business's financial health at a specific point in time, showing what your company owns (assets), what it owes (liabilities), and the net worth (equity) of the business. It helps potential investors and lenders assess your business's stability and ability to meet long-term obligations.

Key elements of the balance sheet include:

- **Assets**: These are resources your business owns that have value, such as cash, inventory, equipment, and property.
  - o **Example**: If you own a manufacturing facility for your eco-friendly packaging company, that would be listed as an asset on your balance sheet.
- **Liabilities**: These are your business's obligations, such as loans, accounts payable, and other debts.

- o **Example**: If you've taken out a business loan to finance production equipment, that would be listed as a liability.

- **Equity**: This represents the net worth of your business—essentially what's left over after subtracting liabilities from assets. It shows what the business is worth to its owners or shareholders.

Example of a balance sheet:

Assets	Liabilities	Equity
Cash: $50,000	Loan: $100,000	Owner's Equity: $50,000
Inventory: $40,000	Accounts Payable: $30,000	
Equipment: $60,000		
Total: $150,000	**Total: $130,000**	**Total: $50,000**

This simple balance sheet shows a healthy business with more assets than liabilities and a solid equity position.

4. Break-Even Analysis: When Will You Be Profitable?

The break-even analysis is a critical part of your financial projections that shows when your business will cover its costs and start making a profit. It's calculated by determining the point at which your total revenue equals your total expenses—essentially when your business breaks even.

To calculate your break-even point, use the following formula:

Break-even point = Fixed costs / (Price per unit – Variable cost per unit)

- **Fixed costs**: These are expenses that remain constant regardless of sales volume, such as rent, salaries, and insurance.

- **Variable costs**: These are costs that fluctuate based on production or sales, such as materials and shipping.

- **Price per unit**: This is the amount you charge customers for each product or service.

- **Example**: If your eco-friendly packaging company has fixed costs of $100,000, sells products for $10 per unit, and has variable costs of $5 per unit, the break-even point is:

Break-even point = $100,000 / ($10 – $5) = 20,000 units

This means you need to sell 20,000 units to cover your costs and begin making a profit.

5. Funding Requirements: What Do You Need to Succeed?

The final element of your financial projections is outlining your funding requirements—how much capital you need to start or grow your business and how you plan to use it. Investors want to know how their money will be spent and what returns they can expect.

- **Startup costs**: List all the initial costs needed to launch your business, such as equipment, inventory, marketing, and hiring staff.

  - **Example**: "To launch our eco-friendly packaging company, we require $250,000 in startup capital. This will be allocated to purchasing manufacturing equipment ($100,000), initial inventory ($50,000), marketing and brand development ($50,000), and working capital for the first six months of operations ($50,000)."

- **Funding sources**: Specify where the funding will come from—whether you're seeking investment, applying for a loan, or using personal savings.

- **Returns**: If seeking investment, outline the expected return on investment (ROI) for potential investors, showing when they can expect to see a return on their capital.

Conclusion: Financial Projections as a Blueprint for Growth

Your financial projections are the backbone of your business plan, providing a detailed blueprint of how your vision will translate into financial success. By forecasting revenue, managing cash flow, and presenting a solid balance sheet, you demonstrate to investors and stakeholders that your business is financially viable and capable of growth.

Creating realistic and data-driven financial projections also gives you the tools to manage your business effectively, guiding your decisions and helping you

Quick Tips and Recap

- **Set realistic revenue goals**: Base your sales projections on thorough market research and realistic growth expectations, not just optimistic assumptions.

- **Know your costs**: Accurately estimate your **Cost of Goods Sold (COGS)** and **operating expenses** to ensure that your profit projections are grounded in reality.

- **Monitor cash flow**: Keep a close eye on cash flow to ensure you have enough liquidity to cover expenses, even if revenue fluctuates.

- **Break-even analysis is key**: Calculate your **break-even point** to understand how many sales you need to cover your costs and start making a profit.

- **Use financial templates**: Leverage financial statement templates (income statement, balance sheet, and cash flow) to standardize your projections and ensure clarity for investors.

- **Prepare for funding**: Clearly outline your startup or growth capital requirements and explain how you plan to use the funds to achieve financial success.

- **Test different scenarios**: Develop multiple financial projections (best-case, worst-case, and realistic scenarios) to prepare for market fluctuations and unexpected challenges.

- **Update your projections regularly**: Financial forecasts should be updated frequently to reflect current market conditions, sales trends, and operational changes.

By following these tips, you can create a solid financial plan that not only supports your business strategy but also builds confidence with potential investors and stakeholders.

CHAPTER TWELVE

First Impressions: Perfecting the Executive Summary

"An executive summary should capture the essence of your business with clarity and flair—think of it as your chance to make a powerful first impression." — DAVID OGILVY, ADVERTISING PIONEER

Welcome to the world of executive summaries, where you get to dazzle your audience with a snapshot of your business brilliance, all within a few tantalizing paragraphs. Think of it as your business's elevator pitch—only this time, you're in a skyscraper, and you have just seconds to impress. It's the art of summarizing your grand vision with the finesse of a magician pulling a rabbit out of a hat, but with fewer animals and more strategic finesse.

In this chapter, we'll dive into the secrets of crafting an executive summary that's not just a bland overview but a compelling appetizer that leaves your readers craving the full feast of your business plan. You'll learn how to distill your business's essence into a punchy, engaging summary that highlights the key points—your mission, vision, and unique selling proposition—without bogging down in the nitty-gritty details.

Imagine your executive summary as the headline of a blockbuster movie trailer—short, snappy, and irresistibly intriguing. It should make investors and stakeholders think, "I need to see more of this!" So, grab your creative hat and get ready to transform your business plan's opening act into a showstopper that ensures your first impression is nothing short of spectacular.

Crafting a Compelling Hook: Grabbing Attention from the Start

The first few sentences of your executive summary are crucial—they determine whether your reader will be engaged or distracted. In the fast-paced world of business, attention is a precious commodity, and you have mere seconds to grab it. The hook is your opportunity to make a powerful first impression, setting the tone for the rest of your business plan and sparking interest in what's to come.

A compelling hook should be clear, concise, and engaging. It needs to communicate the core value of your business in a way that's hard to ignore. Think of it as the headline of your business plan, designed to pique curiosity and make investors or stakeholders think, "I need to know more about this."

1. Start with a Bold Statement

One of the most effective ways to grab attention is to start with a bold, powerful statement that immediately highlights the importance of your business. This could be an eye-opening statistic, a striking fact about the market, or a statement that illustrates the problem your business is solving.

- **Example**: "Every year, over 8 million tons of plastic waste end up in the ocean, and our company is on a mission to change that. With our innovative biodegradable packaging solutions, we aim to reduce plastic waste and help businesses make eco-friendly choices without compromising on quality."

This kind of statement grabs attention by showing the urgency of the problem and positioning your business as a solution from the very beginning. It's bold, relevant, and immediately highlights the value your business brings to the table.

2. Highlight Your Unique Value Proposition

Another approach is to lead with your Unique Selling Proposition (USP)—the one thing that sets your business apart from the competition. By showcasing what makes your business different and why it's valuable, you position yourself as a standout in a crowded market.

- **Example**: "In a market dominated by traditional packaging solutions, our company offers the first fully customizable, biodegradable packaging that costs 20% less than conventional alternatives."

This statement emphasizes what makes your business unique and immediately differentiates you from competitors, capturing the reader's interest in your innovative approach.

3. State the Problem and Present Your Solution

One of the simplest yet most effective hooks is to outline a clear problem in the market and position your business as the solution. This approach works well because it taps into a fundamental truth about entrepreneurship: successful businesses solve real problems.

- **Example**: "Small businesses struggle to find affordable, eco-friendly packaging options, often sacrificing sustainability for cost. Our company solves this by providing affordable, sustainable packaging solutions tailored to the needs of small and mid-sized businesses."

By presenting the problem and solution in one punchy sentence, you quickly demonstrate why your business is relevant and needed in the marketplace.

4. Use a Compelling Question

Opening with a thought-provoking question can instantly engage your audience by making them think about the issue your business addresses. This works particularly well when the question leads directly to the solution your business offers.

- **Example**: "What if your business could reduce plastic waste by 50% while saving money on packaging costs? With our innovative biodegradable packaging solutions, that's exactly what we offer."

This approach puts the reader in the mindset of imagining possibilities and invites them to continue reading to find out how your business can deliver on this potential.

5. Keep It Short and Impactful

No matter which strategy you use, your hook should be short, impactful, and easy to understand. Avoid overcomplicating your opening with technical jargon or unnecessary details. The goal is to intrigue and engage—to get your reader invested in learning more about your business.

Remember, you're writing for an audience that may be reviewing multiple business plans, so brevity is key. Your hook should offer enough information to grab attention without overwhelming the reader. Aim for two to three sentences that capture the essence of your business.

6. Create an Emotional Connection

In addition to facts and figures, consider adding an emotional element to your hook. People are more likely to invest in businesses that inspire them or resonate with their values. If your business has a social mission, a story about how it helps people or impacts the world positively can create a powerful connection with your reader.

- **Example**: "Imagine a world where every package you receive doesn't contribute to the growing waste problem. Our biodegradable packaging solutions not only help businesses reduce their environmental impact but also give consumers peace of mind that their choices are making a difference."

This statement appeals to both the logical and emotional side of your audience, encouraging them to support a business with a positive social impact.

Conclusion: Make It Memorable

Your hook is the gateway to the rest of your business plan, and it needs to leave a lasting impression. Whether you lead with a bold statement, highlight your unique value proposition, or present a compelling question, your goal is to draw your reader in and make them want to learn more.

By crafting a strong, concise, and engaging opening, you set the stage for a compelling executive summary that showcases the brilliance of your business and makes a powerful first impression.

Highlighting Key Points: Summarizing Your Business's Core Elements

Once you've captured your reader's attention with a compelling hook, it's time to highlight the key points that define your business. The executive summary is a snapshot of your entire business plan, so it needs to include the essential elements of your company in a way that is clear, concise, and engaging. Think of this section as giving your audience the most important details upfront—just enough to intrigue them and encourage them to dive deeper into your business plan.

The goal is to summarize your core elements in a way that communicates the strength of your business without overwhelming the reader with too much detail. Here are the core elements you should include and how to structure them.

1. Mission Statement: What is Your Business's Purpose?

Your mission statement should provide a clear and concise description of your business's purpose—why your company exists and what it seeks to achieve. It sets the tone for everything that follows and helps the reader understand your company's core values and long-term vision.

- **Example**: "Our mission is to provide sustainable, affordable packaging solutions that help small businesses reduce their environmental impact and meet the growing demand for eco-friendly products."

This mission statement not only explains what the company does but also highlights its commitment to sustainability and small businesses, creating a sense of purpose that investors and stakeholders can rally behind.

2. Products or Services: What Are You Offering?

Next, briefly describe what your business offers—whether it's a product, service, or solution. Focus on the unique aspects of your offerings and how they meet the needs of your target market. This is where you get to showcase your unique selling proposition (USP)—what sets your business apart from the competition.

- **Example**: "We offer a line of customizable, biodegradable packaging made from plant-based materials, designed to meet the needs of businesses seeking affordable, eco-friendly alternatives to traditional packaging."

This description is short, but it highlights the uniqueness of the product (customizable, biodegradable packaging) and positions the company as a solution to a specific problem (affordable eco-friendly alternatives).

3. Target Market: Who Are Your Customers?

It's important to define your target market clearly. Investors and stakeholders want to know who your customers are, how large your market is, and why your product or service is relevant to them. In this section, focus on the specific group or groups of people or businesses that your company serves.

- **Example**: "Our primary customers are small to mid-sized businesses in the food and beverage industry that are looking for sustainable packaging solutions. With the increasing consumer demand for eco-friendly products, this market is projected to grow by 15% annually."

This gives the reader a clear idea of the target audience and provides context on the market's growth potential, which strengthens the case for your business's viability.

4. Competitive Advantage: What Sets You Apart?

Every successful business has something that makes it stand out from the competition. In this section, summarize your competitive advantage—the feature or aspect of your business that gives you an edge in the marketplace. It could be a unique product, a superior customer experience, a new technology, or a cost advantage.

- **Example**: "Unlike traditional packaging companies, we offer fully customizable designs at prices that are 20% lower than other eco-friendly packaging options on the market, allowing small businesses to reduce their costs while promoting sustainability."

By emphasizing both customization and affordability, this business positions itself as an attractive option for small businesses looking for flexibility and cost savings.

5. Business Model: How Will You Make Money?

Provide a brief explanation of your business model—how your company will generate revenue. This could include direct sales, subscription services, licensing, or any other monetization strategy. Make sure to highlight why this model is scalable and sustainable over the long term.

- **Example**: "We generate revenue through direct B2B sales of our packaging products, offering both one-time purchases and a subscription service for businesses that need consistent monthly supply."

This demonstrates that the company has multiple revenue streams and highlights the subscription model as a way to ensure ongoing, predictable income.

6. Financial Snapshot: How Will You Achieve Profitability?

While you don't need to provide full financial projections in your executive summary, offering a brief financial snapshot gives investors a quick understanding of your company's current and projected financial health. Highlight your revenue goals, profitability timeline, and any key financial milestones you expect to hit.

- **Example**: "We are projecting $500,000 in revenue in our first year, with an anticipated growth rate of 30% year-over-year. We expect to break even by the end of Year 2 and reach profitability in Year 3."

This summary reassures readers that you've considered the financials carefully and have a plan for reaching profitability, which is critical for investors.

7. Growth Strategy: What Are Your Plans for the Future?

Finally, summarize your growth strategy. How will you scale your business, increase your market share, or expand your product offerings? This section provides insight into your long-term vision and helps readers understand how you plan to grow and adapt to changing market conditions.

- **Example**: "Over the next five years, we plan to expand our product line to include reusable packaging and enter international markets, starting with Europe. We will also invest in automated manufacturing to scale production as demand grows."

By outlining clear growth plans, this section demonstrates that your business is not just focused on short-term gains but has a forward-thinking strategy for long-term success.

Conclusion: Crafting a Clear and Concise Overview

When summarizing the core elements of your business in the executive summary, clarity is key. Focus on delivering the most important information in a way that is easy to digest and engaging. Each element—mission statement, products, target market, competitive advantage, business model, financial snapshot, and growth strategy—should be addressed concisely, without diving into too much detail.

By highlighting these key points, you give your audience a clear understanding of your business's value, its potential for growth, and why it's worth investing in. The goal is to inspire confidence and encourage readers to explore the full business plan.

Demonstrating Market Opportunity: Proving the Need for Your Business

A critical component of any executive summary is the market opportunity—the part where you prove that there's a real demand for your product or service and show that your business is well-positioned to meet that demand. Demonstrating market opportunity is about convincing investors, lenders, or stakeholders that you've identified a gap in the market and that your business can fill it profitably.

In this section, you'll provide a snapshot of the market conditions, customer demand, and trends that create an opening for your business to thrive. By doing this effectively, you reassure readers that you've done your research and that there's a clear path to success.

1. Quantifying the Market: Show the Size and Growth Potential

One of the most persuasive ways to demonstrate market opportunity is to quantify the size of the market and its growth potential. Use industry data, reports, and research to show the reader how big the market is and how fast it's growing. Numbers and statistics give credibility to your claims and help paint a clearer picture of the opportunity.

- **Example**: "The global sustainable packaging market is currently valued at $220 billion and is projected to grow at a compound annual growth rate (CAGR) of 7.7% over the next five years. With increasing regulatory pressure and consumer demand for eco-friendly alternatives, the market for biodegradable packaging solutions is expected to expand significantly."

This statement demonstrates that the business is tapping into a rapidly growing industry, backed by credible data that points to future growth. Investors are more likely to get excited about a business that's positioned in an expanding market.

2. Identifying Market Trends: Align with Emerging Needs

Markets don't exist in a vacuum—trends and shifts in consumer behavior, technology, and regulations can create new opportunities. By identifying and aligning your business with these emerging trends, you can prove that you're not only solving a current problem but also positioning yourself for future success.

- **Example**: "As consumers become increasingly aware of environmental issues, demand for sustainable packaging has surged. A recent survey found that 72% of consumers are willing to pay more for products with eco-friendly packaging. Additionally, stricter regulations in the EU and U.S. banning single-use plastics are creating a growing demand for biodegradable solutions."

This highlights specific trends—consumer demand for sustainable products and regulatory changes—that directly support the need for the business's offerings. Tying your business to real-world trends demonstrates that you understand the market's direction and are poised to take advantage of it.

3. Tackling Customer Pain Points: Solving Key Problems

A compelling market opportunity often starts with a pain point or problem that is widespread but inadequately addressed. Clearly identifying these pain points and showing how your business solves them is key to proving market demand. Explain why current solutions fall short and why your business offers a superior alternative.

- **Example**: "Small and mid-sized businesses in the food and beverage industry are struggling to find affordable, eco-friendly packaging options that meet their sustainability goals without cutting into profit margins. Current solutions are often expensive or not customizable enough to meet the needs of smaller businesses. Our biodegradable packaging offers a cost-effective and customizable alternative, tailored specifically to this underserved market segment."

By pinpointing a specific problem that customers face and showing how existing solutions don't fully address it, you create a compelling case for why your product is needed. You position your business as the solution to a market gap that others have failed to address.

4. Mapping the Competition: Finding Gaps and Opportunities

While it's important to acknowledge the competitive landscape, you should also highlight areas where your competitors are falling short or markets that remain underserved. This allows you to demonstrate how your business can capitalize on these gaps and capture market share.

- **Example**: "The majority of sustainable packaging providers target large corporations, leaving smaller businesses without affordable options. By focusing on the specific needs of small to mid-sized companies, we address an underserved market that has been largely ignored by larger competitors."

This shows that while there may be competition in the sustainable packaging market, there's a specific niche that remains untapped, giving your business a unique opportunity to thrive.

5. Market Segmentation: Targeting the Right Audience

Market opportunity isn't just about showing that a market exists; it's about proving that your business is focused on the right segment of the market. Investors want to know that you've zeroed in on an audience with both a need for your product and the willingness to pay for it.

Clearly defining your target market segment helps show that you understand where the biggest opportunity lies and that you've tailored your offering to that audience.

- **Example**: "Our primary target market consists of small to mid-sized businesses in the organic food sector, a market that is growing at 8.5% annually. These companies are particularly focused on sustainability, with 80% of organic food producers indicating that eco-friendly packaging is a top priority for their brand image."

By segmenting the market, you show that you've done your homework and are targeting a specific audience with high potential, rather than taking a one-size-fits-all approach. Investors will see this as a focused and strategic effort.

6. Backing Up Claims with Research and Data

To further strengthen your case, back up your claims with reliable research, data, and market insights. Using credible sources like industry reports, surveys, and government statistics adds weight to your arguments and reassures readers that your projections are based on facts, not assumptions.

- **Example**: "According to a report by Global Market Insights, the biodegradable packaging industry is expected to surpass $12 billion by 2027, driven by increasing consumer demand and regulatory pressures. Furthermore, a Nielsen study indicates that 81% of consumers globally believe companies should help improve the environment, reinforcing the trend toward eco-friendly packaging."

Citing specific studies or reports gives your business plan **authority** and demonstrates that your market opportunity is based on data-driven insights. It helps build investor confidence that the opportunity is real and substantial.

Conclusion: Convincing Readers of the Market's Potential

Demonstrating market opportunity is all about showing that your business is entering the right market at the right time with a product or service that solves a real problem. By quantifying the market size, identifying key trends, addressing customer pain points, and highlighting gaps in the competitive landscape, you can paint a clear picture of the need for your business.

In the executive summary, this section should be concise but persuasive, giving readers enough evidence to believe in the potential of your business without overwhelming them with too many details. The goal is to prove that the demand exists and that your business is uniquely positioned to capture that demand, making it an exciting and valuable opportunity for investors.

Concluding with Impact: Inspiring Confidence and Excitement

The final section of your executive summary is your chance to leave a lasting impression. You've already captured attention with a compelling hook, summarized your business's core elements, and demonstrated market opportunity. Now, it's time to tie everything together in a way that inspires confidence and excitement in your reader, whether they're a potential investor, partner, or stakeholder.

A strong conclusion doesn't just recap your key points—it emphasizes the vision for your business's future and the path to success. This is where you remind your audience why your business is not only a solid investment but also an exciting opportunity that has the potential to achieve great things.

Here are some tips on how to finish your executive summary with impact.

1. Restate Your Vision with Clarity and Confidence

In your conclusion, restate the vision of your business—your ultimate goal and what you're aiming to achieve. Investors and stakeholders want to know that you have a clear direction and that you're confident in your ability to execute on your plan.

- **Example**: "Our vision is to revolutionize the packaging industry by offering businesses sustainable, affordable alternatives that not only reduce environmental impact but also enhance their brand value. With a commitment to innovation and quality, we're poised to lead the way in making eco-friendly packaging the industry standard."

This restates the company's bold, ambitious vision and reminds the reader of its purpose, highlighting the potential impact the business can have on the market and the world.

2. Highlight Your Milestones and Achievements

If your business has already reached important milestones—such as securing partnerships, hitting revenue targets, or completing product development—this is the perfect place to mention them. These achievements demonstrate that you've made progress and that your business is capable of delivering on its promises.

- **Example**: "In just six months, we've secured partnerships with over 50 businesses, launched a successful pilot program, and achieved 20% month-over-month revenue growth. These early successes validate our market demand and reinforce our ability to scale quickly."

By pointing out real accomplishments, you build credibility and show that your business has momentum.

3. Present a Path to Profitability

Investors are keen to know how—and when—your business will become profitable. In this section, briefly highlight your path to profitability and any major financial projections that can help reassure readers that your business will generate returns.

- **Example**: "With a projected annual growth rate of 30%, we expect to reach profitability by the end of Year 2. Our strong early traction and scalable business model position us for rapid expansion, and we're confident in our ability to deliver substantial returns to our investors."

This statement gives the reader a **clear timeline** and sets expectations for when the business will start generating profits.

4. Outline Your Funding Needs and How You'll Use It

If you're seeking funding, this is the moment to state how much capital you need and what it will be used for. Be clear and specific, and tie the funding back to your growth strategy. Investors want to know how their money will be put to work and what milestones it will help you achieve.

- **Example**: "To accelerate our growth, we are seeking $500,000 in funding to expand our production capabilities, scale our sales team, and invest in targeted marketing initiatives. This funding will allow us to increase our market share and reach profitability within the next two years."

By clearly stating your funding needs and connecting them to specific goals, you help investors understand how their investment will contribute to your business's success.

5. Create Excitement About the Future

End on a high note by expressing your enthusiasm for the future and what's possible for your business. The goal is to inspire excitement and confidence—your audience should walk away feeling that this is a business they want to be a part of.

- **Example**: "With the increasing global shift toward sustainability, the timing has never been better for our business. We're excited about the future and are ready to seize this opportunity to reshape the packaging industry. With the right partners and investment, we believe we can achieve exponential growth and make a lasting impact on both the market and the environment."

This statement creates a sense of urgency and possibility, making the reader eager to learn more about the business's potential.

Quick Tips and Recap

- **Start with a compelling hook**: Capture your reader's attention from the first sentence with a bold statement, a thought-provoking question, or your unique selling proposition.

- **Summarize your core elements**: Include your mission statement, products or services, target market, competitive advantage, and business model in a concise, engaging way.

- **Demonstrate market opportunity**: Prove the demand for your business with credible data, trends, and insights, and clearly explain how your business meets customer needs.

- **Restate your vision**: Remind readers of your long-term vision and the impact your business aims to make in the market.

- **Highlight key achievements**: If applicable, mention any important milestones or successes that demonstrate your business's potential.

- **Show your path to profitability**: Provide a quick snapshot of your financial projections, showing when you expect to break even and achieve profitability.

- **Clarify your funding needs**: Be specific about how much funding you need and how you plan to use it to grow your business.

- **End on an inspiring note**: Conclude with excitement and confidence, leaving your reader eager to engage with the rest of your business plan.

By following these tips, your executive summary will make a powerful first impression, setting the stage for a compelling business plan that captures attention and inspires action.

CHAPTER THIRTEEN

Pitch Perfect: Crafting Proposals and Presentations

"A great pitch isn't just about presenting ideas; it's about making your audience feel they can't afford to miss out."— JOE SUGARMAN, ADVERTISING EXPERT

Welcome to the dazzling world of proposals and presentations, where your business ideas are transformed into a performance so compelling that even your cat would pause its nap to pay attention. Crafting these masterpieces is like hosting a show where you're the star performer, the scriptwriter, and the director—all rolled into one.

In this chapter, we'll explore how to turn your ideas into presentations that don't just convey information but dazzle your audience. Picture it as your moment in the spotlight, where every slide is a scene, every bullet point is a plot twist, and every piece of data is a dramatic reveal. Whether you're pitching to investors or presenting to clients, your goal is to make your proposals so irresistible that your audience can't help but say "yes" before you've even finished.

We'll cover how to structure your presentation like a great story—engaging from the start, building up to a climax, and wrapping up with a resolution that leaves them wanting more. You'll learn to combine clarity with charisma, making sure that your pitch doesn't just inform but also entertains and persuades. So, get ready to take center stage and deliver a performance that makes your business ideas sing like a chart-topping hit.

Structuring Your Story: Creating a Clear Engaging Narrative

The key to a successful proposal or presentation lies in how well you tell the story of your business idea. Every great pitch follows a clear, compelling narrative that draws the audience in, keeps them engaged, and builds toward a persuasive conclusion. Your goal is to make your ideas come to life through a well-structured story that your audience can easily follow and, more importantly, get excited about.

In this section, we'll explore how to structure your proposal or presentation like a great story—captivating from the start, logically organized, and ending with a memorable call to action.

1. Start with a Hook: Grab Attention Instantly

Just like any good story, your presentation needs to capture attention right from the start. The opening of your proposal or presentation is your opportunity to set the tone, spark curiosity, and make your audience want to hear more.

- **Begin with a bold statement or fact**: Start with something that immediately resonates with your audience. This could be a surprising statistic, a compelling problem, or a bold vision for the future. Make it relevant to your audience's interests and keep it concise.
  - o **Example**: "Did you know that 80% of businesses that fail cite poor cash flow management as the primary reason? Our

305

company is on a mission to change that by providing intuitive financial solutions that help small businesses thrive."

- **Ask a thought-provoking question**: Opening with a question encourages the audience to engage mentally and think about how your solution might address their needs or concerns.

  o **Example**: "What if you could cut your packaging costs by 30% while reducing your environmental footprint? We've developed a solution that does exactly that."

The goal is to set the stage for the rest of your presentation by creating intrigue and laying the foundation for your key points.

2. Establish the Problem: Identifying the Need or Challenge

Once you have your audience's attention, the next step is to clearly articulate the problem or challenge your business addresses. This is where you establish why your product or service is needed and why it's worth investing in.

- **Define the problem in relatable terms**: Use clear, concise language to describe the problem you're solving. Be specific and use data to back up your points if possible.

  o **Example**: "In the United States alone, businesses are spending over $10 billion annually on outdated, unsustainable packaging solutions. This is not only costly but also damaging to their brand image in a market increasingly focused on sustainability."

- **Show why the problem matters**: Explain why this issue is important to your audience, whether it's a pain point they experience, a gap in the market, or an emerging trend they need to be aware of. The more personal and relevant the problem feels to them, the more engaged they'll be.

This section helps create a sense of urgency—you're showing your audience that the problem exists and that something needs to be done about it.

3. Present Your Solution: The Hero of the Story

Now that you've outlined the problem, it's time to introduce your solution. This is the heart of your story—the part where your product or service steps in to solve the problem in a unique, compelling way.

- **Clearly define your solution**: Explain exactly what your product or service is and how it works. Be specific and avoid overly technical jargon—keep it simple and relatable.

  - **Example**: "Our biodegradable packaging is made from plant-based materials that reduce carbon emissions by 40% compared to traditional plastic packaging. It's fully customizable, affordable, and designed to meet the needs of small to mid-sized businesses."

- **Emphasize your unique value proposition**: Highlight what makes your solution stand out. What differentiates your business from competitors? What's your competitive edge?

  - **Example**: "Unlike competitors, we offer packaging that is not only eco-friendly but also costs 20% less, making it an affordable solution for businesses committed to sustainability without sacrificing profit margins."

This is your opportunity to show that **you have the solution** to the problem and that your approach is better, faster, or more innovative than others in the market.

4. Highlight Benefits: What's in It for Them?

After presenting your solution, take a moment to highlight the benefits and show the impact it will have on your audience or their business. This is where you translate features into tangible results.

- **Focus on key benefits**: Clearly explain how your solution solves the problem and improves your audience's situation. Whether it's saving time, reducing costs, increasing efficiency, or enhancing sustainability, focus on the benefits that matter most to your audience.

- o **Example**: "With our packaging, businesses can expect to reduce their packaging costs by up to 30% and boost their brand's reputation with eco-conscious consumers."

- **Use real-world examples or testimonials**: If possible, provide evidence of your solution's success, such as case studies, testimonials, or performance data.

  - o **Example**: "One of our clients, a mid-sized organic food company, cut their packaging costs by 25% and increased customer satisfaction by 15% after switching to our eco-friendly packaging."

This section helps your audience visualize the positive impact of your solution and understand how it directly benefits them.

5. Build Toward a Climax: Why Now?

As you move through your presentation, build momentum by reinforcing the need for action. This is the climax of your story—the point where your audience sees that the time to act is now.

- **Explain why the timing is right**: Highlight any market trends, emerging opportunities, or shifts in consumer behavior that make your solution timely and relevant.

  - o **Example**: "With governments worldwide cracking down on plastic waste and consumers demanding more sustainable products, the market for eco-friendly packaging is growing faster than ever. Now is the perfect time for businesses to make the switch."

This creates a sense of urgency and positions your solution as the answer to an immediate need.

6. End with a Strong Resolution: Call to Action

Every great story has a powerful ending, and in your presentation, this comes in the form of a clear, actionable next step. This is your call to action—the moment where you tell your audience exactly what you want them to do.

- **Be specific**: Whether you're asking for funding, a partnership, or a sale, make it clear what action you're asking for and why it's important.

  - ○ **Example**: "We're seeking $500,000 in funding to scale our production capabilities and bring our eco-friendly packaging solutions to more businesses across the country. Your investment will help us meet growing demand and create a more sustainable future for packaging."

- **Leave them with a memorable takeaway**: End with a powerful statement that reinforces the value of your business and reminds them why your solution matters.

  - ○ **Example**: "Together, we can reduce plastic waste, improve business efficiency, and build a more sustainable future—one package at a time."

A strong, confident close will leave your audience inspired, excited, and ready to take action.

Conclusion: Telling a Story That Resonates

Crafting a clear, engaging narrative is the key to delivering a winning proposal or presentation. By structuring your pitch like a story—with a hook, a clear problem, a compelling solution, and a call to action—you ensure that your audience stays engaged from start to finish.

Remember, every story is an opportunity to connect with your audience on a deeper level. Whether you're pitching to investors or presenting to potential clients, structure matters—and when done well, it will leave your audience wanting more and eager to take the next step with you.

Visuals that Wow: Designing Slides And Proposals That Stand Out

Visuals are one of the most powerful tools you have to make your proposal or presentation memorable and impactful. Well-designed visuals help simplify complex information, capture attention, and keep your audience engaged. In a world where attention spans are short, effective visuals can be the difference between a pitch that resonates and one that falls flat.

In this section, we'll explore how to design visually compelling slides and proposals that not only convey your message clearly but also add an extra layer of professionalism and polish to your presentation. Remember, your visuals should complement your narrative, not overwhelm it.

1. Keep It Clean and Simple: Less Is More

When it comes to visuals, simplicity is key. Overcrowded slides or pages filled with too much text can confuse or overwhelm your audience. The goal is to create a clean, easy-to-follow design that enhances your message, not distracts from it.

- **Limit text on slides**: Avoid cramming too much information onto a single slide. Use bullet points or short phrases rather than full paragraphs. Your slides should support what you're saying, not serve as a script.

  o **Example**: Instead of including three dense paragraphs about your product's benefits, use three bullet points to highlight the top advantages.

- **Use whitespace strategically**: Whitespace (empty space) is an important design element that gives your visuals room to breathe and helps guide the viewer's eye to the most important points. Don't be afraid of empty space—it creates a sense of clarity and focus.

- **Limit each slide to one key idea**: Focus on communicating one idea per slide. If you have multiple points to make, spread them across several slides rather than squeezing everything onto one. This helps your audience absorb information more easily.

  o **Example**: If you're explaining your revenue model, break it down into bite-sized steps over multiple slides instead of covering it all at once.

2. Use High-Quality Images and Graphics

Visuals are more than just words on a screen. Incorporating images, charts, and infographics can make your presentation more dynamic and engaging. However, it's important to use visuals thoughtfully—choose images that enhance your message and keep the design professional.

- **Use relevant, high-quality images**: Choose images that directly relate to your content. High-resolution, professional-looking images create a polished, credible impression. Avoid low-quality, grainy images or irrelevant stock photos.

    o **Example**: If you're pitching a sustainable product, include images that reflect your eco-friendly mission, such as visuals of renewable materials or clean environments.

- **Incorporate icons and infographics**: Icons and infographics are excellent tools for simplifying complex information. They can help you break down data, illustrate processes, or highlight key points in a visually appealing way.

    o **Example**: Instead of listing the steps of a process in text form, use a visual flowchart or infographic to map out each stage.

- **Be consistent with visuals**: Use a consistent style throughout your presentation. Stick to a unified color scheme, font selection, and image style to create a cohesive and professional look. Avoid mixing too many fonts or colors, as this can make your slides look cluttered or amateurish.

3. Use Data Visualizations for Impact

Numbers are important in any business proposal or presentation, but raw data alone can be difficult to interpret. Data visualizations—like charts, graphs, and tables—can help you present your data in a way that's clear, compelling, and easy to understand.

- **Choose the right type of chart**: Different types of charts serve different purposes. Use the one that best suits your data:

    o **Bar or column charts** are ideal for comparing quantities across different categories.

    o **Line charts** work well for showing trends over time.

    o **Pie charts** are great for illustrating proportions or percentages.

- ○ **Example**: If you're showing sales growth over time, a line chart will clearly illustrate the trend. If you're breaking down market share, a pie chart will effectively visualize the percentage each player holds.

- **Keep data visualizations simple**: While charts and graphs are great tools, it's important not to overcomplicate them. Stick to two or three key data points per chart, and make sure labels and numbers are large enough to be read easily from a distance.

  - ○ **Example**: Don't crowd your graph with too many lines or categories—focus on the most relevant data to your audience.

4. Leverage Color for Emphasis and Branding

Color is a powerful tool for guiding attention, evoking emotion, and reinforcing your brand identity. However, it needs to be used thoughtfully to avoid overwhelming the viewer.

- **Stick to a consistent color palette**: Choose a palette that reflects your brand's colors and stick to it throughout your presentation. This creates a sense of consistency and professionalism.

  - ○ **Example**: If your brand colors are green and blue, incorporate these colors into your headings, icons, and graphics. Avoid introducing too many new colors, as this can disrupt the flow and look unprofessional.

- **Use color to highlight key points**: Color can help guide your audience's attention. Use bold colors sparingly to emphasize the most important data points or elements, like highlighting a percentage increase or drawing attention to a specific part of a chart.

  - ○ **Example**: If you're showing a comparison chart, use a bold color for your company's numbers to make them stand out, while keeping competitors' data in a more neutral color.

- **Be mindful of readability**: Always ensure that your text is readable against the background color. For example, light text on a dark background can work well, but avoid low-contrast combinations like dark text on a dark background or light text on a light background.

5. Ensure Your Slides Flow Smoothly

Just as the narrative structure of your presentation needs to flow logically, so should the visual flow of your slides. Each slide should naturally lead into the next, maintaining a rhythm that keeps your audience engaged without abrupt transitions.

- **Transition smoothly between topics**: Use slides to create visual breaks and transitions between different sections of your presentation. This helps the audience understand when you're moving from one idea to the next and makes the overall structure clearer.

  o **Example**: If you're moving from the problem to the solution, use a simple transition slide with a clear headline like, "Introducing Our Solution."

- **Use consistent slide templates**: To ensure visual consistency, use the same template for similar slides (e.g., all "data" slides use the same layout, all "title" slides have the same format). This creates a seamless experience and avoids jarring shifts in design.

6. Tailor Your Visuals to Your Audience

Always design your presentation with your audience in mind. Visuals that work for a room full of tech-savvy investors might not be as effective for a broader, non-technical audience. Tailor your slides to ensure that they speak directly to the people you're presenting to.

- **Simplify for general audiences**: If your audience is less familiar with technical jargon or detailed data, focus on simple, high-level visuals that communicate the core message clearly.

- **Get detailed for experts**: If you're presenting to industry insiders, you may want to include more in-depth data visualizations or technical diagrams. However, always ensure your visuals are still clean and digestible.

Conclusion: Visuals That Elevate Your Story

Well-designed visuals can take your proposal or presentation from good to great, enhancing your message and keeping your audience engaged. By keeping your design clean, using high-quality images and data visualizations, and maintaining a consistent style, you'll create a visually appealing, professional presentation that supports your narrative without overshadowing it.

Remember, visuals should complement your story, not compete with it. Use them strategically to clarify complex information, emphasize key points, and make your presentation stand out—leaving a lasting impression on your audience.

Mastering Delivery: Engaging Your Audience with Confidence and Charisma

Crafting a compelling proposal or presentation is only half the battle; delivering it with confidence and charisma is what truly brings it to life. The way you present can be just as important as the content itself. Engaging your audience means building a connection, communicating your message effectively, and leaving a memorable impression that compels them to take action.

In this section, we'll explore the techniques that will help you master your delivery—from body language and voice control to audience interaction and managing nerves. Whether you're pitching to investors, clients, or a room full of colleagues, your delivery can be the key to winning them over.

1. Own the Room: Project Confidence from the Start

First impressions matter, and the moment you step up to present, your audience will begin to form an opinion about your credibility. Confidence is contagious; if you project confidence, your audience is more likely to trust what you're saying and engage with your message.

- **Start with a strong posture**: Stand tall, with your shoulders back and feet shoulder-width apart. Good posture not only helps you appear more confident but also improves your breathing and voice projection.

- o **Example**: Before starting, take a deep breath, smile, and make eye contact with your audience. This creates an immediate sense of control and composure.

- **Use open body language**: Keep your gestures natural and open. Avoid crossing your arms, fidgeting, or putting your hands in your pockets. These behaviors can signal discomfort or uncertainty.

- **Make eye contact**: Engaging with your audience through eye contact helps build a personal connection and shows that you're confident in your message. Try to make eye contact with different people in the room, rather than focusing on just one person or the screen.

  - o **Tip**: If making direct eye contact feels uncomfortable, look just above your audience's heads or focus on a friendly face.

2. Control Your Voice: Speak Clearly and with Purpose

Your voice is one of the most powerful tools you have when delivering a presentation. How you say something can be just as important as what you say. A strong, clear voice helps convey confidence and authority, while varying your tone keeps your audience engaged.

- **Speak clearly and at a moderate pace**: Speaking too quickly can make it difficult for your audience to follow along, while speaking too slowly can lose their attention. Aim for a moderate pace that allows your audience to absorb your message.

  - o **Example**: Practice your presentation out loud several times before the actual event, adjusting your speed until it feels natural and conversational.

- **Use tone variation**: Avoid a monotone delivery by varying your tone to emphasize key points. Raising or lowering your voice at the right moments can add energy and make your presentation more dynamic.

  - o **Tip**: When introducing an exciting or important point, speak with a slightly elevated tone to convey enthusiasm. Conversely, when discussing something serious, lower your tone to add gravity.

- **Pause for impact**: Don't be afraid to pause. Pausing after key points gives your audience a moment to digest information and creates emphasis. It also gives you time to breathe and collect your thoughts.

  - o **Example**: After sharing a powerful statistic or presenting your solution, pause for a moment. This gives your audience time to fully absorb the information before you continue.

3. Engage with Your Audience: Make It a Conversation

A great presentation feels less like a lecture and more like a **conversation**. Engaging your audience by involving them in the discussion helps maintain their interest and makes your message more memorable.

- **Ask rhetorical questions**: Pose questions that make your audience think or reflect on what you're saying. Even if they're not answering out loud, questions can mentally engage your audience and make your points more relatable.

  - o **Example**: "How much time could your business save if you automated this process?" This kind of question encourages your audience to think about their own experiences and connect with your solution.

- **Invite audience interaction**: Depending on the setting, you can invite your audience to participate by asking for a show of hands or encouraging questions. This creates a more dynamic and interactive atmosphere.

  - o **Example**: "How many of you have faced this challenge in your business? Let's talk about how we can solve it together."

- **Use storytelling to connect**: People remember stories far better than they remember facts and figures. Share personal anecdotes, client success stories, or real-world examples that make your points come to life.

  - o **Example**: "One of our clients was spending hours every week managing inventory manually. After switching to our automated system, they saved 10 hours per week, allowing them to focus on growing their business."

4. Use Body Language to Reinforce Your Message

Your nonverbal communication is just as important as what you say. Positive body language helps reinforce your message and keep your audience engaged, while negative body language can detract from your credibility.

- **Use gestures naturally**: Hand gestures can help emphasize key points and make your presentation more dynamic. However, be mindful not to overuse them or make overly large gestures that might seem exaggerated.

  - o **Tip**: Practice your presentation in front of a mirror or record yourself to observe your gestures. Aim for movements that feel natural and support your message without distracting from it.

- **Move with purpose**: If you're presenting in a large space, consider moving around the stage to engage different parts of the audience. However, make sure your movement is purposeful and not overly repetitive.

  - o **Example**: If you're transitioning to a new section of your presentation, take a few steps to the side. This signals to your audience that you're moving to a new topic and keeps their attention.

5. Manage Nerves and Stay Calm

Even seasoned presenters get nervous, but the key is learning how to manage your nerves so that they don't interfere with your performance. The more you can stay calm and centered, the better you'll be able to deliver your message with confidence and clarity.

- **Breathe deeply**: Deep, steady breaths help calm your nerves and keep your voice strong. If you feel anxious before or during your presentation, take a moment to breathe deeply, in through your nose and out through your mouth.

   o   **Tip**: Practice deep breathing exercises before your presentation to calm your nerves and steady your breathing.

- **Focus on your message, not yourself**: Shift your focus away from your own nervousness and instead concentrate on delivering value to your audience. By focusing on the message you're sharing, you'll feel more centered and less self-conscious.

   o   **Example**: Remind yourself that you're the expert in the room and that your audience is there to learn from you. This mental shift can help reduce anxiety.

- **Practice, practice, practice**: The best way to build confidence and reduce nervousness is to practice your presentation multiple times. The more familiar you are with your material, the more natural and comfortable you'll feel during delivery.

   o   **Tip**: Practice in front of friends, family, or colleagues who can give you feedback, or record yourself and watch it back to identify areas for improvement.

Conclusion: Delivering with Confidence and Charisma

Mastering your delivery is about more than just conveying information—it's about building a connection with your audience, engaging them with your message, and leaving them inspired to take action. By using confident body language, controlling your voice, interacting with your audience, and staying calm under pressure, you can deliver a presentation that's not only persuasive but also memorable.

With practice and attention to these techniques, you'll be able to captivate your audience, make a powerful impression, and ensure that your proposals and presentations hit the mark every time.

Closing Strong: Ending with a Call to Action That Seals the Deal

The final moments of your presentation or proposal are your last chance to leave a lasting impact. A powerful **conclusion** not only summarizes the key points you've made but also motivates your audience to take action. Whether you're pitching for funding, seeking a partnership, or aiming for a sale, your closing should inspire confidence and create a sense of urgency.

In this section, we'll explore how to close your presentation with a strong, memorable call to action (CTA) that encourages your audience to move forward with you.

1. Summarize Your Key Points

Before you dive into your call to action, take a moment to recap the main points of your presentation. This doesn't mean rehashing everything in detail, but rather, briefly restating the most important ideas to ensure they stick in your audience's mind.

- **Highlight the problem and your solution**: Remind your audience of the challenge or need you've identified and how your business provides the perfect solution.

  - **Example**: "To recap, businesses today are struggling to find affordable, eco-friendly packaging solutions that meet their sustainability goals. Our innovative packaging addresses this problem by offering a customizable, biodegradable option that reduces costs by 20%."

- **Emphasize the benefits and value**: Quickly touch on the key benefits your solution provides and why it's the best choice for your audience.

  - **Example**: "With our solution, businesses can save time, reduce waste, and enhance their brand's reputation for sustainability, all while increasing profitability."

By restating these key points, you reinforce the value of your proposal and ensure your audience is clear on the impact your solution can have.

2. Make Your Ask Clear and Direct

After summarizing your key points, transition smoothly into your call to action. This is the part where you tell your audience exactly what you want from them. Be clear, specific, and confident in your request, leaving no room for ambiguity.

- **Tailor your CTA to your audience**: Depending on the nature of your presentation, your CTA might be asking for funding, requesting a meeting, securing a sale, or forming a partnership. Whatever it is, make sure it's actionable and tailored to the specific goals of your presentation.

  - **Example** (For investors): "We're seeking $500,000 in funding to scale production and expand into new markets. Your investment will help us meet the growing demand for sustainable packaging solutions and position us for long-term growth."

  - **Example** (For a sale): "We're offering an exclusive 20% discount for early adopters who sign up within the next 30 days. This is the perfect opportunity to join us in reducing waste and boosting brand sustainability."

- **Create urgency**: A good CTA often includes a sense of urgency that encourages the audience to take action now, rather than waiting. This could be tied to limited-time offers, early-bird incentives, or the unique opportunity your proposal offers.

  - **Example**: "With the eco-friendly packaging market growing by 10% each year, now is the time to act. We're on the verge of a major market shift, and your investment can help us lead that transformation."

3. Leave Them Inspired and Excited

Your final words should leave your audience feeling inspired and excited about the possibilities your business offers. This is your chance to create an emotional connection and remind them why your proposal matters.

- **Express your passion and vision**: Share your excitement for the future and remind your audience of the larger impact your business can have.

- o **Example**: "At [Your Company], we believe that businesses can make a real difference in the fight against plastic waste. Together, we can build a future where sustainability is the standard, not the exception. We're excited to partner with you in making that vision a reality."

- **End on a high note**: Finish with a strong, uplifting statement that leaves a positive impression. Your goal is to ensure that your audience walks away feeling motivated and ready to engage further with your business.

  - o **Example**: "We're ready to take the next step in revolutionizing the packaging industry, and we'd love to have you on board. Let's make the future greener—together."

By leaving your audience with a clear action and a sense of excitement, you increase the likelihood that they'll follow through and take the next step.

4. Follow Up After the Presentation

Even the best presentations benefit from a timely follow-up. After delivering your call to action, ensure that you have a clear plan for following up with your audience. Whether it's sending a thank-you email, scheduling a follow-up meeting, or providing additional information, proactive follow-up shows your professionalism and commitment.

- **Tip**: Have a follow-up plan in place before your presentation, including key contacts and a timeline for reaching out. Be prompt but not pushy, and ensure that any follow-up communication reinforces the main points of your presentation.

Conclusion: Seal the Deal with Confidence

The way you end your presentation can make all the difference. A strong, clear call to action combined with a memorable and inspiring conclusion will leave your audience feeling excited about the possibilities your business offers—and ready to take the next step.

By summarizing your key points, making a direct ask, and expressing enthusiasm for the future, you create a powerful close that seals the deal and motivates your audience to take action. Whether you're seeking investment, partnerships, or sales, mastering the art of the close will ensure your proposals and presentations leave a lasting impact, driving your business toward success.

Quick Tips and Recap

- **Start strong**: Capture your audience's attention from the very beginning with a bold statement, question, or compelling hook.

- **Structure your presentation like a story**: Build your narrative with a clear beginning, middle, and end, leading up to a powerful conclusion.

- **Use simple and clean visuals**: Design slides that are visually appealing and easy to follow, with minimal text and impactful images or data.

- **Speak with confidence and clarity**: Use your voice effectively, varying your tone and pace to maintain engagement, and pause for emphasis when needed.

- **Engage your audience**: Make your presentation interactive by asking questions, encouraging participation, and maintaining eye contact to create a connection.

- **Control your body language**: Use open, confident gestures and good posture to reinforce your message and project authority.

- **Make your call to action clear**: Be specific about what you want your audience to do, and create a sense of urgency or opportunity around your request.

- **End with inspiration**: Leave your audience feeling excited about your proposal by concluding with a strong, memorable statement that emphasizes your vision and passion.

- **Follow up after the presentation**: Ensure that you have a plan to follow up with your audience to continue the conversation and solidify their commitment.

By mastering these tips, you'll be equipped to deliver proposals and presentations that not only inform but also inspire and motivate your audience to take action.

CHAPTER FOURTEEN

The Art of the Deal: Effective Communication and Negotiation

"Effective communication turns negotiations into win-win situations; it's all about making everyone feel they've gained something valuable."— LEE CLOW, ADVERTISING LEGEND

Welcome to the thrilling world of communication and negotiation, where your words are your most powerful tools and your charm is your secret weapon. Think of it as a high-stakes game of chess, but with fewer pawns and more power moves. This is where you transform mere conversations into artful dialogues and negotiations into masterful deals.

In this chapter, we'll dive into the fine art of persuasion and negotiation with the finesse of a seasoned diplomat. Imagine your communication strategy as a symphony—every word and gesture perfectly orchestrated to create harmony and achieve your goals. You'll learn how to craft messages that resonate, how to listen with the keen ear of a maestro, and how to negotiate like a pro who's always three steps ahead.

We'll explore techniques for turning tough conversations into opportunities and transforming disagreements into agreements. With a dash of charisma and a sprinkle of strategy, you'll find yourself navigating negotiations like a virtuoso, leaving a trail of satisfied partners and closed deals in your wake. So, put on your best negotiation face, and let's turn every conversation into a chance to score big!

Crafting Your Message: Community with Clarity and Confidence

In any negotiation or business conversation, how you communicate can make or break a deal. It's not just about what you say, but how you say it. The key to success lies in crafting your message with clarity, confidence, and purpose. Whether you're delivering a pitch, proposing a solution, or negotiating terms, your words need to be intentional, persuasive, and easy to understand.

In this section, we'll explore how to communicate with precision and make sure your message resonates with your audience, setting the stage for successful negotiations and deals.

1. Know Your Goal: Be Clear About Your Intentions

Before you enter any conversation, it's essential to know exactly what you want to achieve. Whether you're closing a deal, negotiating terms, or resolving a conflict, being clear on your goals ensures that your message stays focused and purposeful.

- **Identify your key points**: What are the most important things you want to communicate? Boil your message down to two or three key takeaways to avoid overwhelming your audience with too much information.

    o **Example**: If you're negotiating a business partnership, your key points might be the mutual benefits, your vision for the collaboration, and the specific terms you want to achieve.

- **Tailor your message to your audience**: Understanding who you're talking to allows you to adjust your tone, language, and focus. Are you speaking to a potential investor, a client, or a colleague? Each audience requires a slightly different approach.

  - **Example**: When talking to an investor, focus on ROI and growth potential. When speaking to a client, emphasize value and results.

2. Keep It Simple and Direct: Avoid Jargon and Ambiguity

Clear communication is often the most effective communication. When crafting your message, simplicity is key. Avoid industry jargon, unnecessary complexity, or vague language that could confuse or alienate your audience.

- **Use clear, concise language**: Focus on delivering your message in simple, straightforward terms. The clearer your communication, the more likely it is that your audience will understand and align with your point of view.

  - **Example**: Instead of saying, "We aim to optimize our supply chain to facilitate resource reallocation for enhanced productivity," say, "We plan to improve our supply chain to reduce costs and increase efficiency."

- **Be direct about what you want**: Don't beat around the bush—get to the point quickly. Let your audience know what you're asking for or proposing from the start.

  - **Example**: "We're proposing a partnership where we handle distribution in exchange for a 20% share of revenue."

By keeping your language simple and direct, you not only avoid confusion but also project confidence and authority.

3. Frame Your Message Positively: Focus on Solutions

Effective communicators know how to frame their message in a way that emphasizes positives rather than negatives. Even if you're discussing challenges or tough situations, the key is to shift the focus toward solutions and opportunities rather than dwelling on problems.

- **Present challenges as opportunities**: Reframe problems as chances to create value or achieve growth. This shows that you're proactive and solution-oriented, which can be more persuasive to the other party.

    o **Example**: Instead of saying, "Our competitors are outpacing us in market share," you could say, "We have an opportunity to capture market share by adopting a more aggressive marketing strategy."

- **Focus on the benefits**: Whether you're proposing an idea, asking for something, or negotiating terms, always highlight the benefits of your message. Help your audience see what's in it for them.

    o **Example**: "By partnering with us, you'll gain access to our distribution network, which will help you reach new customers and increase your market presence."

By framing your message positively, you create a more inviting conversation that encourages agreement and collaboration.

4. Be Confident in Your Delivery: Own Your Message

No matter how clear and well-crafted your message is, it won't resonate unless you deliver it with confidence. Confidence shows that you believe in what you're saying and that you're capable of backing up your claims. Here's how to ensure your delivery matches the strength of your message:

- **Use a strong, steady tone**: Speak in a clear, steady voice that projects confidence. Avoid raising your voice too much or using a questioning tone unless you're genuinely asking a question. A confident tone shows you're in control of the conversation.

    o **Example**: Instead of saying, "I think we should consider this approach?" say, "This approach will help us achieve our goals more effectively."

- **Watch your body language**: Nonverbal cues are just as important as the words you use. Stand or sit tall, maintain eye contact, and use open gestures to reinforce your confidence. Avoid fidgeting or crossing your arms, as these can signal uncertainty or defensiveness.

  o **Example**: When making a key point, use subtle hand gestures to emphasize your words and lean slightly forward to show engagement.

- **Avoid filler words**: Words like "um," "uh," "like," and "you know" can undermine your message and make you seem unsure of yourself. Practice speaking clearly and concisely, especially when delivering important points.

  o **Tip**: If you need a moment to collect your thoughts, pause briefly rather than using filler words.

5. Adapt to Feedback: Stay Flexible and Responsive

Effective communication is a two-way street. While it's important to have a well-crafted message, you also need to be flexible and adapt based on the feedback and reactions you get from your audience.

- **Be open to questions**: Encourage your audience to ask questions or seek clarification. This helps ensure that they fully understand your message and can provide valuable feedback or insights.

  o **Example**: "Does this approach make sense to you? I'm happy to explain any part of it in more detail."

- **Listen and adjust**: Pay attention to verbal and nonverbal cues from your audience. If you notice confusion, disengagement, or disagreement, be prepared to adjust your approach or clarify your message. This demonstrates that you're listening and willing to collaborate.

  o **Tip**: If someone seems uncertain, ask a follow-up question to explore their concerns, like "How do you feel about this part of the proposal?"

By staying flexible and responsive to feedback, you create a more collaborative and effective communication dynamic.

Conclusion: Communicate with Clarity and Purpose

In the world of business and negotiation, your words can be your most powerful asset—when used wisely. By crafting a clear, confident message that's tailored to your audience and delivered with precision, you set yourself up for success in any negotiation or conversation.

Remember to keep your language simple, frame your message positively, and project confidence through both your words and body language. And most importantly, stay open to feedback and adapt when necessary. With these techniques, you'll be able to communicate with clarity and purpose, turning everyday conversations into opportunities to achieve your goals.

The Power of Active Listening: Understanding Before You Persuade

While delivering your message with clarity and confidence is important, the real art of communication and negotiation lies in listening. In high-stakes conversations, it's tempting to focus on persuading the other party, but true power comes from understanding their needs, concerns, and motivations first. Active listening isn't just about hearing words; it's about picking up on tone, emotion, and underlying concerns, and using that information to shape a more compelling argument.

In this section, we'll explore how active listening can help you become a more effective communicator and negotiator. By learning to understand before you persuade, you create a collaborative environment where the other party feels heard and valued, which can ultimately lead to stronger agreements and partnerships.

1. What Is Active Listening?

Active listening goes beyond simply hearing someone speak. It involves fully focusing on the speaker, engaging with their message, and responding in a way that shows you understand their point of view. In negotiations, active listening helps you gain valuable insights into the other party's goals, concerns, and potential objections, giving you the tools to shape your responses more effectively.

- **Engage fully**: Make an effort to give the speaker your undivided attention. This means not interrupting, avoiding distractions (like checking your phone), and using nonverbal cues (like nodding) to show that you're listening.

  o **Tip**: Maintain eye contact, lean slightly forward, and nod occasionally to show you're actively engaged in the conversation.

- **Listen to understand, not just respond**: Often, we listen only with the intent to reply, but active listening requires that you focus on understanding the speaker's perspective before formulating your response.

  o **Example**: "What I'm hearing is that you're concerned about the project timeline. Can you tell me more about what specific challenges you see in meeting the deadline?"

By listening to understand, you create a space where the other party feels heard, which makes them more open to considering your perspective in return.

2. Ask Clarifying Questions: Dig Deeper into Their Needs

Asking clarifying questions is a key part of active listening. It shows that you're genuinely interested in understanding the speaker's point of view and allows you to uncover deeper motivations or concerns that might not be immediately obvious. These insights can be incredibly valuable in negotiations, helping you identify areas of alignment or possible compromise.

- **Ask open-ended questions**: These questions encourage the other party to elaborate on their thoughts and feelings, giving you more context and understanding.

  o **Example**: "Can you explain a bit more about what's most important to you in this deal?" or "What are your biggest priorities for this partnership?"

- **Clarify uncertainties**: If something isn't clear, ask for clarification. This not only prevents misunderstandings but also signals that you care about getting the details right.

  o **Example**: "I just want to make sure I understand—are you saying that the current pricing structure won't work because of budget constraints, or is it more about timing?"

By asking clarifying questions, you dig beneath the surface and get to the heart of what really matters to the other party, allowing you to address their concerns more effectively.

3. Listen for Underlying Emotions and Concerns

In any negotiation, it's essential to listen not only to what is being said but also to how it's being said. Pay attention to the other party's tone of voice, body language, and emotional cues to understand the full context of their message. Often, people's concerns or reservations aren't explicitly stated but can be inferred through these nonverbal signals.

- **Watch for nonverbal cues**: Notice whether the speaker's body language matches their words. Are they saying they're comfortable with a proposal, but their crossed arms or hesitant tone suggest otherwise?

  o **Example**: If someone agrees to a point but looks uncomfortable or sighs, you might say, "I noticed you seem hesitant. Is there something about the proposal that's giving you pause?"

- **Acknowledge emotions**: If you sense frustration, excitement, or concern in the other party's tone, address it. Acknowledging emotions helps build rapport and shows that you're paying attention to their full experience, not just the words they're saying.

  o **Example**: "I can tell that this delay is really frustrating for you, and I understand how important it is to stay on schedule. Let's see if we can find a way to keep things moving."

Understanding the emotions behind the words allows you to respond in a way that is empathetic and thoughtful, which can ease tension and build trust.

4. Paraphrase and Reflect: Confirm Understanding

One of the most powerful active listening techniques is paraphrasing what the other person has said to confirm your understanding. By summarizing their points in your own words, you show that you've truly listened and are making an effort to grasp their perspective. It also gives the other party a chance to correct any misunderstandings before moving forward.

- **Paraphrase key points**: After the other party has explained their position, summarize what you've heard to ensure you're both on the same page.

  - **Example**: "So, just to make sure I understand correctly, you're saying that you're willing to move forward with the deal if we can extend the payment terms to 60 days instead of 30, is that right?"

- **Reflect emotions**: In addition to paraphrasing facts, you can reflect the emotions you've picked up on. This can be particularly helpful in situations where the other party may not have explicitly expressed their feelings.

  - **Example**: "It sounds like you're feeling uncertain about committing to this timeline because of your current workload. Is that accurate?"

Paraphrasing and reflecting back what you've heard helps ensure that you're both aligned and provides a strong foundation for continuing the conversation.

5. Use What You've Learned to Persuade

Once you've actively listened and gathered valuable insights into the other party's needs and concerns, you can tailor your arguments and proposals to address those specific points. By incorporating what you've learned through active listening, you demonstrate that you're collaborative and flexible, which can make your arguments more persuasive and increase the likelihood of reaching an agreement.

- **Address their concerns directly**: If the other party has expressed a specific concern or need, show them how your solution addresses it.

- ○ **Example**: "I understand that timing is critical for you, and that's why we're proposing a phased rollout to ensure we meet your deadlines without sacrificing quality."

- **Highlight shared goals**: By identifying common ground and emphasizing shared goals, you can create a sense of alignment and cooperation.

  - ○ **Example**: "It sounds like we both want to ensure a smooth implementation with minimal disruption to your team. Let's work together on a schedule that meets both our needs."

By using the information you've gathered through active listening, you can create proposals that are more likely to resonate with the other party and lead to successful outcomes.

Conclusion: Listen First, Persuade Second

Active listening is the foundation of effective communication and negotiation. By truly hearing and understanding the other party's perspective before trying to persuade them, you build trust, gain valuable insights, and create a more collaborative environment.

By asking clarifying questions, paying attention to emotions, paraphrasing to confirm understanding, and using what you've learned to shape your proposals, you'll not only become a better listener but also a more persuasive negotiator. In the end, understanding before you persuade paves the way for stronger agreements and more successful outcomes in any negotiation.

Mastering the Negotiation Dance: Strategies for Creating Win-Win Outcomes

Negotiation is often seen as a tug-of-war, but the most successful deals happen when both parties walk away feeling like they've gained something valuable. In business, the goal is not just to win at the other party's expense but to find a solution where everyone benefits—the true art of creating a win-win outcome.

In this section, we'll explore strategies that will help you master the delicate balance of negotiation. Whether you're discussing terms with a client, bargaining with a supplier, or closing a deal with an investor, these techniques will help you negotiate agreements that satisfy both sides, ensuring long-term partnerships and mutual success.

1. Do Your Homework: Preparation Is Key

Before entering any negotiation, it's essential to prepare thoroughly. Understanding your own goals and limits, as well as the other party's, allows you to negotiate from a position of strength. Preparation shows that you're serious, informed, and ready to engage in a meaningful discussion.

- **Understand your objectives**: What are you hoping to achieve from the negotiation? Clearly define your ideal outcome, acceptable compromises, and absolute limits (your bottom line). This will help guide your strategy.

    o **Example**: If you're negotiating a partnership deal, your ideal outcome might be a 50-50 revenue split, but you're willing to go as low as 40-60 if other terms are favorable.

- **Research the other party's needs**: Understanding the other side's motivations, goals, and potential constraints allows you to anticipate what they'll ask for and what you can offer in return. The more you know about their business, their market, and their pressures, the better equipped you'll be to find common ground.

    o **Example**: If you know that the other party is struggling with high production costs, you might offer a solution that reduces their expenses in exchange for favorable pricing terms.

- **Prepare for objections**: Anticipate the other party's concerns and objections, and be ready with solutions or compromises. This helps keep the conversation moving forward, even if disagreements arise.

    o **Example**: If you expect pushback on pricing, prepare alternative payment structures, such as a discount for early payment or flexible installment options.

2. Create a Collaborative Atmosphere: It's Not a Battle

One of the most important mindsets in negotiation is to view it as a collaborative effort rather than a battle. Instead of positioning yourself as an adversary, focus on building a relationship where both sides work together to find a mutually beneficial solution.

- **Use inclusive language**: Words matter. Instead of saying "I need" or "you must," use language that positions both parties as partners working toward a shared goal.

  - **Example**: "How can we structure this deal so that it benefits both of us?" or "Let's find a solution that works for both our teams."

- **Seek common ground early**: Start by discussing the areas where you already agree. Finding common ground helps create a positive tone and builds momentum toward resolving the more challenging issues.

  - **Example**: "It sounds like we both agree that the timeline is critical. Now, let's figure out how we can ensure the budget meets both of our needs."

- **Frame the negotiation as problem-solving**: Instead of viewing the negotiation as a win-lose scenario, position it as a problem you're solving together. This encourages creative solutions and collaboration rather than confrontation.

  - **Example**: "We're facing a challenge with the delivery schedule, but if we can work together on logistics, I think we can find a way to meet the deadline."

3. Make Concessions Wisely: Trade, Don't Give Away

In any negotiation, you'll need to make concessions, but the key is to do so in a way that creates value for both sides. When you make a concession, aim to get something in return rather than giving up something without a trade-off.

- **Don't make concessions too early**: Resist the urge to offer concessions right away, especially if you're trying to build leverage. Wait until you've gathered enough information to know what the other party values most, and then use concessions strategically.

- o **Example**: If the other party wants a discount on your services, don't agree to it immediately. Instead, ask what's most important to them and offer the discount in exchange for a longer-term contract.

- **Tie concessions to specific requests**: When you make a concession, clearly link it to something you need in return. This keeps the negotiation balanced and ensures that both parties are gaining something.

- o **Example**: "I'm willing to reduce the price by 10%, but in return, I'd need a commitment for at least a 12-month contract."

- **Give smaller concessions first**: Start with smaller, less critical concessions before moving to the bigger ones. This allows you to maintain leverage while showing flexibility.

- o **Example**: "We can adjust the delivery schedule slightly if that helps, but I'd need to revisit the cost structure if we're changing the timeline."

By making concessions wisely, you protect your interests while showing a willingness to work together.

4. Look for Creative Solutions: Think Beyond the Basics

Win-win outcomes often come from thinking outside the box. Instead of getting stuck on a specific issue, look for creative solutions that satisfy both parties. This requires flexibility, creativity, and a willingness to explore options that may not have been obvious at the start.

- **Expand the options**: If the negotiation hits a roadblock, think about what other variables you can introduce to the conversation. This could involve adjusting payment terms, offering additional services, or exploring new ways to collaborate.

- o **Example**: If you're stuck on price, consider offering something of value beyond just cost, like free training, extended warranties, or a bundled package that provides more value at the same price point.

- **Use "if-then" propositions**: If you're unsure whether the other party will accept your proposal, offer conditional agreements. This opens the door to creative solutions while ensuring that both sides' needs are met.

    o **Example**: "If you can increase the order size, then I can offer you a larger discount."

- **Identify non-monetary value**: Not every concession has to be financial. Offering non-monetary value can help you reach a win-win outcome without sacrificing profits.

    o **Example**: "We can't lower the price any further, but we can offer additional customization options that add value to your product."

Creative solutions help both sides walk away feeling satisfied, even if the original terms couldn't be met.

5. Know When to Walk Away: Protect Your Bottom Line

Not every negotiation will result in a deal, and that's okay. Part of being an effective negotiator is knowing when it's time to walk away. If the other party's demands are unreasonable or the deal simply doesn't make sense for your business, it's better to step back than to agree to terms that don't align with your goals.

- **Recognize your BATNA**: BATNA stands for Best Alternative to a Negotiated Agreement. It's the fallback plan you'll rely on if the current negotiation doesn't result in a deal. Knowing your BATNA gives you confidence and clarity about when to walk away.

    o **Example**: "If we can't agree on the terms today, we have a backup supplier who can meet our needs, but I'd prefer to work with you if we can find common ground."

- **Stay firm on your non-negotiables**: While flexibility is key to a win-win outcome, there will always be certain terms that you can't compromise on, such as price thresholds or specific delivery requirements. Identify these non-negotiables early and be prepared to walk away if they're not met.

- o **Example**: "Our budget can't exceed $50,000 for this project. If we can't make it work within that range, we'll need to explore other options."

- **Remain professional and open to future opportunities**: Even if the negotiation doesn't result in a deal, keep the relationship positive and professional. Leaving the door open for future opportunities allows you to revisit the conversation if circumstances change.

- o **Example**: "I understand that we're not able to come to an agreement today, but I'd love to stay in touch and explore other opportunities to work together in the future."

Knowing when to walk away protects your business from making bad deals while maintaining positive relationships for future negotiations.

Conclusion: Creating Win-Win Outcomes in Negotiation

Mastering the negotiation dance means understanding that the goal isn't to "win" at the expense of the other party, but to create a solution where everyone benefits. By preparing thoroughly, fostering a collaborative atmosphere, making strategic concessions, exploring creative solutions, and knowing when to walk away, you can negotiate deals that strengthen relationships and lead to long-term success.

Negotiating with a win-win mindset ensures that both sides leave the table feeling valued and satisfied, paving the way for more successful partnerships and future deals.

Closing the Deal: Turning Conversations into Commitments

Closing a deal is the moment where all the preparation, communication, and negotiation come together. It's the final step in transforming discussions into agreements and conversations into concrete commitments. But closing a deal requires more than simply agreeing to terms—it's about instilling confidence in the other party, ensuring clarity, and securing a commitment that sticks. In this section, we'll explore the strategies for closing a deal effectively, ensuring that both parties walk away satisfied and ready to move forward.

1. Recognize the Right Moment to Close

Knowing when to close a deal is critical. If you push too early, you risk leaving unresolved concerns on the table; if you wait too long, the opportunity might slip away. The key is to recognize the signals that indicate your counterpart is ready to commit.

- **Watch for buying signals**: These are verbal or nonverbal cues that indicate the other party is ready to move forward. They might ask detailed questions about implementation, request next steps, or start talking in terms of "we" instead of "you."

  - **Example**: "How soon can we get the contract signed?" or "We'd need to have the first shipment delivered by the 15th. Is that possible?"

- **Summarize agreed-upon terms**: Before moving to the close, briefly summarize what's been agreed upon to ensure that both parties are aligned. This reinforces the progress you've made and sets the stage for finalizing the deal.

  - **Example**: "So, we've agreed on a 12-month contract with quarterly reviews and a 5% discount for early payment. Does that cover everything from your perspective?"

By recognizing when the conversation has naturally reached a point of agreement, you can move to the close with confidence.

2. Use a Direct and Confident Close

Once you've identified the right moment, it's time to move in with a direct and confident close. This is the point where you ask for the commitment and transition from discussing possibilities to finalizing the deal. A clear, decisive close leaves little room for hesitation and signals that you're ready to move forward.

- **Use confident language**: Instead of asking whether the other party is ready to move forward, assume that they are. This creates momentum and signals that you're both on the same page.

    o **Example**: "Let's go ahead and get the contract signed so we can start implementing the plan."

- **Offer options to close**: If the other party seems hesitant, offer closing options to give them flexibility. This allows them to feel in control of the decision while still moving toward a commitment.

    o **Example**: "Would you prefer to sign the contract today, or would it be easier to send it over by email for you to review one last time?"

- **Address any last-minute concerns**: Sometimes, the other party may have lingering questions or concerns that haven't been fully addressed. Invite them to voice any final issues so you can resolve them before closing.

    o **Example**: "Before we finalize everything, is there anything else you'd like to clarify or discuss?"

A direct, confident close demonstrates that you're serious about the deal and ready to move to the next phase.

3. Provide Clear Next Steps

After securing verbal agreement, the next step is to turn that agreement into action. Providing clear next steps ensures that both parties know exactly what happens after the deal is closed and helps avoid any misunderstandings or delays.

- **Outline immediate actions**: Clearly communicate what will happen next, whether that's signing a contract, making a payment, or setting up a meeting to finalize details.

    o **Example**: "Great! I'll send over the final contract today, and once it's signed, we can schedule the onboarding session for next week."

- **Set a timeline**: Providing a specific timeline helps keep things on track and ensures that both parties are committed to moving forward within an agreed-upon timeframe.

  o **Example**: "Let's aim to have everything signed and the first payment processed by the end of the week. Does that timeline work for you?"

- **Assign responsibilities**: Make it clear who is responsible for each action item. This ensures that nothing falls through the cracks and that both sides are accountable for keeping the process moving.

  o **Example**: "I'll handle sending the contract, and if you could send over the payment details, we'll be all set to proceed."

Providing clear next steps not only solidifies the deal but also sets the tone for a smooth and professional relationship moving forward.

4. Solidify the Commitment with a Written Agreement

Verbal agreements are important, but in business, written agreements are essential. Once both parties have agreed on the terms, make sure to formalize the deal in writing. This ensures that everything is clearly documented and helps prevent any misunderstandings or disputes down the line.

- **Send a formal contract**: As soon as possible, follow up on the verbal agreement with a formal contract or agreement that outlines the terms discussed. Be prompt in sending it to maintain momentum and show professionalism.

  o **Example**: "I'll have the contract drafted and sent to you by the end of the day. Let's aim to have it signed by Friday so we can move forward."

- **Include key details**: Make sure the contract includes all the critical details discussed during the negotiation, including pricing, deadlines, deliverables, and any special terms or conditions.

- ○ **Tip**: It's a good idea to have a standard contract template ready to go, so you can quickly customize it based on the specific deal and avoid delays.

- **Confirm receipt and agreement**: Once the contract is sent, follow up to confirm that it's been received and that there are no issues or questions. This helps ensure that the deal moves forward smoothly.

  - ○ **Example**: "Just checking in to make sure you received the contract. Let me know if you have any questions or if everything looks good to sign."

By formalizing the commitment in writing, you protect both parties and ensure that the agreement is clear, transparent, and legally binding.

5. Maintain Momentum Post-Deal

Closing the deal is just the beginning of your relationship with the other party. After the deal is finalized, it's important to maintain momentum and follow through on your commitments. This helps build trust and sets the stage for a successful, long-term partnership.

- **Follow up promptly**: After the contract is signed, follow up with a message that reiterates your excitement about the deal and outlines the next steps in more detail. This keeps the momentum going and reassures the other party that you're committed to delivering on your promises.

  - ○ **Example**: "We're thrilled to be working with you! Now that everything is signed, we'll move forward with setting up the kickoff meeting next week. I'll send over the details by tomorrow."

- **Deliver on your promises**: Make sure that your first actions after the deal are delivered on time and as promised. This establishes your credibility and sets the tone for a positive working relationship.

  - ○ **Example**: If you promised to send onboarding materials or set up a meeting, make sure these actions happen promptly and efficiently.

- **Stay in communication**: Regular updates after the deal is closed help reinforce the relationship and show that you're proactive and engaged. Keep the lines of communication open to ensure a smooth process.

    o **Example**: "Just wanted to give you an update—we've completed the initial setup, and everything is on track for our next milestone. Let me know if you need anything in the meantime."

By maintaining momentum and staying proactive, you solidify the relationship and ensure that the deal transitions smoothly into successful implementation.

Conclusion: Closing with Confidence and Commitment

Closing a deal is more than just securing an agreement—it's about turning words into action and ensuring that both parties are confident in the path forward. By recognizing the right moment to close, delivering a direct and confident close, providing clear next steps, formalizing the agreement in writing, and maintaining momentum post-deal, you create a solid foundation for a successful partnership.

Mastering the art of closing the deal ensures that your negotiations result in real, actionable commitments, paving the way for long-term success and strong business relationships. Whether you're finalizing a contract or securing a handshake agreement, these strategies will help you close the deal with confidence and clarity.

Quick Tips and Recap

- **Recognize buying signals**: Watch for cues that the other party is ready to commit, such as detailed questions or agreement on key terms.

- **Use confident, direct language**: Move the conversation toward closure with clear and assertive statements like, "Let's go ahead and finalize this."

- **Summarize agreed terms**: Ensure clarity by briefly recapping what's been agreed upon before moving to the close.

- **Offer closing options**: If the other party hesitates, give them choices to encourage commitment, such as signing now or reviewing the contract before the final signature.

- **Provide clear next steps**: Outline exactly what needs to happen next, who is responsible, and the timeline for moving forward.

- **Formalize the agreement**: Always send a written contract or agreement to solidify the verbal commitment and ensure clarity on all terms.

- **Maintain momentum and trust**: Follow up promptly, deliver on promises, and keep regular communication to ensure a smooth transition and reinforce the relationship.

By following these quick tips, you'll master the art of closing deals with confidence and professionalism, ensuring clear commitments and lasting business success.

CHAPTER FIFTEEN

Rules of the Game: Navigating Legal and Regulatory Waters

"Mastering the legal landscape is about knowing the rules and using them to your advantage."— CLAUDE HOPKINS, ADVERTISING PIONEER

A h, the legal and regulatory landscape—where paperwork meets peril and compliance is your compass. Navigating this terrain is a bit like playing a game of chess with a twist: the board changes, the rules are complex, and every move has consequences. But fear not! With the right strategies, you'll master the game and avoid the legal quicksand that could otherwise sink your business dreams.

In this chapter, we'll demystify the legal jungle, turning labyrinthine regulations into a navigable map. Think of legal compliance as your business's safety net— essential for keeping your operation smooth and your reputation intact. We'll tackle everything from licensing to contracts with the precision of a seasoned guide, ensuring you dodge pitfalls and sidestep snares along the way.

You'll learn to view legal regulations not as roadblocks, but as the rules of the game that, when understood, can help you play smarter and win bigger. By the end, you'll be well-versed in how to leverage legal knowledge to your advantage, turning potentially daunting obstacles into strategic opportunities. So, gear up, stay sharp, and let's conquer the regulatory maze with confidence and a touch of flair!

Understanding Business Structures: Choosing the Right Legal Entity

One of the first and most important decisions you'll make as an entrepreneur is choosing the legal structure for your business. This decision impacts everything from your day-to-day operations to your taxes and personal liability. The right structure will set the foundation for your business, helping you operate smoothly and protecting you from potential risks down the road.

In this section, we'll break down the most common business structures, explain their pros and cons, and help you choose the one that best fits your needs.

1. Sole Proprietorship: Simplicity with Full Control

A sole proprietorship is the simplest and most common type of business structure, particularly for small businesses and solo entrepreneurs. In this structure, the business is not a separate legal entity—the owner is personally responsible for all aspects of the business.

- **Advantages**:
    - **Simplicity**: It's easy and inexpensive to set up, with minimal paperwork and no formal registration required in most cases.
    - **Full control**: As the sole owner, you have complete control over all business decisions.
    - **Tax benefits**: Your business income is reported on your personal tax return, simplifying the tax filing process.

- **Disadvantages**:

    o **Unlimited personal liability**: You are personally liable for all the business's debts and legal obligations. If the business fails or gets sued, your personal assets (like your home and savings) are at risk.

    o **Limited growth potential**: It can be difficult to raise capital because banks and investors typically prefer more formal business structures.

    o **Limited ability to bring in partners**: Since the business is tied to you personally, it's harder to bring in additional owners.

Is it right for you?

A sole proprietorship is ideal if you're starting a small business with low risk, minimal capital needs, and no plans to scale quickly. It's perfect for freelancers, consultants, or solo service providers.

2. Partnership: Sharing Ownership and Responsibility

A partnership is a business owned by two or more people. There are two types of partnerships: general partnerships(where partners share equal responsibility) and limited partnerships (where some partners have limited liability and a more passive role).

- **Advantages**:

    o **Shared responsibility**: You share the workload, financial commitment, and decision-making with one or more partners.

    o **Pooling resources**: Partners can contribute different skills, expertise, and capital to the business.

    o **Tax benefits**: Like sole proprietorships, partnerships benefit from pass-through taxation, meaning profits and losses are reported on the personal tax returns of the partners.

- **Disadvantages**:

  - **Joint liability**: In a general partnership, all partners are personally liable for the business's debts and legal issues, including the actions of other partners.

  - **Potential conflicts**: Decision-making and sharing profits can lead to disagreements if partners don't have clear agreements in place.

  - **Limited growth potential**: Similar to sole proprietorships, partnerships may struggle to attract investors or raise large amounts of capital.

Is it right for you?

A partnership is suitable for businesses with two or more people who want to share the responsibilities and risks of ownership. It's a good option for professionals like lawyers, accountants, or consultants who want to pool resources and skills.

3. Limited Liability Company (LLC): Protection and Flexibility

A limited liability company (LLC) offers the best of both worlds—it combines the simplicity of a sole proprietorship or partnership with the liability protection of a corporation. LLC owners (called "members") are not personally liable for the company's debts or lawsuits.

- **Advantages**:

  - **Limited liability**: Your personal assets are protected from the business's debts and legal issues, as long as the LLC is properly maintained.

  - **Flexible management**: LLCs can be managed by the owners or by appointed managers, allowing flexibility in how the business is run.

  - **Pass-through taxation**: Profits and losses pass through to the members' personal tax returns, avoiding double taxation (unlike corporations).

- **Disadvantages**:

  - **More paperwork and costs**: Setting up and maintaining an LLC involves more legal paperwork and fees compared to a sole proprietorship or partnership.

  - **Self-employment taxes**: In most cases, LLC members must pay self-employment taxes on their share of the profits, which can be higher than the taxes paid by shareholders of a corporation.

Is it right for you?

An LLC is a great choice for small to medium-sized businesses looking for liability protection while maintaining flexibility in how they operate. It's ideal for entrepreneurs who want to minimize their personal risk without the formalities of a corporation.

4. Corporation: Liability Protection with Growth Potential

A corporation is a separate legal entity from its owners (called shareholders). It provides the highest level of personal liability protection but also involves the most paperwork and regulatory oversight. Corporations can be divided into C corporations and S corporations, each with different tax rules.

- **Advantages**:

  - **Limited liability**: Shareholders are not personally liable for the business's debts or legal issues, beyond their investment in the company.

  - **Ability to raise capital**: Corporations can issue stock, making it easier to raise large amounts of capital from investors.

  - **Perpetual existence**: The corporation continues to exist even if the owners change or leave the business.

- **Disadvantages**:

  - **Double taxation**: In a C corporation, the company's profits are taxed at the corporate level, and then again when dividends are paid to shareholders. (S corporations avoid this, but have restrictions on the number of shareholders.)

- o **Complexity and costs**: Corporations require more paperwork, including annual reports, board meetings, and regulatory compliance. They also tend to have higher setup and maintenance costs.

- o **Less flexibility**: Corporations are subject to more rigid structures, with formalities like appointing directors and officers, maintaining bylaws, and holding shareholder meetings.

Is it right for you?

A corporation is ideal for businesses that plan to grow significantly, raise capital from investors, or go public. It's best suited for larger businesses or startups looking to scale quickly, especially those with complex operations.

5. Choosing the Right Structure for Your Business

The right legal structure for your business depends on several factors, including the size and nature of your business, your growth plans, your appetite for risk, and the level of personal liability protection you need.

Ask yourself these questions:

- How much personal liability am I willing to accept?

- Do I plan to raise capital from investors?

- How much flexibility do I need in managing the business?

- What are my long-term goals for the company's growth and ownership structure?

Choosing the right business structure is crucial because it affects your taxes, personal liability, and ability to raise capital. If you're unsure which structure is best for you, consult with a lawyer or accountant to help guide your decision.

Conclusion: Laying the Foundation for Success

Choosing the right legal structure is the foundation of your business, influencing everything from taxes to personal liability to how you manage the company. By understanding the advantages and disadvantages of each structure, you can make an informed decision that sets your business up for long-term success. Whether you start small with a sole proprietorship or aim to grow with a corporation, selecting the right legal entity is a critical first step in building a strong, sustainable business.

▶ When it comes to choosing the right business structure, making the right decision is crucial—it's the foundation upon which your empire will stand. For an in-depth look at business structures, along with essential template agreements, check out our book from the Empire Builders Series: Masterclasses in Business Law—**Brick by Brick**: The Entrepreneur's Guide to Constructing a Company. It offers a step-by-step guide to building your company the right way, ensuring you have a solid legal foundation for long-term success.

Contracts 101: Building Strong Agreements

Contracts are the backbone of every business relationship. They serve as a legally binding agreement that defines the terms, obligations, and expectations between two or more parties. Whether you're dealing with clients, partners, employees, or vendors, having a well-drafted contract is essential for protecting your business, minimizing risk, and ensuring smooth operations. In this section, we'll break down the basics of building strong contracts that safeguard your interests and foster successful collaborations.

1. Why Contracts Matter

A contract is more than just a formality—it's a critical tool for ensuring that everyone involved understands their roles and responsibilities. It also provides legal protection in case disputes arise. Without a clear contract, misunderstandings can lead to disagreements, missed deadlines, or even lawsuits.

- **Clarity**: Contracts clearly outline what each party is agreeing to, minimizing confusion and ambiguity.

- **Legal protection**: In the event of a breach, a contract provides legal grounds for resolving the issue, either through negotiation, mediation, or in court.

- **Professionalism**: Using contracts in business dealings shows that you take your relationships seriously and that you're organized and prepared.

Key takeaway: Always use contracts for any formal business agreement, no matter how small. Verbal agreements leave too much room for misunderstanding and legal issues.

2. Key Elements of a Strong Contract

While every contract will differ based on the type of agreement, certain core elements should always be included. These ensure the contract is complete, legally binding, and protects your interests.

- **Offer and Acceptance**: The contract should clearly state the offer being made and the acceptance of that offer by the other party. This forms the basic agreement between both sides.

    o **Example**: "We agree to provide consulting services for six months, starting on [date], in exchange for a payment of $5,000 per month."

- **Consideration**: This refers to what each party will give or receive. It could be money, goods, services, or something else of value.

    o **Example**: "In exchange for delivering the product by [date], we will pay the full amount of $10,000 upon receipt."

- **Roles and Responsibilities**: Clearly define who is responsible for what. Outline the scope of work, deadlines, and any specific tasks or deliverables expected from each party.

    o **Example**: "The contractor will provide design services as outlined in the attached scope of work, and the client agrees to supply all necessary materials by [date]."

- **Termination Clause**: This specifies the conditions under which the contract can be terminated by either party. It may include notice periods, reasons for termination, and any fees associated with early termination.

  - **Example**: "Either party may terminate this contract with 30 days' written notice. Early termination by the client will result in a termination fee of 25% of the remaining contract value."

- **Confidentiality or Non-Disclosure Agreement (NDA)**: If you're sharing sensitive information with the other party, a confidentiality clause ensures they won't disclose or misuse that information.

  - **Example**: "Both parties agree to keep confidential all trade secrets, proprietary information, and financial details obtained during the course of this contract."

▶ A Unilateral Confidential Agreement can be found in the **Appendix**. If you are interested in receiving an electronic copy of this document, please email us at documents@AuthorsDoor.com with the subject line "Request for Unilateral Confidential Agreement." Upon receiving your email, we will promptly send you a Microsoft Word copy of the document. **Disclaimer:** Please note that all agreements are provided for informational purposes only and should not be construed as legal advice. We recommend consulting with a qualified attorney to ensure that any legal documents or decisions are tailored to your specific circumstances.

- **Dispute Resolution**: Include a clause that outlines how disputes will be resolved, whether through mediation, arbitration, or litigation.

  - **Example**: "In the event of a dispute, the parties agree to first attempt resolution through mediation before pursuing legal action."

- **Signatures and Dates**: Every contract must be signed and dated by all parties to be legally binding. Ensure that all relevant parties have signed the contract and that it includes the date of execution.

Key takeaway: A strong contract covers all essential elements, leaving no room for ambiguity or uncertainty.

3. Common Types of Business Contracts

Understanding the types of contracts commonly used in business can help you draft the right agreements and avoid costly mistakes. Here are some of the most frequently used business contracts:

- **Service Agreements**: These contracts outline the terms between a service provider and a client, detailing the scope of services, timelines, and payment terms.

    o **Example**: If you hire a marketing consultant, you'll use a service agreement to define what services they'll provide, how long the project will take, and how much they'll be paid.

- **Partnership Agreements**: For businesses with multiple owners or partners, a partnership agreement defines each partner's rights, responsibilities, and share of profits and losses.

    o **Example**: If you're entering into a joint venture with another company, you'll use a partnership agreement to establish ownership percentages, roles, and decision-making authority.

- **Sales Contracts**: These agreements are used to outline the terms of selling goods or services. They include pricing, delivery terms, and warranties.

    o **Example**: If you're selling products to a retailer, a sales contract will specify the quantity, pricing, and delivery schedule.

- **Non-Disclosure Agreements (NDAs)**: NDAs protect sensitive information by legally binding the recipient to keep the information confidential.

    o **Example**: If you're sharing trade secrets with a potential business partner or employee, you'll use an NDA to ensure they don't disclose your confidential information to others.

▶ A Mutual Confidential Agreement can be found in the **Appendix**. If you are interested in receiving an electronic copy of this document, please email us at documents@AuthorsDoor.com with the subject line "Request for Mutual Confidential Agreement." Upon receiving your email, we will promptly send you a Microsoft Word copy of the document. **Disclaimer:** Please note that all agreements are provided for informational purposes only and should not be construed as legal advice. We recommend consulting with a qualified attorney to ensure that any legal documents or decisions are tailored to your specific circumstances.

- **Employment Contracts**: These outline the terms of employment between an employer and an employee, including salary, benefits, job responsibilities, and termination policies.

  o **Example**: If you hire a new team member, an employment contract will define their role, salary, work expectations, and how either party can terminate the agreement.

- **Lease Agreements**: If your business rents office or retail space, a lease agreement outlines the terms, including rent, duration, maintenance responsibilities, and any specific lease terms.

  o **Example**: Leasing a commercial office space will require a lease agreement that details the rental price, term length, and property use rules.

Key takeaway: Familiarize yourself with the types of contracts relevant to your business to ensure that every agreement is legally sound and protects your interests.

4. Tips for Drafting and Reviewing Contracts

Whether you're drafting a contract yourself or reviewing one provided by another party, there are key best practices to follow. A poorly written contract can lead to confusion, disputes, or worse—legal action.

- **Be clear and specific**: Avoid vague or ambiguous language. Contracts should clearly define the expectations, rights, and obligations of both parties.

- o **Example**: Instead of writing, "The service provider will deliver the project in a reasonable time," write, "The service provider will deliver the project by August 31, 2026."
- **Get everything in writing**: Verbal agreements are difficult to enforce. Always put agreements in writing, even for small or informal deals.
  - o **Example**: If you agree to modify a contract, ensure that the changes are made in writing and signed by both parties.
- **Review carefully before signing**: Never sign a contract without reading it thoroughly and ensuring you understand all its terms. If you're unsure about any section, consult a lawyer.
  - o **Tip**: Pay extra attention to clauses about termination, payment terms, and liability—these are often areas where disputes arise.
- **Amend as necessary**: If circumstances change, or if you need to modify any part of the agreement, ensure that amendments are properly documented, signed, and attached to the original contract.
  - o **Example**: "This amendment modifies the original contract dated June 1, 2024, extending the delivery date to September 15, 2024."

Key takeaway: A well-drafted contract should be clear, specific, and leave no room for interpretation. Always review contracts carefully before signing and amend them as needed to reflect changes.

▶ When it comes to publishing contracts, understanding the fine print is essential to protecting your rights and interests. For a comprehensive guide to navigating publishing agreements and access to template contracts, explore our book from the Empire Builders Series: Masterclasses in Business Law— **Legal Ink**: Navigating the Legalese of Publishing. This resource will help you confidently negotiate terms, avoid common pitfalls, and ensure your publishing journey is legally sound.

5. When to Involve a Lawyer

While you might feel comfortable drafting simple contracts yourself, there are times when hiring a lawyer is crucial. A business lawyer can help you avoid pitfalls, ensure compliance with laws, and negotiate more favorable terms.

- **Complex agreements**: If the contract involves complicated terms, large sums of money, or multiple parties, it's wise to consult with a lawyer to ensure that everything is properly documented.

  - o **Example**: If you're negotiating a major partnership deal or entering into a licensing agreement, legal expertise can help you avoid costly mistakes.

- **Dispute resolution**: If a contract dispute arises, a lawyer can help resolve the issue and protect your business from legal liability.

  - o **Example**: If a client refuses to pay, a lawyer can help you pursue legal action and navigate the contract's dispute resolution process.

Key takeaway: Don't hesitate to involve a lawyer when dealing with complex contracts, high-stakes agreements, or any situation where legal risks are involved.

Conclusion: Building Contracts That Protect and Propel Your Business

Strong contracts are the foundation of successful business relationships. By understanding the key elements of a contract, using clear and specific language, and knowing when to consult a lawyer, you can build agreements that protect your business, reduce risk, and create mutual trust with partners, clients, and employees.

Whether you're drafting a service agreement, negotiating a partnership, or signing a lease, having well-constructed contracts ensures that your business operates smoothly and legally. Properly managed contracts aren't just legal documents—they're powerful tools for building a thriving business.

Licensing and Compliance: Staying on the Right Side of the Law

Running a business isn't just about having a great product or service—it's also about ensuring you're operating within the legal boundaries. Licensing and compliance are critical elements in this process, as they help you avoid fines, legal troubles, or even the shutdown of your business. Navigating the world of business licenses, permits, and regulations can seem complex, but staying compliant ensures that your business can grow without unnecessary risk.

In this section, we'll explore the essentials of business licensing and compliance, guiding you through the steps needed to keep your business in good standing with regulatory authorities.

1. Understanding Business Licenses and Permits

Depending on the nature of your business, you may be required to obtain one or more licenses or permits to operate legally. These requirements can vary based on your industry, location, and business activities. Failing to secure the necessary licenses can lead to hefty fines, penalties, or even a shutdown.

- **Business Licenses**: A general business license allows you to operate legally within your city, county, or state. It's typically one of the first licenses any business will need.

    o **Example**: If you're starting a retail store or an online business, your local government may require you to obtain a general business license before you can begin selling.

- **Industry-Specific Licenses**: Certain industries require additional licenses beyond the general business license. This could include healthcare, financial services, food service, alcohol sales, or construction.

    o **Example**: A restaurant owner will need a food service license, health permits, and possibly a liquor license if they plan to serve alcohol.

- **Environmental and Safety Permits**: Businesses that handle hazardous materials, generate waste, or impact the environment may need specific environmental permits. Similarly, construction or manufacturing businesses may need safety permits to comply with health and safety regulations.

  o **Example**: A construction company may need a building permit, an environmental impact permit, and an OSHA safety permit for certain projects.

- **Home-Based Business Permits**: If you're running a business out of your home, you may need a special home-based business permit, particularly if you have employees or clients visiting your home.

  o **Example**: If you're a freelance graphic designer working from home, your local municipality may require a home occupation permit to ensure your business doesn't disrupt your neighborhood.

Key takeaway: Always check with your local, state, and federal authorities to ensure you have the right licenses and permits before starting your business. It's essential to understand which ones apply to your industry and location.

2. How to Obtain the Right Licenses

Securing the correct licenses and permits for your business isn't a one-size-fits-all process. The requirements depend on your industry and location, but the general steps below can help guide you through the process.

- **Research local requirements**: Start by researching your city and county's business license requirements. Most local government websites provide resources or databases to help you determine which licenses and permits apply to your business.

  o **Tip**: Your city's business development office can be a great resource for understanding local requirements and getting the necessary paperwork.

- **Check state and federal requirements**: Some industries, like healthcare, finance, and alcohol sales, may require state or federal licenses. Check with your state's department of commerce or licensing agency to see what's required for your business type.

- o **Example**: A financial advisor may need state registration with the securities commission and possibly federal licenses from the Financial Industry Regulatory Authority (FINRA).

- **Apply for your business license**: Once you know what licenses and permits you need, gather the required documents, complete the application, and pay any associated fees. The application process may vary by location, so be sure to follow all instructions carefully.

  - o **Tip**: Processing times can vary, so apply well before your expected launch date to avoid delays in starting your business.

- **Keep licenses up to date**: Business licenses often need to be renewed annually or bi-annually. Failing to renew your licenses can result in penalties, fines, or the suspension of your business operations.

  - o **Tip**: Mark renewal deadlines on your calendar or set reminders so you don't miss important dates.

Key takeaway: Always research the specific licenses and permits required for your industry and location. Follow through with applications and renewals to avoid costly mistakes and ensure uninterrupted business operations.

3. Staying Compliant with Regulations

Once you've obtained the necessary licenses and permits, the next step is ensuring your business stays compliant with relevant laws and regulations. Compliance helps you avoid fines, penalties, and legal actions, and ensures that your business is operating ethically and responsibly.

- **Employment Laws**: If you have employees, you must comply with labor laws related to wages, benefits, workplace safety, and anti-discrimination practices. This may include adhering to minimum wage laws, overtime rules, and providing workers' compensation insurance.

- o **Example**: If your business employs more than 50 people, you may be required to offer health insurance under the Affordable Care Act (ACA).

- **Tax Compliance**: In addition to filing your business taxes, you'll need to ensure you're withholding the correct amounts for employee payroll taxes and paying any applicable state or local taxes.

  - o **Tip**: Work with a tax professional to ensure you're meeting all your tax obligations, from income tax to sales tax to employment tax.

- **Data Privacy and Security**: If your business collects customer data, you must comply with data protection regulations, such as the General Data Protection Regulation (GDPR) for EU citizens or the California Consumer Privacy Act (CCPA) for California residents. These laws outline how you can collect, store, and use personal data.

  - o **Example**: An e-commerce store must ensure that customer credit card information is securely encrypted and that privacy policies are clear and compliant with relevant laws.

- **Industry-Specific Regulations**: Many industries are heavily regulated, and you'll need to stay compliant with industry-specific laws. This is particularly true for healthcare, financial services, food and beverage, and real estate.

  - o **Example**: A healthcare business must comply with the Health Insurance Portability and Accountability Act (HIPAA), which governs how patient information is handled and protected.

Key takeaway: Stay on top of your industry's regulatory environment and ensure your business is compliant with labor, tax, data privacy, and industry-specific regulations. Non-compliance can lead to costly penalties and damage to your reputation.

4. Keeping Up with Regulatory Changes

Regulations can change over time, especially as industries evolve or new laws are introduced. Staying on top of these changes is crucial for maintaining compliance and ensuring your business doesn't face unexpected legal challenges.

- **Subscribe to industry newsletters and updates**: Many industry organizations, trade associations, and government agencies offer newsletters or alerts to help businesses stay informed of regulatory changes. Signing up for these updates can keep you informed about new requirements or deadlines.

  - **Example**: The Small Business Administration (SBA) provides updates on federal regulatory changes, while local chambers of commerce often track changes in local and state regulations.

- **Consult with legal and compliance experts**: Regularly working with a business attorney or compliance expert can help you navigate complex regulatory environments. These professionals can provide guidance on new laws, help with audits, and ensure you're meeting all legal requirements.

  - **Tip**: Consider setting up annual compliance audits with a lawyer to ensure all aspects of your business are in line with the latest regulations.

- **Stay proactive**: Don't wait until you're notified of non-compliance to act. Regularly review your business practices, update licenses, and address compliance issues before they become bigger problems.

  - **Tip**: Set reminders to periodically check for updates on relevant regulations, especially if you operate in a fast-changing industry like tech or finance.

Key takeaway: Staying compliant is an ongoing process. Regularly check for regulatory updates, consult with experts, and be proactive in ensuring your business operations are up to code.

Conclusion: Compliance Is Key to Long-Term Success

Licensing and compliance might not be the most glamorous part of running a business, but they're absolutely essential. By ensuring that your business has the proper licenses and adheres to local, state, and federal regulations, you create a solid foundation for growth while avoiding legal trouble. From securing business licenses to staying compliant with tax, labor, and data privacy laws, taking the time to navigate the regulatory landscape is a critical investment in your business's long-term success.

By being diligent, staying informed, and working with experts when needed, you'll ensure that your business operates smoothly and stays on the right side of the law. Compliance isn't just about avoiding fines—it's about building a reputable and sustainable business.

Intellectual Property: Protecting Your Ideas and Brand

Your business's ideas, products, and brand are some of its most valuable assets, and intellectual property (IP) laws are designed to protect them. From your company's name and logo to the unique products or services you create, intellectual property ensures that others can't steal or misuse what you've worked hard to build. Protecting your IP not only safeguards your business but also gives you the legal foundation to enforce your rights, prevent infringement, and maintain a competitive edge.

In this section, we'll explore the various types of intellectual property and how to protect your business's innovations, creations, and brand identity.

1. Understanding the Different Types of Intellectual Property

There are several different types of intellectual property, each designed to protect a specific kind of asset. It's essential to understand which types apply to your business so that you can take the appropriate steps to secure your rights.

- **Trademarks**: A trademark protects your brand's identity, including logos, names, slogans, and any other distinctive marks associated with your business. Registering a trademark prevents others from using similar marks that could confuse customers.

- o **Example**: If you've created a unique logo for your business or developed a catchy slogan, a trademark protects it from being copied by competitors.

- **Copyrights**: Copyright law protects original works of authorship, such as written content, music, art, software code, and videos. Copyright gives you the exclusive right to use, reproduce, and distribute your creative work.

- o **Example**: If you've written a book, created marketing content, or produced a video, copyright protects your work from unauthorized use.

- **Patents**: A patent protects inventions or processes, giving you the exclusive right to make, use, or sell your invention for a set period (usually 20 years). Patents are typically used for new products, processes, or technologies.

- o **Example**: If your business has developed a groundbreaking new product or manufacturing process, a patent ensures competitors can't copy or sell it without your permission.

- **Trade Secrets**: Trade secrets include confidential business information, such as formulas, processes, or customer lists, that give your company a competitive advantage. Unlike patents, trade secrets are protected indefinitely as long as they remain confidential.

- o **Example**: The recipe for Coca-Cola is a famous trade secret that is carefully protected to maintain the company's competitive edge.

Key takeaway: Identifying which types of intellectual property apply to your business is the first step in protecting your assets. Ensure you understand the difference between trademarks, copyrights, patents, and trade secrets to secure the appropriate protections.

2. How to Protect Your Intellectual Property

Once you've identified your intellectual property, the next step is securing the proper protections. The process varies depending on the type of IP, but each requires proactive steps to ensure your business is legally covered.

- **Registering Trademarks**: To protect your brand's name, logo, or slogan, you'll need to register it as a trademark with the United States Patent and Trademark Office (USPTO) or your country's equivalent. Trademark registration provides legal protection and makes it easier to enforce your rights in case of infringement.

  - o **Tip**: Before filing a trademark application, conduct a thorough search to ensure your mark isn't already in use by another business. The USPTO's online database can help you with this.

▶ When it comes to trademark protection, safeguarding your brand is essential to building a lasting empire. For a deeper dive into trademark strategies and to access template agreements, explore our book from the Empire Builders Series: Masterclasses in Business Law—**Mark Your Territory**: Navigating Trademarks in the Modern Marketplace. This book will help you secure your brand, avoid legal pitfalls, and position your business for long-term recognition and success.

- **Securing Copyrights**: In the U.S., copyright protection automatically applies as soon as an original work is created, but registering it with the U.S. Copyright Office provides additional legal benefits, including the ability to sue for damages in case of infringement.

  - o **Example**: If you've written original content or developed software, register it with the Copyright Office to strengthen your legal protection and establish proof of ownership.

▶ When it comes to copyright protection, ensuring your creative assets are properly safeguarded is vital to building your empire. For an in-depth exploration of copyright strategies and access to template agreements, check out our book from the Empire Builders Series: Masterclasses in Business

Law—**Beyond the Pen**: Copyright Strategies for Modern Creators. This book equips you with the tools to protect your intellectual property, navigate legal complexities, and unlock the full value of your creations.

- **Filing for Patents**: Patents are more complex and time-consuming to obtain than other forms of IP. You'll need to file a detailed patent application with the USPTO (or the relevant patent office in your country), including technical descriptions and drawings of your invention. If granted, you'll receive exclusive rights to your invention for up to 20 years.

  o **Tip**: Consider consulting a patent attorney, as the application process can be complicated and costly. A professional can help you navigate the legal requirements and ensure your invention is fully protected.

- **Protecting Trade Secrets**: To protect trade secrets, it's essential to implement internal safeguards, such as confidentiality agreements (NDAs) for employees, partners, and contractors. Ensure that any sensitive information is restricted to only those who need to know.

  o **Tip**: Regularly review and update confidentiality agreements to reflect changes in your business or its trade secrets.

Key takeaway: Securing your intellectual property requires formal registration in many cases. Take proactive steps to file trademarks, copyrights, or patents, and establish safeguards for trade secrets to protect your business's most valuable assets.

3. Enforcing Your Intellectual Property Rights

Once you've protected your intellectual property, you must remain vigilant in enforcing your rights. Infringement—whether it's someone using your trademark, copying your content, or selling a similar invention—can harm your business's reputation and profitability. Taking swift legal action can deter infringement and protect your business.

- **Monitor for Infringement**: Regularly monitor your industry, competitors, and the marketplace for potential infringement on your intellectual property. This can be done by conducting searches online, reviewing trademark filings, and keeping an eye on competitors' products or marketing materials.

- o **Example**: Use Google Alerts or hire a trademark watch service to notify you if your business name or product is being used without your permission.

- **Send Cease-and-Desist Letters**: If you discover that someone is infringing on your intellectual property, your first step is typically to send a cease-and-desist letter. This is a formal legal demand that the infringer stop using your IP and take corrective action. In many cases, this will resolve the issue without the need for litigation.

  - o **Tip**: A lawyer can help you draft a strong cease-and-desist letter, ensuring that it clearly outlines the infringement and the legal consequences if the infringer does not comply.

- **Take Legal Action When Necessary**: If the infringer does not comply with the cease-and-desist letter, you may need to file a lawsuit to enforce your rights. This could include suing for damages, seeking an injunction to stop the infringing activity, or negotiating a settlement.

  - o **Example**: If a competitor starts using a name similar to your trademarked brand, and refuses to stop after receiving a cease-and-desist letter, you can file a lawsuit to prevent further infringement and potentially recover damages.

Key takeaway: Protecting your intellectual property doesn't stop after you secure it—you must actively monitor and enforce your rights to maintain the integrity and value of your IP.

4. The Benefits of Strong Intellectual Property Protections

Having strong intellectual property protections in place offers several benefits for your business. Not only do they provide legal safeguards, but they can also enhance your business's credibility, attract investment, and create additional revenue streams.

- **Increase Business Value**: Registered IP rights add significant value to your business, making it more attractive to investors, partners, and potential buyers. A well-protected brand or patented product can give you a competitive edge and increase your market valuation.

    o **Example**: If you're seeking investment or considering selling your business, having registered trademarks, patents, or copyrights can significantly boost your company's appeal and market value.

- **Generate Revenue**: Intellectual property can be licensed or sold to others, creating additional revenue streams for your business. For example, you can license your patented technology to other companies in exchange for royalties, or allow another business to use your trademark in a specific market.

    o **Example**: A software company may license its proprietary technology to third-party developers for a fee, generating ongoing revenue without the need for direct sales.

- **Build Brand Credibility**: Trademarks help establish a strong, recognizable brand identity that builds trust with customers. When customers see a trademarked logo or name, they know they're purchasing from a legitimate, trusted business.

Key takeaway: Strong intellectual property protections not only defend your ideas but also enhance your business's overall value, offering long-term strategic and financial benefits.

Conclusion: Protecting and Leveraging Your Intellectual Property

Intellectual property is one of the most valuable assets your business can possess, and protecting it is essential to your long-term success. By understanding the different types of IP—trademarks, copyrights, patents, and trade secrets—and securing legal protections, you can prevent others from stealing or misusing your innovations, brand, and creative works.

Staying proactive in enforcing your IP rights and leveraging them to generate additional revenue or build your brand will further strengthen your business. With a solid intellectual property strategy, you'll safeguard your company's unique ideas and products while positioning yourself for growth and success in the marketplace.

Quick Tips and Recap

- **Identify your intellectual property**: Determine which assets—such as logos, brand names, inventions, written content, or trade secrets—need protection.

- **Register trademarks and copyrights**: Secure legal protection for your brand identity, creative works, and business name by registering them with the appropriate authorities.

- **File for patents**: If you've developed a unique invention or process, consider filing for a patent to ensure exclusive rights for up to 20 years.

- **Protect trade secrets**: Implement confidentiality agreements and internal safeguards to keep sensitive business information, such as formulas or processes, secure.

- **Monitor for infringement**: Regularly check for unauthorized use of your intellectual property and take action when needed to protect your rights.

- **Send cease-and-desist letters**: If infringement occurs, start by sending a formal notice demanding the infringing party stop their actions before pursuing legal action.

- **Leverage your IP for growth**: Intellectual property can add significant value to your business and can be licensed or sold to generate additional revenue.

- **Stay proactive and enforce your rights**: Continuously monitor your IP portfolio and take steps to protect and enforce it when necessary.

By following these tips, you'll ensure your business's ideas and brand are safeguarded, providing a strong foundation for long-term success.

PART FOUR

Taking Action

Welcome to the thrilling climax of your business journey—where all those grand plans and brilliant strategies finally get their moment in the spotlight! This is where the rubber meets the road, and your ideas morph from mere words on paper into action-packed reality. Think of this part as the grand finale of a fireworks show: it's time to light the fuse and watch your plans explode into dazzling success. In this section, we'll cover the art of turning strategy into execution with flair and finesse. From launching your initiatives to tackling obstacles head-on, you'll learn how to make every move count and keep your momentum rolling. So, strap in, because it's time to take action and make your business dreams not just a possibility, but a spectacular reality!

CHAPTER SIXTEEN

Launch Sequence: Kicking Off Your Business

"Launching your business is like a grand performance—every detail matters, and first impressions are everything."— LEO BURNETT, ADVERTISING LEGEND

L adies and gentlemen, the countdown is over—it's launch time! Picture this: you're the captain of a rocket ship, your business is the spacecraft, and today, you're blasting off into the stratosphere of entrepreneurial success. This is no ordinary launch; it's a full-throttle, high-octane event where every detail counts, from the ignition sequence to the final liftoff.

In this chapter, we'll navigate the exhilarating final steps before your business soars into the market. You'll learn how to prepare for lift-off with precision and style, ensuring your launch isn't just a flash in the pan but a grand spectacle. We'll cover everything from assembling your launch team and fine-tuning your messaging to managing that all-important initial blast of visibility.

Think of it as orchestrating a rock concert—your business's debut should be loud, memorable, and make everyone in the audience want an encore. So, fasten your seatbelt, check your checklist, and get ready to make an unforgettable entrance. Your business is about to take flight, and the sky's the limit!

Assembling Your Launch Team: Building the Crew for Success

Every successful launch, whether it's a product, service, or full business, requires a solid team of individuals working together toward the same goal. Much like the crew of a spaceship, each person plays a crucial role in ensuring a smooth takeoff and successful mission. Assembling your launch team is about choosing the right people with the skills, knowledge, and dedication needed to make your business debut an unforgettable event.

In this section, we'll explore how to build the perfect team for your business launch and ensure that each person knows their role in the countdown to success.

1. Identify the Key Roles for Your Launch

The first step in assembling your launch team is understanding the specific roles you'll need to cover every aspect of your business's debut. Each business is unique, and the size and scope of your launch will determine the roles required. However, here are some common roles that are essential for most business launches:

- **Project Manager**: The captain of your launch team. This person will oversee the entire process, ensure deadlines are met, and coordinate between different team members. The project manager keeps the launch on track, manages resources, and ensures everything runs smoothly on the big day.

    o **Key tasks**: Coordinating timelines, managing communication, handling logistics, and troubleshooting issues as they arise.

- **Marketing and PR Lead**: Responsible for generating buzz and getting your message out to the public. This person oversees your marketing campaigns, social media strategy, and PR outreach, ensuring that your launch gets maximum visibility.

- o **Key tasks**: Crafting marketing materials, managing social media accounts, coordinating with press and influencers, and handling pre-launch promotions.

- **Brand and Content Manager**: This person is in charge of your brand's messaging, content creation, and overall tone. They ensure that every piece of communication reflects your business's identity and vision.

- o **Key tasks**: Developing launch content, writing press releases, creating website copy, and managing visual assets like logos and branding materials.

- **Sales or Business Development Lead**: If your launch involves direct sales (whether online or in person), this person will handle the customer outreach and ensure that sales processes are smooth and effective.

- o **Key tasks**: Managing the sales team, setting up sales funnels, handling pre-orders, and ensuring that customer service is ready for launch day.

- **Tech Support**: For digital businesses or launches with an online component, having tech support on hand is essential. This team member handles your website, ensures online platforms function properly, and resolves any technical issues during the launch.

- o **Key tasks**: Website development, troubleshooting technical problems, managing the online store or digital platforms, and ensuring your launch goes off without a hitch.

Key takeaway: Understand the key roles that are necessary for your specific business launch, and assign each role to a qualified person who can own it and deliver results.

2. Choosing the Right People for the Job

Once you've identified the roles you need, it's time to fill them with the right people. Choosing the right individuals can make the difference between a smooth launch and a chaotic one. Look for team members who are not only skilled in their area but are also reliable, proactive, and able to work under pressure.

- **Look for experience**: When building your launch team, try to choose people with relevant experience. Whether it's a previous business launch or expertise in a specific field (e.g., marketing, sales, logistics), experienced team members will be able to anticipate challenges and solve problems quickly.

  - o **Tip**: If you don't have the budget for full-time staff, consider hiring freelancers, consultants, or part-time workers who specialize in launch-related tasks.

- **Prioritize communication and collaboration skills**: A successful launch requires seamless communication between all team members. Choose people who can collaborate effectively, share updates clearly, and adapt quickly to new information.

  - o **Example**: Your marketing lead and content manager should work closely to ensure that all promotional materials align with the brand message and marketing strategy.

- **Delegate with trust**: Trust is key to building an effective launch team. Assign tasks and give your team members the autonomy to manage their responsibilities. Micromanaging can slow things down, while empowering your team builds confidence and speeds up the process.

  - o **Tip**: Set clear expectations, but allow your team the freedom to come up with creative solutions and manage their own areas of responsibility.

Key takeaway: Choose skilled, communicative, and reliable people for each role, and ensure that they're capable of working independently while collaborating with the rest of the team.

3. Setting Clear Goals and Expectations

Once your team is assembled, you'll need to set clear goals and expectations for each member. A launch is a fast-paced, high-pressure environment, so everyone must understand what's expected of them, how they contribute to the overall launch, and what the timeline looks like.

- **Define success metrics**: For each role, define specific goals or success metrics. For example, your marketing lead's goal may be to generate 5,000 new leads before launch day, while your tech support team's goal could be ensuring 100% uptime for your website during launch.

  o **Example**: "Our marketing goal is to reach 10,000 people through social media ads and get 1,000 sign-ups for the early access list."

- **Create a detailed timeline**: Break down the launch process into key milestones and deadlines. Provide your team with a detailed timeline that outlines when each task should be completed and what deliverables are due at each stage.

  o **Tip**: Use project management tools like Trello, Asana, or Monday.com to assign tasks, track progress, and ensure everyone stays on the same page.

- **Communicate regularly**: Establish regular check-ins or meetings to discuss progress, address any issues, and ensure that everyone is aligned. This keeps the team focused and allows for adjustments as needed.

  o **Example**: Schedule a weekly team meeting to review the status of each task, update timelines, and troubleshoot potential bottlenecks.

Key takeaway: Set clear, measurable goals for each team member, create a detailed timeline for the launch, and maintain open communication throughout the process.

4. Handling Last-Minute Challenges: Keeping Teams Focused

No matter how well you plan, unexpected challenges can arise in the final countdown to your launch. The key to navigating these hurdles is staying calm, keeping your team focused, and being prepared to adapt as needed.

- **Encourage problem-solving**: Empower your team to solve problems on their own without waiting for approval. This not only speeds up the resolution process but also builds confidence in the team's ability to handle issues as they arise.

  - o **Tip**: Create a decision-making hierarchy so that team members know when to escalate issues and when they can handle them independently.

- **Stay flexible**: While it's important to have a solid plan, flexibility is equally essential. If something doesn't go as expected, be ready to adapt, make quick decisions, and keep the team motivated through any last-minute changes.

  - o **Example**: If a marketing campaign isn't generating as many leads as anticipated, pivot by exploring new platforms or adjusting the messaging based on feedback.

- **Keep morale high**: Launches can be stressful, but keeping morale high is crucial to maintaining productivity. Celebrate small wins along the way, acknowledge the hard work of your team, and create a positive atmosphere that keeps everyone motivated.

  - o **Tip**: Even something as simple as a shout-out during a team meeting or offering lunch on a busy day can boost team morale and keep spirits high.

Key takeaway: Be prepared for last-minute challenges, encourage quick problem-solving, stay flexible with your plan, and keep morale high to ensure a successful launch.

Conclusion: Your Launch Crew Is the Key to Success

Assembling the right team is a critical step in ensuring a successful business launch. With skilled, reliable team members in place, clear goals and expectations set, and regular communication flowing, you'll be well on your way to making your launch day an unforgettable success. A strong team can help navigate last-minute challenges, keep everything on track, and ensure that your business takes off with precision and confidence.

Remember, your team is your crew, and together, you'll pilot your business into the market with the energy and excitement it deserves.

Crafting a Compelling Launch Message: Telling Your Story

Your launch message is the heart of your business's debut—it's how you introduce yourself to the world, capture attention, and communicate the essence of your brand. A compelling launch message isn't just about what you're selling; it's about telling the story of your business, connecting emotionally with your audience, and making them believe in what you stand for. A great story resonates, sticks with people, and makes them eager to be part of your journey.

In this section, we'll explore how to craft a compelling launch message that not only tells your story but also excites and engages your audience.

1. Start with Your "Why"

At the core of every successful business is a strong purpose—the "why" behind what you do. Your launch message should start by explaining this purpose and helping your audience understand the reason your business exists. People aren't just drawn to products or services; they're drawn to purpose and passion.

- **Why does your business exist?** What problem are you solving, and why is it important to you and your customers? Starting with your "why" creates an emotional connection and makes your audience care about what you're offering.

    - **Example**: "At [Business Name], we believe that everyone deserves access to affordable, high-quality skincare products made from natural ingredients. We started this journey because we saw a gap in the market for products that are both effective and eco-friendly."

- **Tell your origin story**: Share the story of how and why your business came to be. This humanizes your brand and helps people relate to you on a personal level.

    o   **Example**: "Our founder, Sarah, struggled with skin sensitivities for years, trying product after product with no success. Frustrated by the lack of natural options, she decided to create her own line of skincare products—made from ingredients that nourish without irritation."

Key takeaway: Start your launch message by focusing on your business's purpose and the problem you're solving. This will engage your audience emotionally and make them want to support your journey.

2. Highlight What Makes You Unique

Once you've established your "why," it's time to show your audience what makes your business stand out from the competition. What's your unique selling proposition (USP)? What differentiates your product, service, or brand from others in the market? In a crowded marketplace, your launch message needs to clearly communicate why customers should choose you over others.

- **Focus on your unique value**: Whether it's superior quality, innovative technology, ethical practices, or an unbeatable customer experience, highlight what makes your business unique.

    o   **Example**: "Unlike mass-produced products, our skincare line is handcrafted in small batches using only sustainably sourced ingredients, ensuring the highest quality and the lowest environmental impact."

- **Address customer pain points**: Show how your business directly solves your target audience's pain points or unmet needs.

    o   **Example**: "We know that finding skincare that's both effective and gentle on sensitive skin can feel impossible. That's why we created a formula that's free from harsh chemicals and allergens, so you can get the results you want without the irritation."

- **Stand for something**: Consumers today want to support businesses that align with their values. If your business is socially or environmentally responsible, incorporates ethical sourcing, or supports a cause, make that a central part of your launch message.

- o **Example**: "With every purchase, we donate a portion of our profits to organizations that protect endangered rainforests, because we believe in beauty that's good for you and the planet."

Key takeaway: Emphasize what makes your business different and why customers should choose you. This is the core of your competitive advantage.

3. Keep It Clear and Concise

Your launch message should be clear, concise, and easy to understand. While it's tempting to include every detail about your business, keeping things focused and streamlined ensures that your audience grasps the most important points quickly. A great launch message gets to the heart of your story without overwhelming people with unnecessary information.

- **Simplify your message**: Aim for clarity over complexity. Use straightforward language that anyone can understand—avoid jargon or buzzwords that could confuse or alienate your audience.
  - o **Example**: Instead of saying, "We offer a highly synergistic array of botanical extracts designed to optimize dermal regeneration," say, "We use natural plant-based ingredients to give your skin a healthy, glowing appearance."

- **Focus on key takeaways**: Your launch message should answer three essential questions:

1. What is your business or product?
2. Why should people care?
3. How can they benefit from it?
   - o **Example**: "At [Business Name], we offer handmade skincare products that are 100% natural and free from harmful chemicals. Our mission is to help people achieve healthy, radiant skin while reducing their environmental footprint."

- **Call to action**: End your message with a clear call to action (CTA), telling your audience what to do next. Whether it's visiting your website, signing up for a newsletter, or attending a launch event, make it easy for people to engage with you.

  - **Example**: "Ready to experience the difference? Visit our website to shop our collection and enjoy 20% off your first purchase during launch week!"

Key takeaway: Keep your message simple, clear, and focused on the key takeaways. End with a compelling call to action to drive engagement.

4. Create an Emotional Connection

Storytelling is one of the most powerful ways to engage your audience on an emotional level. Your launch message should not only convey facts and information but also spark emotions like excitement, inspiration, or curiosity. When your audience feels emotionally connected to your brand, they're more likely to become loyal customers and advocates.

- **Use relatable language**: Speak directly to your target audience's needs, desires, and emotions. Show empathy for their challenges and demonstrate that you understand their problems.

  - **Example**: "We know how frustrating it is to try product after product without seeing real results. That's why we've spent years perfecting a formula that actually works—and we can't wait for you to try it."

- **Inspire your audience**: Use language that evokes positive emotions like hope, inspiration, and excitement. Show how your product or service can improve their lives.

  - **Example**: "Imagine waking up to clear, glowing skin every morning, knowing that the products you use are good for your body and the planet. That's what we want for you."

- **Share your passion**: Let your excitement and passion for your business shine through. When your audience sees how much you care about what you're offering, they'll feel more invested in your success.

o **Example**: "We're more than just a skincare brand—we're a movement. We believe in creating beauty products that don't just make you look good, but feel good too. Join us on this journey to healthier, happier skin."

Key takeaway: Craft a message that connects with your audience on an emotional level, using storytelling, relatable language, and an inspiring tone.

5. Ensure Consistency Across All Channels

Your launch message should be consistent across all platforms—whether it's your website, social media, email campaigns, or press releases. Consistency helps reinforce your message, build brand recognition, and create a unified experience for your audience.

- **Align your messaging**: Make sure that the language, tone, and key points of your launch message are consistent across all channels. Whether someone reads a tweet, an email, or a press release, the core message should be the same.

  o **Example**: If your core message is about eco-friendly skincare, all your channels should highlight this focus, from social media posts to product descriptions.

- **Use visual consistency**: In addition to your written message, your visuals (logos, colors, fonts) should also be consistent. This reinforces your brand identity and makes your launch more cohesive.

  o **Example**: Use the same color palette, fonts, and style for all launch materials, from your website to social media graphics and email templates.

Key takeaway: Consistency across all platforms ensures that your audience gets a unified and memorable brand experience.

Conclusion: Tell a Story That Resonates
Crafting a compelling launch message is about more than just explaining your product or service—it's about telling a story that resonates with your audience, highlights your uniqueness, and connects emotionally. By starting with your

"why," focusing on what makes you special, and keeping your message clear, you'll create a powerful launch message that engages, inspires, and drives action.

Remember, your launch message sets the tone for your brand's future. Make it memorable, authentic, and exciting—and watch your business take off with a story that people want to be part of.

Generating Buzz: Marketing and Promoting Your Big Day

Your business launch is a major event, and like any big event, you want as many eyes on it as possible. Generating buzz is all about building excitement and anticipation, creating a buzzworthy atmosphere that gets people talking, sharing, and eagerly awaiting your launch day. From leveraging social media to crafting email campaigns, you'll need a solid marketing and promotional strategy that ensures your launch doesn't just go off quietly but makes a loud, memorable impact.

In this section, we'll dive into how to create marketing campaigns that get people excited, build momentum leading up to your launch, and ensure your big day is one to remember.

1. Build Anticipation with a Pre-Launch Campaign

Before your actual launch day, it's crucial to start building excitement and awareness. A pre-launch campaign can tease your audience with what's to come, getting them curious and eager for more. The more anticipation you build before launch, the more successful your big day will be.

- **Create teaser content**: Share sneak peeks, behind-the-scenes looks, and hints about your launch. This could be anything from photos of your product in development to glimpses of your new website. Teasers build curiosity and make people excited to see the final reveal.

  - **Example**: Share a social media post with the caption, "Something exciting is coming... Stay tuned for the big reveal on [launch date]!"

- **Countdown to launch**: Implement a countdown to your launch day. You can do this through social media posts, emails, or even a countdown timer on your website. A countdown adds urgency and keeps your audience engaged as the big day approaches.

  o **Tip**: Consider creating a countdown graphic or video to use across your channels, counting down the days or hours until launch.

- **Offer early access or exclusive previews**: Reward your most loyal followers or subscribers by giving them early access or exclusive sneak peeks. This not only makes them feel valued but also generates buzz as they share their excitement with others.

  o **Example**: "Sign up for our email list to get an exclusive early look at our new collection before anyone else!"

Key takeaway: A pre-launch campaign builds anticipation and excitement, making your audience eager for your official launch.

2. Leverage Social Media to Create Hype

Social media is one of the most powerful tools for generating buzz and getting the word out about your launch. With billions of users across platforms like Instagram, Twitter, Facebook, and TikTok, social media gives you the ability to reach a vast audience and create excitement in real-time.

- **Choose the right platforms**: Not every social media platform will be right for your business. Focus on the platforms where your target audience is most active, whether that's Instagram for a fashion brand or LinkedIn for a B2B service.

  o **Example**: If you're launching a fashion line, Instagram and TikTok may be your best bets for reaching visually driven audiences, while LinkedIn would be ideal for a professional consulting service.

- **Create shareable content**: Social media thrives on content that people want to share. Create engaging, visually appealing posts, videos, and stories that encourage your followers to share with their networks. The more your audience shares, the bigger your launch buzz will become.

- o **Example**: Post a teaser video of your product with a question like, "Guess what's coming soon? Share your guesses in the comments and tag a friend who would love this!"

- **Collaborate with influencers**: Partnering with influencers or social media personalities can dramatically increase your reach and credibility. Influencers have built-in audiences who trust their recommendations, making them ideal partners for promoting your launch.

- o **Tip**: Choose influencers who align with your brand's values and target audience. Their followers should match the type of customers you want to attract.

- **Use hashtags and challenges**: Create a unique hashtag for your launch and encourage your audience to use it when posting about your business. You can also launch a challenge or giveaway that incentivizes followers to engage with your content.

- o **Example**: Run a contest where followers post a photo or video using your hashtag for a chance to win early access or a free product. This builds engagement and creates user-generated content for your brand.

Key takeaway: Use social media strategically by creating shareable content, partnering with influencers, and encouraging engagement with challenges and hashtags.

3. Engage with Your Audience through Email Marketing

While social media is great for building buzz, email marketing remains one of the most effective tools for directly reaching your audience. With email, you have the ability to nurture relationships, build excitement, and guide potential customers through the launch journey.

- **Build an email list early**: Before your launch, focus on growing your email list with interested subscribers. You can collect emails by offering incentives like early access, exclusive discounts, or downloadable content.

- o **Example**: "Sign up for our email list and get 15% off your first purchase when we launch!"

- **Create a pre-launch email sequence**: A well-designed email sequence can build anticipation and keep your audience engaged leading up to your launch. Use a series of emails to introduce your brand, tease your product or service, and offer exclusive information or deals.

  - o **Example**: Send a three-part email sequence:

    1. "We're launching soon! Here's what you need to know."

    2. "Sneak peek! Here's what you can expect on launch day."

    3. "The big day is almost here! Don't miss out."

- **Launch day email**: On the day of your launch, send a high-energy, action-driven email announcing that your product or service is officially live. Include a clear call to action that directs readers to your website, store, or event.

  - o **Tip**: Make your launch day email stand out by using bold visuals, a countdown timer, or a limited-time offer that creates urgency.

- **Follow up with post-launch emails**: After the initial launch, follow up with thank-you emails to those who participated, and offer any post-launch promotions to continue driving engagement.

  - o **Example**: "Thank you for being part of our launch! Here's 10% off your next purchase as a token of our appreciation."

Key takeaway: Use email marketing to build and nurture your audience before, during, and after the launch, creating a direct and personal connection with potential customers.

4. Generate Press Coverage and Publicity

Getting media attention can amplify your launch and expose your business to a much wider audience. Press coverage not only builds credibility but can also generate significant buzz if your story resonates with journalists, bloggers, or industry influencers.

- **Craft a compelling press release**: A well-written press release can attract media outlets and bloggers to cover your launch. Make sure your press release highlights the unique aspects of your business and why it's newsworthy.

  - o **Example**: "Local Entrepreneur Launches Eco-Friendly Skincare Line Designed for Sensitive Skin" could be a compelling angle for a beauty brand with a focus on sustainability.

- **Target the right publications**: Research publications, websites, and blogs that cater to your target audience. Focus on media outlets that are relevant to your industry or location.

  - o **Example**: If you're launching a tech startup, pitch your story to tech blogs or business publications like TechCrunch or Forbes. For a local restaurant opening, reach out to food blogs or local news outlets.

- **Offer exclusive stories or interviews**: Journalists love getting exclusive content or interviews with founders. Offer to share your personal story, behind-the-scenes insights, or an exclusive look at your launch to generate more interest.

  - o **Example**: "We'd love to give your readers an exclusive first look at our new product launch and share our founder's story about creating a business during the pandemic."

- **Leverage social proof**: If you can secure endorsements from influencers, early customer testimonials, or partnerships with well-known brands, use that social proof to strengthen your pitch to the press.

    o   **Tip**: Include any customer reviews, influencer partnerships, or notable collaborations in your press materials to show that your business is already generating excitement.

Key takeaway: Press coverage can help take your launch to the next level. Write a compelling press release, target relevant outlets, and offer exclusive stories to gain media attention.

Conclusion: Make Your Launch a Buzzworthy Event
Generating buzz for your launch is all about building anticipation, creating excitement, and engaging your audience through strategic marketing efforts. Whether it's through pre-launch campaigns, social media hype, email marketing, or press coverage, the goal is to make your launch a highly visible, memorable event that captures the attention of your target audience.

By leveraging a mix of marketing tactics—teasing your launch, collaborating with influencers, nurturing your email list, and reaching out to the press—you'll ensure that your launch is not only successful but also the talk of the town. The more buzz you create, the more likely your business is to hit the ground running with energy and momentum!

Managing Your Launch Day: Executing with Precision and Poise

Launch day is the culmination of all your hard work—the moment when your business finally steps into the spotlight. The key to a successful launch day lies in execution. Everything you've planned, from your marketing campaigns to team coordination, needs to come together seamlessly. While launch day can be exhilarating, it's also high-pressure, which means staying calm, organized, and adaptable is crucial.

In this section, we'll cover how to manage your launch day with precision and poise, ensuring that every detail is executed smoothly and that your business makes a memorable debut.

1. Stick to the Plan—but Be Ready to Adapt

By the time launch day arrives, you should have a clear, detailed plan in place for how the day will unfold. However, no matter how well you've planned, it's essential to remain flexible and ready to adapt if unexpected challenges arise. The key is to stick to the structure of your plan while being agile enough to handle any last-minute changes.

- **Review your launch checklist**: Before the big day, go through your launch checklist to ensure all tasks are completed, from content uploads to system tests. This will help you feel confident that everything is in place for a smooth launch.

  - o **Tip**: Break your checklist into time slots so you know exactly when each step needs to happen—whether it's sending out your launch email, posting on social media, or going live on your website.

- **Anticipate potential issues**: While it's impossible to predict every issue, thinking through possible problems (such as website crashes, shipping delays, or social media hiccups) will help you prepare backup solutions. Have your tech support or customer service team on high alert to address any issues quickly.

  - o **Example**: "If our website goes down due to high traffic, we'll redirect visitors to a temporary page with instructions on how to place orders manually or contact support."

- **Stay calm under pressure**: Launch day can feel overwhelming, but maintaining a calm, solution-oriented mindset will help you and your team handle any challenges that arise. If something doesn't go according to plan, stay focused on problem-solving rather than panicking.

  - o **Tip**: Designate a point person to handle unexpected issues so that the rest of the team can focus on their tasks without getting derailed.

Key takeaway: Stick to your launch day plan, but be flexible and ready to adapt to any unforeseen challenges that may arise.

2. Keep Your Audience Engaged Throughout the Day

The momentum of your launch doesn't stop once you hit the "go live" button. Keeping your audience engaged throughout launch day is crucial for building excitement, driving sales, and ensuring a strong start for your business.

- **Post live updates**: Use social media to share real-time updates, behind-the-scenes content, and moments of celebration. Live updates give your audience a sense of being part of the launch and can drive more engagement throughout the day.

  - **Example**: "We're officially LIVE! Shop now and use code LAUNCHDAY for 15% off your first order. Here's a sneak peek of our launch event—come celebrate with us!"

- **Host a launch event or livestream**: Consider hosting a virtual or in-person event to celebrate your launch. A livestream on Instagram, Facebook, or YouTube allows you to engage directly with your audience, answer questions, and share more about your business in an interactive format.

  - **Tip**: Plan a special announcement or product demonstration during the event to encourage people to tune in and engage.

- **Monitor and respond to feedback**: Engage with your customers in real time by monitoring comments, messages, and reviews throughout the day. Responding promptly to feedback—whether it's a question about a product or a technical issue—shows that you're attentive and ready to help.

  - **Example**: "Thanks for your feedback! We're so excited you love the product. Let us know if you have any questions, and enjoy your 10% off coupon for being part of our launch."

Key takeaway: Keep your audience excited and engaged throughout launch day with real-time updates, events, and responsive communication.

3. Maintain Clear Communication with Your Team

Your team is the backbone of your launch day success. While each member may be focused on their individual tasks, ensuring that everyone stays in communication is key to coordinating efforts and tackling challenges as a united front.

- **Use a communication platform**: Set up a dedicated platform for internal communication, such as Slack, Microsoft Teams, or a group chat. This will allow your team to share updates, ask questions, and address any issues quickly without disrupting the overall workflow.

  o **Tip**: Create different channels for specific tasks or departments (e.g., marketing, tech support, customer service) to keep conversations organized and focused.

- **Hold a morning kickoff meeting**: Before the official launch begins, gather your team for a quick kickoff meeting to review the schedule, confirm that everyone is ready, and set the tone for the day. This is also a good time to reiterate key goals and responsibilities.

  o **Tip**: Keep this meeting short and focused to ensure everyone can jump right into their tasks after the briefing.

- **Schedule check-ins throughout the day**: Depending on the length and complexity of your launch, schedule brief check-ins at key points in the day. These touchpoints allow you to assess progress, address any issues, and adjust as needed.

  o **Example**: "Let's check in at noon to review initial sales numbers and see if we need to adjust our social media posts based on engagement."

Key takeaway: Keep your team connected with clear, real-time communication and regular check-ins to ensure a smooth launch.

4. Track and Measure Performance in Real Time

To understand the success of your launch day and make any necessary adjustments, it's important to track and measure key performance metrics in real time. By monitoring the data as it unfolds, you can quickly identify what's working well and where you might need to pivot.

- **Monitor website traffic and sales**: Use tools like Google Analytics, Shopify analytics, or your website's built-in reporting system to track real-time website traffic, user behavior, and sales performance. Keep an eye on how many visitors are converting to customers and which pages are performing best.

    o **Tip**: Set up goals and funnels in Google Analytics to track specific actions (e.g., completed purchases, sign-ups) and identify drop-off points.

- **Track social media engagement**: Use social media analytics to measure engagement on your launch day posts. Track likes, comments, shares, and clicks to see which content is resonating most with your audience.

    o **Example**: "Our Instagram Stories are driving the most clicks to the website—let's post more behind-the-scenes content throughout the day."

- **Evaluate email performance**: If you're running an email campaign, monitor open rates, click-through rates, and conversion rates in real time. This will help you understand which emails are performing best and where there's room for improvement.

    o **Tip**: If an email is underperforming, consider sending a follow-up email later in the day with a stronger call to action or incentive.

Key takeaway: Track performance metrics in real time to make data-driven decisions and optimize your launch as it unfolds.

5. Celebrate the Wins and Reflect on Lessons Learned

At the end of launch day, it's important to take a moment to celebrate your wins—both big and small. Launching a business is no small feat, and acknowledging the hard work and success of your team will boost morale and set a positive tone for the next phase of your business journey.

- **Celebrate with your team**: Whether it's a virtual toast, a team shoutout, or a celebratory social media post, make sure to take time to appreciate your team's efforts. Celebrating the launch fosters a sense of accomplishment and keeps team morale high.

  - **Example**: "We did it! Huge thanks to the entire team for making today such a success. Here's to many more milestones ahead!"

- **Reflect on lessons learned**: While it's important to celebrate, it's also valuable to reflect on any lessons learned during the launch. What went well? What could have been improved? Use these insights to refine your strategies for future launches or business operations.

  - **Tip**: Schedule a debrief with your team after launch day to discuss both successes and areas for improvement. This reflection will help you continue to grow and evolve your business.

- **Keep momentum going**: Just because launch day is over doesn't mean the excitement should stop. Keep the momentum going by planning post-launch promotions, following up with customers, and maintaining engagement with your audience.

  - **Example**: "Thank you for making our launch a success! Stay tuned for upcoming offers and new product releases—this is just the beginning!"

Key takeaway: Celebrate your launch day successes, reflect on the lessons learned, and maintain momentum as you continue to grow your business.

Conclusion: Execute with Confidence and Precision

Launch day is a defining moment for your business, and executing with precision and poise ensures that your hard work pays off. By sticking to your plan, keeping your audience engaged, maintaining clear communication with your team, and tracking performance in real time, you'll set the stage for a successful launch.

Remember to celebrate your achievements, learn from any challenges, and keep the excitement alive even after launch day ends. With the right preparation, adaptability, and teamwork, your business will take off with the confidence and success it deserves.

Quick Tips and Recap

- **Stick to your launch plan, but stay flexible**: Follow your schedule and checklist, but be prepared to adapt to last-minute challenges with quick, solution-oriented thinking.

- **Build anticipation with a pre-launch campaign**: Use teasers, sneak peeks, and countdowns to generate excitement before your launch day.

- **Leverage social media and real-time updates**: Engage your audience with live posts, behind-the-scenes content, and even a launch day event or livestream.

- **Use clear internal communication**: Keep your team connected through communication tools and schedule regular check-ins to address issues quickly.

- **Track key performance metrics in real-time**: Monitor website traffic, sales, social media engagement, and email performance throughout the day to make informed adjustments.

- **Celebrate your wins and learn from challenges**: Acknowledge the hard work of your team, reflect on the lessons learned, and keep the momentum going post-launch.

By following these tips, you'll ensure a smooth, engaging, and successful launch day that leaves a lasting impression on your audience and sets your business up for continued growth.

CHAPTER SEVENTEEN

Keeping Score: Monitoring and Managing Performance

"Keeping score in business means continuously monitoring and managing performance to not only meet targets but to exceed them, ensuring strategic growth and operational excellence." — INDRA NOOYI, FORMER CEO OF PEPSICO AND INFLUENTIAL BUSINESS EXECUTIVE

Welcome to the scoreboard of business—where keeping an eye on your metrics is less about crunching numbers and more about celebrating your victories and learning from your missteps. Imagine you're the coach of a high-stakes game, and your team's performance stats are your playbook. Here, you'll master the art of monitoring and managing performance with the precision of a sports analyst and the enthusiasm of a fan at the championship finals.

In this chapter, we'll dive into the nitty-gritty of tracking your business's health, from key performance indicators to actionable insights. Think of it as your business's personal trainer regimen—regular check-ins, adjustments, and plenty of encouragement to ensure you're always on top of your game.

We'll explore how to set up your performance dashboard, interpret your data like a pro, and pivot when necessary without losing momentum. So, grab your whistle and clipboard, because it's time to manage your business's performance like a championship coach—cheering on your successes and fine-tuning your strategy to keep winning!

Identifying Key Performance Indicators (KPIs): Measuring What Matters

In any business, there are countless metrics you could track, but the key to effective performance management is focusing on the metrics that truly matter—Key Performance Indicators (KPIs). KPIs are the specific, measurable values that demonstrate how effectively your business is achieving its objectives. Think of KPIs as your business's scorecard, helping you gauge success and identify areas that need improvement.

In this section, we'll explore how to identify the most relevant KPIs for your business, ensuring that you're not just measuring numbers, but tracking the metrics that have a direct impact on your success.

1. Align KPIs with Business Goals

The first step in identifying the right KPIs is to make sure they are directly aligned with your overall business goals. Every KPI you track should reflect progress toward achieving your most critical objectives. Whether your goal is to increase revenue, improve customer satisfaction, or optimize operational efficiency, your KPIs should serve as measurable indicators of your progress.

- **Ask yourself**: What are the most important outcomes for my business? Is it growth in revenue, customer acquisition, product development, or something else? Your KPIs should provide a clear picture of how well you're moving toward these goals.

- o **Example**: If your primary goal is to grow revenue by 20% this year, a relevant KPI might be monthly revenue growth rate or customer lifetime value. If customer satisfaction is a priority, you might track Net Promoter Score (NPS) or customer retention rate.

- **Avoid vanity metrics**: Vanity metrics are numbers that look good on paper but don't provide meaningful insights into your business's actual performance. Likes, views, or social media followers can be vanity metrics if they don't contribute to your bottom line. Instead, focus on metrics that tie back to your goals.

  - o **Example**: Instead of measuring website traffic as a standalone metric, track conversion rates—the percentage of website visitors who become paying customers. This metric directly reflects the effectiveness of your website in driving sales.

Key takeaway: Choose KPIs that are directly tied to your business goals, avoiding vanity metrics that don't provide actionable insights.

2. Choose Quantifiable and Actionable KPIs

Effective KPIs should be quantifiable and actionable, meaning they provide clear, measurable data that you can act upon. Vague or subjective metrics won't give you the insights needed to make strategic decisions. The best KPIs are specific, measurable, and easy to track.

- **Be specific**: Define your KPIs as clearly as possible. Vague goals like "improve customer service" aren't actionable, but a specific KPI like average response time for customer inquiries provides a measurable, trackable target.

  - o **Example**: Instead of tracking "increased brand awareness," track brand mentions on social media or referral traffic to see exactly how often people are talking about and engaging with your brand.

- **Ensure measurability**: Every KPI should have a clear, numerical value that you can measure over time. Whether it's percentages, dollar amounts, or raw numbers, make sure your KPIs are easy to track with the data you have available.

- o **Example**: Track monthly recurring revenue (MRR) if you run a subscription-based business, or return on ad spend (ROAS) if you invest heavily in digital advertising.

- **Actionable insights**: KPIs should inform decisions. If a KPI doesn't help you make changes to improve performance, it's not a valuable metric. For every KPI, consider what actions you can take if the metric improves, declines, or stays flat.

- o **Example**: If your customer churn rate increases, it signals that you need to dive deeper into why customers are leaving and what changes you can make to improve retention.

Key takeaway: Choose KPIs that are specific, measurable, and actionable, allowing you to track progress and make data-driven decisions.

3. Focus on Leading and Lagging Indicators

KPIs can be broadly categorized into leading and lagging indicators. Understanding the difference between the two will help you track performance holistically and make proactive adjustments when necessary.

- **Leading indicators**: These are forward-looking metrics that predict future performance. They give you an early warning about where things are headed, allowing you to make adjustments before outcomes are fully realized.

- o **Example**: If you want to increase sales, a leading indicator could be the number of new sales leads or website conversions, as these activities directly impact future revenue.

- **Lagging indicators**: These metrics reflect past performance and outcomes. They show you the results of actions that have already taken place. While lagging indicators are great for measuring success, they don't provide early insights into potential problems.

> o **Example**: Monthly sales revenue or profit margin are lagging indicators because they show the results of your business activities over a specific period, but they don't predict future sales.

- **Balance both**: To get a full picture of your business's performance, track both leading and lagging indicators. Leading indicators help you anticipate changes, while lagging indicators measure your actual results.

  > o **Example**: For a marketing campaign, a leading indicator might be email open rates or click-through rates, while a lagging indicator would be the number of conversions or total revenue generated.

Key takeaway: Track both leading and lagging indicators to anticipate future trends and measure past performance.

4. Monitor KPIs Regularly and Adjust When Necessary

Tracking KPIs isn't a one-time exercise—it requires regular monitoring and adjustment. As your business evolves, your goals and priorities may shift, which means your KPIs may need to change too. Consistently reviewing your KPIs ensures that you stay aligned with your objectives and can pivot when necessary.

- **Set a review schedule**: Decide how often you'll review your KPIs—whether it's daily, weekly, monthly, or quarterly. The frequency depends on the type of business you run and how quickly things change. Regular reviews allow you to stay on top of performance and make timely adjustments.

  > o **Tip**: For fast-moving aspects of your business (like online sales or marketing campaigns), daily or weekly tracking might be necessary. For long-term metrics (like customer retention or annual revenue), monthly or quarterly reviews may suffice.

- **Analyze trends over time**: One month of data won't tell you the whole story. Track your KPIs over time to identify patterns and trends that can inform your business decisions. A slight dip in sales one month might not be concerning, but a downward trend over several months is worth investigating.

- o **Example**: If you notice a steady increase in customer acquisition cost (CAC), it may signal that your marketing strategies are becoming less efficient, and you'll need to rethink your approach.

- **Be willing to adjust**: If a KPI no longer aligns with your goals or isn't providing useful insights, don't be afraid to change or replace it. As your business grows and your priorities evolve, so should your KPIs.

  - o **Example**: If you initially tracked total website visits, but now you want to focus more on engagement, you might shift your focus to bounce rate or time on page instead.

Key takeaway: Regularly monitor your KPIs, track trends over time, and be ready to adjust your metrics as your business evolves.

Conclusion: Measure What Matters for Sustainable Growth

Identifying the right KPIs is crucial for monitoring your business's performance and ensuring you're on the right path toward achieving your goals. By aligning your KPIs with your business objectives, choosing quantifiable and actionable metrics, balancing leading and lagging indicators, and regularly reviewing your data, you can effectively measure progress, identify opportunities for improvement, and steer your business toward sustainable growth.

Your KPIs should serve as a clear roadmap, helping you celebrate your successes and course-correct when necessary. When you measure what matters, you're equipped with the insights you need to make smart, data-driven decisions that propel your business forward.

Building Your Performance Dashboard: A Centralized View of Success

A performance dashboard is your business's control center—a visual tool that consolidates all of your key metrics into one easy-to-read display. By centralizing your Key Performance Indicators (KPIs) in a single location, you can monitor the health of your business at a glance, quickly spot trends, and identify areas that need attention. Think of it as the dashboard in a car: it gives you real-time feedback on how everything is running, so you can make adjustments before problems arise.

In this section, we'll explore how to build an effective performance dashboard that provides a comprehensive and centralized view of your business's success, empowering you to make data-driven decisions with confidence.

1. Select the Right Metrics for Your Dashboard

Your performance dashboard should be focused on the most important KPIs that drive your business forward. It's easy to get overwhelmed by too much data, so the key is to be selective about the metrics you include. Make sure your dashboard reflects the KPIs that give you the clearest insights into how your business is performing in relation to your goals.

- **Prioritize essential KPIs**: Start by identifying the 5 to 10 most critical KPIs that represent the health of your business. These might include metrics related to sales, customer satisfaction, operational efficiency, or financial performance.

  - o **Example**: For an e-commerce business, essential KPIs might include monthly revenue, conversion rate, average order value, and cart abandonment rate.

- **Customize for different teams**: Depending on your business structure, different teams (such as marketing, sales, or operations) may need different dashboards. Customize dashboards to show the KPIs that are most relevant to each team's responsibilities and goals.

  - o **Example**: A marketing dashboard might include website traffic, social media engagement, and email open rates, while a sales dashboard might focus on lead conversion rate, monthly sales, and sales pipeline value.

- **Avoid overloading with data**: While it's tempting to track every possible metric, overloading your dashboard with too much data can make it difficult to focus on what matters most. Keep it simple and focused, ensuring the dashboard provides clarity and insight at a glance.

Key takeaway: Focus on the essential KPIs that give you the clearest picture of your business's performance, and customize dashboards for different teams if needed.

2. Choose the Right Tools to Build Your Dashboard

Creating an effective performance dashboard requires the right tools to gather, visualize, and analyze your data. There are various software platforms available that make it easy to create dynamic, real-time dashboards. The key is to choose a tool that integrates with your existing systems and provides easy-to-understand visuals.

- **Use a dashboard platform**: Many tools can help you build your dashboard, from business intelligence platforms to more straightforward software designed specifically for dashboard creation. Popular options include Google Data Studio, Tableau, Power BI, Klipfolio, and Geckoboard.

  - **Tip**: Choose a tool that integrates seamlessly with your data sources, such as your CRM, website analytics, or accounting software, so you can automate data updates in real time.

- **Consider cloud-based solutions**: Cloud-based dashboards allow for real-time access to data and can be easily shared with team members. This is especially important if your team is working remotely or across different locations.

  - **Example**: **Google Data Studio** is a cloud-based platform that allows you to pull in data from various sources (like Google Analytics, Google Ads, and spreadsheets) to create shareable dashboards.

- **Look for customizable templates**: Most dashboard platforms offer customizable templates that make it easy to create a professional-looking dashboard without starting from scratch. Customize your dashboard with the right widgets, charts, and tables that best represent your KPIs.

o **Tip**: Use a mix of visual elements, such as bar charts, line graphs, and heat maps, to make data easy to interpret at a glance.

Key takeaway: Choose a dashboard tool that integrates with your existing systems, offers cloud-based access, and allows for customization to reflect your specific KPIs.

3. Design for Clarity and Ease of Use

Your dashboard should be designed to deliver information quickly and clearly. The design and layout of your dashboard are just as important as the data itself. A well-organized, visually appealing dashboard allows you and your team to grasp key insights in seconds, without having to sift through complicated spreadsheets or reports.

- **Use a clean, simple layout**: Group related metrics together, and use consistent formatting to create a cohesive and easy-to-navigate dashboard. Avoid clutter or overwhelming visuals that make it difficult to interpret the data.

  o **Example**: Group your financial KPIs (like revenue and profit margins) in one section and your customer engagement metrics (like customer satisfaction and NPS scores) in another, using headings or color coding to differentiate sections.

- **Make key metrics stand out**: Use larger fonts, bold colors, or highlight features to make the most important KPIs stand out on the dashboard. This ensures that the metrics you need to focus on are front and center.

  o **Tip**: If you're tracking performance against targets, consider using progress bars, goal indicators, or color-coded visuals (like red for below target and green for above target) to easily see how you're performing.

- **Incorporate real-time data**: If possible, set up your dashboard to pull in real-time data, so you always have the most up-to-date information at your fingertips. This allows you to respond quickly to changes in performance, whether positive or negative.

    o   **Example**: An e-commerce company might track real-time sales and inventory levels on its dashboard to quickly adjust marketing campaigns or restock products.

Key takeaway: Design your dashboard for simplicity, clarity, and ease of use, ensuring that the most important metrics are prominently displayed and easy to understand.

4. Make Your Dashboard Actionable

The ultimate goal of your performance dashboard is not just to monitor data but to drive action. A great dashboard allows you to quickly assess the health of your business and empowers you to make informed, data-driven decisions. To ensure your dashboard is actionable, it should highlight key trends, anomalies, and opportunities for improvement.

- **Track progress against goals**: Your dashboard should display how each KPI is performing against its target or goal. This makes it easy to see whether you're on track to meet your objectives or if adjustments are needed.

      o   **Example**: If one of your goals is to increase monthly recurring revenue by 10%, your dashboard should show both your current MRR and your progress toward that 10% goal.

- **Identify trends and patterns**: Use your dashboard to spot trends over time, whether it's seasonal changes in customer behavior or long-term growth in a particular area. Recognizing trends can help you anticipate future challenges or opportunities.

      o   **Tip**: Use line charts or trend graphs to visualize how your KPIs are performing over time, making it easier to identify upward or downward trends.

- **Set alerts for key metrics**: Some dashboard tools allow you to set alerts or notifications if a particular KPI goes outside of a predefined range. This ensures you're notified immediately if something requires attention, such as a sudden drop in sales or an unexpected increase in customer churn.

○ **Example**: If your customer support team's average response time exceeds 24 hours, set an alert to notify you so you can address the issue before it impacts customer satisfaction.

Key takeaway: Ensure your dashboard is actionable by tracking progress against goals, identifying trends, and setting alerts for critical metrics that require immediate attention.

Conclusion: Your Dashboard as a Strategic Tool

A well-built performance dashboard is one of the most powerful tools you can use to monitor and manage your business's performance. By selecting the right metrics, using the right tools, designing for clarity, and making the dashboard actionable, you'll have a centralized view of success that helps you stay on top of your goals and respond quickly to changes in performance.

Your dashboard should not only provide a real-time snapshot of how your business is performing but also empower you to make informed decisions that drive growth, efficiency, and success. With a clear, effective dashboard in place, you'll be equipped to navigate your business toward long-term sustainability and achievement.

Interpreting Data: Turning Metrics into Actionable Insights

Collecting data through KPIs and performance dashboards is a crucial part of managing your business, but the real value comes from interpreting that data and using it to make strategic decisions. Numbers on their own are just numbers—your goal is to turn those metrics into actionable insights that can help you improve performance, identify opportunities, and address challenges before they become bigger issues.

In this section, we'll explore how to analyze and interpret your data effectively, allowing you to go beyond the numbers and use data to inform meaningful actions that drive your business forward.

1. Look for Trends Over Time

One of the most important aspects of data interpretation is recognizing trends. Tracking KPIs over time allows you to see patterns in performance that might not be obvious from a single data point. Whether it's seasonal sales spikes, long-term growth, or gradual decline in customer satisfaction, understanding trends helps you predict future outcomes and make proactive adjustments.

- **Compare historical data**: Use historical data to identify whether your KPIs are moving in the right direction. For example, comparing quarterly revenue growth from this year to last year can give you a clearer picture of long-term performance and growth.

  o **Example**: If you notice a consistent uptick in sales during the holiday season, you might decide to increase inventory or launch more aggressive marketing campaigns during that time to capitalize on the trend.

- **Spot emerging trends early**: Sometimes, small fluctuations in your data can signal larger trends on the horizon. Paying attention to small but consistent changes can help you anticipate issues before they fully materialize.

  o **Example**: If you see a steady increase in customer acquisition cost (CAC) over the past few months, it may signal that your marketing strategies are becoming less efficient, allowing you to adjust your approach early on.

Key takeaway: Track your metrics over time to identify trends and patterns that can help you predict future outcomes and make informed decisions.

2. Identify and Investigate Anomalies

Not all data will follow predictable patterns. Occasionally, you'll encounter anomalies—sudden spikes or drops in your KPIs that don't align with the usual trends. While some anomalies might be positive (like a sudden increase in sales after a successful marketing campaign), others could indicate potential problems that need to be addressed.

- **Isolate the cause of the anomaly**: When you notice an anomaly in your data, dig deeper to uncover the underlying cause. Anomalies might result from external factors (like seasonal changes or unexpected events) or internal issues (like a breakdown in operations or a marketing misstep).

  o **Example**: If your website traffic suddenly drops, investigate whether there were any changes to your SEO strategy, technical issues on your website, or shifts in customer behavior.

- **Act quickly on negative anomalies**: Negative anomalies, like a drop in sales or a spike in customer complaints, should be addressed immediately. Pinpointing the cause allows you to take corrective action before the issue worsens.

  o **Example**: A sudden drop in customer satisfaction scores may indicate a problem with product quality or customer service. Quickly addressing the issue can help you avoid long-term damage to your brand.

- **Leverage positive anomalies**: Not all anomalies are bad—sometimes, you'll experience a positive spike in a metric like sales or engagement. When this happens, investigate what caused the spike and see if it's something you can replicate.

  o **Example**: If your social media engagement doubles in a single week, review the content you posted during that period to understand what resonated with your audience and apply similar strategies moving forward.

Key takeaway: Investigate anomalies in your data, both positive and negative, to uncover the causes and take action accordingly.

3. Break Down the Numbers with Segmentation

Not all data is created equal, and sometimes your overall metrics can hide important insights. By segmenting your data, you can break down large metrics into smaller, more specific groups, allowing you to see trends and patterns that would otherwise go unnoticed.

- **Segment by customer demographics**: Analyze your KPIs by different demographic segments, such as age, location, or purchase history, to better understand who your most valuable customers are and where potential growth opportunities lie.

    o **Example**: If your average order value (AOV) is higher among customers aged 25-34, you might decide to tailor more marketing efforts toward this age group to maximize sales.

- **Segment by product or service**: Break down your metrics by specific product lines or services to understand which areas of your business are performing best. This can help you identify where to invest more resources or where improvements are needed.

    o **Example**: If you're running an online store, segmenting your sales data by product can reveal which items are your top performers and which ones might need promotional support to boost sales.

- **Segment by marketing channel**: Understanding which marketing channels are driving the most traffic, engagement, or conversions can help you optimize your marketing spend and focus on the channels that are delivering the best results.

    o **Example**: If your return on ad spend (ROAS) is significantly higher on Facebook than on Google Ads, you might decide to allocate more budget to Facebook campaigns to maximize your marketing ROI.

Key takeaway: Use segmentation to break down your data by customer demographics, product lines, or marketing channels for deeper insights and more targeted strategies.

4. Make Data-Driven Decisions

Once you've identified trends, anomalies, and key insights through segmentation, the next step is to act on those insights. The ultimate goal of data interpretation is to turn metrics into concrete, data-driven decisions that improve your business's performance. This might involve adjusting your strategy, reallocating resources, or setting new goals based on what the data reveals.

- **Turn insights into actions**: For each key insight you discover, ask yourself what action you can take to either capitalize on an opportunity or address an issue. Whether it's doubling down on a successful marketing channel or addressing customer feedback, your data should inform every strategic decision.

  o **Example**: If you discover that your customer retention rate is declining, you might decide to implement a loyalty program or enhance your post-purchase follow-up process to encourage repeat business.

- **Use A/B testing to validate decisions**: When trying new strategies based on your data, consider running A/B tests to validate your decisions. This allows you to experiment with different approaches and see which one delivers the best results before committing fully.

  o **Example**: If your data suggests that changing the layout of your website could improve conversions, A/B test different layouts to see which one performs best before rolling it out across your site.

- **Regularly review and adjust your strategies**: Data is dynamic, and your strategies should be too. Regularly review your performance data to ensure that your decisions are still aligned with your goals and that you're making the necessary adjustments as your business evolves.

  o **Tip**: Set up quarterly or monthly strategy reviews where you assess your key KPIs, discuss what's working and what's not, and adjust your plans accordingly.

Key takeaway: Turn your insights into actionable, data-driven decisions that improve performance, validate them through testing, and continuously review your strategies for optimal results.

Conclusion: Turning Metrics into Meaningful Action

Interpreting data is about much more than just tracking numbers—it's about understanding the story behind those numbers and using that understanding to make informed, strategic decisions. By identifying trends, investigating anomalies, breaking down your data through segmentation, and acting on insights, you can turn raw data into actionable intelligence that drives your business forward.

The key to successful data interpretation is not just looking at the numbers but asking the right questions: What is this data telling me? How can I use this information to improve performance? By embracing a data-driven mindset, you'll be able to continuously optimize your business, seize opportunities, and stay ahead of the competition.

Course-Correcting: Adjusting Strategies Based on Performance

No business strategy is set in stone. Even the most well-crafted plans may need adjustments based on real-world performance. The key to long-term success is having the ability to course-correct—to make changes to your strategies based on the data and insights you gather from tracking performance. Being proactive and adaptable is essential in a dynamic business environment, where market conditions, customer behaviors, and competition are constantly evolving.

In this section, we'll explore how to use your performance metrics to guide strategic adjustments, helping you stay on track toward your goals and ensure continued growth.

1. Recognize When Course Corrections Are Needed

The first step in course-correcting is recognizing when a strategy isn't working as expected. Metrics and KPIs are your early warning system, signaling when it's time to make changes. While small fluctuations in performance can be normal, consistent underperformance is a sign that a deeper adjustment is needed.

- **Set performance thresholds**: Establish clear performance thresholds or benchmarks for each KPI. If your metrics fall below these thresholds consistently, it's a sign that your current strategy needs to be reevaluated.

  o **Example**: If your customer acquisition cost (CAC) increases above your target range for several months in a row, it could mean that your marketing efforts are becoming less efficient, prompting a shift in strategy.

- **Listen to leading indicators**: Leading indicators, which predict future performance, are particularly valuable in signaling when a course correction is needed. If leading indicators like website traffic or lead generation start to decline, it's an early sign that you need to take action before these trends affect lagging indicators like revenue.

  o **Example**: If your lead conversion rate starts dropping, it's a signal to review your sales funnel or marketing campaigns to identify where potential customers are falling off.

- **Use customer feedback**: Data from customer surveys, reviews, or support interactions can provide qualitative insights that highlight areas where your strategy isn't meeting expectations. This feedback can help you pinpoint where course corrections are needed.

  o **Tip**: If customer complaints about delivery times increase, it might be time to reevaluate your supply chain or logistics strategy.

Key takeaway: Regularly monitor your metrics and set performance thresholds to recognize when a strategy isn't working as expected. Pay attention to leading indicators and customer feedback for early warning signs.

2. Analyze the Root Cause of Underperformance

Before making any changes to your strategy, it's important to thoroughly understand the root cause of underperformance. Adjustments based on incomplete or superficial analysis may not solve the underlying issue and could even exacerbate it. A data-driven approach helps you pinpoint the exact problem so you can make targeted changes.

- **Look for patterns**: When you notice underperformance in a particular KPI, review the data over time to identify patterns or trends that could be contributing to the issue.

  o **Example**: If your customer churn rate has been steadily increasing, break down the data by customer segments, product categories, or subscription types to identify which areas are driving the most churn.

- **Conduct a root cause analysis**: Use techniques like the 5 Whys (asking "why" multiple times to drill down into the cause) or a fishbone diagram to map out potential causes of underperformance. This methodical approach helps you explore all possible contributing factors, from operational inefficiencies to changes in customer preferences.

  o **Example**: If your sales conversion rate is declining, asking "Why?" might lead you to discover that a recent website update caused confusion in the checkout process, deterring customers from completing their purchase.

- **Consider external factors**: Not all performance issues are internal. Sometimes external factors like market changes, new competitors, or economic shifts can impact your performance. Stay aware of external trends and how they might be influencing your business.

  o **Example**: If your product sales are declining, consider whether new competitors have entered the market or if there are seasonal factors influencing customer behavior.

Key takeaway: Conduct a root cause analysis to fully understand the reasons for underperformance. Use data and feedback to identify patterns and external factors that could be influencing your results.

3. Test and Implement Strategic Adjustments

Once you've identified the root cause of an issue, it's time to make strategic adjustments. However, rather than making sweeping changes all at once, it's often better to test smaller, more targeted adjustments first. This approach allows you to evaluate the effectiveness of the change before implementing it on a larger scale.

- **Start with small changes**: When making adjustments, start small and test different approaches to see what works best. This could mean adjusting your messaging, experimenting with a new marketing channel, or changing your product offerings slightly. By starting small, you reduce the risk of negative outcomes.

  o **Example**: If your email open rates are declining, you could test different subject lines or email formats to see which one resonates better with your audience before overhauling your entire email marketing strategy.

- **Use A/B testing**: A/B testing is a powerful way to evaluate different strategies side by side. By testing two variations (A and B) on different segments of your audience, you can quickly determine which one performs better and make data-backed decisions.

  o **Example**: If you're considering changing your pricing strategy, A/B test different price points with two customer groups to see which results in higher sales or customer satisfaction.

- **Measure the impact of changes**: Once you've implemented a change, track your KPIs closely to measure the impact. This will allow you to assess whether the adjustment is having the desired effect or if further refinements are needed.

  o **Example**: After changing your social media strategy, measure the impact on engagement rate and referral traffic to see if the new approach is delivering better results.

Key takeaway: Test small, targeted changes first, use A/B testing when possible, and track the impact of your adjustments on performance to ensure the changes are effective.

4. Remain Flexible and Ready to Pivot

The ability to pivot—or make a significant change in strategy when necessary— is essential in the fast-moving world of business. While smaller course corrections may solve many issues, there are times when a more significant shift in direction is required. This might involve repositioning your product, entering a new market, or adopting a new business model altogether.

- **Know when to pivot**: Pivoting is often necessary when you're consistently missing your performance goals despite making smaller adjustments. It could also be the right move if your market is shifting dramatically or if new opportunities emerge that could redefine your business's success.

  o **Example**: If a competitor launches a groundbreaking product that disrupts your market, you may need to pivot by offering a new feature or service that differentiates your brand.

- **Evaluate the potential impact**: Before making a major pivot, evaluate the potential risks and rewards. Consider how the pivot will affect your current customer base, operational processes, and financial performance. A well-executed pivot can open up new opportunities, but a poorly planned one can create additional challenges.

  o **Example**: If you're pivoting to offer a subscription-based service instead of one-time purchases, consider how this will affect your cash flow, marketing strategies, and customer retention efforts.

- **Be proactive, not reactive**: While it's important to respond to changes in performance, try to stay ahead of the curve by anticipating future challenges and opportunities. A proactive approach allows you to pivot on your terms rather than reacting to external pressures.

  o **Example**: If you anticipate that customer preferences are shifting toward eco-friendly products, consider pivoting your product line to focus on sustainability before your competitors do.

Key takeaway: Know when to pivot by evaluating long-term trends and performance. Stay flexible and open to making significant changes when necessary to capitalize on new opportunities or respond to market shifts.

Conclusion: Course-Correcting for Long-Term Success

Course-correcting is a critical part of managing your business's performance and ensuring that you stay on track to meet your goals. By recognizing when adjustments are needed, conducting thorough root cause analyses, testing and implementing strategic changes, and knowing when to pivot, you can keep your business agile and responsive to both internal performance metrics and external market conditions.

Remember, the key to successful course corrections is flexibility. By continuously monitoring your data, learning from your results, and remaining open to change, you'll position your business to adapt and thrive, no matter what challenges come your way. With the ability to course-correct effectively, you'll be equipped to navigate your business through growth, uncertainty, and beyond.

Quick Tips and Recap

- **Set performance thresholds**: Establish benchmarks for each KPI to identify when your strategy isn't working and adjustments are needed.

- **Track leading and lagging indicators**: Pay attention to leading indicators to catch issues early and lagging indicators to assess overall outcomes.

- **Conduct root cause analysis**: Use methods like the "5 Whys" to drill down and find the real reason for underperformance before making changes.

- **Test small changes first**: Start with targeted adjustments and A/B testing to evaluate different strategies before committing to larger changes.

- **Monitor the impact of adjustments**: Continuously track KPIs to ensure that changes lead to improved performance and course-correct as needed.

- **Be ready to pivot**: If smaller changes aren't delivering results, consider making a significant shift in strategy to better align with market conditions or opportunities.

By regularly reviewing your performance data and making strategic adjustments, you'll ensure that your business stays agile, responsive, and on track for long-term success.

CHAPTER EIGHTEEN

Shift Gears: Mastering the Art of the Pivot

"Mastering the art of the pivot in business is about recognizing when the path you're on isn't leading you towards your goals and having the courage to take a new direction for better outcomes."— ERIC RIES, ENTREPRENEUR AND AUTHOR OF THE LEAN STARTUP

Welcome to the thrilling world of the pivot, where agility and adaptability are your best friends, and change is not just inevitable but an opportunity. Think of pivoting as the business equivalent of a high-speed car chase—swift, decisive, and often unexpected. In this chapter, we'll delve into the art of shifting gears with finesse, ensuring that when life throws you a curveball, you dodge it and come out ahead.

Imagine you're dancing on a slippery floor—one wrong move, and you could stumble. But with the right moves, you glide gracefully, turning obstacles into opportunities. We'll explore how to read the market signals, adjust your strategy on the fly, and turn potential setbacks into springboards for success.

You'll learn how to execute a pivot that's not just a reaction but a calculated, strategic shift that keeps you in the game and ahead of the competition. So, get ready to embrace change like a pro and make every pivot a power move on the path to business greatness!

Recognizing the Need for a Pivot: When to Shift Strategies

In business, staying on course is important, but knowing when to pivot is equally crucial for long-term success. A pivot isn't about abandoning your core idea; it's about adjusting your strategy to better align with market conditions, customer needs, or internal realities. But how do you know when it's time to make that shift? In this section, we'll explore the key signs that indicate a pivot is necessary and help you decide when to make a strategic change to keep your business moving forward.

1. Stagnant or Declining Growth

One of the clearest signs that a pivot might be necessary is when your business is experiencing stagnant or declining growth. If your sales, customer base, or market presence isn't expanding despite consistent efforts, it's a signal that your current strategy may no longer be effective. Businesses that once thrived may hit a plateau, and continuing with the same approach may lead to further decline.

- **Key metrics to monitor**: Keep an eye on metrics like revenue growth, customer acquisition rate, and market share. If these metrics have been flat or declining for a sustained period, it could be a sign that the market is no longer responding to your current offering or that you're out of sync with changing customer needs.

  - **Example**: If your product has seen consistent sales for several years but suddenly experiences a sharp decline, it may indicate that customer preferences have shifted or new competitors are disrupting your market.

- **Evaluate customer behavior**: Are customers showing less interest in your product or service? Look for changes in customer engagement, purchase frequency, or satisfaction. If you're seeing more churn or lower repeat purchase rates, it might be time to reevaluate your strategy.

Key takeaway: A sustained period of stagnant or declining growth is one of the clearest signs that a pivot may be necessary. Monitor your key growth metrics closely to spot when your current strategy is no longer working.

2. Shifts in Market Demand

Markets are constantly evolving, and what was once in high demand can quickly become obsolete. When market demand shifts, businesses must adapt or risk being left behind. A pivot may be needed if you notice that the market is trending in a different direction than when you first launched your business.

- **Analyze industry trends**: Stay informed about broader industry trends that could signal a change in customer preferences or technology. Innovations, emerging technologies, or shifts in societal behavior can quickly alter the landscape of your market.

  o **Example**: If you're in the tech industry and a new disruptive technology like AI or blockchain emerges, it could signal a shift in what customers expect, prompting you to pivot your product development toward these new trends.

- **Competitor activity**: Keep an eye on competitors. If you notice that competitors are innovating or shifting their focus, it may indicate that they've detected a change in market demand. Don't wait until you're losing customers to realize the market has evolved.

- **Customer feedback**: Listen to your customers. They often provide the first indicators of a shift in demand. If you're hearing recurring complaints, suggestions, or requests for features that your current offering doesn't address, it might be time to pivot to meet their evolving needs.

  o **Example**: If customers consistently ask for a more sustainable or eco-friendly version of your product, it could indicate a growing trend in environmental consciousness that your business needs to address.

Key takeaway: Pay attention to shifts in market demand by monitoring industry trends, competitor actions, and customer feedback. When demand moves in a different direction, be ready to pivot to meet new market expectations.

3. New Opportunities or Unmet Needs

Sometimes, the need for a pivot comes not from a problem, but from an exciting new opportunity. Unmet needs in the market or new growth opportunities can provide a compelling reason to shift your business strategy. If you've identified a gap in the market that your business is uniquely positioned to fill, pivoting can help you capitalize on that opportunity before someone else does.

- **Spotting unmet needs**: Unmet needs often become apparent through market research, customer feedback, or your own observations as an industry insider. Look for pain points or frustrations that customers consistently mention, but that aren't being adequately addressed by existing products or services.

  - **Example**: If you notice that a specific group of customers is using your product in ways you didn't originally anticipate, it could signal an unmet need that you can pivot to serve directly.

- **Emerging markets**: Sometimes a pivot is necessary to take advantage of an emerging market that's ripe for innovation. Whether it's expanding into a new geographical area, targeting a different demographic, or offering a new product line, pivoting into an emerging market can open up significant growth opportunities.

  - **Example**: If your business has been successful domestically but you identify a growing demand for your product in international markets, a pivot could involve expanding your business to meet this new opportunity.

Key takeaway: Don't just pivot to solve problems—pivot to seize new opportunities. Look for unmet needs in the market and emerging opportunities that align with your business's strengths.

4. Internal Struggles and Operational Inefficiencies

A pivot may also be necessary when internal factors, such as operational inefficiencies, resource constraints, or team misalignment, are hindering your ability to execute your current strategy effectively. If your business is facing recurring internal challenges that are holding you back from achieving growth, it may be time to rethink your approach.

- **Operational bottlenecks**: If inefficiencies in your operations are consistently slowing down production, increasing costs, or reducing quality, it's a sign that your current model may not be sustainable. A pivot could involve rethinking your supply chain, outsourcing certain functions, or adopting new technologies to streamline operations.

  - ○ **Example**: If your current manufacturing process can't scale to meet growing demand, pivoting to a more efficient production method or partnering with a larger supplier could resolve the bottleneck and position your business for growth.

- **Resource misalignment**: If your team is stretched too thin or struggling to execute the business's core tasks, it may indicate that your current strategy is misaligned with your available resources. Pivoting to a more focused or scalable model can help you optimize your resources and achieve better results.

  - ○ **Example**: If your team is spending too much time on low-value activities, a pivot might involve outsourcing non-core tasks and focusing more on high-impact projects that align with your business's strengths.

Key takeaway: Internal struggles and operational inefficiencies are signs that your current strategy may not be sustainable. Look for opportunities to pivot toward a more streamlined, scalable approach that aligns with your resources and capabilities.

Conclusion: Know When It's Time to Pivot
Recognizing the need for a pivot is a critical skill in business. Whether it's due to declining growth, shifting market demand, new opportunities, or internal struggles, knowing when to shift gears can make the difference between

stagnation and long-term success. By closely monitoring your performance metrics, staying attuned to market changes, and being proactive in addressing both challenges and opportunities, you can pivot strategically and position your business for continued growth.

A successful pivot isn't about abandoning your vision—it's about adapting it to better fit the evolving landscape, making sure your business remains competitive, relevant, and poised for future success.

Evaluating Pivot Opportunities: Choosing the Right Direction

When you've identified the need for a pivot, the next critical step is choosing the right direction. Pivoting isn't just about change for the sake of change—it's about making a calculated, strategic decision that aligns with your long-term goals and maximizes your chances of success. Evaluating potential pivot opportunities means weighing the risks and rewards, analyzing market fit, and determining whether the pivot will improve your position in the market. In this section, we'll explore how to evaluate different pivot opportunities and make the best choice for your business.

1. Assess Alignment with Your Core Mission and Values

When considering a pivot, it's important to evaluate whether the new direction aligns with your business's core mission and values. A successful pivot shouldn't stray too far from your brand's identity or what makes your business unique. Instead, it should build on the foundation you've already established, leveraging your existing strengths.

- **Revisit your mission**: Ask yourself whether the pivot supports your long-term vision for the company. Does this opportunity still allow you to fulfill your mission, or will it require a complete overhaul of your business's identity?

  o **Example**: If your company's mission is to deliver sustainable products, pivoting into a new market or product category should still align with your commitment to sustainability. A pivot that goes against your core values, such as introducing non-eco-friendly products, could confuse your customer base and dilute your brand.

- **Leverage existing strengths**: Ensure that the pivot leverages your business's core competencies. You don't want to pivot into a direction that requires you to build entirely new capabilities unless you have the resources and time to do so. The best pivots allow you to use your current skills, infrastructure, and resources in a new way.

  - o **Example**: If your strength is exceptional customer service, you might pivot to offer a new service or product that still emphasizes personalized support rather than entering a market that prioritizes automation and self-service.

Key takeaway: Make sure your pivot aligns with your company's mission, values, and strengths. The right pivot should build on what you already do well, not force you to reinvent your entire business model.

2. Analyze Market Demand and Fit

Before committing to a pivot, it's essential to analyze the market to ensure there is enough demand to justify the shift. A pivot that doesn't address a clear market need, or that enters a market already saturated with competitors, is unlikely to succeed. Understanding the size of the opportunity and how well your business fits into the new market is key.

- **Conduct market research**: Research the potential market for your pivot. Are there enough customers who need or want the new product or service you're considering? Is the market growing, stable, or declining? Look for data that supports the viability of the opportunity.

  - o **Example**: If you're considering pivoting from a B2C model to a B2B model, conduct market research to understand the size of the B2B market, the types of companies that would benefit from your offering, and the challenges they face that your business could solve.

- **Evaluate competition**: Consider the level of competition in the market. A pivot into a highly competitive space could make it difficult to differentiate your business, while a pivot into an underserved niche may present more opportunities for growth.

  o **Example**: If you're thinking about launching a subscription box service, but the market is flooded with similar offerings, you'll need to evaluate whether you can offer something truly unique or if you'd be better off exploring a less crowded niche.

- **Test for product-market fit**: Consider running small tests or pilot programs to evaluate whether your pivot is likely to succeed in the new market. This could include soft launches, focus groups, or surveys to gather feedback from potential customers.

  o **Example**: If you're pivoting to offer a new product line, start with a limited release or crowdfunding campaign to gauge demand and gather early feedback before fully committing to the pivot.

Key takeaway: Thoroughly analyze market demand, competition, and fit before making a pivot. Conduct research, test the waters, and ensure there's enough demand to support the shift.

3. Evaluate the Risks and Rewards

All pivots come with inherent risks, but the potential rewards can make it worth the effort. Weighing the risks and rewards of each pivot opportunity is crucial to making an informed decision. You need to understand not only what you stand to gain but also what you're risking by making the shift—and how to mitigate those risks.

- **Assess the potential rewards**: Start by evaluating the upside of the pivot. What new opportunities does it open up? How could it accelerate your growth or position you better in the market? Look at both the short-term benefits (e.g., increased revenue, new customer segments) and the long-term potential (e.g., industry leadership, expanded market share).

o **Example**: A pivot into an emerging market with little competition could provide rapid growth and position your business as an early leader in the space, creating a lasting competitive advantage.

- **Identify potential risks**: Every pivot comes with risks. These could include alienating your existing customers, stretching your resources too thin, or entering a market with more challenges than you anticipated. Consider the financial, operational, and reputational risks involved in making the pivot.

  o **Example**: If you pivot to a new product line, you risk losing focus on your core offering and alienating customers who prefer your original product. Consider whether the potential gain from the pivot outweighs the risk of losing existing customers.

- **Create a risk mitigation plan**: Once you've identified the risks, create a plan to minimize them. This could include setting contingency plans, securing additional resources, or preparing a phased approach to the pivot to reduce the impact on your business.

  o **Example**: If you're worried about alienating your existing customer base, you might introduce the new product line gradually and offer incentives or personalized support to keep your current customers engaged during the transition.

Key takeaway: Weigh the risks and rewards carefully before committing to a pivot. Understand both the potential benefits and the risks, and create a plan to mitigate those risks as much as possible.

4. Assess the Impact on Your Team and Resources

A pivot can have significant implications for your team and resources, from shifting focus to reallocating budgets. Before making a final decision, consider whether your team has the capacity to handle the pivot and whether you have the financial resources and operational support to execute the change effectively.

- **Evaluate team capacity**: Consider whether your current team has the skills and capacity to handle the pivot. Will the shift require additional training, new hires, or restructuring? Ensure that your team is aligned with the new direction and ready to take on new challenges.

- o **Example**: If your pivot involves adopting new technology or expanding into a new market, make sure your team has the expertise to manage the transition. You may need to invest in training or bring in new talent to support the pivot.

- **Examine resource allocation**: Pivots often require reallocating resources, whether it's adjusting budgets, shifting focus away from existing projects, or investing in new tools and technology. Assess whether you have the financial and operational resources to support the pivot without sacrificing other critical areas of your business.

- o **Example**: If you're pivoting to a new product line, you may need to redirect resources from marketing or R&D. Ensure that you're not underfunding other vital aspects of your business in the process.

- **Plan for operational changes**: Pivots can also impact your day-to-day operations, from supply chain adjustments to changes in customer service protocols. Consider how the pivot will affect your current operations and plan for any necessary changes in advance.

- o **Example**: If you're moving from a traditional sales model to a subscription-based service, you'll need to adjust your billing, customer support, and fulfillment processes to align with the new model.

Key takeaway: Ensure your team and resources are capable of handling the pivot. Consider the need for additional training, resource allocation, and operational changes to ensure a smooth transition.

Conclusion: Choose the Right Pivot with Confidence

Evaluating pivot opportunities is about finding the right balance between alignment with your core mission, market demand, risk management, and resource readiness. By carefully analyzing each opportunity, testing for market fit, and understanding the potential impact on your team and operations, you can make a confident decision that positions your business for future growth.

A successful pivot isn't just about responding to challenges—it's about seizing new opportunities, adapting to changing conditions, and making strategic decisions that keep your business relevant, competitive, and profitable.

Executing a Successful Pivot: Planning and Communication

No business strategy is set in stone. Even the most well-crafted plans may need adjustments based on real-world performance. The key to long-term success is having the ability to course-correct—to make changes to your strategies based on the data and insights you gather from tracking performance. Being proactive and adaptable is essential in a dynamic business environment, where market conditions, customer behaviors, and competition are constantly evolving.

Once you've identified the need for a pivot and chosen the right direction, the next step is executing the pivot effectively. A successful pivot requires meticulous planning, clear communication, and strategic execution to ensure that your business adapts smoothly to the new direction without losing momentum or alienating key stakeholders. In this section, we'll explore how to plan and communicate your pivot to ensure it's carried out efficiently and embraced by your team, customers, and partners.

1. Create a Clear and Detailed Pivot Plan

A successful pivot begins with a well-defined plan that outlines every step of the transition. This plan should address not only what will change but also how those changes will be implemented, the timeline for each phase, and the resources needed to support the pivot. The more comprehensive and detailed your plan, the smoother the transition will be.

- **Break it down into phases**: Depending on the scale of the pivot, it's often best to break the transition down into smaller, manageable phases. This allows you to implement changes gradually, assess their impact, and adjust as needed.

  o **Example**: If you're pivoting to introduce a new product line, the first phase might involve market testing and feedback, the second phase could be product development, and the final phase might be a full-scale launch.

- **Set clear goals and milestones**: Establish specific, measurable goals for each phase of the pivot. These goals will help you track progress and ensure that you're staying on track throughout the process.

  - o **Example**: If your pivot involves entering a new market, set milestones like securing your first 100 customers in the new market, establishing key partnerships, or achieving a specific revenue target within the first six months.

- **Plan for contingencies**: No pivot is without challenges, so it's important to anticipate potential roadblocks and plan for contingencies. Identify the key risks associated with the pivot and develop backup strategies to mitigate those risks.

  - o **Example**: If your pivot involves outsourcing production to a new supplier, have alternative suppliers lined up in case your primary partner faces delays or quality issues.

Key takeaway: Create a detailed pivot plan that includes clear phases, goals, milestones, and contingency plans to ensure a smooth and strategic transition.

2. Communicate Transparently with Your Team

Effective communication is critical to the success of any pivot. Your team needs to fully understand the reasons for the pivot, how it will affect their roles, and what the new strategy entails. Clear, transparent communication helps to build buy-in and ensure that everyone is aligned with the new direction.

- **Explain the "why" behind the pivot**: Begin by communicating the reasons for the pivot. Whether it's a response to market changes, customer needs, or new opportunities, your team needs to understand the rationale behind the decision. Transparency fosters trust and helps your team see the pivot as a strategic move rather than a reactionary one.

  - o **Example**: "We're pivoting to focus on our subscription model because we've identified growing demand for recurring services in our market. This will allow us to build stronger

427

customer relationships and create a more predictable revenue stream."

- **Clarify the impact on roles and responsibilities**: A pivot can lead to shifts in roles and responsibilities, so it's important to clarify how the pivot will affect each team member. Outline any new roles that will be created, and provide training or resources if necessary to support your team in adapting to the new direction.

  o **Example**: If your sales team will need to shift from selling one-off products to subscription services, ensure they receive the necessary training and resources to succeed in this new model.

- **Provide regular updates**: As the pivot progresses, keep your team informed of key milestones, challenges, and successes. Regular updates ensure that everyone is on the same page and can address any concerns or questions that arise during the transition.

  o **Tip**: Hold weekly or biweekly team meetings to review progress, celebrate wins, and discuss any adjustments that need to be made to the pivot plan.

Key takeaway: Communicate openly and frequently with your team, explaining the reasons for the pivot, clarifying new roles, and providing regular updates to keep everyone aligned and engaged.

3. Manage Stakeholder Expectations

In addition to your internal team, your external stakeholders—such as customers, investors, partners, and suppliers—also need to be kept in the loop about your pivot. Managing these relationships with care is essential to ensure that your pivot doesn't cause confusion, concern, or misalignment with key stakeholders.

- **Communicate with customers**: If the pivot will affect your customers (e.g., changes to products, services, or pricing), communicate with them clearly and proactively. Explain how the pivot will benefit them, address any potential concerns, and provide a timeline for the changes. Transparency builds trust and ensures that your customers stay loyal throughout the transition.

     o   **Example**: "We're excited to announce that we're expanding our product line to better meet your needs. Here's what's changing, and here's how it will improve your experience with us."

- **Keep investors and partners informed**: If your pivot requires additional resources or changes in direction that affect your investors or partners, make sure to communicate these changes early on. Provide them with data or insights that support the pivot, and outline how the new strategy will drive future growth and value.

     o   **Example**: If your pivot requires additional funding, share a revised financial plan with your investors, detailing how the pivot will increase revenue or market share and outlining the expected return on investment.

- **Strengthen supplier relationships**: If the pivot impacts your suppliers or operational partners, make sure they're aware of any changes in demand, production schedules, or product specifications. This ensures that you can maintain smooth operations during the pivot.

     o   **Example**: If you're launching a new product line, communicate with your suppliers about potential increases in order volume, quality requirements, or changes in delivery timelines.

Key takeaway: Proactively communicate with customers, investors, partners, and suppliers to manage expectations, maintain trust, and ensure alignment throughout the pivot process.

4. Monitor Progress and Adjust as Needed

Executing a successful pivot requires ongoing monitoring to ensure that the strategy is working and that you're on track to achieve your goals. Regularly reviewing your progress allows you to identify any issues early and make adjustments before they become major obstacles.

- **Track key performance indicators (KPIs)**: Set specific KPIs to measure the success of your pivot and track them regularly. These could include customer acquisition, sales growth, market share, or other relevant metrics depending on the nature of your pivot.

- o **Example**: If your pivot involves introducing a subscription service, track KPIs such as subscriber growth, monthly recurring revenue (MRR), and churn rate to measure the success of the new model.

- **Gather feedback and iterate**: Don't hesitate to make adjustments to your pivot strategy based on feedback from your team, customers, or stakeholders. Be open to iterating on the plan if certain aspects of the pivot aren't working as expected.

  - o **Tip**: Hold regular check-ins with your team to gather feedback on what's working and what's not. Use this feedback to refine your approach and address any roadblocks.

- **Celebrate wins and learn from challenges**: As you execute the pivot, celebrate key milestones and successes along the way. Acknowledging progress keeps your team motivated and builds confidence in the new direction. Similarly, learn from any challenges or setbacks and use them as opportunities to improve.

  - o **Example**: If the initial phase of your pivot achieves its goals (e.g., a successful product launch), take time to celebrate with your team and share the positive results with stakeholders.

Key takeaway: Monitor KPIs, gather feedback, and adjust your pivot strategy as needed. Celebrate successes and use challenges as learning opportunities to refine your approach.

Conclusion: Plan and Communicate for a Seamless Pivot

Executing a successful pivot requires careful planning, clear communication, and a commitment to monitoring and adjusting along the way. By creating a detailed pivot plan, communicating openly with your team and stakeholders, and tracking progress regularly, you'll ensure that your pivot is not only well-executed but also embraced by everyone involved.

The key to a seamless pivot is flexibility—being willing to adapt as you go and making sure everyone is aligned with the new direction. With the right strategy in place, your pivot can unlock new growth opportunities, improve your market position, and set your business on a path to long-term success.

Learning from the Pivot: Measuring Success and Iterating

Once you've executed your pivot, the journey doesn't end there. A successful pivot is not just about changing direction—it's about measuring the impact, learning from the experience, and continuously iterating to refine your approach. Whether the pivot brings immediate success or presents unexpected challenges, the key is to use the results as a learning opportunity to improve your strategy and ensure long-term growth.

In this section, we'll explore how to measure the success of your pivot, learn from the outcomes, and iterate on your approach to keep your business on the path to success.

1. Define Metrics of Success

The first step in measuring the effectiveness of your pivot is defining what success looks like. Success metrics will depend on the nature of your pivot—whether you've shifted your product offering, entered a new market, or changed your business model. Clear, measurable objectives help you evaluate whether the pivot is achieving the intended results.

- **Set clear KPIs**: Establish specific key performance indicators (KPIs) to track the success of your pivot. These should align with your overall business goals and reflect both the short-term and long-term impact of the pivot.

    - **Example**: If your pivot involves shifting to a subscription-based business model, KPIs could include monthly recurring revenue (MRR), subscriber growth, and customer churn rate.

- **Measure customer response**: Customer feedback is an essential metric for evaluating the success of your pivot. Track metrics related to customer satisfaction, engagement, and retention to understand how well your new strategy is resonating with your target audience.

- o **Example**: Post-pivot, send surveys or conduct focus groups to gather feedback on how customers are responding to your new product or service. Are they satisfied with the changes? Are there areas for improvement?

- **Assess financial performance**: Financial metrics are critical for determining whether the pivot is delivering the expected return on investment. Track sales growth, profit margins, cash flow, and overall profitability to ensure that your pivot is contributing to the financial health of your business.

  - o **Example**: If your pivot involves expanding into a new market, measure how much revenue the new market generates compared to your existing markets.

Key takeaway: Define clear KPIs, measure customer response, and assess financial performance to determine whether your pivot is achieving its goals.

2. Evaluate the Impact of the Pivot

Once you've gathered data on your KPIs, it's time to evaluate the overall impact of the pivot. Did the pivot lead to the desired outcomes? Were there any unexpected results, both positive and negative? By analyzing the data, you can identify what worked, what didn't, and where improvements can be made.

- **Identify successes and challenges**: Review your KPIs to identify which aspects of the pivot were successful and which areas fell short. Celebrate the wins, but also take the time to understand the challenges or setbacks you encountered.

  - o **Example**: If your pivot led to a successful product launch but sales didn't meet expectations, analyze whether the pricing strategy, marketing efforts, or customer education were factors that contributed to lower-than-expected sales.

- **Compare pre- and post-pivot performance**: A useful way to evaluate the impact of a pivot is to compare key metrics before and after the pivot.

This allows you to see how your business has evolved and whether the pivot has led to measurable improvements in performance.

- o **Example**: If your pivot was aimed at increasing customer retention, compare your **customer retention rate** pre- and post-pivot to see if the changes made a positive impact.

- **Gather qualitative feedback**: In addition to quantitative data, gather qualitative feedback from both your team and your customers. This feedback can provide valuable insights into how the pivot was perceived, what could be improved, and what elements were particularly effective.

- o **Tip**: Hold debrief sessions with your team to discuss the execution of the pivot and gather their thoughts on what went well and what could be improved. Similarly, engage with customers through surveys or interviews to get their perspectives.

Key takeaway: Evaluate the pivot's overall impact by analyzing both quantitative KPIs and qualitative feedback. Identify successes and challenges to better understand how the pivot performed.

3. Learn from the Process

Every pivot, whether it meets all expectations or presents unforeseen challenges, is an opportunity to learn and grow. By reflecting on the process, you can uncover valuable lessons that will guide future strategic decisions. The ability to learn from the experience is what separates businesses that thrive from those that stagnate.

- **Reflect on what worked**: Take time to reflect on what aspects of the pivot worked well. Whether it was your team's adaptability, a particular marketing strategy, or a product feature that resonated with customers, understanding these successes will help you replicate them in the future.

- o **Example**: If your marketing campaign for the pivot was highly effective in driving customer engagement, analyze the elements that made it successful, such as messaging, channels used, or timing, and apply those lessons to future campaigns.

- **Identify areas for improvement**: No pivot is without its challenges. Reflect on what didn't go as planned, and identify the root causes of any issues you encountered. Use this information to improve your future pivots and business strategies.

    o **Example**: If your supply chain struggled to keep up with demand post-pivot, work on strengthening relationships with suppliers, improving forecasting, or exploring new logistics partners to avoid similar challenges in the future.

- **Create a playbook for future pivots**: The insights you gain from this pivot can serve as a valuable resource for future pivots or strategic shifts. Document the key takeaways, including what worked, what didn't, and any best practices that emerged during the process.

    o **Tip**: Develop a "pivot playbook" that outlines lessons learned, successful strategies, and key action steps that can be used as a reference for future pivots or major business changes.

Key takeaway: Learn from the pivot by reflecting on both the successes and challenges, and create a playbook of best practices to guide future pivots and strategic decisions.

4. Iterate and Refine Your Approach

A pivot is rarely a one-and-done process. As you evaluate the success of your pivot and learn from the outcomes, you may find opportunities to iterate and refine your approach. Continuous iteration ensures that your business remains agile and adaptable to further changes in the market or customer needs.

- **Test new ideas**: After analyzing the pivot's performance, you may identify areas that could be further optimized or improved. Don't be afraid to test new ideas, tweak your strategies, and iterate on your approach to maximize success.

    o **Example**: If the pivot to a subscription model was moderately successful but customers are requesting more flexibility, consider testing different subscription tiers or payment plans to enhance the offering.

- **Stay responsive to market changes**: Even after a successful pivot, the market will continue to evolve. Stay responsive to emerging trends, customer feedback, and industry changes so that you can iterate on your strategy and remain competitive.

  o **Example**: If a new competitor enters the market post-pivot, consider refining your marketing message or product features to better differentiate your brand and capture customer attention.

- **Revisit KPIs regularly**: As part of the iteration process, revisit your KPIs regularly to ensure that you're on track to meet your goals. Continuous monitoring allows you to make adjustments quickly and keep your business aligned with its strategic objectives.

  o **Tip**: Schedule monthly or quarterly KPI reviews to assess the ongoing performance of your pivot and identify areas where further refinements may be needed.

Key takeaway: The pivot doesn't end with execution—iterate and refine your approach based on what you've learned. Stay responsive to market changes and continuously improve your strategy to maximize long-term success.

Conclusion: Measure, Learn, and Iterate for Long-Term Success

The success of a pivot is not determined solely by its immediate outcomes but by your ability to measure performance, learn from the experience, and iterate for continuous improvement. By defining clear success metrics, evaluating the impact of the pivot, reflecting on key takeaways, and refining your approach, you'll ensure that your business remains agile and adaptable in a fast-changing market.

Remember, a pivot is a strategic shift that requires thoughtful planning and execution, but it also offers an opportunity for growth and innovation. With the right approach to measuring success and learning from the process, every pivot can become a stepping stone to greater business success and resilience in the future.

Quick Tips and Recap

- **Define clear KPIs**: Set measurable goals and key performance indicators (KPIs) to track the success of your pivot.

- **Evaluate customer response**: Gather feedback from your customers to understand how well your pivot is being received and where improvements can be made.

- **Compare pre- and post-pivot performance**: Use your performance data to assess whether the pivot has led to measurable improvements in key areas like sales, customer satisfaction, and market position.

- **Reflect on successes and challenges**: Identify what worked well and what didn't, using these insights to refine your approach and guide future decisions.

- **Create a pivot playbook**: Document key lessons learned, successful strategies, and best practices for future pivots or business shifts.

- **Iterate and refine**: Continuously monitor performance and be prepared to make adjustments based on new insights or market changes.

By following these tips, you'll be able to measure the success of your pivot, learn from the process, and iterate for continuous improvement, ensuring long-term success and adaptability.

CHAPTER NINETEEN

Scaling New Heights: Strategies for Growth

"Scaling new heights in business requires not just vision but also a robust strategy that includes scalability from the start, turning small wins into major growth opportunities." — REID HOFFMAN, ENTREPRENEUR AND CO-FOUNDER OF LINKEDIN

Welcome to the summit of business success, where scaling new heights is less about climbing ladders and more about reaching for the stars with a well-packed parachute. In this chapter, we're talking about growth strategies that'll have your business soaring to new altitudes, leaving competitors in your rearview mirror.

Think of it as upgrading from a cozy cabin to a penthouse suite—suddenly, you've got more space, a better view, and room to invite even more guests to the party.

We'll explore how to expand your reach, scale operations, and leverage opportunities with the same finesse as a seasoned mountaineer.

You'll learn how to set ambitious goals, identify high-impact strategies, and build a growth plan that's as robust as it is thrilling. With the right approach, scaling up becomes less of a daunting climb and more of an exhilarating ascent. So strap on your gear, chart your course, and get ready to conquer new heights in style!

Setting Scalable Goals: Building a Blueprint for Expansion

Scaling your business requires more than just ambition—it demands a clear, actionable plan that is grounded in scalable goals. These goals are your blueprint for expansion, giving you a roadmap to grow sustainably without overwhelming your team or resources. In this section, we'll explore how to set effective, growth-oriented goals that are both bold and achievable, helping you steer your business to new heights with confidence.

1. Define What Growth Looks Like for Your Business

Before you can scale, you need a clear understanding of what growth means for your business. This will vary depending on your industry, business model, and long-term objectives. For some businesses, growth might mean increasing revenue, while for others it could mean expanding market share, scaling production, or even increasing customer loyalty.

- **Revenue-based growth**: Many businesses focus on increasing their top-line revenue as a key measure of growth. This could involve increasing sales of existing products, expanding into new markets, or launching new product lines.

    o **Example**: If your goal is to double your revenue over the next two years, you need a clear plan for how to achieve that—whether through new product launches, geographic expansion, or other growth levers.

- **Market expansion**: Growth doesn't always mean more sales; it can also involve entering new markets, either by geographic expansion or by targeting new customer segments.

  o **Example**: Expanding into international markets might be your next step. Identify which markets are most aligned with your product or service and develop a strategy to penetrate those areas.

- **Operational growth**: For many businesses, scaling means increasing operational capacity to meet higher demand. This could involve automating processes, expanding your team, or improving supply chain efficiency.

  o **Example**: If you're a manufacturer, scaling may involve investing in new equipment to increase production capacity, reducing lead times, and improving logistics.

Key takeaway: Clearly define what growth means for your business—whether it's revenue growth, market expansion, or scaling operations. This will guide the rest of your goal-setting process.

2. Make Your Goals Ambitious Yet Achievable

Growth goals should be ambitious enough to push your business forward, but realistic enough to remain achievable. This balance between aspiration and practicality is crucial for keeping your team motivated while avoiding burnout or resource strain.

- **Set SMART goals**: When setting growth targets, follow the SMART framework—goals that are Specific, Measurable, Achievable, Relevant, and Time-bound.

  o **Example**: Instead of saying "We want to increase revenue," aim for something more precise: "We want to increase revenue by 20% in the next 12 months by expanding into two new markets."

- **Break down long-term goals into smaller milestones**: Scaling can feel daunting if you're only focusing on massive, long-term targets. Break your big goals into smaller, more manageable milestones that can be tracked and celebrated along the way.

- o **Example**: If your long-term goal is to expand into five new markets, start by setting a milestone of entering one market within six months, then scaling from there.

- **Balance ambition with capacity**: Make sure that your goals align with your business's current capacity. Do you have the resources, talent, and systems in place to meet your growth targets? If not, scaling goals may need to include investments in infrastructure or talent acquisition.

- o **Example**: If you plan to grow sales by 50%, assess whether your team, supply chain, and technology can support that growth. If not, part of your growth goal should be to improve those areas before scaling sales.

Key takeaway: Use SMART goals to set ambitious but realistic growth targets. Break long-term goals into smaller milestones and ensure that your resources can support the desired expansion.

3. Align Your Growth Goals with Your Business Strategy

Growth goals should align seamlessly with your overall business strategy. This ensures that your growth efforts are cohesive and that every step you take is contributing to your broader objectives. If your growth goals don't align with your strategy, you risk wasting resources or pursuing growth for the wrong reasons.

- **Evaluate current strengths and weaknesses**: Review your current business strategy to identify your strongest areas of opportunity for growth. Build your goals around these areas, leveraging what you already do well.

- o **Example**: If your customer service is a major differentiator, consider scaling by offering new services that deepen customer relationships or increase lifetime value.

- **Stay true to your mission**: As you scale, it's important not to lose sight of your company's mission and values. Your growth goals should reflect the core of what makes your business unique, ensuring that scaling doesn't dilute your brand identity or customer experience.

- o **Example**: If sustainability is central to your brand, your growth goals should include ways to scale operations while maintaining or improving your environmental impact.

- **Ensure market alignment**: Growth should be driven by customer demand and market opportunities, not by internal ambition alone. Conduct market research to ensure that your growth goals are aligned with what the market needs and can support.

- o **Example**: If your goal is to grow sales by 30%, research whether there is sufficient demand in your target markets to support that level of growth.

Key takeaway: Ensure your growth goals align with your overall business strategy, leveraging strengths, staying true to your mission, and responding to market demand.

4. Track Progress and Adjust as Needed

Once your scalable goals are set, it's important to track progress regularly and be willing to adjust as needed. Growth isn't always linear, and there will be times when you need to pivot or refine your approach to stay on track.

- **Set up key performance indicators (KPIs)**: Use KPIs to track progress toward your growth goals. These could include revenue, customer acquisition, market share, or other relevant metrics. Regularly review these KPIs to ensure that you're moving in the right direction.

- o **Example**: If your goal is to increase online sales, track KPIs like website traffic, conversion rates, and average order value to measure progress.

- **Be flexible with your timeline**: While it's important to have deadlines, understand that scaling often involves unforeseen challenges. Be prepared to adjust your timeline or strategies if you encounter unexpected roadblocks.

- o **Example**: If your goal was to launch in a new market within six months but supply chain issues arise, adjust your timeline to ensure you can still meet your goals without compromising quality.

- **Iterate and improve**: Growth goals should be dynamic, not static. As you scale, gather data, listen to feedback, and continuously refine your goals to reflect new insights and changing conditions.

  - o **Example**: If your new product line is gaining traction faster than expected, adjust your goals to reflect the opportunity for faster expansion in that category.

Key takeaway: Track your progress using KPIs, remain flexible with timelines, and iterate on your goals as needed to adapt to changing conditions.

Conclusion: Build Your Blueprint for Sustainable Growth
Setting scalable goals is the foundation of a successful growth strategy. By defining what growth looks like, making goals both ambitious and realistic, aligning them with your business strategy, and tracking progress regularly, you can build a blueprint for expansion that will guide your business to new heights.

Growth is an exhilarating journey, but it requires focus, flexibility, and a clear roadmap. With scalable goals in place, you'll be well-equipped to chart your path to success and take your business to the next level.

Optimizing Operations: Creating Efficient Systems for Growth

As your business scales, operational efficiency becomes the backbone that supports sustainable growth. Without streamlined processes and systems in place, scaling can quickly lead to chaos, inefficiency, and even a decline in product or service quality. Optimizing your operations is essential to ensure that your business can handle increased demand while maintaining profitability, customer satisfaction, and team morale. In this section, we'll explore how to build scalable, efficient systems that support long-term growth.

1. Streamline Processes and Eliminate Bottlenecks

Scaling effectively means ensuring that your operations can run smoothly at a larger scale without slowing down due to inefficiencies or bottlenecks. Start by reviewing your existing processes to identify areas where delays, redundancies, or other inefficiencies may be holding you back.

- **Map out current processes**: Begin by mapping out your current workflows across different departments, from production to customer service to sales. This will help you visualize how work moves through your organization and identify where things may be slowing down.

    o **Example**: If your product fulfillment process involves multiple manual steps, such as data entry or checking inventory by hand, this could become a bottleneck as order volumes increase.

- **Identify and eliminate inefficiencies**: Once you've mapped out your processes, look for areas where tasks can be automated, streamlined, or eliminated entirely. Often, inefficiencies are the result of outdated methods or unnecessary layers of complexity.

    o **Example**: If your sales team is spending hours on manual follow-ups, consider using customer relationship management (CRM) software to automate follow-up emails and track interactions.

- **Standardize processes for consistency**: As you scale, it's important to ensure that your team is following consistent, standardized processes. This minimizes errors, reduces training time for new hires, and ensures that tasks are completed efficiently across the organization.

    o **Example**: Create standard operating procedures (SOPs) for repetitive tasks, such as onboarding new clients or processing returns. This helps maintain consistency and reduces the learning curve for new team members.

Key takeaway: Streamline and standardize your processes to eliminate inefficiencies and ensure that your operations can scale smoothly without bottlenecks.

2. Leverage Automation for Greater Efficiency

Automation is one of the most powerful tools for optimizing operations as your business grows. By automating repetitive or time-consuming tasks, you can free up your team to focus on higher-value activities, reduce the risk of errors, and increase the overall speed of your operations.

- **Automate repetitive tasks**: Look for areas of your business that involve repetitive, manual work, such as invoicing, data entry, scheduling, or email communications. Automating these tasks with the right tools can significantly increase efficiency and reduce operational costs.

    o **Example**: Use automated invoicing software to generate and send invoices automatically, reducing the need for manual oversight and speeding up payment collection.

- **Integrate systems to improve data flow**: Automating isn't just about replacing individual tasks with software; it's also about ensuring that your various systems work together seamlessly. Integrating your tools— such as accounting software, CRM systems, and marketing platforms— can improve data flow, reduce duplication, and provide real-time visibility into business performance.

    o **Example**: Integrating your e-commerce platform with your inventory management system can ensure that stock levels are updated automatically when orders are placed, reducing the risk of overselling or stockouts.

- **Scale customer service with automation**: As your business grows, handling customer inquiries and support requests manually can quickly become overwhelming. Implementing chatbots, automated ticketing systems, or AI-driven support tools can help you scale customer service without sacrificing quality.

    o **Example**: Use a chatbot on your website to handle common customer inquiries, such as tracking orders or answering frequently asked questions, while freeing up human agents for more complex issues.

Key takeaway: Leverage automation to reduce manual tasks, improve data flow between systems, and scale customer service, allowing your business to grow efficiently without adding unnecessary overhead.

3. Enhance Supply Chain and Inventory Management

Efficient supply chain and inventory management are critical to scaling your business successfully, especially if you're dealing with physical products. Without a solid system in place, scaling can lead to stockouts, delays, or excess inventory that ties up capital.

- **Implement real-time inventory tracking**: As your business grows, real-time inventory tracking becomes essential to avoid stock shortages or overstocking. Implement systems that allow you to monitor inventory levels across warehouses, suppliers, or retail locations in real-time, enabling you to respond quickly to changes in demand.

    o **Example**: Use an inventory management platform that integrates with your e-commerce and point-of-sale systems, ensuring that inventory levels are updated instantly as sales are made.

- **Diversify your supply chain**: Relying on a single supplier can leave your business vulnerable to disruptions. As you scale, consider diversifying your supply chain by sourcing from multiple suppliers, both locally and internationally. This provides greater flexibility and reduces the risk of supply chain bottlenecks.

    o **Example**: If you're scaling your product line, establish relationships with multiple manufacturers to ensure that you can meet demand even if one supplier experiences delays.

- **Optimize inventory levels**: Excess inventory ties up valuable capital, while stockouts can lead to lost sales. As you scale, it's important to optimize your inventory levels based on accurate demand forecasting and historical sales data.

o **Example**: Use demand forecasting tools to predict which products will sell in higher volumes during certain seasons, and adjust your inventory levels accordingly.

Key takeaway: Implement real-time inventory tracking, diversify your supply chain, and optimize inventory levels to ensure that your supply chain can support growth without delays or disruptions.

4. Scale Your Team and Resources Strategically

As your business grows, so will your need for additional talent and resources. However, scaling your team too quickly can lead to inefficiencies, while scaling too slowly can prevent you from keeping up with demand. It's important to approach scaling your team and resources strategically, ensuring that you have the right people and tools in place to support growth.

- **Hire for key roles as needed**: Instead of hiring in bulk, focus on filling key roles that will have the greatest impact on your ability to scale. This might involve hiring specialists in areas like operations, marketing, or finance, who can help guide your business through the next phase of growth.

  o **Example**: If you're expanding into a new market, consider hiring a local market expert who can navigate regulatory requirements and establish key relationships.

- **Outsource or delegate non-core tasks**: To keep your team focused on high-impact work, consider outsourcing non-core tasks that are time-consuming or outside your team's expertise. This allows you to scale more efficiently without adding significant overhead.

  o **Example**: If you're spending too much time on administrative tasks like payroll or bookkeeping, consider outsourcing those functions to an external provider.

- **Invest in scalable technology and infrastructure**: As your team grows, ensure that you have the right technology and infrastructure to support collaboration, communication, and productivity. This might involve

446

investing in project management tools, cloud-based systems, or communication platforms that can scale with your business.

    o   **Example**: Use cloud-based project management software to keep your team aligned, especially as remote work becomes more common and your team expands across locations.

Key takeaway: Scale your team and resources strategically, hiring for key roles, outsourcing non-core tasks, and investing in scalable technology to support long-term growth.

Conclusion: Build Efficient Systems for Sustainable Growth

Scaling your business is about more than just increasing revenue—it requires building efficient, scalable systems that can handle the increased complexity and demand. By streamlining processes, leveraging automation, optimizing supply chain management, and scaling your team strategically, you'll ensure that your operations can support sustainable growth without sacrificing quality or efficiency.

The key to optimizing operations is a combination of smart planning, the right tools, and continuous improvement. With these elements in place, you'll be well-positioned to handle the challenges of scaling and reach new heights in your business.

Expanding Your Market Reach: Strategies for Capturing New Audiences

As your business grows, one of the most powerful ways to scale is by expanding your market reach and capturing new audiences. Whether through geographic expansion, targeting new customer segments, or diversifying your product offerings, broadening your market presence can significantly boost revenue and create new opportunities for long-term success. In this section, we'll explore strategies for expanding your market reach and capturing the attention of new audiences.

1. Target New Geographic Markets

One of the most common ways to expand your market reach is by entering new geographic markets, either domestically or internationally. Geographic expansion allows you to tap into new customer bases, diversify your revenue streams, and increase brand visibility.

- **Research market potential**: Before expanding into a new region, conduct thorough research to ensure that there is enough demand for your product or service. Analyze local consumer behavior, competition, and economic conditions to assess whether the market is a good fit for your business.

  - o **Example**: If you're considering expanding internationally, research the regulatory environment, cultural preferences, and potential barriers to entry in your target country. Look for underserved markets where your product or service could fill a gap.

- **Localize your marketing and messaging**: When entering a new geographic market, it's important to tailor your marketing and messaging to resonate with local audiences. This could involve translating content, adjusting your brand messaging to fit cultural norms, or using region-specific marketing channels.

  - o **Example**: If you're expanding into a Spanish-speaking market, consider localizing your website, social media, and advertising content in Spanish to connect more effectively with the local audience.

- **Leverage local partnerships**: Establishing relationships with local partners can accelerate your entry into a new market. These partners could include distributors, retailers, influencers, or industry leaders who can help you navigate the local landscape and build credibility.

  - o **Example**: Partner with a local distributor to handle logistics and distribution in the new market, allowing you to focus on marketing and customer acquisition.

Key takeaway: Expanding into new geographic markets requires thorough research, localized marketing, and strategic partnerships to ensure a successful entry and sustained growth.

2. Target New Customer Segments

If your current market is saturated or you've already achieved strong penetration, the next step in expanding your reach could involve targeting new customer segments. This strategy allows you to diversify your audience and tap into new opportunities without necessarily entering new geographic markets.

- **Identify underserved segments**: Look for customer segments that are underserved by your current offerings but could benefit from your product or service. These segments might have different needs, preferences, or pain points than your existing customers.

  - **Example**: If you sell fitness equipment primarily to young adults, consider targeting seniors with products designed specifically for their fitness needs. This allows you to capture a new audience without significantly changing your core product.

- **Adapt your product or service**: To appeal to a new customer segment, you may need to adapt your product or service to better meet their needs. This could involve offering new features, creating tailored versions of your product, or adjusting your pricing model to fit the segment's preferences.

  - **Example**: If you're targeting budget-conscious customers, you might introduce a more affordable version of your product or offer flexible payment options to make it more accessible.

- **Tailor your marketing efforts**: When targeting new segments, it's essential to tailor your marketing messages and campaigns to resonate with their specific values, interests, and challenges. Understand their motivations and craft messaging that speaks directly to their needs.

  - **Example**: If you're targeting busy professionals, emphasize the convenience and time-saving aspects of your product in your marketing materials, as these factors are likely to appeal to this audience.

Key takeaway: Targeting new customer segments allows you to diversify your audience and revenue streams. Focus on identifying underserved segments, adapting your product, and tailoring your marketing to appeal to their unique needs.

3. Diversify Your Product or Service Offerings

Expanding your market reach doesn't always mean finding new customers—it can also involve offering new products or services to your existing audience. By diversifying your offerings, you can increase customer lifetime value, deepen customer loyalty, and open up new revenue streams.

- **Offer complementary products or services**: Think about how you can expand your product or service portfolio by offering complementary items that enhance the value of your core offering. This allows you to cross-sell or upsell to your existing customer base, increasing average order value and customer retention.

  o **Example**: If you sell skincare products, consider launching a complementary line of beauty accessories or tools, such as facial rollers or cleansing brushes, to offer your customers a complete skincare solution.

- **Introduce new product lines**: Launching new product lines or variations of your existing products can help you capture new audiences or meet evolving customer preferences. Look for trends in your industry or feedback from customers that indicate demand for additional offerings.

  o **Example**: If your clothing brand primarily sells casual wear, consider introducing an activewear line to capitalize on the growing demand for fitness and athleisure products.

- **Explore subscription or membership models**: Another way to diversify your offerings and expand your reach is by introducing subscription or membership models. This provides a predictable revenue stream while offering your customers convenience and added value.

- o **Example**: If you sell specialty coffee, you could offer a subscription service that delivers new blends to customers' doors every month, creating a recurring revenue model and deepening customer loyalty.

Key takeaway: Diversifying your product or service offerings allows you to expand your market reach within your existing customer base while capturing new audiences with complementary products or new lines.

4. Leverage Digital Marketing to Reach a Wider Audience

As your business grows, one of the most cost-effective and scalable ways to expand your market reach is through *digital marketing*. By leveraging digital channels, you can connect with potential customers far beyond your current geographic or demographic boundaries, growing your audience in a targeted and measurable way.

- **Utilize social media marketing**: Social media platforms offer a powerful way to reach new audiences, build brand awareness, and engage with customers. Focus on creating engaging, shareable content that resonates with your target audience and encourages them to spread the word.

  - o **Example**: Run targeted social media ad campaigns on platforms like Instagram or Facebook, using audience insights to reach specific demographics or interest groups that align with your product or service.

- **Invest in SEO and content marketing**: Search engine optimization (SEO) and content marketing are long-term strategies that can help you capture organic traffic and reach new audiences through search engines. By creating valuable, relevant content that addresses the needs and interests of your target audience, you can position your business as an authority and attract potential customers.

- o **Example**: Write blog posts, guides, or how-to articles that answer common questions or solve problems your audience faces. Optimize these pieces for relevant search terms to drive traffic to your website.

- **Run targeted paid advertising**: Paid advertising on platforms like Google Ads, Facebook Ads, and LinkedIn allows you to reach highly specific audiences with targeted messages. These platforms enable you to segment your audience based on demographics, interests, behaviors, and even past interactions with your brand.

  - o **Example**: Use retargeting ads to reach potential customers who have visited your website but didn't make a purchase, reminding them of your products and encouraging them to return.

- **Leverage influencer partnerships**: Partnering with influencers who align with your brand can help you tap into new audiences by leveraging their existing followers and credibility. Influencer marketing is particularly effective for reaching niche audiences that are hard to access through traditional advertising.

  - o **Example**: Collaborate with a popular lifestyle or beauty influencer to promote your product through sponsored posts, product reviews, or giveaways, helping you reach their engaged audience.

Key takeaway: Leverage digital marketing channels—such as social media, SEO, content marketing, and paid advertising—to reach new audiences and expand your brand's visibility on a scalable, global level.

Conclusion: Expand Your Market Reach Strategically

Expanding your market reach is a critical component of scaling your business. By targeting new geographic markets, identifying underserved customer segments, diversifying your product offerings, and leveraging digital marketing strategies, you can capture new audiences and unlock new growth opportunities.

The key to successful expansion is strategy—each move should be carefully researched and aligned with your overall business goals. With the right approach, you can expand your reach in ways that not only grow your revenue but also strengthen your brand, diversify your customer base, and position your business for long-term success.

Leveraging Partnerships and Alliances: Collaborating for Greater Impact

As your business scales, leveraging partnerships and strategic alliances can be one of the most effective ways to expand your reach, grow your market presence, and enhance your competitive advantage. Collaboration allows you to tap into new networks, share resources, and create synergies that drive mutual growth. In this section, we'll explore how to identify, form, and manage strategic partnerships that can help your business reach new heights.

1. Identify Potential Partnership Opportunities

Before you can leverage partnerships, you need to identify the right opportunities. Not all collaborations will be beneficial, so it's crucial to find partners whose goals, values, and strengths align with yours. Think about how a partnership can fill gaps in your business, complement your offerings, or give you access to new customers.

- **Look for complementary businesses**: The best partnerships are often between businesses that offer complementary products or services, allowing each to provide more value to their customers. For example, if you sell fitness equipment, a partnership with a company that sells health supplements could create a mutually beneficial offering for customers.

  - **Example**: A software company that specializes in project management could partner with a business offering team collaboration tools, allowing both companies to offer integrated solutions for their customers.

- **Focus on shared audiences**: Seek out partnerships with businesses or influencers that target similar customer segments. By aligning with partners who already serve your target audience, you can quickly expand your reach and increase brand visibility.

o **Example**: If your business caters to busy professionals, you might partner with a productivity app to offer bundled solutions that help customers streamline their workday.

- **Explore industry alliances**: Industry partnerships, such as collaborating with trade organizations, industry influencers, or professional associations, can help you establish credibility, build trust, and gain access to new market segments.

  o **Example**: Join forces with an industry trade association to co-host webinars, events, or workshops, positioning your business as a thought leader and expanding your audience.

Key takeaway: Identify potential partners that offer complementary products or services, share a similar target audience, and align with your values and business goals to create impactful collaborations.

2. Develop a Win-Win Partnership Strategy

Once you've identified potential partners, the next step is to develop a mutually beneficial partnership strategy. Successful partnerships should be structured so that both parties gain value—whether through shared resources, increased visibility, or access to new markets. The key is to create a win-win scenario that ensures long-term collaboration and success.

- **Define shared goals**: A successful partnership begins with clearly defined goals that benefit both parties. Start by identifying what each partner hopes to achieve through the collaboration, such as expanding market reach, enhancing product offerings, or increasing brand awareness. Ensure that these goals are aligned to prevent any potential conflicts or misaligned expectations.

  o **Example**: If your goal is to expand into a new geographic market, your partner's goal might be to gain access to your customer base for a new product they're launching. By working together, both companies can achieve their objectives.

- **Clarify roles and responsibilities**: To avoid confusion or misunderstandings, clearly outline the roles and responsibilities of each partner in the collaboration. This includes defining who will lead specific tasks, how resources will be shared, and how results will be measured.

- o **Example**: In a co-marketing campaign, one partner may be responsible for content creation while the other handles distribution and promotion. Clarifying these roles from the outset ensures a smooth execution of the strategy.

- **Establish metrics for success**: Just as with any business initiative, it's important to establish metrics for measuring the success of the partnership. Whether it's increased sales, new customer acquisition, or enhanced brand visibility, set clear KPIs (key performance indicators) to track progress and ensure both parties are benefiting from the collaboration.

- o **Example**: If the goal of your partnership is to increase leads, track the number of new leads generated from joint campaigns, webinars, or cross-promotions to measure the effectiveness of the collaboration.

Key takeaway: Develop a win-win partnership strategy by setting shared goals, clarifying roles and responsibilities, and establishing clear metrics for success to ensure long-term collaboration and mutual benefit.

3. Co-Marketing and Cross-Promotion

One of the most effective ways to leverage partnerships is through co-marketing and cross-promotion. By joining forces with another business, you can expand your audience reach, enhance brand credibility, and drive more sales with joint marketing efforts. Co-marketing allows both partners to share resources and costs while reaping the benefits of greater visibility and engagement.

- **Launch joint campaigns**: Co-marketing campaigns are a great way to introduce your partner's audience to your brand and vice versa. This could include launching joint product bundles, co-branded content, or exclusive offers for each other's customers.

- o **Example**: If you're a skincare brand partnering with a beauty influencer, you could create a co-branded beauty routine kit featuring your products, promoted through the influencer's channels and your own.

- **Host joint events or webinars**: Collaborating with partners on events, webinars, or workshops can provide valuable content for both audiences while establishing your business as an expert in your industry. Events also offer opportunities to engage with new customers in a meaningful way.

  - o **Example**: Co-host a webinar with your partner on a topic that resonates with both audiences, such as "How to Boost Productivity with the Right Tools" if you're in the software or tech space.

- **Cross-promote on digital channels**: Use your partner's digital channels to promote your business, and do the same for them. This could include sharing social media posts, newsletters, blog content, or even running paid ads that feature both brands.

  - o **Example**: Collaborate with a partner to run a cross-promotional email campaign, where each business sends a dedicated email promoting the other's products or services to their email list, offering exclusive discounts or promotions.

Key takeaway: Co-marketing and cross-promotion allow you to reach new audiences and drive growth through joint campaigns, events, and promotions. Leverage digital channels to share resources and amplify your reach.

4. Foster Long-Term Collaborative Relationships

Partnerships that deliver the most value are those built on long-term collaboration. While short-term partnerships can yield quick wins, ongoing relationships allow you to build trust, adapt to new opportunities, and continue growing together over time.

- **Maintain open communication**: Strong partnerships rely on clear and consistent communication. Keep the lines of communication open with your partners, regularly checking in on progress, challenges, and new opportunities for collaboration. This helps build trust and ensures that both parties are aligned on future goals.

- o **Example**: Schedule regular meetings or calls with your partner to discuss performance, upcoming initiatives, and any adjustments needed to maximize the impact of your collaboration.

- **Adapt to new opportunities**: As your businesses evolve, so too should your partnership. Be open to new ideas, market shifts, or changes in customer needs that could lead to fresh opportunities for collaboration. This adaptability allows your partnership to remain relevant and continue delivering value over time.

  - o **Example**: If a new trend emerges in your industry, explore how you and your partner can pivot or enhance your existing collaboration to capitalize on the trend.

- **Celebrate shared successes**: Acknowledge and celebrate the successes of your partnership to reinforce the value of the collaboration. Whether it's hitting a joint sales target, launching a successful campaign, or expanding into a new market together, celebrating these wins helps strengthen the partnership and motivates both parties to continue working together.

  - o **Example**: Host a joint event or release a case study showcasing the results of your collaboration, highlighting the mutual benefits and positive outcomes.

Key takeaway: Foster long-term collaborative relationships by maintaining open communication, adapting to new opportunities, and celebrating shared successes. Ongoing partnerships can provide sustained value and growth for both parties.

Conclusion: Collaborate for Greater Impact and Growth

Leveraging partnerships and alliances is a powerful way to expand your business's reach, drive growth, and create greater value for your customers. By identifying complementary partners, developing a win-win strategy, co-marketing to expand your audience, and fostering long-term relationships, you can unlock new opportunities and accelerate your growth trajectory.

The key to successful partnerships is *mutual benefit*—both parties should gain value, whether through shared resources, new customers, or enhanced brand visibility. When done right, partnerships can amplify your business's impact, helping you scale faster and more efficiently while building lasting relationships in the process.

Quick Tips and Recap

- **Identify complementary partners**: Collaborate with businesses or influencers offering products that complement yours, allowing both parties to enhance value and reach new audiences.

- **Develop a win-win strategy**: Ensure both parties benefit by setting shared goals, clarifying roles, and defining metrics to track success.

- **Leverage co-marketing and cross-promotion**: Use joint campaigns, events, and cross-promotion on digital channels to reach wider audiences with minimal extra effort.

- **Foster long-term relationships**: Build lasting partnerships through open communication, regular check-ins, and adapting to new opportunities as they arise.

- **Align partnership goals with customer needs**: Focus on collaborations that enhance customer experience by offering more comprehensive solutions or exclusive deals.

- **Explore industry collaborations**: Partner with trade organizations or industry influencers to boost credibility and access new markets through co-hosted events or content.

- **Share resources for efficiency**: Pool resources like marketing tools or distribution networks to cut costs and improve operational efficiency for both partners.

- **Celebrate and review success**: Regularly review the partnership's performance, celebrate milestones, and refine strategies for future collaborations.

CHAPTER TWENTY

Beyond the Horizon: Planning for the Long-Term

"Planning for the long-term isn't about predicting the future, but about preparing to adapt to whatever the future holds, ensuring sustainability and resilience in an ever-changing world." — JEFF BEZOS, FOUNDER AND FORMER CEO OF AMAZON

Welcome to the crystal ball of business strategy, where planning for the long-term is less about fortune-telling and more about meticulous map-making. In this chapter, we're venturing beyond the immediate, into the realm where future-proofing your business is as thrilling as plotting your course to uncharted territories.

Picture yourself as the captain of a ship navigating through uncharted waters. You're not just focused on the next wave but plotting a course that'll see you through stormy seas and sunny skies alike. We'll dive into the art of crafting a long-term vision that's both aspirational and actionable, ensuring you're not just riding the waves but steering your vessel with purpose.

You'll learn how to anticipate future trends, build resilient strategies, and position your business for sustained success. So, grab your compass and telescope, because it's time to look beyond the horizon and set sail towards a future that's as promising as it is exciting!

Crafting a Long-Term Vision: Setting Your Business's North Star

At the heart of every successful business is a long-term vision—a guiding principle that serves as the North Star, leading the company forward, no matter the obstacles along the way. Crafting a long-term vision is about more than just setting goals for the future; it's about defining a purpose that will inspire, direct, and unify every part of your business. This vision gives you and your team a clear understanding of where the company is headed and why it exists beyond profit.

1. Define Your Business's Purpose and Core Values

Before you can set your long-term vision, it's crucial to understand the purpose of your business. This isn't just about what your business does, but why it exists in the first place. A powerful vision reflects the core values that define your business's identity and mission, ensuring that as you grow and expand, you remain true to your foundational principles.

- **Ask yourself key questions**: What problem is your business solving? How are you making a difference in your industry or community? What values drive your decisions? These questions help clarify your purpose, allowing you to build a vision that is both meaningful and aligned with your long-term goals.

  - **Example**: If your company focuses on eco-friendly products, your vision might be centered around sustainability and reducing environmental impact. A long-term vision could be: "To lead the market in sustainable products that improve daily life without harming the planet."

460

- **Inspire with values, not just profits**: A compelling vision should go beyond profit-driven goals. It should inspire your team, customers, and stakeholders by highlighting the values your company stands for and the positive impact it hopes to make.

  o **Example**: A tech company might frame its vision as "Empowering people to solve problems through innovative technology," which emphasizes purpose and innovation over simply being profitable.

Key takeaway: Define your business's purpose and core values to create a meaningful long-term vision that inspires and aligns your team and stakeholders.

2. Set Ambitious, Yet Achievable Long-Term Goals

Your long-term vision should be aspirational, but it must also be actionable. It's essential to strike a balance between aiming high and ensuring that your vision is grounded in achievable milestones. A clear, structured path ensures that your team can work towards the vision in tangible, measurable ways.

- **Break your vision into milestones**: While your vision may outline goals that are 10, 15, or even 20 years in the future, it's important to break these down into smaller, more manageable goals. These milestones will serve as checkpoints that keep your business on track toward achieving its larger vision.

  o **Example**: If your vision is to become a global leader in clean energy solutions, your milestones might include expanding into five new markets over the next five years, developing new technologies, or achieving industry certifications that demonstrate your leadership in sustainability.

- **Set SMART goals**: Ensure that your long-term goals are Specific, Measurable, Achievable, Relevant, and Time-bound. This structure helps transform ambitious visions into actionable plans that can be tracked and measured over time.

  o **Example**: Instead of stating, "We want to expand globally," a SMART goal would be, "We will enter three international markets within the next five years, increasing international revenue by 25%."

Key takeaway: Break your long-term vision into SMART goals and actionable milestones to create a roadmap that ensures progress toward achieving your aspirational goals.

3. Communicate the Vision Clearly to Your Team

Your long-term vision will only have an impact if everyone in your business understands it and is committed to it. Clear, consistent communication of your vision ensures that your entire team is aligned and working toward the same goal, creating a unified direction for the company's growth.

- **Make it part of your company culture**: Your long-term vision should be more than just a statement on your website—it should be embedded in your company culture. Regularly reinforce the vision during meetings, employee onboarding, and internal communications to ensure that it's always front of mind.

  o **Example**: Host quarterly "vision alignment" meetings where leadership updates the team on progress toward long-term goals and discusses how day-to-day work is contributing to the bigger picture.

- **Inspire buy-in from every level**: For your vision to take root, it needs buy-in from every level of your organization, from top executives to entry-level employees. Help your team understand how their roles contribute to the long-term vision and celebrate milestones along the way to keep everyone motivated.

  o **Example**: Highlight individual or team contributions that have moved the company closer to its long-term goals in company-wide communications or during team meetings. Recognize efforts that align with the company's vision to create a sense of shared ownership.

Key takeaway: Communicate your long-term vision clearly and consistently to inspire and unify your team, making it an integral part of your company culture and daily operations.

4. Stay Flexible and Open to Evolution

While it's important to have a clear long-term vision, the business landscape is always changing. A truly effective vision should be *flexible* enough to evolve as markets shift, technology advances, and customer needs change. Flexibility allows your business to stay adaptable and resilient, even while remaining committed to its core goals and values.

- **Regularly review and refine your vision**: Set aside time at least once a year to review your long-term vision and assess whether it still aligns with the market environment and your company's trajectory. If necessary, adjust your vision to reflect new opportunities, challenges, or industry shifts.

  o **Example**: If your company originally set a long-term goal of becoming a leader in traditional retail, but the market has shifted to e-commerce, you may need to update your vision to reflect a focus on digital and omnichannel strategies.

- **Be open to feedback**: Encourage feedback from employees, customers, and stakeholders to help refine and evolve your long-term vision. Input from different perspectives can offer valuable insights that you might not have considered, ensuring that your vision remains relevant and inspiring.

  o **Example**: Survey your team or customers every year to gather their perspectives on the company's direction and vision. Use this feedback to make adjustments that keep your business forward-thinking.

Key takeaway: Stay flexible and open to adjusting your long-term vision as markets change and new opportunities arise, while keeping your core values and purpose at the heart of your business.

Conclusion: Create a Vision That Guides Long-Term Success

Crafting a long-term vision is a critical step in guiding your business toward sustained success. By defining your purpose, setting ambitious yet achievable goals, communicating the vision clearly to your team, and remaining flexible as circumstances evolve, you'll create a roadmap that not only inspires but also provides a strategic path to growth. A powerful vision acts as your business's North Star, helping you navigate challenges and capitalize on opportunities as you move confidently toward the future.

Anticipating Market Trends: Staying Ahead of the Curve

In today's fast-paced business landscape, anticipating market trends is one of the most critical elements of long-term success. Being able to identify and capitalize on trends before your competitors gives you a significant edge, positioning your business as a leader rather than a follower. This section focuses on how to track emerging trends, recognize shifts in customer behavior, and proactively adapt your strategy to stay ahead of the curve.

1. Track Industry Developments and Innovations

To stay ahead, it's essential to keep a close watch on the latest developments and innovations within your industry. This means not only staying informed about the competition but also monitoring technological advances, regulatory changes, and shifts in market dynamics that could impact your business.

- **Follow industry publications and thought leaders**: Regularly reading industry-specific journals, blogs, and reports can help you stay updated on the latest trends. Following thought leaders and influencers on social media also provides real-time insights into emerging trends and disruptive technologies.

    o **Example**: A company in the renewable energy sector should track technological advancements in solar power, changes in environmental regulations, and new market entrants to identify opportunities for growth and innovation.

- **Attend industry conferences and events**: Conferences, trade shows, and webinars are excellent opportunities to learn about emerging trends, network with other industry professionals, and gain insight into where the market is heading.

  o **Example**: If you run an e-commerce business, attending an annual e-commerce conference can provide valuable insights into the future of online shopping, including new tools and platforms that can streamline operations and enhance customer experience.

- **Leverage trend forecasting tools**: Tools like Google Trends, Statista, or Gartner's Hype Cycle can help you spot early signs of emerging trends, understand consumer interest, and predict the next big thing. Use data-driven insights to support your trend forecasting efforts.

  o **Example**: If you are in the fashion industry, using Google Trends to monitor the rising popularity of certain styles or fabrics can inform your product development decisions before those trends go mainstream.

Key takeaway: Stay informed about industry developments by following publications, attending events, and using trend forecasting tools to recognize emerging opportunities and innovations.

2. Understand Shifts in Consumer Behavior

Market trends are often driven by changes in consumer behavior. Recognizing and responding to these shifts can open new avenues for growth and innovation. It's essential to keep a close eye on your customers, understanding their evolving needs, preferences, and challenges.

- **Conduct regular market research**: Use surveys, focus groups, and customer interviews to gather feedback and insights into changing customer preferences. Analyzing this data can help you identify emerging trends and adapt your products or services accordingly.

o **Example**: A restaurant chain noticing a shift towards plant-based diets can introduce more vegetarian or vegan menu options to cater to growing demand.

- **Monitor social media and online communities**: Social media platforms and online forums can provide invaluable insights into consumer sentiment, allowing you to spot emerging trends in real-time. By engaging with your audience directly or analyzing discussions, you can identify shifts in behavior that may affect your market.

  o **Example**: A fitness brand that notices an increasing number of conversations about home workouts on platforms like Instagram and Reddit might launch a line of home fitness equipment to meet this demand.

- **Analyze purchasing patterns and consumer data**: Use data analytics to track changes in your customers' buying behaviors, identifying new preferences, product trends, or emerging customer segments. This data-driven approach helps you stay agile and responsive to market shifts.

  o **Example**: A company that sells consumer electronics may notice a spike in demand for smart home devices, leading them to expand their product line to include smart lighting, thermostats, and security systems.

Key takeaway: Monitor shifts in consumer behavior through market research, social media engagement, and data analytics to ensure your business remains in tune with customer needs and preferences.

3. Keep an Eye on Emerging Technologies

Technology is one of the most powerful drivers of market trends. Staying aware of emerging technologies that could disrupt your industry or provide new growth opportunities is crucial for maintaining a competitive edge.

- **Adopt relevant technologies early**: Businesses that are quick to adopt new technologies often gain a significant competitive advantage. Stay open to experimenting with emerging technologies that can improve your operations, customer experience, or product offerings.

○ **Example**: Retail companies that embraced e-commerce and mobile shopping early on were better positioned to meet customer needs during the shift toward online shopping, particularly during times of disruption like the COVID-19 pandemic.

• **Invest in research and development (R&D)**: Consider allocating resources to R&D to explore how emerging technologies like artificial intelligence (AI), machine learning, blockchain, or automation can benefit your business. Keeping R&D as a core part of your strategy ensures that you're not just following trends, but actively contributing to innovation.

○ **Example**: A healthcare company that invests in AI-driven diagnostics may be able to offer faster, more accurate results than competitors, positioning itself as a leader in the industry.

• **Collaborate with tech innovators**: Forge partnerships with technology providers, startups, or research institutions to stay at the forefront of innovation. These partnerships can help you explore new ways to incorporate cutting-edge technology into your business model.

○ **Example**: A logistics company partnering with a drone technology startup could pioneer faster, more efficient delivery methods, setting itself apart from traditional delivery services.

Key takeaway: Stay informed about emerging technologies, adopt them early, and explore R&D or partnerships to integrate innovation into your business model.

4. Proactively Adapt Your Strategy to Market Shifts

It's not enough to just recognize market trends—you need to proactively adapt your strategy to capitalize on them. Being agile and ready to pivot in response to changes in the market ensures that you remain competitive and relevant in the long term.

• **Build flexibility into your business model**: Ensure that your business model is adaptable, allowing you to shift resources, adjust your product offerings, or pivot strategies quickly when new trends emerge. This flexibility helps you respond to changes without disrupting your entire operation.

- o **Example**: A company offering subscription boxes may initially target fitness enthusiasts but could quickly adapt to trends by introducing boxes for other niches like beauty or mental wellness.

- **Diversify revenue streams**: One way to adapt to market shifts is by diversifying your revenue streams. By expanding your offerings or entering new markets, you reduce your reliance on a single source of income, making your business more resilient to changes.

- o **Example**: A publishing company may start offering digital e-books, audiobooks, and online courses to diversify its income streams in response to the decline in print sales.

- **Stay ahead of the competition**: Monitor your competitors closely to see how they are responding to emerging trends. Use this information to differentiate your business and take a proactive approach to meeting market demand before others can catch up.

- o **Example**: If your competitors are slow to adopt AI-driven customer service tools, quickly integrating AI chatbots into your customer service can position your business as a leader in customer experience.

Key takeaway: Proactively adapt your business strategy to capitalize on emerging trends, build flexibility into your business model, and stay ahead of the competition by being agile and innovative.

Conclusion: Lead the Market by Staying Ahead of Trends

Anticipating market trends is essential for staying competitive and positioning your business for long-term success. By tracking industry developments, understanding shifts in consumer behavior, staying on top of emerging technologies, and adapting your strategy proactively, you'll be able to stay ahead of the curve and capitalize on new opportunities. Businesses that are quick to recognize and respond to trends can navigate changes in the market more effectively and lead their industries into the future.

Building Resilience: Preparing for Challenges and Uncertainty

In today's unpredictable business environment, building resilience is essential to ensure that your business can withstand challenges and uncertainty. Resilience goes beyond simply responding to crises—it's about creating a strong foundation that allows your business to adapt, recover, and emerge stronger when faced with obstacles. Whether it's market volatility, economic downturns, or unexpected disruptions, resilient businesses are prepared to face the unknown and continue thriving.

This section will explore strategies for building resilience by strengthening your business model, developing contingency plans, and fostering a culture of adaptability and agility.

1. Diversify Revenue Streams to Reduce Dependency

One of the most effective ways to build resilience is by diversifying your revenue streams. Relying on a single source of income can make your business vulnerable to external shocks, such as market downturns or shifts in consumer demand. Diversification not only reduces risk but also creates new opportunities for growth and stability.

- **Expand product or service offerings**: Consider how you can introduce new products or services that complement your existing offerings. By doing so, you spread your risk across multiple revenue streams rather than depending on one main product or market.

  o **Example**: A fitness studio that primarily offers in-person classes could diversify by adding online classes, merchandise, and wellness coaching services, ensuring continued income even if one revenue stream is impacted.

- **Enter new markets**: Expanding into new geographic regions or customer segments can also help you diversify your revenue. Different markets may be affected by economic changes or trends in varying ways, allowing your business to balance risk across different areas.

- Example: A software company that initially targets small businesses could begin offering enterprise solutions to larger corporations, thereby increasing market reach and revenue stability.

- **Create recurring revenue models**: Subscription-based or membership models provide a steady, predictable income stream that can help cushion your business during periods of uncertainty. Recurring revenue models also help build long-term relationships with customers, contributing to customer loyalty.

  - Example: A company selling digital tools could introduce a subscription model for premium features, creating consistent monthly income while diversifying away from one-time sales.

Key takeaway: Diversify your revenue streams by expanding offerings, entering new markets, or creating subscription models to reduce dependency and build financial resilience.

2. Develop Robust Contingency Plans

No business is immune to challenges, but businesses that prepare for potential disruptions are more likely to recover quickly. A *contingency plan* acts as a safety net, allowing you to navigate unexpected events with minimal disruption. Having a well-thought-out plan in place ensures that your business can remain operational, even during crises.

- **Identify potential risks**: Begin by identifying the risks your business is most likely to face. These could include economic downturns, supply chain disruptions, natural disasters, cybersecurity threats, or industry-specific challenges. By understanding the risks, you can proactively plan for them.

  - Example: If your business is reliant on international suppliers, a potential risk could be disruptions in the supply chain due to political instability or shipping delays.

- **Create response strategies for key risks**: For each identified risk, develop a specific response strategy. This should outline the steps you'll take to mitigate the impact of the event, ensure business continuity, and protect your assets. Assign roles and responsibilities within your team so that everyone knows their part in the plan.

  o **Example**: If you're concerned about potential supply chain disruptions, a response strategy could involve securing backup suppliers, increasing inventory levels of key materials, or diversifying your supplier network.

- **Test and update your plans regularly**: It's important to regularly test and update your contingency plans to ensure they remain relevant as your business evolves and external conditions change. Schedule periodic reviews and simulations to assess how well your business would respond to a disruption.

  o **Example**: Conduct an annual "disaster recovery" drill where you simulate a key risk, such as a cyberattack or a sudden loss of a supplier, to test the effectiveness of your contingency plan and make adjustments where needed.

Key takeaway: Develop and regularly update contingency plans by identifying key risks, creating response strategies, and testing your plans to ensure they're effective during times of uncertainty.

3. Build a Financial Safety Net

Having a strong financial safety net is one of the most critical aspects of business resilience. It ensures that your business has the cash flow and resources to survive during challenging times, whether due to market downturns, sudden expenses, or a drop in revenue. Financial resilience allows you to weather short-term challenges while maintaining long-term growth.

- **Maintain healthy cash reserves**: Building and maintaining cash reserves ensures that your business has liquidity to cover unexpected expenses, such as operational disruptions, equipment failures, or a temporary loss of sales. Aim to have enough cash on hand to cover at least three to six months of operating expenses.

○ **Example**: A retail business might set aside a portion of profits each month into a dedicated emergency fund, which can be accessed in the event of store closures or unexpected costs.

- **Establish access to credit lines or funding**: In addition to cash reserves, it's wise to establish access to credit lines or secure funding options that you can tap into during emergencies. This provides flexibility in times of financial strain, allowing your business to continue operating without significant disruptions.

○ **Example**: A manufacturing company might secure a revolving line of credit from a financial institution, giving it the option to borrow funds quickly in case of equipment breakdowns or unexpected raw material shortages.

- **Diversify financial investments**: To further protect your business's finances, consider diversifying your investments across different asset types. This reduces exposure to risk and provides additional financial security in case one investment area is negatively impacted by market changes.

○ **Example**: Instead of keeping all profits in a single business savings account, a company might diversify its reserves by investing in short-term bonds, stocks, or other low-risk financial instruments.

Key takeaway: Build a financial safety net by maintaining healthy cash reserves, establishing access to credit, and diversifying financial investments to ensure your business can weather financial uncertainties.

4. Foster a Culture of Adaptability and Agility

Resilient businesses are adaptable and agile, able to quickly respond to changing conditions and seize new opportunities when they arise. A strong internal culture that prioritizes innovation, flexibility, and problem-solving helps your team navigate challenges with confidence and resilience.

- **Empower employees to make decisions**: Encourage decision-making at all levels of the organization to enable fast responses to changes and challenges. By giving employees the autonomy to solve problems and adapt to new circumstances, your business can react more quickly to disruptions.

- o **Example**: A customer service team might be empowered to resolve client issues on the spot, without needing managerial approval, allowing for faster resolutions and a more agile response to customer feedback.

- **Encourage continuous learning and innovation**: Promote a culture of continuous learning where employees are encouraged to develop new skills, stay informed about industry trends, and experiment with new ideas. This not only prepares your team to adapt but also fosters innovation that can lead to new opportunities.

- o **Example**: A tech company might hold regular "innovation days" where employees are encouraged to brainstorm new solutions to existing challenges or explore emerging technologies that could benefit the business.

- **Be open to pivoting your strategy**: Building resilience means being willing to pivot your business strategy when necessary. Encourage a flexible mindset that allows your business to quickly shift direction in response to market changes or customer needs.

- o **Example**: A restaurant that experiences declining dine-in customers might pivot by offering meal kits for delivery or launching virtual cooking classes, ensuring continued revenue despite changes in consumer behavior.

Key takeaway: Foster a culture of adaptability and agility by empowering employees, encouraging continuous learning, and staying open to strategic pivots to navigate challenges with ease.

Conclusion: Build Resilience for Long-Term Success

Building resilience is a proactive process that ensures your business can withstand and thrive in the face of challenges and uncertainty. By diversifying your revenue streams, developing robust contingency plans, building a financial safety net, and fostering a culture of adaptability, you create a foundation that allows your business to not only survive but grow during difficult times. With resilience as a core part of your business strategy, you'll be better equipped to handle whatever comes your way and position your business for long-term success.

Sustaining Growth: Strategies for Long-Term Success

Achieving growth is one thing; sustaining it over the long term is another challenge entirely. Sustaining growth requires a delicate balance between expanding your business and maintaining its core strengths, all while adapting to changing markets and customer needs. In this section, we'll explore the key strategies that successful businesses use to sustain growth over time, ensuring continued profitability, innovation, and market leadership.

1. Focus on Continuous Innovation

One of the most critical factors in long-term success is the ability to continuously innovate. Businesses that fail to evolve and offer new solutions risk becoming stagnant, while those that prioritize innovation stay competitive and attract new customers. By fostering a culture of innovation, your business can adapt to changing markets and meet emerging customer needs.

- **Invest in research and development (R&D)**: Regularly investing in R&D allows your business to explore new technologies, products, and processes that can fuel growth. Stay ahead of industry trends by constantly seeking ways to improve your offerings or create new ones.

  o **Example**: A company in the technology space could allocate resources to R&D to explore advancements in AI and automation, positioning itself as a leader in the future of tech innovation.

- **Encourage a culture of innovation**: Create an environment where employees feel encouraged to share new ideas and experiment with fresh approaches. Make innovation a part of your company's DNA by celebrating creativity and rewarding risk-taking.

- o **Example**: Google's "20% time" initiative allows employees to spend 20% of their work hours on passion projects, which has led to the development of major innovations like Gmail and Google News.

- **Stay customer-focused**: Innovation should always be tied to customer needs and desires. Use customer feedback to drive your innovation efforts, ensuring that new products or services provide real value to your audience.

  - o **Example**: A beauty brand could introduce eco-friendly packaging in response to growing consumer demand for sustainable products, aligning its innovations with customer preferences.

Key takeaway: Prioritize continuous innovation by investing in R&D, fostering a culture of creativity, and staying customer-focused to drive long-term growth.

2. Diversify Revenue Streams

To ensure long-term growth, it's essential to diversify your revenue streams. Relying on a single product, service, or market can make your business vulnerable to shifts in demand, competition, or economic conditions. Diversification provides stability and allows you to explore new opportunities without losing focus on your core business.

- **Introduce new products or services**: Expanding your product or service offerings is one of the most straightforward ways to diversify revenue. Look for ways to solve new problems or address additional needs within your existing customer base.

  - o **Example**: A fitness company that sells workout equipment might introduce a subscription service for virtual fitness classes, offering customers ongoing value and creating a recurring revenue stream.

- **Expand into new markets**: Geographical expansion can be an effective way to sustain growth. By entering new markets—whether domestic or international—you can increase your customer base and reduce reliance on a single region.

- o **Example**: A food brand that has found success in the U.S. might explore opportunities in international markets, such as launching its products in Europe or Asia, to capitalize on global demand.

- **Leverage partnerships and collaborations**: Strategic partnerships can open new avenues for revenue generation. Collaborating with complementary businesses allows you to reach new audiences and expand your offerings.

- o **Example**: A travel company could partner with a hotel chain to offer exclusive vacation packages, creating a new source of revenue for both companies while enhancing customer experiences.

Key takeaway: Diversify revenue streams by introducing new products, expanding into new markets, and leveraging partnerships to reduce risk and ensure sustained growth.

3. Build Strong Customer Relationships

Loyal customers are the backbone of sustained growth. Retaining your existing customers and deepening those relationships can often be more profitable than acquiring new ones. Focusing on customer loyalty and retention ensures that your business enjoys a steady stream of repeat business, while strong customer relationships can lead to valuable referrals and brand advocacy.

- **Deliver exceptional customer service**: Exceptional service creates lasting relationships with customers, turning one-time buyers into loyal advocates. Ensure your customer service is proactive, responsive, and consistent across all touchpoints.

- o **Example**: An e-commerce retailer might implement a customer support system with 24/7 chat availability and follow-up emails to ensure customers are fully satisfied with their purchases.

- **Create loyalty programs**: Reward your loyal customers with programs that incentivize repeat business, whether through discounts, points, or exclusive perks. This keeps your brand top of mind and encourages long-term customer retention.

  o **Example**: A coffee shop could implement a rewards app that gives customers points for every purchase, redeemable for free drinks or special offers, creating an incentive to return regularly.

- **Engage through personalized marketing**: Use customer data to tailor your marketing efforts and create personalized experiences for your audience. Personalized marketing increases engagement and strengthens customer loyalty by showing that you understand and value their preferences.

  o **Example**: An online clothing retailer might send personalized emails suggesting new arrivals based on past purchases or browsing behavior, increasing the likelihood of repeat sales.

Key takeaway: Build long-term customer relationships by delivering exceptional service, creating loyalty programs, and using personalized marketing to engage your audience.

4. Ensure Operational Scalability

Sustaining growth isn't just about generating more sales—it's about ensuring that your operations can scale efficiently to handle increased demand. If your business can't scale without sacrificing quality or customer experience, growth will be unsustainable. Ensuring operational scalability means creating systems, processes, and infrastructure that can expand as your business grows.

- **Invest in automation and technology**: As your business grows, manual processes can become bottlenecks. Investing in automation and technology allows you to scale your operations without a proportional increase in labor costs. Look for ways to streamline tasks like order fulfillment, customer service, and inventory management.

○ **Example**: A fulfillment center might invest in automated packing machines to handle increased orders during peak seasons, ensuring that orders are processed quickly and efficiently without adding more staff.

- **Outsource non-core functions**: As your business scales, it can become more efficient to outsource non-core functions, such as IT, accounting, or logistics. This allows your team to focus on strategic activities that directly impact growth.

  ○ **Example**: A growing e-commerce business might outsource its shipping and fulfillment to a third-party logistics provider, enabling it to scale its operations while focusing on marketing and product development.

- **Monitor performance and make data-driven decisions**: Use key performance indicators (KPIs) and data analytics to monitor the scalability of your operations. Regularly assess your operational efficiency and make data-driven decisions to optimize processes.

  ○ **Example**: A company could track its inventory turnover rate to identify inefficiencies in the supply chain and make adjustments to meet increasing customer demand without overstocking.

Key takeaway: Ensure operational scalability by investing in automation, outsourcing non-core functions, and using data to optimize processes and maintain quality as your business grows.

Conclusion: Sustain Growth for Long-Term Success

Sustaining growth over the long term requires a multi-faceted approach that includes continuous innovation, diversified revenue streams, strong customer relationships, and scalable operations. By focusing on these key strategies, your business can maintain momentum and adapt to changing market conditions while delivering consistent value to your customers. Long-term success isn't just about growth—it's about building a business that can thrive and evolve, no matter what challenges come your way.

Quick Tips and Recap

- **Prioritize continuous innovation**: Regularly invest in R&D and foster a culture that encourages creativity, helping your business stay ahead of the competition and meet evolving customer needs.

- **Diversify revenue streams**: Expand your product or service offerings, enter new markets, and leverage strategic partnerships to minimize risk and create steady growth.

- **Build strong customer relationships**: Focus on exceptional customer service, loyalty programs, and personalized marketing to drive retention and convert customers into long-term advocates.

- **Ensure operational scalability**: Invest in automation and technology, outsource non-core functions, and optimize processes to scale efficiently while maintaining high quality.

- **Stay customer-focused with feedback**: Regularly gather and act on customer feedback to ensure your business continues to meet their needs and evolves in line with changing preferences.

- **Monitor performance metrics**: Track key performance indicators (KPIs) such as revenue growth, customer acquisition costs, and operational efficiency to make data-driven decisions and stay on course.

- **Be adaptable and agile**: Keep your business flexible, able to pivot quickly in response to changes in the market, consumer behavior, or economic conditions to ensure continued relevance.

- **Plan for long-term financial stability**: Maintain healthy cash reserves, secure credit lines, and diversify investments to weather unforeseen challenges and ensure steady, sustainable growth.

By following these strategies, you'll be equipped to sustain growth, adapt to changing conditions, and build a foundation for long-term business success and profitability.

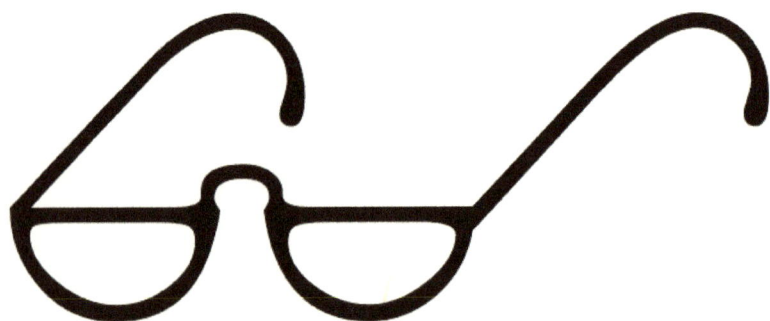

Conclusion

Focus, Action, and Growth—Building Your Future Business

Congratulations—you've made it to the final section of your roadmap to entrepreneurial success. Throughout this book, we've explored the key strategies and tools needed to bring your business idea to life—from crafting a practical business plan to launching with purpose and scaling with efficiency. The journey of building a business is not just a one-time achievement but an ongoing process of innovation, adaptation, and growth.

This abridged edition has focused on the essential building blocks—cutting through unnecessary complexity so you can move forward with clarity and purpose. Every entrepreneur's path is filled with challenges and opportunities, but with a strong foundation, a clear plan, and a resilient mindset, you are prepared to take on whatever lies ahead.

Your Path Forward

The lessons in these pages are not static—they are guiding principles designed to grow with you as your business evolves. Success isn't about perfection or luck;

it's about strategic decisions, consistent action, and a commitment to long-term growth. The tools and frameworks you've gained here are your foundation. From here, it's about taking the first step, then the next, until your idea becomes a thriving reality.

Embrace Clarity and Purpose

At the heart of every great business is a clear vision—one that goes beyond profits to make a meaningful impact. Whether you aim to solve a problem, improve lives, or leave a mark on your community, your purpose will guide your actions and inspire others to follow your journey.

Flexibility for Growth and Change

Success isn't a straight path—it's a series of twists, turns, and moments that require flexibility. As you build, remember that every challenge is an opportunity to grow. Be open to change, willing to pivot, and always keep learning. Your business plan isn't set in stone—it's a living document that grows with you, evolving as you navigate new opportunities and challenges.

Resources for Deeper Insight

While this abridged edition delivers core strategies, the case studies originally included can now be found in the companion Empire Blueprint Series. These volumes explore over 200 real-world stories from entrepreneurs who've built, grown, and scaled businesses successfully. Use them as additional inspiration, reference points, and learning opportunities as you continue on your entrepreneurial journey.

Start Where You Are—Act Now

The road to success begins with action. Don't wait for the perfect moment—there's no such thing. Start small, make progress every day, and trust that the journey will unfold as it should. With the tools in this book, you have what you need to turn your vision into reality.

Your Future Empire Awaits

The journey from idea to empire may not be easy, but it will be worth it. By focusing on what matters most—your vision, strategy, and action—you can build a business that grows, scales, and leaves a lasting impact. Whether you're starting fresh or refining a venture, you now have a roadmap to guide your way.

So, what's your next step? Take action. Your business is waiting to be built, and the future is yours to shape. Let's get started.

Where Do We Go From Here?

As you reach the end of this book, you're probably asking, "What's next?" You've laid the groundwork for turning your ideas into a business empire, but the journey doesn't end here. In fact, this is just the beginning. Whether you're refining your business model, preparing for rapid growth, or navigating the complexities of the marketplace, the next steps in your entrepreneurial journey will require new knowledge and strategies. That's why the Empire Builders Series: Masterclasses in Business and Law continues to equip you with the tools you need to scale your business and protect your intellectual property along the way.

You've made it to the end of *From Idea to Empire: Abridged Edition*, but your journey is just beginning. The tools, frameworks, and strategies within this book are only the foundation of your entrepreneurial success. The next step is to put what you've learned into action—refining your business model, preparing for growth, and staying agile in a constantly evolving market.

For those looking for deeper inspiration and practical insights, the Empire Blueprint Series: Case Studies for Business Success offers over 200 real-world examples of how entrepreneurs overcame challenges, built thriving ventures, and scaled their businesses strategically. If you're ready to dive deeper into these stories, the companion volumes are a perfect next step.

Additionally, if you're building a business that involves creative assets—like content, products, or intellectual property—securing legal protection is essential. Look out for upcoming books in the Empire Builders Series: Masterclasses in Business and Law, which will explore strategies for copyright protection, legal compliance, and safeguarding your unique creations.

The journey from idea to empire requires ongoing learning, persistence, and flexibility. Keep moving forward with confidence, knowing that the resources and knowledge in this series will continue to support you along the way. Whether you're just starting out or scaling your operations, the Empire Builders Series is here to provide you with expert guidance at every stage.

Remember, success isn't just a one-time achievement—it's about continuous growth, resilience, and long-term impact. Your business future is bright, and the possibilities are limitless. Take the first step today, and let this book serve as your roadmap for every challenge and opportunity to come.

Final Conclusion: The Journey Starts Here

Congratulations! You've completed *From Idea to Empire: Abridged Edition*—a streamlined guide designed to give you the essential strategies needed to launch and grow your business. But this isn't the end; it's just the beginning of a long and rewarding entrepreneurial journey. Whether you are refining your vision, launching your first product, or planning for future growth, this book has provided the tools to start building your dream.

The real magic happens now—when you put these strategies into action. Entrepreneurship is not a destination but a continuous process of learning, adapting, and evolving. As you move forward, embrace every challenge as an opportunity to grow, and stay focused on your long-term goals.

If you're seeking deeper insights, the Empire Blueprint Series: Case Studies for Business Success is the next step. With over 200 real-world success stories, those volumes offer inspiration and practical advice from entrepreneurs who have built thriving enterprises. These case studies complement what you've learned here, providing tangible examples of how strategies come to life.

Remember, success doesn't happen overnight. The key is to keep moving forward, step by step, with clarity, purpose, and resilience. Your business will evolve, and so will you. Stay flexible, stay motivated, and don't be afraid to pivot when needed.

This journey is yours to shape. Armed with your business plan and the insights from this book, you have everything you need to build something extraordinary. Now it's time to take action—because your empire awaits.

Conclusion

The future is in your hands. Go build it.

READ ON for a bonus chapter!

The Entrepreneur's Toolkit: Essential Resources for Ongoing Growth

"Tools and resources are the keys to unlocking your business's full potential."— ANN HANDLEY, MARKETING EXPERT

Welcome to the ultimate gadget lab for entrepreneurs, where the tools aren't just shiny—they're your secret weapons for ongoing success. Think of this chapter as your business's personal toolkit, packed with everything from high-tech gadgets to nifty tricks that'll make your entrepreneurial journey smoother than a freshly polished espresso machine.

We're talking about resources that are as essential as a good cup of coffee—things like productivity apps that keep you on track, financial tools that make budgeting feel less like a chore, and networking platforms that turn casual chats into lucrative opportunities.

Whether you're scaling up or simply keeping things running smoothly, these tools will help you stay sharp, efficient, and always one step ahead. So, get ready to dive into your toolkit, armed with the knowledge and resources you need to keep growing and thriving like the savvy entrepreneur you are!

Productivity Powerhouses: Apps and Tools to Streamline Your Workflow

In the fast-paced world of entrepreneurship, time is your most valuable resource. Managing your daily tasks, meetings, projects, and communications efficiently can make all the difference between staying ahead of the curve and falling behind. Luckily, there are productivity apps and tools designed to streamline your workflow, help you stay organized, and free up time for strategic thinking and innovation. In this section, we'll explore essential tools that will supercharge your productivity and keep your business running smoothly.

1. Project Management Tools: Stay Organized and On Track

As your business grows, managing multiple projects, teams, and deadlines becomes more complex. Project management tools help you organize tasks, assign responsibilities, set deadlines, and track progress, ensuring everyone stays on the same page.

- **Trello**: Trello uses a visual "board" and "card" system to organize tasks. It's an intuitive tool for tracking to-dos, project progress, and team assignments. You can break down larger tasks into subtasks, set due dates, and even collaborate with your team in real time.

  - o **Example**: A marketing team can use Trello to manage their content calendar, creating cards for each piece of content, assigning team members, and tracking the progress from brainstorming to publication.

- **Asana**: Asana is a robust project management tool that allows you to manage projects with timelines, task lists, and collaborative features. It's perfect for keeping track of long-term goals and daily tasks alike, with options for setting milestones and deadlines.

- **Example**: A product development team can use Asana to map out the development cycle for a new product, tracking everything from initial concept to launch while ensuring that deadlines are met and dependencies are managed.

- **Monday.com**: Monday.com offers a highly customizable interface for managing projects. You can create workflows for any kind of project, track tasks with visual timelines, and automate repetitive processes, making it a powerful tool for scaling operations.

  - **Example**: A customer service team can use Monday.com to track client requests and feedback, ensuring that issues are addressed in a timely manner and resolutions are tracked for future reference.

Key takeaway: Project management tools like Trello, Asana, and Monday.com keep your projects organized and on track, helping you manage deadlines, collaborate effectively, and ensure tasks don't fall through the cracks.

2. Time Management and Focus Apps: Maximize Productivity

Entrepreneurs often juggle multiple responsibilities at once, and staying focused is key to getting everything done. Time management tools help you manage your day effectively by tracking how you spend your time and improving focus.

- **RescueTime**: RescueTime tracks the time you spend on different apps, websites, and tasks throughout the day. It provides detailed reports on where your time goes, helping you identify inefficiencies and distractions that may be holding you back.

  - **Example**: If you notice that you're spending too much time on email and social media, RescueTime can help you refocus your time on high-priority tasks and reduce distractions.

- **Focus@Will**: This app uses scientifically designed music to help you concentrate and stay productive for longer periods. It's great for deep work sessions where you need to block out distractions and focus on completing a task.

o **Example**: A business owner working on a strategic plan might use Focus@Will to create an environment conducive to uninterrupted focus, improving productivity during key planning hours.

- **Toggl**: Toggl is a time-tracking app that helps you measure how much time you're spending on specific tasks. It's ideal for freelancers or entrepreneurs who need to track billable hours or simply want to ensure they're using their time efficiently.

  o **Example**: A freelance graphic designer can use Toggl to track time spent on client projects, ensuring accurate billing and insights into how long similar projects typically take.

Key takeaway: Time management tools like RescueTime, Focus@Will, and Toggl help you stay focused, manage distractions, and make sure your time is spent efficiently on high-impact tasks.

3. Communication Tools: Streamline Team Collaboration

Smooth, effective communication is the backbone of any successful team. Communication tools help you stay connected, facilitate real-time collaboration, and reduce the clutter of endless email chains.

- **Slack**: Slack is a messaging platform designed to replace emails and foster real-time communication between teams. You can organize conversations into channels, integrate with other tools (like Google Drive or Trello), and keep communications organized and easy to find.

  o **Example**: A marketing team can use Slack channels to manage communication on different projects, keeping conversations about social media, advertising, and content strategy separate yet accessible.

- **Zoom**: Zoom has become the go-to tool for virtual meetings, whether you're connecting with remote team members, clients, or partners. Its video conferencing capabilities, screen sharing, and webinar options make it an essential tool for any modern business.

o **Example**: A team spread across different locations can use Zoom to conduct weekly video meetings, ensuring everyone stays aligned on goals and progress no matter where they are.

- **Microsoft Teams**: Microsoft Teams combines chat, video conferencing, and file sharing into one tool, making it easy for teams to collaborate on projects, share updates, and manage documents. It's particularly useful for businesses that already use the Microsoft Office suite.

  o **Example**: A product development team might use Microsoft Teams to store and collaborate on project documents, conduct virtual meetings, and communicate updates all within one platform.

Key takeaway: Communication tools like Slack, Zoom, and Microsoft Teams streamline collaboration, reduce email clutter, and help teams stay connected and efficient, regardless of location.

4. File Management and Storage: Keep Documents Accessible

In the digital age, keeping your files organized, secure, and easily accessible is crucial to smooth operations. Cloud-based file storage tools ensure that your team can access important documents from anywhere, while also maintaining security and version control.

- **Google Drive**: Google Drive offers cloud-based file storage and real-time collaboration on documents, spreadsheets, and presentations. It's easy to share files with team members, control permissions, and keep everything organized in folders.

  o **Example**: A marketing team might store their content calendar, campaign assets, and analytics reports on Google Drive, ensuring everyone has access to the latest versions and can collaborate in real time.

- **Dropbox**: Dropbox offers secure file storage and easy sharing across teams. It's particularly useful for businesses that need to store large files like videos, high-resolution images, or other media assets.

o **Example**: A design agency could store client portfolios, high-resolution design files, and contracts in Dropbox, ensuring that both the team and clients can access them anytime.

- **OneDrive**: Microsoft OneDrive integrates with the Office 365 suite, offering seamless cloud storage and collaboration on documents. It's a great choice for businesses that rely heavily on Word, Excel, and PowerPoint, providing easy access to files across devices.

o **Example**: A consulting firm might store all client presentations and financial spreadsheets on OneDrive, making them accessible to the entire team and allowing for real-time updates.

Key takeaway: File management tools like Google Drive, Dropbox, and OneDrive keep your documents secure, accessible, and organized, enabling smooth collaboration across teams and devices.

Financial Wizards: Tools for Budgeting, Forecasting, and Cash Flow Management

Keeping your business's finances in order is crucial to ensuring long-term success. From managing day-to-day expenses to planning for future growth, having the right financial tools at your disposal can make budgeting, forecasting, and cash flow management much more manageable. In this section, we'll explore the top financial tools that will help you take control of your business finances, giving you the insights you need to make informed decisions and keep your company on track.

1. Budgeting Tools: Stay on Top of Expenses

Proper budgeting ensures that your business stays financially healthy and ready to meet its goals. With budgeting tools, you can track expenses, allocate resources effectively, and avoid overspending by keeping a close eye on where your money goes.

- **QuickBooks**: QuickBooks is one of the most popular financial tools for small businesses. It offers robust budgeting features, allowing you to create budgets, categorize expenses, and monitor your financial health in real-time. You can also generate detailed reports to see how your spending aligns with your budget and make adjustments as needed.

- o **Example**: A small retail business could use QuickBooks to track daily expenses, monitor inventory costs, and generate monthly budget reports to keep spending under control.

- **Xero**: Xero is a cloud-based accounting tool that provides excellent budgeting and expense tracking features, perfect for businesses that need to manage multiple accounts or track cash flow across different departments. Xero also integrates seamlessly with other apps, making it easy to manage your finances from anywhere.

  - o **Example**: A tech startup might use Xero to manage budgets across various projects, ensuring that spending stays aligned with overall company goals and avoiding unnecessary expenses.

- **FreshBooks**: FreshBooks is an intuitive accounting and budgeting platform that helps small businesses and freelancers track expenses, manage invoices, and monitor overall financial health. Its user-friendly interface makes budgeting simple for entrepreneurs with minimal accounting experience.

  - o **Example**: A freelance web designer can use FreshBooks to create a budget for ongoing projects, track expenses, and ensure profitability by comparing actual costs against projected income.

Key takeaway: Budgeting tools like QuickBooks, Xero, and FreshBooks help you stay on top of your expenses, ensuring your business operates within its means and is prepared for future growth.

2. Forecasting Tools: Plan for Future Growth

Financial forecasting is essential for long-term planning. Forecasting tools allow you to predict revenue, model different growth scenarios, and make informed decisions about scaling your business. By analyzing historical data, these tools help you plan for both opportunities and challenges, ensuring that you're prepared for whatever comes next.

- **Float**: Float integrates with accounting software like Xero and QuickBooks to provide real-time cash flow forecasting. With Float, you can model different scenarios, such as changes in sales or expenses, and see how they will affect your future cash flow, allowing you to plan ahead with confidence.

  - o **Example**: A SaaS company could use Float to forecast cash flow based on various subscription growth models, helping them plan when to invest in additional staff or marketing.

- **LivePlan**: LivePlan is a business planning tool that offers powerful forecasting features. It helps you create detailed financial projections, from revenue forecasts to break-even analyses, based on historical data and growth assumptions. LivePlan also includes templates for creating professional business plans that can be shared with investors.

  - o **Example**: A bakery expanding to multiple locations could use LivePlan to forecast sales and expenses for each new store, allowing them to plan cash flow needs and avoid overextending financially.

- **PlanGuru**: PlanGuru is designed for small businesses and startups that need robust financial forecasting capabilities. With tools for budgeting, forecasting, and financial analysis, PlanGuru helps you create accurate financial projections for up to 10 years in the future, making it ideal for businesses planning long-term growth.

  - o **Example**: A manufacturing company could use PlanGuru to project revenue based on seasonal trends, ensuring they have the cash flow to meet peak production demands without overcommitting resources during slower periods.

Key takeaway: Forecasting tools like Float, LivePlan, and PlanGuru help you predict future revenue and cash flow, allowing you to make informed decisions and plan for sustainable growth.

3. Cash Flow Management: Keep the Money Moving

Cash flow is the lifeblood of any business. Proper cash flow management ensures that you have enough money on hand to meet short-term obligations, while still investing in long-term growth. With the right tools, you can monitor your cash flow in real-time, identify potential cash shortages, and avoid costly financial surprises.

- **Pulse**: Pulse is a cash flow management tool specifically designed for small businesses and startups. It provides a simple, clear interface to track your cash flow in real-time, helping you anticipate cash shortages or surpluses and adjust your spending accordingly.

  - **Example**: A small agency could use Pulse to track its cash flow and determine when it's safe to invest in new software, hire additional staff, or pursue new business opportunities without risking liquidity issues.

- **Fathom**: Fathom integrates with accounting software to provide detailed insights into your financial performance, including cash flow analysis. It also offers visual reporting, making it easy to spot trends and potential cash flow issues before they become critical.

  - **Example**: A growing e-commerce business could use Fathom to analyze cash flow and create visual reports for investors, helping them make data-driven decisions about future investments in inventory or marketing.

- **Zoho Books**: Zoho Books is a full-featured accounting software with built-in cash flow management tools. It allows you to track income, expenses, and cash flow, while offering insights into where you can optimize spending to improve liquidity.

  - **Example**: A digital marketing firm could use Zoho Books to monitor cash flow as projects are completed, ensuring they always have enough cash on hand to cover payroll and operational expenses.

Key takeaway: Cash flow management tools like Pulse, Fathom, and Zoho Books help you monitor your cash flow, avoid shortages, and ensure you have the liquidity to meet both short-term and long-term financial needs.

4. Invoicing and Payment Tools: Ensure Timely Payments

Staying on top of invoicing and payments is crucial to maintaining healthy cash flow. Invoicing and payment tools streamline the billing process, ensure timely payments, and reduce the time you spend chasing down unpaid invoices.

- **Wave**: Wave is a free invoicing tool that helps small businesses and freelancers create professional invoices, send them to clients, and track payments. It also integrates with payment processors, allowing clients to pay directly through the platform.

  - o **Example**: A freelance photographer can use Wave to send invoices immediately after a photoshoot and receive payments online, reducing the time between project completion and payment.

- **FreshBooks**: FreshBooks not only offers accounting features but also has a comprehensive invoicing system that automates the entire process. You can set up recurring invoices, send reminders, and accept online payments, making it easier to manage billing without missing a beat.

  - o **Example**: A graphic design firm might use FreshBooks to send monthly retainer invoices to clients, set up automatic payment reminders, and track which invoices are overdue.

- **Square Invoices**: Square Invoices provides an easy-to-use platform for sending invoices and accepting payments, both online and in person. The platform offers options for recurring billing, payment tracking, and automated reminders, helping businesses stay on top of invoicing.

  - o **Example**: A small restaurant offering catering services might use Square Invoices to manage invoices for catering events, ensuring clients receive their bills immediately and payments are processed promptly.

Key takeaway: Invoicing tools like Wave, FreshBooks, and Square Invoices simplify the billing process, improve cash flow, and ensure timely payments, helping you avoid financial delays and maintain steady revenue.

Conclusion: Master Your Finances with the Right Tools

Managing your business's finances doesn't have to be overwhelming. With the right financial tools, you can take control of your budgeting, forecasting, and cash flow, ensuring your business stays financially healthy and prepared for growth. Whether you're tracking expenses, predicting future revenue, or ensuring timely payments, these tools make financial management easier and more efficient, allowing you to focus on what truly matters—growing your business. By integrating these financial wizards into your toolkit, you'll be ready to tackle any financial challenge with confidence and clarity.

Networking and Collaboration Platforms: Expanding Your Professional Circle

In the entrepreneurial world, your network is your net worth. Building strong relationships with other professionals, potential partners, and customers can open doors to new opportunities, insights, and collaborations that accelerate your business growth. In this section, we'll explore the best networking and collaboration platforms that will help you connect with the right people, expand your professional circle, and collaborate effectively with your team and industry peers.

1. LinkedIn: The Go-To Professional Networking Hub

When it comes to professional networking, LinkedIn is the undisputed leader. With over 700 million members, LinkedIn is the platform for building connections, sharing industry knowledge, and creating professional opportunities. Whether you're seeking partners, mentors, employees, or potential clients, LinkedIn offers the tools to expand your network and build your brand.

- **Create a standout profile**: Your LinkedIn profile serves as your digital business card. Ensure that your profile is polished and up-to-date, showcasing your expertise, accomplishments, and what your business offers.

> o **Example**: An entrepreneur launching a new tech startup might optimize their LinkedIn profile with keywords related to their industry and include case studies or projects that demonstrate their expertise.

- **Join industry-specific groups**: LinkedIn groups are an excellent way to connect with like-minded professionals in your niche. Engage in discussions, share insights, and ask questions to deepen your knowledge and build relationships with other industry experts.

> o **Example**: A marketing consultant could join groups related to digital marketing, where they can share expertise, discuss trends, and connect with potential clients looking for marketing advice.

- **Leverage LinkedIn's messaging and content-sharing features**: Use LinkedIn's messaging feature to reach out to potential collaborators or clients. Additionally, sharing articles, blog posts, and videos through your feed positions you as a thought leader and keeps you top of mind for your network.

> o **Example**: A business coach might share weekly tips on leadership and productivity, establishing credibility while providing value to their connections.

Key takeaway: LinkedIn is a powerful networking tool that allows you to build relationships, share your expertise, and connect with professionals in your industry to expand your professional circle.

2. Slack Communities: Collaborate and Connect with Industry Peers

While Slack is often known for its internal team collaboration features, it's also a great way to network through communities that are organized around shared interests or industries. Slack communities allow you to collaborate, exchange ideas, and network with people in your field in real time.

- **Join public Slack communities**: There are countless public Slack communities organized by industry, role, or interests. These communities provide a platform for you to ask questions, share resources, and participate in discussions with peers from around the globe.

  o **Example**: A SaaS founder could join a Slack community like SaaS Founders, where they can discuss growth strategies, share challenges, and connect with other entrepreneurs facing similar hurdles.

- **Leverage direct messaging and private groups**: Slack allows for quick, direct communication with members, and many communities also offer smaller, topic-specific channels. These smaller groups create deeper, more meaningful connections over shared professional challenges or goals.

  o **Example**: A startup founder might join a channel dedicated to funding strategies, connecting with other entrepreneurs who are seeking or sharing advice on raising capital.

- **Use Slack for collaboration with external partners**: Beyond joining industry communities, Slack is a great tool for collaborating with external teams, partners, or contractors. Create dedicated channels for specific projects, share files, and communicate in real time to keep everyone aligned.

  o **Example**: A design agency could create a shared Slack workspace with a client to streamline project collaboration and communication without the need for long email threads.

Key takeaway: Slack communities and channels provide valuable opportunities for networking with peers, collaborating in real time, and building relationships with like-minded professionals.

3. Meetup: Expand Your Network Through Local Events

Meetup is a platform that connects people based on shared interests, offering opportunities to attend or host in-person and virtual events. For entrepreneurs looking to grow their network, Meetup provides access to thousands of groups and events tailored to specific industries or professional goals.

- **Find and attend industry events**: By joining Meetup groups in your area of interest, you can attend local or virtual events designed to connect professionals and foster collaboration. These events range from workshops and seminars to networking mixers and industry talks.

  o **Example**: A product manager could attend product management workshops through Meetup, where they can network with other professionals, share best practices, and gain new insights.

- **Host your own events**: If you're looking to position yourself as a leader in your field or build connections within your community, consider hosting your own events on Meetup. Hosting a networking event or workshop can help you build relationships while showcasing your expertise.

  o **Example**: A digital marketing strategist could host a free online workshop on social media marketing trends, attracting other professionals in the industry and creating potential business opportunities.

- **Engage in virtual meetups**: If attending in-person events isn't possible, Meetup's virtual events allow you to connect with professionals from around the world. Virtual meetups give you access to a broader network and can lead to collaborations or partnerships beyond your local area.

  o **Example**: An entrepreneur in New York could join a virtual meetup focused on sustainability trends, networking with professionals from different industries and locations, potentially leading to new ideas or collaborations.

Key takeaway: Meetup allows you to expand your network by attending or hosting events, giving you access to local and global professionals who share your interests and goals.

4. Clubhouse: Voice-Driven Networking and Collaboration

Clubhouse is a voice-driven social networking platform that allows entrepreneurs to join live discussions, participate in Q&A sessions, and network with professionals in real-time audio rooms. It's like being at a virtual conference, where conversations flow naturally, and you can jump in to share your thoughts or listen to experts in your industry.

- **Join industry-specific rooms**: Clubhouse has rooms dedicated to virtually every industry and topic imaginable, from entrepreneurship and tech to personal development and leadership. Joining these rooms allows you to listen to conversations led by experts, ask questions, and connect with like-minded professionals.

  - o **Example**: A tech entrepreneur could join a room focused on AI advancements, listen to experts in the field, and connect with potential collaborators or investors interested in cutting-edge technology.

- **Host your own rooms or panels**: If you want to share your expertise, consider hosting your own Clubhouse room. Whether it's leading a discussion or hosting a panel of experts, this is a great way to build authority in your field and connect with an engaged audience.

  - o **Example**: A wellness coach might host a weekly Clubhouse room where they discuss mindfulness practices, inviting other coaches and wellness enthusiasts to join the conversation.

- **Network with people in real-time**: Unlike other social media platforms, Clubhouse's audio-only format creates a more personal, real-time interaction. You can ask questions, offer insights, and build relationships through natural conversations with professionals from around the globe.

  - o **Example**: A fashion designer could network with industry insiders by joining rooms dedicated to fashion trends, asking for advice, and sharing their own experiences, potentially leading to new partnerships or opportunities.

Key takeaway: Clubhouse offers a unique, real-time platform for networking and collaboration through live audio conversations, allowing you to engage directly with industry experts and peers.

5. Collaboration Tools: Work Together Seamlessly

While networking platforms are essential for building relationships, collaboration tools ensure that you can work together effectively with the connections you've made. Whether you're partnering with another business or working remotely with a distributed team, the right collaboration tools make all the difference in executing projects smoothly.

- **Google Workspace**: Google Workspace (formerly G Suite) offers a suite of cloud-based collaboration tools, including Google Docs, Google Sheets, and Google Drive. Teams can work together on documents in real time, share files, and keep projects organized, all while ensuring that everyone is on the same page.

  o **Example**: A content team working on a large marketing campaign might use Google Docs to draft and edit copy together in real time, streamlining collaboration and eliminating version control issues.

- **Trello**: Trello's visual boards make collaboration easy by organizing tasks and allowing team members to contribute, update progress, and add feedback in one place. It's a flexible tool for managing joint projects, even when team members are working in different locations.

  o **Example**: A startup might use Trello to manage a product launch, assigning tasks to marketing, development, and design teams while keeping everything organized in one shared workspace.

- **Notion**: Notion is an all-in-one workspace that combines note-taking, project management, and collaboration tools. It allows teams to organize information, collaborate on tasks, and store important documents in one place, making it ideal for cross-functional projects.

o **Example**: A remote team might use Notion to create a shared knowledge base, collaborate on product roadmaps, and manage project timelines, ensuring that all team members have access to critical information.

Key takeaway: Collaboration tools like Google Workspace, Trello, and Notion ensure that you can work seamlessly with your team and external partners, even when working remotely or across different time zones.

Conclusion: Build Strong Networks for Long-Term Success
Networking and collaboration are the keys to long-term success in any business. By leveraging platforms like LinkedIn, Slack, Meetup, Clubhouse, and essential collaboration tools, you can expand your professional circle, build meaningful relationships, and create opportunities for growth. Whether you're attending virtual events, joining discussions, or working together on shared projects,

Marketing Marvels: Tools for Boosting Visibility and Engaging Customers

In today's competitive marketplace, simply having a great product or service isn't enough. You need a strong marketing strategy and the right tools to reach your target audience, engage customers, and build lasting relationships. In this section, we'll explore the best marketing tools to boost your business's visibility, drive customer engagement, and generate leads, ensuring that your brand stays top of mind for your audience.

1. Email Marketing: Build Relationships and Drive Conversions

Email marketing remains one of the most powerful tools for nurturing customer relationships and driving sales. With the right email marketing platform, you can send personalized, automated messages, track engagement, and create targeted campaigns that speak directly to your customers' needs.

- **Mailchimp**: One of the most popular email marketing tools, Mailchimp offers a user-friendly interface for creating automated email campaigns, newsletters, and personalized emails. Its robust analytics and segmentation features allow you to target specific customer groups, improving open rates and conversions.

- o **Example**: An e-commerce business might use Mailchimp to send personalized product recommendations based on a customer's previous purchases, driving repeat sales and increasing customer loyalty.

- **ConvertKit**: ConvertKit is an email marketing tool built for creators and small businesses. It offers powerful automation features, allowing you to build sales funnels, segment your audience, and send targeted emails based on customer behavior. It's ideal for entrepreneurs who want to turn leads into paying customers.

  - o **Example**: A course creator could use ConvertKit to build an email sequence that nurtures leads through free content, leading them to sign up for a paid course.

- **ActiveCampaign**: ActiveCampaign combines email marketing, automation, and CRM features, making it a versatile tool for businesses looking to manage their customer relationships and communications in one place. It's perfect for businesses that want to send personalized, behavior-driven emails.

  - o **Example**: A software company could use ActiveCampaign to track user behavior on their platform and send automated emails that help guide users through the onboarding process, increasing customer retention.

Key takeaway: Email marketing platforms like Mailchimp, ConvertKit, and ActiveCampaign help you create targeted, personalized campaigns that build relationships and drive conversions.

2. Social Media Management Tools: Streamline Online Presence

Social media is an essential part of any modern marketing strategy, but managing multiple platforms can be time-consuming. Social media management tools allow you to schedule posts, track engagement, and manage all your social channels from one place, ensuring that your online presence remains consistent and engaging.

- **Hootsuite**: Hootsuite is a comprehensive social media management tool that supports scheduling, monitoring, and analyzing posts across multiple platforms, including Facebook, Twitter, Instagram, and LinkedIn. Its analytics features allow you to track the performance of your content and optimize future posts.

  o **Example**: A small business could use Hootsuite to schedule a week's worth of social media content in advance, ensuring a consistent posting schedule without having to manually post each day.

- **Buffer**: Buffer is another popular social media management tool known for its simplicity and ease of use. It allows you to schedule posts across various platforms, analyze performance, and engage with your audience from one dashboard. It's a great option for businesses focused on creating engaging content.

  o **Example**: A fashion brand could use Buffer to schedule Instagram posts, monitor the performance of different campaigns, and adjust their content strategy based on which posts generate the most engagement.

- **Later**: Later is a visual-first social media scheduling tool, making it ideal for brands that rely on platforms like Instagram and Pinterest. With its drag-and-drop calendar, you can plan and preview your content ahead of time, ensuring your visual brand stays cohesive and consistent.

  o **Example**: A lifestyle influencer could use Later to plan a month's worth of Instagram content, ensuring that their posts align with upcoming promotions and partnerships.

Key takeaway: Social media management tools like Hootsuite, Buffer, and Later help you streamline your online presence by scheduling posts, tracking performance, and managing multiple platforms from one dashboard.

3. SEO Tools: Improve Your Search Visibility

To attract new customers, your business needs to be discoverable through search engines. SEO tools help you improve your search engine rankings, analyze your website's performance, and optimize your content for the keywords your audience is searching for.

- **SEMrush**: SEMrush is a comprehensive SEO tool that offers keyword research, site audits, and competitor analysis. It helps you identify the most valuable keywords for your business and optimize your website to improve your search rankings. SEMrush also provides insights into your competitors' strategies, helping you stay ahead in your niche.

  - o **Example**: A digital marketing agency might use SEMrush to audit a client's website, identify SEO issues, and suggest improvements to boost search visibility and attract more organic traffic.

- **Ahrefs**: Ahrefs is a powerful tool for SEO and backlink analysis. It allows you to track keyword rankings, analyze competitor content, and find backlink opportunities to improve your website's authority. With Ahrefs, you can track how well your content is performing and adjust your strategy accordingly.

  - o **Example**: A blog-driven business could use Ahrefs to discover new content ideas by analyzing what's working for competitors, as well as tracking the performance of their existing blog posts.

- **Moz**: Moz offers a suite of SEO tools, including keyword research, site audits, and link building. Its easy-to-use interface and detailed insights make it an excellent choice for businesses that are new to SEO but want to improve their search engine visibility and drive organic traffic.

  - o **Example**: A local bakery might use Moz's local SEO tools to optimize their website for local search terms, ensuring they rank higher in Google's results when customers search for "bakeries near me."

Key takeaway: SEO tools like SEMrush, Ahrefs, and Moz help you improve your website's search visibility, drive organic traffic, and stay ahead of competitors by optimizing your content and keywords.

4. Content Marketing Platforms: Create Value, Not Just Noise

Content marketing is all about delivering value to your audience through educational, entertaining, or inspiring content. Content marketing platforms allow you to create, distribute, and manage content that resonates with your audience, builds trust, and positions your brand as an authority in your industry.

- **HubSpot**: HubSpot is an all-in-one inbound marketing platform that offers tools for blogging, content creation, social media, and email marketing. It's designed to help businesses attract, engage, and delight customers with valuable content that leads to conversions. HubSpot also provides analytics to track content performance.

  - **Example**: A B2B software company could use HubSpot to create in-depth blog posts on industry trends, distribute them via email marketing, and track which posts generate the most leads.

- **CoSchedule**: CoSchedule is a content marketing platform that helps businesses plan, create, and publish content more efficiently. It offers editorial calendar tools, social media scheduling, and team collaboration features, making it easy to manage all aspects of your content marketing in one place.

  - **Example**: A nonprofit organization might use CoSchedule to plan its blog content, schedule social media posts, and ensure that all campaigns are aligned with upcoming fundraising events.

- **ClearVoice**: ClearVoice is a content creation platform that connects businesses with freelance writers, editors, and content creators. It's ideal for companies that need help producing high-quality content at scale. The platform also offers collaboration and workflow tools for managing content production from ideation to publication.

○ **Example**: A healthcare company could use ClearVoice to hire expert writers to create educational articles on wellness topics, helping them engage with their audience while building credibility in their industry.

Key takeaway: Content marketing platforms like HubSpot, CoSchedule, and ClearVoice help you create valuable, targeted content that resonates with your audience, builds trust, and drives engagement.

5. Analytics Tools: Measure What Matters

Understanding the performance of your marketing efforts is essential to improving them. Analytics tools provide insights into what's working, what's not, and where you should focus your efforts. By analyzing data from your website, social media, and email campaigns, you can make data-driven decisions to optimize your strategy.

- **Google Analytics**: Google Analytics is a must-have tool for any business looking to track website traffic, user behavior, and conversion rates. It provides a detailed view of how visitors are interacting with your site, allowing you to see which marketing channels are driving the most traffic and conversions.

  ○ **Example**: An e-commerce store might use Google Analytics to track where their customers are coming from—whether through social media, organic search, or paid ads—and adjust their marketing strategy to focus on the most effective channels.

- **Kissmetrics**: Kissmetrics is an analytics platform that tracks user behavior and engagement across your website and marketing campaigns. It helps you understand how users move through your sales funnel and which touchpoints lead to conversions, making it easier to optimize your customer journey.

  ○ **Example**: A subscription-based service could use Kissmetrics to track how users interact with their website before signing up, helping them identify any drop-off points in the funnel and make improvements to increase conversions.

- **Hotjar**: Hotjar provides heatmaps, session recordings, and feedback tools that show you how users are interacting with your website. It's a great tool for identifying pain points in your site's user experience and making data-driven decisions to improve your site's design and functionality.

  o **Example**: A travel agency could use Hotjar to track how visitors navigate their booking process, identifying areas where users get stuck or abandon their bookings and making adjustments to improve the user experience.

Key takeaway: Analytics tools like Google Analytics, Kissmetrics, and Hotjar help you measure the effectiveness of your marketing efforts, providing actionable insights that guide data-driven decision-making and optimize your strategy.

Conclusion: Empower Your Marketing Strategy with the Right Tools
Building a successful marketing strategy requires the right combination of tools to reach and engage your audience, optimize your content, and measure your success. With the marketing marvels covered in this section—whether it's email marketing, social media management, SEO optimization, content creation, or analytics—you can create a comprehensive, data-driven approach to boosting visibility and driving customer engagement. Armed with these tools, your marketing efforts will be more targeted, efficient, and impactful, ensuring your brand stays top of mind and your business continues to grow.

Learning and Growth Resources: Staying Informed and Inspired

As an entrepreneur, continuous learning and staying up to date with industry trends are crucial to your success. Whether it's mastering new skills, gaining insights into the latest business strategies, or staying motivated, learning and growth resources provide the knowledge and inspiration you need to keep evolving. In this section, we'll explore platforms, tools, and resources that help you stay informed and inspired as you grow your business.

1. Online Learning Platforms: Upskill and Stay Competitive

In the rapidly changing business world, acquiring new skills and staying ahead of trends can make a significant difference. Online learning platforms offer a flexible way to learn from experts, master new topics, and apply these skills to your business.

- **Udemy**: Udemy is one of the largest online learning platforms, offering courses on a wide range of topics from digital marketing to financial management. With thousands of courses available, you can learn from experts in various fields and apply the knowledge directly to your business.

  - **Example**: A startup founder looking to improve their digital marketing skills could enroll in a Udemy course on SEO and social media marketing to help their business gain more visibility online.

- **Coursera**: Coursera partners with top universities and institutions to offer professional development courses and certifications. With access to courses from Ivy League schools and global organizations, Coursera provides deep insights into business, technology, and personal development.

  - **Example**: An entrepreneur could take a course on business analytics from a top university to better understand data-driven decision-making, giving them a competitive edge in their industry.

- **LinkedIn Learning**: LinkedIn Learning (formerly Lynda.com) offers on-demand courses focused on business, technology, and creative skills. The platform is integrated with LinkedIn, allowing you to showcase completed courses and certifications on your profile.

  - **Example**: A small business owner could use LinkedIn Learning to take a course on leadership and team management, applying these skills to create a more efficient and motivated team.

Key takeaway: Online learning platforms like Udemy, Coursera, and LinkedIn Learning allow you to acquire new skills and stay competitive in the fast-paced business environment.

2. Business and Industry News: Stay Updated on Trends

Keeping up with the latest business news and industry trends helps you stay informed and make better decisions. Business news platforms and resources keep you updated on market changes, emerging technologies, and new opportunities.

- **Harvard Business Review (HBR)**: HBR provides articles, case studies, and reports on a wide range of business topics, including leadership, strategy, innovation, and management. It's a go-to resource for thought-provoking insights that help entrepreneurs navigate the complex world of business.

  - **Example**: A CEO could read HBR articles on leadership and strategy to gain insights into best practices, helping them refine their approach to managing their team and scaling their business.

- **TechCrunch**: If your business is in the tech space, TechCrunch is an essential resource for staying up to date with industry developments, startup news, and tech innovations. TechCrunch covers everything from product launches to funding rounds, giving you a pulse on the latest trends.

  - **Example**: A tech entrepreneur could follow TechCrunch to stay informed about competitor product releases, venture capital movements, and emerging trends in AI or blockchain.

- **Entrepreneur.com**: Entrepreneur is a leading publication dedicated to startup culture, business innovation, and personal growth. It features stories from successful entrepreneurs, as well as tips, advice, and insights into managing and scaling a business.

  - **Example**: A founder could use Entrepreneur.com to read about successful startups, learning from their experiences and applying these lessons to their own business journey.

Key takeaway: Staying informed through platforms like Harvard Business Review, TechCrunch, and Entrepreneur.com helps you make strategic decisions and keep pace with the latest industry developments.

3. Podcasts and Audiobooks: Learn on the Go

For busy entrepreneurs, podcasts and audiobooks are an excellent way to absorb new knowledge and insights during commutes, workouts, or downtime. These audio resources offer a wealth of information on entrepreneurship, leadership, business strategies, and personal growth.

- **The Tim Ferriss Show**: Hosted by best-selling author Tim Ferriss, this podcast features interviews with high achievers from various fields, including business, sports, entertainment, and science. Guests share their tactics, routines, and philosophies for success, providing valuable lessons for entrepreneurs.

    o **Example**: A small business owner could listen to an episode featuring a successful startup founder, gaining insights into productivity, overcoming challenges, and scaling a business.

- **How I Built This**: Hosted by NPR's Guy Raz, "How I Built This" tells the stories behind the people who created some of the world's best-known companies. Each episode offers a deep dive into the journey of building a successful business, including the challenges and triumphs along the way.

    o **Example**: An aspiring entrepreneur could listen to episodes featuring well-known founders like Howard Schultz (Starbucks) or Sara Blakely (Spanx) to gain inspiration and learn from their experiences.

- **Audible**: Audible offers a wide selection of audiobooks covering business topics, leadership, productivity, and personal development. Listening to audiobooks is a great way to keep learning while multitasking.

    o **Example**: An entrepreneur could listen to audiobooks like *The Lean Startup* by Eric Ries or *Good to Great* by Jim Collins during their morning commute to stay inspired and learn new strategies for growing their business.

Key takeaway: Podcasts and audiobooks offer entrepreneurs a convenient way to learn and stay motivated, with access to expert insights and real-world business stories while on the go.

4. Online Communities and Forums: Engage with Like-Minds

Sometimes, the best learning comes from real-time conversations with peers. Online communities and forums provide platforms for entrepreneurs to ask questions, share experiences, and collaborate on solving challenges. These communities create opportunities to learn from others and gain diverse perspectives.

- **Reddit (r/Entrepreneur):** Reddit's r/Entrepreneur forum is a large and active community of entrepreneurs from all over the world. Members share advice, ask questions, and discuss a variety of topics related to starting and growing a business. It's a great resource for learning from others' experiences and getting feedback on your ideas.

  - **Example:** A founder facing a specific business challenge could post on r/Entrepreneur to get feedback and solutions from other entrepreneurs who have been through similar situations.

- **GrowthMentor:** GrowthMentor is an online platform where entrepreneurs can connect with experienced mentors in areas like growth marketing, product development, and fundraising. It offers one-on-one sessions with industry experts, providing practical advice and personalized feedback.

  - **Example:** A SaaS startup founder might use GrowthMentor to book a session with a growth expert, learning how to optimize their sales funnel and increase customer retention.

- **Indie Hackers:** Indie Hackers is a community of entrepreneurs building profitable online businesses. It's a space to share your journey, ask questions, and learn from others who are bootstrapping their own ventures. Indie Hackers features interviews, articles, and forums dedicated to entrepreneurial success.

  o   **Example**: A software developer launching a side project could use Indie Hackers to share progress, ask for feedback, and learn about the business models other indie founders have used to achieve success.

Key takeaway: Engaging with online communities like Reddit's r/Entrepreneur, GrowthMentor, and Indie Hackers allows entrepreneurs to learn from peers, collaborate on challenges, and gain practical insights for growing their businesses.

5. Inspiration and Motivation Resources: Stay Driven

Running a business can be mentally and emotionally taxing. Staying motivated through the highs and lows of entrepreneurship requires consistent inspiration and a positive mindset. Inspiration and motivation resources provide that extra push when you need it most.

- **TED Talks**: TED Talks offer short, powerful presentations on a wide range of topics, including business, leadership, innovation, and personal growth. Listening to thought leaders and industry pioneers share their ideas can spark creativity and keep you inspired.

  o   **Example**: A founder feeling overwhelmed could watch a TED Talk on overcoming adversity or leadership, gaining a fresh perspective and renewed motivation to tackle challenges.

- **Medium**: Medium is a platform where professionals, thought leaders, and entrepreneurs write about their experiences, offering inspiration and practical advice. Whether it's an article on leadership or a story about overcoming failure, Medium is full of valuable insights.

  o   **Example**: An entrepreneur experiencing a setback could read articles on Medium about how other business leaders have overcome obstacles, providing motivation to keep pushing forward.

- **Motivational Podcasts (e.g., "The Tony Robbins Podcast")**: For entrepreneurs looking for regular motivation, podcasts like "The Tony

Robbins Podcast" offer actionable advice on business, personal development, and achieving success. Hearing directly from motivational speakers can provide the mental boost you need.

> o **Example**: A business owner facing a difficult decision could listen to an episode of "The Tony Robbins Podcast" for inspiration on overcoming fear and making confident choices.

Key takeaway: Inspiration and motivation resources like TED Talks, Medium, and motivational podcasts help entrepreneurs stay driven, overcome challenges, and remain focused on their goals.

Conclusion: Fuel Your Growth with Learning and Inspiration
Entrepreneurship is a constant learning process, and staying informed and inspired is critical to long-term success. With access to online learning platforms, business news, podcasts, online communities, and inspirational resources, you can keep growing, evolving, and staying ahead of the curve. Whether you're mastering a new skill, staying updated on industry trends, or seeking motivation during tough times, these learning and growth resources will empower you to lead your business to greater heights. Stay curious, keep learning, and continue pushing the boundaries of what's possible for your business.

Quick Tips and Recap

- **Invest in continuous learning**: Use online platforms like Udemy, Coursera, and LinkedIn Learning to gain new skills and stay competitive.

- **Stay informed with industry news**: Follow resources like Harvard Business Review, TechCrunch, and Entrepreneur.com to keep up with trends and market developments.

- **Listen and learn on the go**: Tune into podcasts like *The Tim Ferriss Show* and *How I Built This*, or explore audiobooks through Audible for ongoing inspiration and knowledge.

- **Engage with online communities**: Join forums like Reddit's r/Entrepreneur, Growth Mentor, and Indie Hackers to collaborate, learn from others, and share your journey.

- **Seek inspiration and motivation**: Watch TED Talks, read articles on Medium, or listen to motivational podcasts to stay driven through the ups and downs of entrepreneurship.

- **Participate in real-time learning**: Use platforms like Clubhouse or join virtual meetups to engage in live discussions with industry experts and peers.

- **Curate a personal growth plan**: Set aside time each week to read, listen, or engage with new content that challenges your thinking and fuels your business growth.

- **Stay adaptable**: Use your learning and growth resources to continuously adapt and apply new strategies to your evolving business needs.

By leveraging these learning and growth resources, you'll be better equipped to make informed decisions, stay inspired, and guide your business toward ongoing success.

Appendix

Essential Agreements and Documents

This appendix provides key documents to support your entrepreneurial journey, including **two business plans** to guide strategic growth and **Non-Disclosure Agreements (NDAs)**—both **unilateral** and **mutual**—to protect sensitive information. These templates serve as practical tools to help you plan effectively and safeguard your ideas as you build your empire.

Disclaimer: These documents are provided for informational purposes only and do not constitute legal or financial advice. It is recommended that you consult with a qualified professional to ensure these templates meet your specific needs and comply with local laws and regulations.

▶ If you are interested in receiving an electronic copy of any of the following documents, please email us at documents@AuthorsDoor.com with the subject line "Request for [fill in the blank]." Upon receiving your email, we will promptly send you a Microsoft Word copy of the document. **Disclaimer:** Please note that all agreements are provided for informational purposes only and should not be construed as legal advice. We recommend consulting with a qualified attorney to ensure that any legal documents or decisions are tailored to your specific circumstances.

1. Publishing House Business Plan

The Ridge Publishing Group
2021-2025 Business Plan
Confidential and Proprietary

1.0 EXECUTIVE SUMMARY

The Ridge Publishing Group (RPG), spearheaded by the dynamic duo of Lori Ann Moeszinger and her husband, Eric Moeszinger, stands at the forefront of innovation in the publishing world. Lori, a serial entrepreneur with a diverse background in business, fashion, law, and multimedia ventures, alongside Eric, brings to life RPG's vision of intertwining literature, film, and interactive entertainment into a cohesive, global brand.

At the heart of RPG lies a diverse portfolio of six distinct imprints alongside its flagship brand, each carving out unique spaces in the literary and entertainment landscapes. These include: (1) Guardians of Biblical Truth Publishing Group, a beacon for those seeking profound, faith-based insights; (2) Hoyle Theology Publisher Group, dedicated to exploring theological wisdom; (3) Documentaries in Print Publishing Group, where real-world narratives meet the page;.(4) Education in Games Publishing Group, merging learning with the joy of gameplay; (5) Urban Chronicles Publishing House, capturing the pulse of city life through storytelling; (6) AuthorsDoor Group, a platform for aspiring and established writers to hone their craft; and (7) Ethan Fox Books, RPG's vibrant subsidiary, which introduces young readers to the joy of storytelling through an interactive online world.

Powerful Business Model

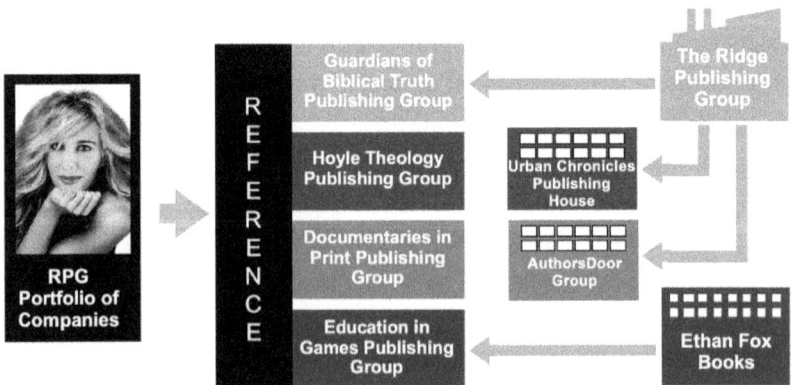

Lori Ann Moeszinger, the visionary behind RPG, is not just the company's backbone; she is a storyteller whose narratives are designed to inspire, challenge, and transform. Writing

Appendix

under various pseudonyms, she navigates themes from biblical insights to publishing expertise with unparalleled versatility. Eric, contributing with his fiction works under E. L. Seer, complements this dynamic, creating a symbiotic blend of fiction and non-fiction that sets RPG apart.

RPG's digital footprint is equally impressive, with five specialized blogs that extend the reach and impact of its publishing mission: (1) Publisher and Her World blog, a precursor to the AuthorsRedDoor blog reboot, this blog offers a unique glimpse into the publishing world, filled with humor, personal insights, and the adventures of Lori and Eric's partnership; (2) Jesus-Says blog, dedicated to the Guardians of Biblical Truth, this platform provides devout insights and discussions on biblical teachings and spirituality; (3) Manhattan Chronicles blog, a fictional exploration of life in Manhattan, offering essays that promise laughter, shock, and self-discovery; (4) Authors Red Door blog, a resource hub for authors, publishers, and creators, featuring teachings from Lori's extensive how-to sell books progressive series and free courses; and (5) Ethan Fox Official KidsStagram blog, an interactive space for young readers, inspired by the Ethan Fox Books franchise, fostering creativity and learning outside the classroom.

RPG's revolutionary business model is designed to thrive under the helm of Lori and Eric Moeszinger. This husband-and-wife team's strategy emphasizes rapid market entry, digital engagement, and long-term earnings potential. RPG is not just a publishing house; it's a platform for change, driven by passion, innovation, and a commitment to storytelling that resonates.

Welcome to The Ridge Publishing Group, where storytelling meets innovation.

1.1   Management by Objectives (MBOs)

At the heart of The Ridge Publishing Group's strategic vision lies a transformative Business Model platform, ingeniously crafted and executed by the powerhouse husband-and-wife team of Eric and Lori Moeszinger. This revolutionary approach is not just about publishing; it's about redefining the industry through agility, innovation, and strategic foresight.

Key Objectives for Unparalleled Success:

- **Diverse Revenue Streams**: By harnessing multiple revenue channels, The Ridge Publishing Group ensures a broad and resilient financial foundation. Our diverse imprints and digital platforms, including an array of specialized blogs and educational resources, cultivate a multifaceted revenue ecosystem that mitigates risk and promotes stability.

- **Scalability and Operating Leverage**: Our business model is designed for scalability, enabling rapid expansion while maintaining low variable costs. This structure allows for significant operating leverage, where the core assets of creativity and intellectual property drive growth, predictable revenue, and high profit margins. The result? A cash flow-positive operation poised for exponential growth.

- **Comprehensive Leadership**: Underpinning our business model is a team of qualified leaders, with Eric and Lori Moeszinger at the helm, embodying the roles of CEO, CBDO, CMO, CSO, COO, CTO, CCGO, CFO, CIO, and CHRO. This unparalleled leadership depth ensures expert oversight across all critical business functions, from strategic marketing to financial management and operational excellence.

From Idea to Empire

- **Innovative Business Model with Built-in Spinoff Strategies**: The Ridge Publishing Group's business model is unprecedented in its integration of in-house publishing with the potential for spinoff ventures. This forward-thinking approach not only solidifies our position in the market but also opens avenues for future expansion and diversification.

In summary, The Ridge Publishing Group stands at the forefront of the publishing industry, not merely participating but actively shaping its future. Our strategic objectives and innovative business model are the bedrock upon which we will build long-term value for our stakeholders, redefine the landscape of publishing, and inspire a new generation of readers and creators.

1.2   Keys to Success

1.2.1. 2021: A Year of Foundations and Firsts for The Ridge Publishing Group

The year 2021 marked a pivotal moment in the journey of The Ridge Publishing Group, a year where visions took form and the foundational stones of our ambitious venture were laid. It was a year of dynamic beginnings, characterized by the launch of several key digital platforms and the debut of groundbreaking literary works that showcase our commitment to diversity, creativity, and innovation in publishing.

In 2021, The Ridge Publishing Group embarked on a pivotal deployment of our digital footprint through the strategic development and launch of key online platforms. Most notably, this included the establishment of the main publisher's website for The Ridge Publishing Group, the entertainment-focused website for Ethan Fox Books, and the engaging Ethan Fox Official KidsStagram blog site. These digital platforms have been meticulously crafted not just as the online representations of our imprints but as vibrant, interactive communities. They serve as a nexus for readers, authors, and creative enthusiasts to discover, engage, and draw inspiration, marking a significant milestone in our journey to connect with and inspire a global audience.

2021 also saw the release of the first books in what promises to be a series of captivating narratives and engaging content across various genres. The Ethan Fox *Original Series* made its debut with "Ethan Fox and the Eyes of the Desert Sand," inviting readers into a world of adventure and mystery. Simultaneously, the educational and entertaining "Wordly Pagemore's Early Worm Activities & Games – The Eyes of the Desert Sand Edition" was launched, aimed at sparking curiosity and a love for learning among young readers. Additionally, the debut illustrated chapter book "Mayhem in the Moongarden" began its journey, offering young audiences a blend of humor, adventure, and imagination.

2021 was a year of laying the groundwork and forging paths into new territories. With each launch and release, The Ridge Publishing Group solidified its commitment to enriching lives through storytelling, education, and entertainment. It was a year that set the stage for growth, innovation, and the realization of our vision to inspire change and empower voices across the globe.

1.2.2. 2022: A Year of Expansion and Innovation at The Ridge Publishing Group

In 2022, The Ridge Publishing Group celebrated a year of significant growth and strategic development. Key among our achievements was the relocation of our headquarters to a vibrant downtown location, positioning us at the heart of the literary and creative communities we serve. This year also saw the release of eagerly anticipated sequels within our beloved Ethan Fox *Original Series*: "Ethan Fox and the Shadow Princess," the second

Appendix

installment in the Ethan Fox *Original Series*, and the next chapter in "Wordly Pagemore's Early Work Activities & Games – The Shadow Princess Edition."

Our commitment to enriching our publishing portfolio was further evidenced by the advancement of several exciting projects in our pipeline. These include personal and impactful narratives like "Autobiography: Total Surrender, My Story and Bonus: Your Life's Blueprint in Seven Steps" and "When Death Knocked at My Door," as well as the innovative "New Narrated Study Bible" series, the comprehensive "Hoyle Theology Encyclopedia" series, and the apologetic "Defending the Faith – Documentaries in Faith." Additionally, we ventured into the realm of interactive entertainment with the development of "Heaven's Seminary," a board game designed to engage and educate through play.

2022 was a year of both deepening and broadening for The Ridge Publishing Group, as we continued to expand our offerings and strengthen our position in the market.

1.2.3. 2023: The Year of Strategic Learning and Preparation at The Ridge Publishing Group

In 2023, The Ridge Publishing Group embarked on a transformative journey of introspection and strategic analysis, dubbing it "The Year of the Assignment." This pivotal year was dedicated to mastering the intricacies of the publishing market, particularly understanding what drives book sales and secures a thriving position in a competitive landscape. Our explorations unveiled the impactful strategy of offering FREE books to capture reader interest, alongside adopting Amazon's rapid release method. Consequently, we strategically postponed the launch of promising series like "The Living Waters" and "The Manhattan Diaries" to 2024, planning for a staggered release to maximize visibility with Amazon's crucial 30-day New Release window.

Further enhancing our approach, we discovered the rejuvenating effect of book bundles on existing publications, breathing new life into our catalog. Beyond these insights, 2023 was also a year of creation, marked by the development of the AuthorsDoor Leadership Program. This comprehensive initiative, featuring three progressive series complete with free courses, and downloadable workbooks, is set for release in the latter half of 2024, promising to enrich our educational offerings.

As we move forward, our pipeline for 2024 is robust, filled with multiple book and series releases that reflect the lessons learned and strategies honed in 2023. This year of deliberate pause and learning has poised The Ridge Publishing Group for a future of dynamic growth and sustained success.

1.2.4. 2024: Embracing Innovation and Multimedia Expansion at The Ridge Publishing Group

In 2024, The Ridge Publishing Group embarked on a transformative journey, shifting from traditional to innovative publishing, a strategic pivot inspired by the fruits from "The Year of the Assignment" in 2023. This year marked a significant reboot in our approach to publishing, digital engagement, and content delivery. We unveiled a revamped publisher website enriched with comprehensive press kits and seamlessly integrated it with a new author-focused platform linked to our light-hearted initiative, The Manhattan Diaries, via our New Youniversity website.

Anticipating the second half of the year, we are set to introduce our bridge platform, AuthorsDoor, which will further enrich our digital ecosystem. In a bold move to align with the evolving multimedia landscape, we transitioned Ethan Fox Books and KidsStagram from book-centric to film-centric sites, laying the groundwork for potential film adaptations and enhancing our engagement with fans through a dedicated Fan Page.

Moreover, 2024 saw the launch of three new blogs: Publisher and Her World, Jesus Says, and Manhattan Chronicles, each designed to cater to distinct audiences and expand our digital footprint. The forthcoming launch of the Authors Red Door blog will complement these efforts, embodying the innovative spirit of our 2023 strategies.

This year's reboot is not merely a change but a reinvention, positioning The Ridge Publishing Group at the forefront of innovative publishing, poised for unprecedented growth and impact in the literary and entertainment sectors.

1.2.5. 2025 and Beyond: Expanding Horizons with The Ridge Publishing Group

As The Ridge Publishing Group looks ahead to 2025 and beyond, we are strategically positioning ourselves to secure a film deal for the acclaimed Ethan Fox *Original Series*, marking a significant leap in the multimedia storytelling realm. Our ambition extends into the educational sector, where we aim to enrich the learning experience from pre-K through 12th grade with innovative educational materials derived from the Ethan Fox Books universe. This initiative reflects our commitment to leveraging our content across diverse platforms and audiences.

Furthermore, the anticipated release of the New Narrated Study Bible showcases our dedication to expanding our publishing portfolio into new genres and formats, offering unique and engaging ways for readers to connect with biblical narratives.

The journey beyond 2025 is poised to unfold with even more groundbreaking projects and collaborations. At The Ridge Publishing Group, our vision is to continually explore, innovate, and inspire, setting new benchmarks in the publishing and entertainment industries. Our forward-thinking strategies and commitment to excellence are the driving forces behind our quest to create impactful stories and educational content that resonate across generations.

2.0   BUSINESS OVERVIEW

2.1   Bridging Innovation in Publishing and Education

The advent of the internet has dramatically reshaped the publishing landscape, enabling authors to self-publish with unprecedented ease, eliminating the traditional constraints of inventory and warehousing. In this evolving ecosystem, The Ridge Publishing Group and the Ethan Fox Books franchise are poised to merge, unlocking vast potential for spinoff ventures that span across the publishing and educational sectors. A prime example of this synergy is our Education in Games initiative, which champions the transformative potential of board games as educational tools, offering an accessible and engaging solution to the educational challenges of our time.

Lori Moeszinger, the visionary behind The Ridge Publishing Group, emphasizes, "While the entertainment value of board games is widely recognized, their potential as a medium for primary through higher education content is a game-changer in addressing our current educational crisis." This innovative approach comes at a critical juncture, as the escalating costs of traditional education increasingly place higher education beyond the reach of many Americans. The trend towards higher education becoming less accessible is further exacerbated by a doubling in student borrowing over the past decade and a bias in financial aid distribution that disadvantages lower-income families.

Appendix

Moreover, the higher education sector is experiencing a period of significant upheaval, with a worrying trend of college consolidations and closures driven by increased regulation and declining enrollments. These challenges have forced many institutions to hike tuition fees, slash faculty positions, and curtail course offerings, merely to remain operational.

At the heart of Education in Games is a mission to revolutionize how education is delivered and perceived. By leveraging board games as a powerful educational platform, we aim to democratize access to knowledge and skills essential for success in the 21st century. Our curriculum not only seeks to level the educational playing field but also to foster cultural understanding, empathy, and a global perspective, equipping students to thrive in an interconnected world. Through Education in Games, The Ridge Publishing Group is not just participating in the publishing and educational arenas; we are setting the stage for a future where learning is inclusive, engaging, and universally accessible.

2.2 The Evolution from Traditional to Self-Publishing

In the realm of traditional publishing, the emphasis on content quality cannot be overstated, with the editorial process playing a pivotal role in shaping a manuscript's success. However, the landscape of publishing has been undergoing a significant transformation, challenging the notion that traditional publishers hold a monopoly over connecting authors with their audience.

Platforms like Amazon, Ingram Content Group, and various aggregators including Smashwords, now Draft2Digital, are redefining the pathway to publication. These entities are democratizing access to the market, offering authors streamlined avenues to publish, market, and distribute their works directly to readers.

This shift towards self-publishing isn't a novel trend but rather an evolution of the indie author movement, which has long championed the autonomy of publishing and selling books without the intermediation of traditional publishing houses. The distinction lies in the self-publisher's dual role as both author and publisher, managing the entire lifecycle of a book from creation to consumer.

The journey to a book's success encompasses far more than just writing; it involves a comprehensive 75 percent effort in editing, designing, managing pre-press and post-press activities, marketing, and much more, with writing accounting for only about 25 percent of the total endeavor.

The advent of platforms such as Amazon KDP, Amazon KDP Print, IngramSpark, and others has further simplified the publishing equation to primarily involve just the author and the reader. For indie authors, the challenge remains to produce compelling, high-quality content that captivates readers. Beyond the creation of content, the focus shifts to effective marketing and global distribution strategies, alongside the continuous process of writing and publishing more works. These developments have not only expanded the opportunities for authors but have also enriched the literary market with a diverse range of voices and stories.

2.3 Ethan Fox Books: A New Contender in the Quest for the Next Fantasy Phenomenon

As the literary and cinematic worlds continue to seek the successor to the Harry Potter phenomenon, a new challenger emerges from The Ridge Publishing Group: E. L. Seer's debut, "Ethan Fox and the Eyes of the Desert Sand." Positioned within the fiercely competitive landscape of crossover fantasy series, this inaugural entry in the Ethan Fox

From Idea to Empire

Original Series is a visually captivating narrative set in a concealed universe with Earth at its core.

In a market where publishers are vying for the next big hit, offering substantial advances for debut novels that captivate young adults and fans across the spectrum of literary and commercial fiction, "Ethan Fox and the Eyes of the Desert Sand" introduces readers to a world brimming with intrigue. The tale of teenagers Ethan and Hayley, drawn together by fate to unravel the story's grand enigma and access to the four elemental worlds of the Chrysalis, is a rich tapestry of characters, creatures, and cosmic dilemmas.

What distinguishes the Ethan Fox series is not just its imaginative setting or the complex web of romance, rivalry, and suspense. It's the depth of its characters – Ethan, Hayley, and even the memorable Gruggins – balanced against the villainous Victor and Daavic, that anchors the narrative's appeal. It's a story where the universe's vastness is matched only by the protagonists' relatability, ensuring readers' investment from the first page.

Amidst the echoes of past contenders like *The Night Circus*, *Legend*, and *The Age of Miracles*, and standing alongside young adult titans like *Percy Jackson* and the *Inheritance Cycle*, the Ethan Fox Books series signals its ambition to carve out its own legacy. Despite the daunting sales figures of these established franchises, The Ridge Publishing Group's innovative approach to marketing – encompassing licensing deals, immersive websites, and community engagement through initiatives like the KidsStagramCLUB and philanthropy – sets the stage for Ethan Fox to captivate a global audience.

With a marketing strategy that mirrors the event-style releases of blockbuster films, The Ridge Publishing Group is not just launching a book series; it's unveiling an experience. The Ethan Fox Books series, with its blend of compelling storytelling and interactive engagement, stands on the threshold of becoming a major cultural phenomenon.

For more insights into the Ethan Fox universe and its burgeoning community, visit our dedicated site and discover how "Ethan Fox and the Eyes of the Desert Sand" is capturing the imaginations of readers worldwide.

3.0 HISTORY AND CURRENT BUSINESS

3.1 Corporate Overview: The Ridge Publishing Group

The Ridge Publishing Group, headquartered in the vibrant city of Coeur d'Alene, Idaho, stands as a premier global entity in the realms of book, film, and board game production. With a strategic focus on becoming the world's leading resource for theology education, The Ridge Publishing Group offers an unparalleled range of products including books, textbooks, documentaries, board games, and card decks. Catering to a diverse audience, our publishing portfolio encompasses fiction, non-fiction, and children's literature across various formats such as hardcover, trade paperback, audio, electronic, and digital.

Our subsidiary, Ethan Fox Books, epitomizes excellence in publishing, delivering an enticing mix of fiction, non-fiction, and children's titles. We are dedicated to crafting educational and entertaining content for both classroom and home environments. Our extensive product line extends to magazines, technology-driven offerings, teacher resources, videos, and toys, all designed to enrich and engage young minds.

Distribution of our products and services spans multiple channels, ensuring accessibility and convenience. From book clubs and fairs to direct-to-home programs, as well as through retail outlets, schools, libraries, and our dedicated website Ethan Fox Books, we aim to reach readers wherever they are, fostering a love for reading and learning across generations.

3.2 Company History

Founded in 2021, The Ridge Publishing Group, from its inception distinguished itself by launching an array of digital platforms and imprints designed to cater to diverse audiences. 2021 saw the unveiling of the Ethan Fox Books *Original Series*, starting with "Ethan Fox and the Eyes of the Desert Sand," marking the Group's foray into creating a significant franchise that seeks to emulate the event-publishing success reminiscent of the Harry Potter series. Alongside, the Group introduced several specialized blogs and educational resources, expanding its footprint in the digital domain.

The subsequent years were characterized by strategic growth and innovation. In 2022, The Ridge Publishing Group relocated its headquarters to a prime downtown location, signaling its expanding influence and operational capabilities. This year also witnessed the release of sequels within the Ethan Fox series and the advancement of various projects in the publishing pipeline, showcasing the Group's commitment to delivering engaging and diverse content.

2023 was designated "The Year of the Assignment," a period of introspective strategy refinement and learning. The Group embraced industry insights, such as the power of free books and Amazon's rapid release strategy, positioning itself for a transformative future. This year was pivotal in laying the groundwork for staggered releases and leveraging book bundles to rejuvenate interest in existing titles.

Embracing the lessons of 2023, 2024 marked a significant reboot from traditional to innovative publishing. The Ridge Publishing Group relaunched its publisher and author websites, introduced new blogs, and pivoted the Ethan Fox Books and KidsStagram sites towards a film-centric approach in anticipation of a future film deal. This year epitomized the Group's adaptive strategies and its drive towards multimedia expansion.

Looking ahead to 2025 and beyond, The Ridge Publishing Group is poised for further evolution, aiming to secure a film deal for the Ethan Fox Books franchise and delve deeper into educational materials for pre-K to 12th grade. With the planned release of the New Narrated Study Bible and continued innovation, the Group is set on a trajectory to redefine publishing and educational entertainment.

Since 2021, The Ridge Publishing Group has not only established itself as a beacon of creativity and innovation but also as a testament to the enduring power of storytelling and education. Through strategic foresight, adaptability, and a passion for enriching lives, the Group continues to pave its way forward, shaping the future of publishing and beyond.

4.0 MARKETING PLANS

As The Ridge Publishing Group navigates the dynamic landscape of the publishing industry, our market strategy is designed to maximize reach, engagement, and conversion across all our platforms and imprints. Drawing from the insights and milestones achieved since our inception in 2021, our marketing plans for the upcoming years are both ambitious and meticulously structured to ensure sustainable growth and market penetration.

4.1 Digital Presence and Content Marketing

Our digital strategy centers on leveraging our websites, specialized blogs, and social media channels to build a strong online presence. With the successful launch and subsequent reboot of our publisher and author websites, including Ethan Fox Books and KidsStagram, we aim to enhance user experience with the interactive content, video trailers, author interviews, and behind-the-scenes glimpses into the making of our books and board games. SEO optimization and content marketing will drive traffic and improve search engine rankings, ensuring visibility for our diverse product offerings.

4.2 Staggered Release Strategy

Learning from the "Year of the Assignment" in 2023, we will implement Amazon's rapid release strategy to keep our titles within the 30-day New Release lists, beginning with "The Living Waters series" and "The Manhattan Diaries series" in 2024. This approach will maintain a constant buzz around our new releases, encouraging ongoing engagement from our audience.

4.3 Interactive and Educational Initiatives

Continuing our commitment to educational enrichment, we will further develop our board game and educational material lines, focusing on pre-K to 12th grade. Our marketing will highlight the educational value of these products, positioning them as essential tools for learning and entertainment, distinct from traditional educational resources.

4.4 Event and Experience Marketing

We will create event-like experiences around major book releases, mirroring the strategy that made the Harry Potter franchise a global phenomenon. This includes book launch events, readings, and interactive online events that bring the world of Ethan Fox and other series to life for fans and new readers alike.

4.5 Licensing and Merchandising

In anticipation of securing a film deal for the Ethan Fox Books franchise, we will explore licensing opportunities and merchandise that can extend the brand's reach. From apparel and accessories to collectibles, our goal is to build a robust merchandise line that fans can embrace.

4.6 Philanthropy and Community Engagement

Our philanthropic efforts, particularly through initiatives like KidsStagram.com/Philanthropy, will continue to play a crucial role in our marketing strategy. By aligning our brand with causes that matter to our readers and the broader community, we will foster goodwill and deepen our market engagement.

4.7 Partnerships and Collaborations

We will seek strategic partnerships with educational institutions, literary festivals, and other cultural events to promote our titles and educational games. Collaborations with influencers, book bloggers, and educators will help amplify our reach and credibility among target audiences.

4.8 Analytics and Feedback Loops

To ensure our marketing strategies remain effective and responsive to market trends, we will employ analytics tools to monitor performance and gather feedback across all

Appendix

channels. This data-driven approach will allow us to refine our tactics, ensuring we remain agile and proactive in our marketing efforts.

In summary, The Ridge Publishing Group's marketing plans are crafted to propel our diverse range of books, educational games, and digital content into the forefront of our target markets. Through innovative strategies, engagement, and a steadfast commitment to quality and community, we are poised to expand our influence and inspire audiences worldwide.

5.0   PRODUCT DEVELOPMENT PLANS

The Ridge Publishing Group, since its foundation in 2021, has embarked on a journey to innovate and inspire across the realms of publishing, education, and entertainment. Our product development strategy is grounded in our mission to deliver compelling content, immersive educational tools, and engaging experiences that cater to a global audience. Herein, we outline our plans for product development, ensuring alignment with market demands and our long-term vision.

5.1   Expanding the Ethan Fox Books Series

Building on the success of the Ethan Fox Books original series, we plan to continue developing this franchise with new titles and spin-offs. Each book will be strategically released to maintain momentum and interest within our target demographics, utilizing insights from our "Year of the Assignment" to optimize launch timings and marketing approaches.

5.2   Educational Board Games and Resources

Leveraging our understanding of the educational sector's needs, we will expand our line of board games and educational resources. These products will focus on delivering key educational outcomes through play, targeting a range of age groups from pre-K through 12th grade. Development will prioritize inclusivity, ensuring that learning materials are accessible and beneficial to diverse learning styles and needs.

5.3   Digital Content and E-Learning Platforms

In response to the growing demand for digital learning solutions, The Ridge Publishing Group will develop interactive e-learning platforms and digital content. This includes expanding our offerings with ebooks, audiobooks, and interactive educational apps that complement our physical products, enhancing the learning experience through technology.

5.4   Film and Multimedia Projects

Anticipating a film deal for the Ethan Fox Books franchise, we will explore the development of related multimedia content, including short films, animated series, and interactive websites. These projects will serve to broaden the franchise's appeal and provide fans with new ways to engage with the Ethan Fox universe.

5.5   New Imprints and Genre Exploration

To diversify our portfolio, The Ridge Publishing Group plans to launch new imprints that cater to niche markets and emerging genres. This includes delving deeper into theology education resources, reflective of our ambition to become the largest theology teaching resource globally. Additionally, we will explore opportunities in genres such as science fiction, fantasy, and non-fiction, identifying gaps in the market where we can introduce innovative and thought-provoking content.

5.6   Licensing and Merchandising

In line with expanding our brand presence, we will actively pursue licensing opportunities to develop merchandise that complements our books series and educational games. This includes apparel, collectibles, and educational kits that enhance the reading and learning experience, driving brand engagement and opening new revenue streams.

5.7   Sustainability and Accessibility

Our product development plans also emphasize sustainability and accessibility. We will explore eco-friendly production methods and materials for our physical products and ensure that our digital offerings are accessible to individuals with disabilities, making our content available to the widest possible audience.

5.8   Continuous Research and Feedback Integration

Understanding that successful product development is an ongoing process, The Ridge Publishing Group will invest in market research and consumer feedback mechanisms. This will enable us to stay ahead of industry trends, adapt to changing consumer preferences, and continuously improve our product offerings based on direct input from our audience.

In conclusion, The Ridge Publishing Group's product development plans are designed to foster growth, innovation, and engagement across our diverse range of offerings. By focusing on quality, relevance, and the integration of new technologies, we are poised to meet the evolving needs of our readers and learners, securing our position as a leader in the publishing and educational sectors.

6.0   SALES / SERVICE PLANS

The Ridge Publishing Group's sales and service strategy is designed to capitalize on our innovative publishing model, diverse product offerings, and the evolving needs of our target markets. Our approach combines direct sales, strategic distribution, and exceptional customer service to foster growth, reader engagement, and brand loyalty.

6.1   Direct Sales and E-commerce Strategy

- **Website Sales**: Our reboot publisher, author, and bridge websites, including Ethan Fox Books and KidsStagram, will serve as primary channels for direct sales – via Amazon.com payment and fulfillment – offering books, board games, and educational materials. Enhanced e-commerce functionality and user experience will facilitate easy navigation and purchasing.

- **Digital Platforms**: Ebooks and audiobooks will be distributed through major online retailers like Amazon, Barnes & Noble, and Apple Books, leveraging their global reach and the popularity of digital reading platforms.

6.2   Distribution and Retail Partnerships

- **Bookstores and Retailers**: We will continue to build and strengthen relationships with national and independent bookstores, as well as with major retail chains, to ensure wide availability of our physical products.

- **Educational Distribution**: For our educational games and materials, partnerships with schools, libraries, and educational institutions will be pursued to integrate our products into classrooms and learning centers.

Appendix

6.3 Subscription Services and Continuity Programs

- Launching subscription services for both books and board games, offering customers exclusive access to new releases, special editions, and members-only content.

- Developing continuity programs that encourage repeat purchases and build a loyal customer base through rewards, discounts, and early access to new products.

6.4 Service and Support

- **Customer Support**: Providing comprehensive customer support through various channels, including phone, email, and social media, ensuring queries and issues are resolved promptly.

- **Community Engagement**: Actively engaging with our readers and users through social media, forums, and events to gather feedback, answer questions, and foster a sense of community around our brands.

6.5 Marketing and Promotional Activities

- Implementing targeted marketing campaigns for new releases, utilizing digital advertising, social media, email newsletters, and press releases to generate buzz and drive sales.

- Organizing book launch events, author signings, and educational workshops to engage directly with our audience and promote our products.

6.6 Feedback and Product Development

- Establishing mechanisms to gather reader and user feedback on our products and services, enabling continuous improvement and innovation in our offerings.

- Involving our community in the product development process through surveys, beta testing of new board games, and crowdsourcing ideas for future book titles or series.

6.7 Licensing and Merchandising

- Exploring licensing deals to extend the reach of our franchises, particularly the Ethan Fox Books series, into merchandise, adaptations, and collaborations that can open additional revenue streams.

6.8 Philanthropic Initiatives

- Enhancing our brand's social impact through philanthropy, such as our work with children's hospitals and educational initiatives, aligning our sales strategies with our commitment to making a positive difference.

In essence, The Ridge Publishing Group's sales and service plans are structured to not only drive revenue and market share but also to deepen our engagement with readers and users, reinforcing our position as a leading innovator in the publishing and educational game industry.

7.0   FUNDING PROPOSAL

The Ridge Publishing Group will self-fund this venture.

8.0   OPERATIONAL OVERVIEW – See Executive Summary herein.

9.0   FINANCIAL PLAN

The Ridge Publishing Group, a general partnership, intends to incorporate in 2024 after it turns a substantial profit, and thereafter, pay the founders accordingly.

2. Strategic Growth Business Plan—hybrid: publishing, e-commerce, and fashion

LA Survival Gear and Prep Writer
2018-2022 Business Plan
Confidential and Proprietary

1.0   EXECUTIVE SUMMARY

LA Survival Gear and Prep Writer (LA SGPW) is founded by serial entrepreneur, Lori Ann, with credentials in business and law; developing and executing an End Times Preparedness Business over the next 60-months, featuring: an End Times Preparedness publishing platform and a fashion and luxury Survival Goods platform. "A designer because it's my first love, but a lot of my time now is dedicated to my life as a publisher and author." The publishing industry continues to be in turmoil with the arrival of the Internet allowing us to create a End Times Preparedness publishing platform with little to no in-house inventory burdens. The fashion industry puts a "premium on charisma over craft" which is LA SGPW's advantage; which allows us to produce high-end fashion functional Survival Gear garments as well as practical and efficient survival merchandise. Together these two LA SGPW worlds will collide creating a mega spin-off opportunity within both industries. All of which offer strong long-term earnings power.

The current total worldwide market for apparel, accessories, and lifestyle amenities is a trillion dollar industry, which represents billions in per annum revenue. For example, in 2009 Polo Ralph Lauren Corp. (NYSE: RL) reported $5.02 billion in annual sales and $4.795 billion in 2010. While Random House and Penguin merge to take on Amazon and Apple, the leaders in the print and eBook revolution, Random House reported revenues of $2.4 billion and operating profit of 161 million. Moreover, there is a current un-met home-grown need to more effectively create and keep jobs within the U.S., treating the underlying unemployment and national debt with a back to basics approach – take care of our own first, and support our global economies second.

LA SGPW has developed a new revolutionary Business Model platform that will single-handedly be ran by a sole business owner, Lori Ann, with its rapid to market cohesive Business Model. LA SGPW's technology will focus on innovations, green technologies, and ethical standards in both the fashion and publishing markets. In addition, LA SGPW will outsource its publishing platform eliminating inventory risks.

Appendix

Powerful Business Model

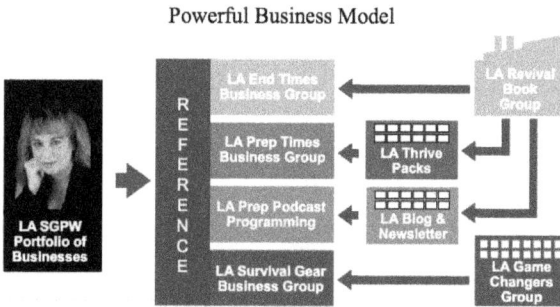

1.1 Objectives (MBOs)

- Multiple revenue streams delivering diversified revenue base.

- Scalable Business Model with significant operating leverage – rapid growth, leveraging core asset, predictable revenue streams, low variable cost, high profit margins, cash flow positive.

- Qualified business owner performing as: CEO, CBO, CMO, CSO, COO, CTO, CCGO, CFO, CIO, CHRO.

- Unprecedented in-house LA SGPW Business Model, which will separate into a mega Spin-Off business, LA Game Changers Group.

1.2 Keys to Success

- Q2' 2018 – Relocate -- LA Prep Writer Business Unit -- Walk-the-Talk documentary

- Q2' 2018 – Launch LA Prep Times business; write Book 3, Living Tactically book series.

- Q2' 2018 – Launch LA Thrive Packs business; write/publish 10-Pack 1 for LA Prep Times, Book 3 up sale.

- Q3' 2018 – Launch LA End Times business; write Books 1 and 2, Messages of the Bible Revealed book series.

- Q1' 2019 – Launch LA Survival Gear business; develop product line, rollout in Q1' 2021.

- Q3' 2019 – Publish LA Prep Times publishing business; Book 3, Living Tactically book series.

- Q3' 2019 – Launch LA Prep Times business; write Books 4 and 5, Living Tactically book series.

- Q3' 2019 – Launch LA Thrive Packs business; write/publish 10-Packs 2 and 3 for Books 4 and 5.

- Q4' 2019 – Publish LA End Times business; Books 1 and 2, Messages of the Bible Revealed book series.

- Q1' 2020 – Develop LA Survival Gear Concept product lines: prototypes, finished goods, etc.

- Q2' 2020 – Launch LA Prep Blog business; write/publish blogs/newsletters seeding LA Prep Podcast business.

- Q3' 2020 – Launch LA Prep Times publishing business, Books 6 and 7, Living Strategically book series.

- Q3' 2020 – Launch LA Thrive Packs business, write/publish 10-Packs 4 through 11 for Books 6 and 7.

- Q4' 2020 – Publish LA Prep Times business; Books 4 and 5, Living Tactically book series.

- Q1' 2021 – Rollout LA Survival Gear business; manufactured product lines; VestPack and DogPack series.

- Q2' 2021 – Launch LA Prep Podcast Programming business; screen-write Podcast episodes.

- Q3' 2021 – Directed-Startup; LA SGPW Holding Group -- Wholesale Distribution and Licensing Agreements.

- Q4' 2021 – Publish LA Prep Times business; Books 6 and 7; Living Strategically book series.

- Q2' 2022 – Acquire Aauvicom Assets 28 Book Titles; Asset Purchase Agreement.

- Q3' 2022 – Rollout LA Revival Book Group; revise/re-publish 28 book titles.

- Q4' 2022 – Exit Plan – Sell off Directed-Startup; LA SGPW Holding Group.

- Q4' 2022 – LA Prep Podcast Programming; ends with The Money Game season; which launches spin-off, LA Game Changers Group business -- *see LA Game Changers Group Business Plan.*

1.3   What We Are About – *something different*

- **Our vision** – Our business offers compelling reasons, solutions and products for every aspect of Prep Times -- the times we live in today -- and End Times -- the time we will soon be living in -- preparedness, all at incredible prices, which provides us with a unique point of differentiation. We produce all-encompassing solutions for planning, designing and prepping for Prep Times and End Times with our books, newsletters, podcasts, and survival gear at affordable prices.

- **Our mission** – The LA SGPW mission is to redefine are way of living, provide quality products, create worlds and invite people to take part in accountability and responsibility. (The importance of the LA SGPW Mission Statement should not be underestimated. The LA SGPW Mission Statement describes the values, services and the business' Mission for the future.).

- **Our key strategies** are, herein, throughout our Business Plan.

- **Our tactics** that are associated with each of these strategies are in our Timetable document.

Appendix

Thus, our working document just says, here's how we are executing against our 2018-2022 Business Plan. "My name is Lori Ann, and I see the fashion and publishing worlds differently. If we are not upsetting someone in business, we are doing something wrong."

1.4   Management Team

The company's current management and execution team is composed of several key proven and successful business entrepreneurs/executives. Each CV below provides an overview of a person's experience and other qualifications.

LORI MOESZINGER, J.D. – FOUNDER, DIRECTOR, CHIEF EXECUTIVE OFFICER

Lori Moeszinger has more than 25 years of executive management experience driving high-tech and start-up companies to commercial success. Ms. Moeszinger is a seasoned entrepreneur with years of fashion, finance and law experience and is currently serving, as the chief designer and publisher of LA SGPW. Formerly, Ms. Moeszinger has held reoccurring management roles, including a six-year tenure at 3Com Corporation and was instrumental in three initial public offerings from 1994 to 2004 and numerous financing ventures. An accomplished author and publisher, Ms. Moeszinger served as president and chief executive officer of Step-by-Step Publications from 1993 to 1997 before being copied by the publishing industry with the *For Dummies*, *Idiots Guides*, and the like book series. Ms. Moeszinger holds a Bachelor's of Science degree in Business with a minor in Accounting and a Doctor of Jurisprudence degree from Lincoln Law School of California.

JOSEPH JONES – CO-FOUNDER

Joe began consulting with Aauvi Group, Inc.'s board of directors in March 2008, Aauvicom Group in 2014 and LA GCG in 2023. As the founder of the Apply Networks Corporation, Joe is the guiding force behind the company's vision to bring innovative and affordable applications to the K-12 educational arena. With a background in application development and a track record of building successful new business ventures, Joe brings to ANC a unique blend of technological and business expertise. Prior to founding ANC, Joe brings over 20 years of experience in all corridors of the Internet and technology sectors. Joe has held positions as CTO and director of application development at Expression Networks, Technology director at New York Times Regional Newspaper Group, and was part of the new product development team at Adobe Systems, Inc.

MARK SMITH, CPA – TARGETING CHIEF FINANCIAL OFFICER

Mark began consulting with the business in March 2019. Mr. Smith currently serves as a certified public accountant for the M. A. Smith full service accounting firm. Mr. Smith specializes in providing resources and expertise clients need to better manage their day-to-day accounting and business operations. Mark's approach is to build partnerships with clients so more time can be focused on clients growing their businesses. Accounting services include: accounting systems, payroll, bookkeeping, and accounting and tax software packages. Tax services include: tax returns, sales tax returns, AMT taxes, audits, representation, and entity filings. Previously, Mark held management roles during his tenure at Ernst & Young.

From Idea to Empire

2.0   Business Overviews

The U.S. market opportunity for LA SGPW is as follows:

2.1   Fashion Industry Market Analysis

The opportunity to build a company really starts with the attractiveness of the market opportunity. Small markets in the fashion industry seldom deliver the opportunity to build big companies. Investors prefer companies that can deliver revenues of $50M to $100M within a 4 to 5 year period. The LA SGPW expectations are to deliver such results. This is only realizable in a large growing market; the fashion and luxury goods industry continues to be a growing trillion-dollar market; fashion and luxury survival goods introduces a whole new market to the industry.

For example, in June 2011, luxury brand Missoni partnered a deal with Target, the trendy discounter; introduced an affordable, limited-edition collection for fashion and home ranging in price from $2.99 to $500.99, with most items less than $40, available Sept. 13 through Oct. 22, 2011 at all Target stores and Target.com – it was an epic success. The retailer has worked with Isaac Mizrahi (before amicably leaving to head the Liz Claiborne line in 2008), Alexander McQueen, Zac Posen, Rodarte, and Proenza Schueller to name a few. Next on the agenda, Neiman Marcus, the luxury chain, and Target, got together for Christmas 2012 in an unprecedented partnership whereby they jointly corralled 24 CFDA designers to create items for a limited-edition holiday collection at all 1,763 Target stores and the 42 Neiman Marcus stores, as well as online – the deal was a flop.

2.1.1   What was the difference about the Missoni for Target launch?

The Missoni for Target launch was an epic success – if you define success by cleaned-out retail shelves and a web site crash. (For the record, at 6 p.m. on Tuesday (the next day), the site was still down.).Target has partnered with designers in the past with varying levels of success, but nothing quite like this.

For starters, the sheer volume and range of Missoni for Target was something to behold: The 400-piece collection included clothing (for men, women, children, and infants), home design, office supplies, shoes, accessories, furniture, and even bikes – one could potentially Missonify their entire world in a single shopping trip. And who wouldn't want to do that? The Lookbook – which was previewed months before the launch – featured every single item in the collection, allowing future Missoni for Target owners to visualize exactly what they will buy and where it will look/go. Essentially, the Lookbook was the equivalent of a catalog (89 pages), with items temporarily out of stock.

The designs were more Missoni than they were Target, showcasing the Italian designer's signature zigzag lines. While the promotional materials did – of course – feature the trademark Target bull's-eye, the color scheme was black and white, not red and white, which signaled a more serious engagement with high style. Case in point, Manhattanites are not usually among Target's audience – there are only two stores in New York City, one in Brooklyn and the other in central Harlem – but the Harlem store was one of the first to sell out. (Even former Real Housewives of New York star and current Skinny girl empress Bethany Frankel was among the shoppers.)

Missoni for Target took full advantage of the myriad bloggers eager to compete for audiences with tidbits of the launch. The campaign was one of dangled carrots and rolling embargoes: Racked.com blogged about the press preview in May, which gave editors and reporters all the secrets of the collection as long as they promised not to tell.

Appendix

The ad campaign – which, naturally, was the subject of a few 'leaked' images – featured Margherita Missoni herself, looked like a series of production stills from a 1960's Avant garde film, and ran in Vogue in August.

Then, there was Marina, literally the biggest blogger in the world: Marina is a 25-foot doll who physically attended fashion week events along with blogging as Missoni for Target's hired brand ambassador. Her blog, titled *All the Way Up Here*, takes perhaps just a page from the book of pint-sized uber-fashionista Tavi Gevinson – with its Instamatic-esque photography and ethereal musings, it aims squarely for a downtown crowd.

It was an awful lot of work, this Missoni for Target launch. But the five-pronged-and-then-some strategy seemed to have worked exactly as planned. And of course, Target in no way anticipated the collection would be sold out shortly after the launch. Not to mention, the eBay resellers turning a profit as well.

3.0 HISTORY AND CURRENT BUSINESS

3.1 Corporate Profile

LA SGPW is part Prep Times and End Times publishing house as well as a joint venture Survival Gear fashion house located in Northern Idaho. The LA PW Publishing Group® business focuses on publishing solution driven books for the times we are living in and the times we will be living in. The LA SG Fashion House® production and manufacturing business produces practical and functional goods (read-to-wear, accessories, bags, pet accessories and others). It is known for its knitwear designs, made from a variety of yarns in colorful patterns. The company was founded by Lori Moeszinger in early 2018 and is currently a sole-proprietorship. Aside from The LA SG product lines, the company has diversified. The LA PW Publishing Group® was initially launched early 2018. It is a content, commerce and technology company that provides consumers access to books, pamphlets, newsletters and other content across its multi-channel distribution platform; comprising several imprints, including production and manufacturing businesses.

3.2 Story Behind the Name

"Many people ask me what drove me to move to North Idaho. The short answer, it was God. Born and raised and living in the Bay Area/Silicon Valley in California -- or the cement jungle as my husband calls it -- I lived like most people: By the time I was 44 years old, I had *three boys* and was on my *third marriage*. I was educated; I had *three degrees*: an associate, bachelors, and Juris Doctor in law. I retired at age 47 to care for my husband's *three parents* before each passed away. We owned our own home, had a couple of cars and were living the American Dream. Yet, something was missing. I was becoming more and more restless, impatient and unhappy. Then one day, out of despair, I found myself throwing up my arms and pleading with God to give me a direction. (Although I have always believed in God I hadn't reached out in a very long time.) And on that day, I kind of stopped everything. (The kids were grown and out of the house; it was just the *three of us*: my husband, our dog and me.) And I just sat still. Something I had not done before. And then, before I knew my journey herein began." – Lori Ann

3.3 Company History

2018 – 2022 annual CEO letters will be available upon request wrapping up each calendar year.

4.0 **MARKETING PLANS**

4.1   LA Prep Writer Publishing Group

The LA PW Publishing Group House will be known as the Go-To medium when addressing peoples anxiety about the current times we are living in today and where we are headed.

4.1.1   Blueprint: Target for LA PW Publishing Group Business Model – 46 Books / Blogs and Podcasts

- End Times Division -- Messages of the Bible Revealed Book Series: 2 Books

- Prep Times Division -- Living Tactically Book Series and Living Strategically Book Series: 5 Books

- 10 Packs for Thriving Division -- Lifestyle Planners: 11 Publications

- LA Revival Book Group Business Unit -- Strategic 2022 Target: 28 Books

- LA Prep Blog Business Unit -- La Newsletter Division

- LA Prep Podcast Business Unit -- Walk-the-Talk Programming

4.2   LA Survival Gear Fashion House

The LA SG Fashion House will be known as a leader in design, marketing and distribution of premium survival gear lifestyle products in four categories: apparel, home, accessories and fragrances. Known as *The MOD Squad*, it is a fashion house that features three young, hip crime fighters: One White, One Black, One Blonde, is our promotional hype-line. The casting is intended to appeal to a youthful, counterculture audience. The visions for each of my collections are going to feel very modern, very cool, completely effortless, and entirely glamorous. The House's primary premise has a lot of Bridgett Bardot in the collections. I'm really doing a little more Tomboy girl meets bad boy. More than anything, it's less girly and feminine and frilly and it's more like, kind of cool and effortless. I think it goes from chic to vacation. The House in and of itself portrays a multicultural society -- much like we have today -- that deals with issues of racial politics, drug culture, and counterculture – hard and soft.

4.2.1   Blueprint: Target for Missoni Business Model – 400 Items / 89 Look Book Pages

Target had been working for Italian luxury knitwear designer, Missoni, for a year to create and launch a line of 400 items unique for the national retailer. Missoni is known for colorful zigzag stripes on items, including knit dresses, tights, sweaters, rain boots, luggage, dinnerware, iPad and iPod covers and even furniture. LA SGPW will execute a similar business model but going beyond: similar to the St. John's Knitwear Look product line business model producing and manufacturing 49 Items / 7 Look Book Pages.

Appendix

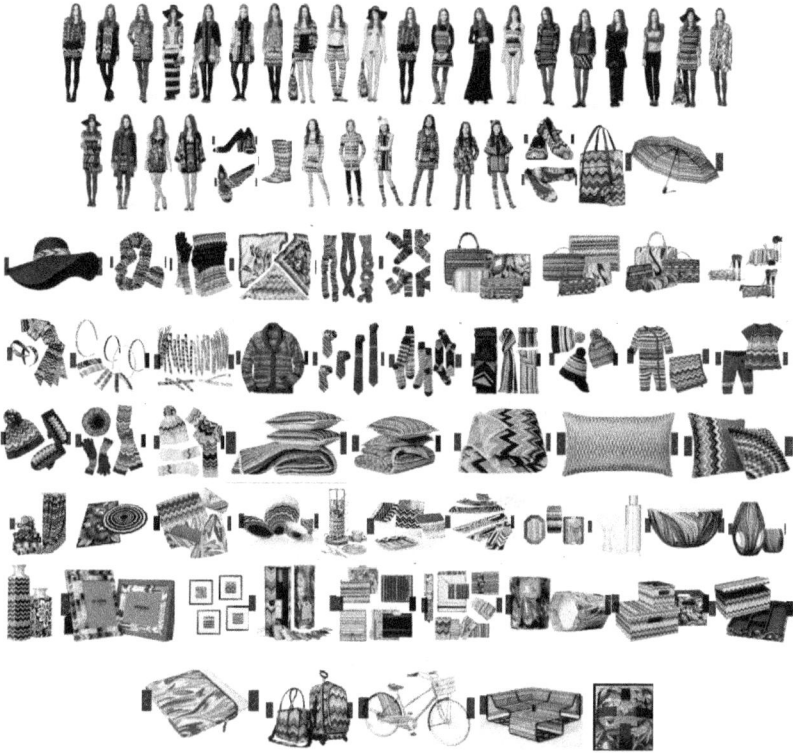

4.2.2 What did Target for Missoni do right?

- **Advertising and promotion helped create demand**. Several weeks in advance of the release of Missoni for Target, Target Inc. launched an onslaught of well-produced TV ads and integrated media promotions. Social media network buzz, increased chatter, and demand was instantaneously created; most of this media is measurable. LA SGPW will doing the same using Blog and Podcast mediums.

- **A sense of urgency drove immediate interest and response**. The products included in Missoni for Target were limited; 400 items to be exact, as were the dates/locations they would be made available – September 13 through October 22 at 1,762 Target stores in the U.S. and online. LA SGPW will doing the same; 49 items to be exact -- January 13, 2021 at social media platforms, blogs and podcast mediums.

- **Sales and distribution alternatives flourished**. Following the site crash, Missoni for Target on eBay saw traction at higher prices, better margins and meeting a further segmented audience's consumer demand. LA SGPW will explore the value of its own eBay store.

- **PR efforts and social media chatter thrusted the campaign into the mass media stratosphere**. The Target site went down at 6AM and it was reported as a headline news story on the Today Show at 7. Coincidence? Hmmmnn. Target also used Facebook posts to keep consumers up to date. LA SGPW will launch its own website and social media stages.

4.2.3 Target for Missoni Ad Campaign Formula

1. **Start a whispering campaign.** PR people and IT people, even remotely associated with the brand, had been telling their audience for months, "Target's about to release a really big designer collaboration. We can't tell you who it is, but it's REALLY big." LA SGPW will repeat this campaign model.

2. **Set up a social media explosion.** When you finally did learn what the big deal was, it wasn't via a press release to your inbox but through Twitter. Target placed a blurb with Vogue, then publicly announced the collaboration on May 4th via Twitter, with a link to Vogue.com: "Target Style – Three words: Missoni for Target. Yes, yes. You did read it right – this September. http://..." It was the perfect pairing of credible, high-end, old-school publication (Vogue) and social media hype juggernauts (Twitter/Facebook). LA SGPW will repeat this social media explosion model.

Missoni Facebook Page

3. **Hold back the photos until it's time.** On a Wednesday, you were allowed to preview the collection in an office building in Manhattan BUT before you could even enter the space, you had to sign a release promising not to take photos or publish any images online... until Target says it's OK. All the other editors – everyone from Conde Nast employees to bloggers – did the same. Of course, this caused everyone to tweet the preview like crazy and maniacally check their in-boxes to see when photos would be available. And when they were, most posted them like everyone else in a heartbeat. (And yes, I did think the collection was pretty cool – there are chevron ottomans, towels, bedding, vases, rugs, shower curtains...there's even a chevron bike!) In short, the landscape has changed since the availability of the Internet. Via networks like Facebook and Twitter, the connection between brand, publication, and consumer feels closer than ever, and (when it's handled capably) the hype seems to effortlessly spin itself. LA SGPW will repeat this preview model.

4. **Spoilers.** The First Missoni for Target Ad Starring Margherita Missoni. Missoni's highly-anticipated gigantic collection for Target will encompass everything from men's and women's clothes to accessories to furniture to candles to bicycles. It's basically a whole lifestyle brand in one collection. So, it's exciting to see how they would translate this into an ad campaign. Some behind-the-scenes shots emerged in May, so we were able to get a glimpse of the Mod '60s-inspired vibe of the campaign and now thanks to Fashionologie we have part of the finished product. We're still dying to see the commercial, but for now here's a glimpse into the

colorful, zig zag-y world of Missoni for Target, starring Margherita herself.

Image of the Day

Target Peterson Milla Hooks fueled the fire for the retailer's Missoni collection By Emma Bazilian. When Target announced that its next big designer collaboration would be with the Italian fashion house Missoni, fashionistas everywhere were thrilled at the prospect of scoring one of the designer's iconic zigzag knits – which usually retail for thousands of dollars – for around $40 a piece. But few could have foreseen the mayhem that would ensue when Target finally released the line last Wednesday: Missoni-crazed customers not only flooded the retailer's stores, but they actually managed to crash its website for most of the day. LA SGPW will create our own Spoiler model much like Missoni did.

Ad of the Day

5. **Sneak peek at the upcoming collection.** The Missoni Collection for Target – The Italian fashion house's signature stripes, zigzags, and vibrant colors are just about to take over one of America's favorite shopping destinations. Here's a sneak peek at the upcoming collection. View slideshow:

Above: Behind-the-scenes footage from the Missoni for Target advertising shoot, featuring Margherita Missoni. Photography by Alex Prager.

Beginning September 13, the wild, psychedelic prints that have made the fashion house Missoni a high-style staple since the 1950s will debut in Target stores across America. With prices ranging from $3 to $600, the collection includes interpretations of Missoni's signature knitwear as well as colorful swirled vases, a graphic umbrella, and even a zigzag-pattern bicycle. "We've had great success with collaborations. We believe they're important in keeping our brand fresh and allow us to reach different audiences," says Margherita Missoni, muse to her mother, creative director Angela Missoni, and the face for the Target-Missoni campaign. "Working with Target, we were able to create a collection that reflects our rich heritage of print, pattern, and color combinations at really affordable prices." Cheap thrills indeed. LA SGPW will create our own Sneak Peak model in advance of January 13, 2020 launch.

6. **Missoni for Target Commercial**. In honor of that rather impressive feat, let's take a look back at one Missoni for Target commercial that got those women salivating weeks ago. For its final campaign for Target, Minneapolis-based agency Peterson Milla Hooks decided to go back to Missoni's roots. The 30-second spot, shot in Milan, Italy, follows the fashion house's heiress and occasionally spokes model Margherita Maccapani Missoni on a very stylish, '60s-inspired spy caper – a throwback to the era when the Missoni label first shot to fame. To the tune of a kitschy 007 soundtrack, Margherita and a pretty blonde associate attempt to pass along a top-secret note while on a sly (and stylish) romp around the city. The brand's signature prints pop up on nearly every surface – from plates to children's clothing and even a bike-showing how the 400-piece collection isn't just fun, but functional, too.

The spy story might be silly, but who cares about secret agents when there's 400 pieces of Missoni to be ogled? The brand's lively prints and bright colors are a perfect fit for PMH's cutesy-chic Target campaigns, and the spot manages to sell a deeply discounted version of the Missoni lifestyle while still looking like a millionbucks. While it might not make you want to go out and cover yourself in head-to-toe zigzags, it's not hard to see what made those site-crashing customers so eager to grab a piece of the fun. LA SGPW will produce our own Commercial model and repeat the Missoni business model.

Fall/Winter 2011 Campaign
Missoni for Target

Campaign Credits, **Models**, Margherita Missoni

Appendix

4.2.4 Pop-Up Stores

LA SGPW will negotiate with vacant venues for 'House of LA Survival Gear Mall' pop-up stores. For example, using the same Midtown space that played host to its Liberty of London pop-up last year, Target upped the ante for its latest designer collection – a collaboration with Italian fashion house Missoni – and built a bigger, bolder experiential effort. The vacant venue, which sits opposite Bryant Park on Sixth Avenue and 42nd Street, was not only transformed into a temporary store bedecked with bull's-eye logos and Missoni's signature pattern, but is also home to "Little Marina," a 25-foot-tall doll that was part of a social media campaign for the launch.

With 400 pieces – apparel and accessories for women, men, girls and baby, as well as home furnishings – the Missoni for Target line is the retailer's largest designer collection to date. To properly showcase this, Target leased the site's second floor, increasing the size of the space by nearly a third, from 5,000 to 8,000 square feet. Event producer David Stark was brought in to build out the space and sought to do so in a manner that wasn't visually excessive.

Photo: Neil Rasmus/BFAnyc.com

"The collection is so strong that it's not hard to bring it to life in a way that is exciting," said Stark, who also created the Liberty of London pop-up and has been working with Target for nearly a decade. "The challenge is that because there are so many patterns, it is quite a sophisticated line you have to walk to make them look incredible. It's easy to have a lot of overload – you have to figure out the fine balance of placement and juxtaposition so that everything has the air to be seen and breathe."

Allowing the collection to flex its muscles, Stark created a setup comparable to a house, or, "Missoni Mall," as some likened it, with the first floor dedicated to smaller goods and decorative objects and the second floor, accessed by stairs, housing bed and bath vignettes.Planning for the project took about eight months, with Target's design and marketing teams traveling to Italy several times to work with the Missoni family, who in turn made visits to the retailer's Minneapolis headquarters. Actual setup took three weeks working with a crew of about 45. Stark estimates the teardown time to be about a week.

Scattered downpours did little to dampen the moods of hundreds of fashion V.I.P.s who turned out for the preview shopping party on Wednesday. To maximize the selling space, celebrity guests – including Joy Bryant, Michelle Trachtenberg, Camilla Belle, Emma Roberts, and Selita Ebanks – entered a covered step-and-repeat erected just outside the pop-up. Such attendees were escorted inside via a separate entrance to see the giant doll. Little Marina, which was created by a Los Angeles-based special effects company is operated by four puppeteers, comes dressed head-to-toe in Missoni for Target and holds an oversize replica of an iPhone. Given its size, the big marionette served as the centerpiece of the space.

"It's always about the buzz and visibility and creating excitement around the launch," Stark said. For the rest of the interior, Stark used the iconic Missoni patterns as a tool to cohesively revamp the raw venue. For example, black-and-white-patterned walls enclose and mask the structural columns. "It's designed in a way that it's supposed to be here," said Stark. "The design is one part married to the architecture of the space and one part bringing the campaign to life." With hundreds of products and multiple bold prints to balance, Stark said the concept of the pop-up actually worked in his favor when it came to mapping out the store design. "You know exactly what you're getting, so you can create displays and a floor plan that's specific to the product," he said. "We really start with the grid and then design very specific fixtures and displays with the product exactly in mind." This included painting the ceiling black to allow for vivid colors of the collection and the oversize ad campaign images – which channel a 1960s Italian film aesthetic – to truly pop.

Ahead of the Missoni for Target's official national launch on September 13, the pop-up show debuted to the public on Fashion's Night Out and was slated to stay open through Saturday, but on Thursday the entire inventory was depleted within an hour, forcing it to close.

4.2.5 Official-Site for Missoni Ad Campaign

For Fall '09, Missoni enlisted the help of Ryan McGinley – the same photog who shot Stella's playful ad – to create an amazing, windblown masterpiece. The campaign features Hanne Gaby Odiele and her luxurious locks, in Missoni's signature knits. Peep the eye-catching, colorful juxtaposition between the soft knits and back truck. Don't her striped blue cardigan and oatmeal leggings look cozy enough to sleep in? LA SGPW will repeat a similar Ad Campaign.

MISSONI

Appendix

5.0 PRODUCT DEVELOPMENT PLANS

Author and Publisher businesses are composed of three processes:

- Design Process: Cover design, a picture says 1,000 words: the cover should clearly speak the content of the book; front and back matter development; storyboarding or drafting the table of contents, draft or write introductory chapters; draft or write manuscript of body of book; draft or write indexes; draft or write appendices; read finished manuscript for completeness; edit or redline manuscript; and rework manuscript.

- Production Process: Production or manufacturing of print and eBooks will be outsourced to Amazon and Smashwords. Production or manufacturing of pamphlets will be done in-house by LA SGPW, includes barcoding, printing, cutting, and binding.

- Marketing Process: The marketing process includes identifying, producing, and promoting books and pamphlets that relate to the company's objectives. Successful marketing requires a thorough knowledge of the business, its image, goals, and capabilities; a description of its target customer by gender, age, income, interests, and lifestyles; and a definition of its market, according to book type and use, price range, size range and figure type, quality, value, and information.

Apparel manufacturing is composed of three processes:

- Design Process: Product development, or the creation of new styles involves a variety of specific operations, developing design ideas—sizes, number of pieces, style, season, wardrobe plan, etc.—each season and/or collection should have a theme, selecting patterns, fabrics, findings, and trimmings that are available and appropriately priced—preshrink after purchase and label, making the first pattern, making fitting adjustments on patterns, lay out pattern, cutting, marking, making a sample garment or prototype, evaluation and refining the fit and design, computing the cost, making a production pattern, making duplicates, and grading the production pattern.

- Production Process: Production, or manufacturing, includes the cutting, sewing, pressing, fitting, accessorizing, signatures, sewing label and packaging of finished garments.

- Marketing Process: The marketing process includes identifying, producing, and promoting products that relate to the company's objectives. Successful marketing requires a thorough knowledge of the business, its image, goals, and capabilities; a description of its target customer by gender, age, income, interests, and lifestyles; and a definition of its market, according to garment type and use, price range, size range and figure type, quality, value, and fashion.

6.0 SALES / SERVICE PLANS

The LA SGPW opportunity includes direct retail sales/services, indirect retail sales, and wholesale sales. Direct sales and services will be offered through our LA SGPW/Exchange – LA SGPW boutique online shopping, pop-up stores, catalog sales, and outsourcing services through LA SGPW House. Indirect sales opportunities include store-in-store pop-ups. Wholesale sales distribution agreements and licensing agreements will be offered through the LA SGPW Holding Group showrooms and studios. LA SGPW will continue to use the Target for Missoni business model to get the word out.

6.1.1   Product Adoption -- LA Prep Writer Business Unit Revenues

- End Times Division -- 2 Books

- Prep Times Division -- 5 Books

6.2.1   Product Adoption -- LA ThrivePacks™ Business Unit Revenues

- 10-Packs for Thriving Division -- 11 Pamphlets

6.3.1   Product Adoption -- LA Prep Blog Business Unit Revenues

- LA Newsletter Division -- Newsletter Subscriptions

6.4.1   Product Adoption -- LA Prep Podcast Business Unit Revenues

- Walk-the-Talk Programming Division -- 7 DVDs: 7 six month Seasons over 3-1/2 years:

- Season 1 -- 26 weekly Episodes -- Living Your Life by Design: markets Books 1, 2 and 3

- Season 2 -- 26 weekly Episodes -- How I Lost 60 Pounds: markets Book 4

- Season 3 -- 26 weekly Episodes -- A Body in Motion! markets Book 4

- Season 4 -- 26 weekly Episodes -- Small Space Gardens: markets Book 5

- Season 5 -- 26 weekly Episodes -- Home-Scale Permaculture: markets Book 5

- Season 6 -- 26 weekly Episodes -- Time: Turn Back Time & Master Time: markets Books 6 and 7

- Season 7 -- 26 weekly Episodes -- The Money Game: markets Books 6 and 7

6.5.1   Product Adoption -- LA Revival Book Group Business Unit Revenues

- Aauvicom Group asset purchase acquisition -- 28 book titles: revise each title and re-publish as new on Amazon and Smashwords

6.6.1   Product Adoption -- LA SGPW Holding Group Business Unit Revenues

- Exit Strategy -- Enter into Distributor Wholesale Agreements and Licensing Agreements for all product lines. This will close the *LA SGPW 5-year 2018-2022 Business Plan* venture. The LA SGPW venture completes a complex seeding program for a subsequent business endeavor, namely, *LA Game Changers Group -- see 3-year 2023-2025 Business Plan.*

6.7.1   Product Adoption -- LA Survival Gear Business Unit Revenues

- PrepPack™ Survival Gear Division -- This division would not make sense unless every Product Adoption Business Unit mentioned previously herein is already in play, i.e., selling. The LA Survival Gear business is an up-selling business model for the LA SGPW Product Adoption Business Units.

Appendix

6.7.2 Pricing Structure

Our pricing structure assumes an average fixed unit price per unit sale for the entire collection line. For example, in the 2019 VestPacks collection there are 7 pieces. Depending on the fabric, attention to detail, and difficulty these prices will differ per unit sale. But on average the price is fixed at $250 per piece.

6.7.3 Size Conversion Chart

Our sales forecast reflects unit sales in 5-sizes: S, M, L, XL, and XXL.

6.7.4 Sales Forecast

Our sales forecast assumes 20% costs and 80% mark up in price, which is a reasonable assumption; the higher our costs per item the more expensive the piece. Costs include labor and materials. We are expecting to increase sales from $1,225,000 in 2021 to more than double this amount year-over-year. (Assumptions in 2021 production assumes selling one each of the 49 piece collection -- produced solely in-house -- at $250 per piece = $12,250 gross sales ($9,800 net sales); however, conservatively speaking, selling 100 each of the 49 piece collection in 2021 would garner $1,225,000 gross sales in our first year or $980,000 net sales.) Assumptions in 2021 and beyond, assume doubling sales year-over-year.

Our business model is repeatable: each year we will produce a *new* 49-piece collection: 7 VestPacks, 7 ScarfPacks, 7 HatPacks, 7 BootTopPacks, 7 DogPacks, 7 Fashion DogPacks, and 7 Dog BedPacks = 49 units. The collections never increase in size. And each year's collection will no longer be available after a new collection is released.

Assumptions in 2021 may be further broken down as follows:

- Q1'2021 – 49 piece collection, producing 100 units of each = 4,900 units (4,900 units at $250 per piece = $1,225,000 gross sales or $980,000 net sales). 4,900 units per year = producing 13.42 units per day.

- Q1'2022 – 49 piece collection, producing 200 units of each = 4,900 units (9,800 units at $250 per piece = $2,450,000 gross sales or $1,960,000 net sales). 4,900 units per year = producing 26.84 units per day.

The growth forecast is in line with the inventory available and expected number of clients' year-after-year, and is relatively low for our industry because we are developing our products in-house. In 2022 we expect growth closer to $3,000,000 with the addition of hiring contractors and opening high-end designer boutiques throughout the United States, to a projected total of $5,000,000 in 2023. Still, we expect to blow through all of these numbers way before these conservative piece-rates and timeframes.

6.7.5 Commercial Websites

Selling through website traffic gives us the opportunity to reach customers at just about any point on the globe. But trading outside of the U.S. entails special issues we won't face with domestic customers: the type of currency we'll use, how we'll ship, and most important, how we can avoid fraud. While anyone around the world can view our website we don't have to agree to sell to overseas customers. We may want to limit sales to domestic customers to avoid headaches in the short-term. Canada is a foreign country for purposes of our selling activities.

The LA SGPW website will be initially developed with few technical resources. A simple hosting provider, Yahoo! Web services, will host the site and provide the technical back end.

The LA SGPW will work with a contracted user interface designer to develop complexity to the website, e.g., music, slideshow capabilities, and more. The user interface designer will work with our Chief Technology Officer and a graphic artist to come up with the website logo, and the website graphics.

Our Chief Technology Officer will do the maintenance of the site. As the website rolls out future development such as newsletters and downloadable articles, a technical resource may need to be contracted to build the trackable download and the newsletter capabilities. LA SGPW can also look into pre-packaged solutions through Yahoo! Web hosting.

6.7.6 Sales Strategy – eBay

eBay is the premier online auction site for buying and selling goods throughout the world. Some sellers are corporations, but the vast majority are individuals. At the start of 2004, there were already 95 million buyers and sellers worldwide on eBay. The total dollar value of goods sold in 2003 was $20 billion. No wonder eBay is one of the most successful stocks traded on Nasdaq.

eBay may have started off as on online garage sale where people were able to sell junk from their attic and basements, but today things are different. Collectibles account for only a small percentage of eBay sales. The vast number of items offered today on eBay are new items, including clothing, DVDs and CDs, and electronics. eBay is a marketplace like no other. According to a 2004 survey by TRUSTe, eBay ranked as the most trusted company among customers—above American Express, Proctor & Gamble, Amazon.com, the U.S. Postal Service, and IBM.

6.7.6.1 Online Auctions

There are ten basic steps to posting items for sale through the online auction process:

1. Decide on the type of auction – (1) a regular auction with a reserve (such as your cost for the item). Also set the auction period, the number of days you want the auction to run. However, using the auction process you don't know at the start what your final selling will be. For example, regular eBay auctions run from 1 day to 10 days. You will need to take care to time your auctions so that they end at a time of day when buyers are online. (2) If you are selling multiple items that are exactly the same, you can use a Dutch auction to sell all of them at once. (3) Or, if you can't stand the uncertainty of the auction process, you can use Buy It Now auctions to sell your items at a fixed price, just like in a store.

2. Research the Item.

3. Photograph the Item.

4. Describe the Item.

5. Pack and Weigh the Item.

6. Listing Products – (1) Select a category, (2) Title and description, (3) pictures and details, (4) payment and shipping, and (5) review and submit. The Seller Form is what you complete to post an item for an auction.

7. After the Sale – contact the buyer.

8. Getting Paid.

9. Leave Feedback.

10. Ship the Item.

eBay does charge sellers to use the amazing website, which is a platform on which to sell goods to the worldwide marketplace. There is a sliding-scale commission that eBay charges only when you sell your item (there's no added fee for shipping). There are three types of eBay fees: (1) Insertion fees – $500 and up would be a fee of $4.80. (2) Additional fees – additional images, super-size an image, etc. (3) Final value fees = $25 to $1,000 = 5.25% of the first $25 ($1.31) plus 2.75% of the remaining closing value; over $1,000 = 5.25% of the first $25 ($1.31) plus 2.75% of the next $25 to $1,000 ($26.81), plus 1.5% of the remaining closing value balance.

6.7.6.2 Online Storefront

Selling on eBay isn't limited to auctions—you can open an online storefront to sell items at fixed prices. eBay stores aren't bricks-and-mortar locations for your business. They're online storefronts at which you can sell items at a fixed price—without listing them for auction. Your eBay store becomes part of the vast eBay mall. eBay stores were started in 2001 as a way to augment auction sales for customers who prefer fixed pricing.

Having an eBay store is a way to bring your business to the next level. It not only opens up another way in which to make money on eBay, but it also creates an image for your business, giving you credibility that can enhance both store and auction sales. An eBay store is made up of customized pages that you create using HTML or eBay provided templates to list the items you have for sale. Obviously, you need to have a number of items to stock your store shelves, or it doesn't pay to start your store. You do not need a professional to set up a store—just follow the eBay instructions. However, if you have the money and want to polish your look, consider working with a company that can upgrade your store's appearance.

6.7.6.3 Stores Versus Auction Format

Having an eBay store isn't mutually exclusive with running auctions. You can and probably should run auctions and also maintain storefronts (through either eBay or your own website) if your selling activities are a high enough level. Each complements the other. Your store drives people to your auctions, and your auctions drive people to your store.

Having a store and conducting auctions that each refer to the other is called cross-promotion—one thing drives another. There is a cross-promotional tool that you can use to simplify your cross-promotions.

As an eBay storeowner, you receive free monthly sales reports.

Before you fully commit to running an eBay store, you can test the waters by taking advantage of the eBay 30-day free-trial period for your store.

6.7.6.4 Opening Your Stores

eBay provides all the instructions you need to proceed. Eligibility requirements for becoming a storeowner are negligble: You only need to have at least 20 feedbacks or to be ID verified (provide your credit card information). Once you decide to open an eBay store, decide on the store level you want. You have three options: (1) Regular storefront – This is a basic storefront with the lowest monthly rent in the form of a monthly subscription fee. (2) Featured store – This is the next step up, to double the size and increase exposure on eBay pages, for five times the cost of the regular storefront. (3) Anchor store – This is the deluxe storefront, with triple the regular size but added customer support and more, for 50 times the cost of the regular store.

6.7.6.5 Store Fees

Several different costs are associated with maintaining an eBay store.

1. Subscription Fee –The main charge is your subscription fee, which you pay each month. Think of this as your monthly rental cost for store space. The higher the rent is, the more space (pages) you get (the first 30 days of any level you select are free): (1) Basic – You get five pages for your listings. Cost: $9.95 per month. (2) Featured – You get 10 pages of listings plus a free subscription to Selling Manager Pro (which normally costs $15.99 per month), increased exposure on eBay store pages, and more. Cost: $49.95 per month. (3) Anchored – This store level is for large, high-volume sellers. The price includes 15 pages of listings, everything available through the Featured store, as well as 24x7 dedicated live customer support from eBay. Cost: $499.95 per month.

2. Insertion Fee – Your second main cost is insertion fees for your listings. Think of this cost as a stocking fee for filling your shelves. You have the space, but you pay for each item you put on your shelf by listing it. Unlike auctions that can run a maximum of 10 days, store items can be listed virtually forever. You can list items as good 'til cancelled (GTC). If you want an item to be in your store until it's sold or you want to de-list it, insert it as good 'til canceled. You pay a fee for this as if you are listing it over and over again every 30 days. The insertion fee covers any quantity of items with a single listing (for example, the same fee applies to 1 or 100 cameras, as long as they are all the same).

3. Closing Value Fees – The third main cost of having a store is the fee you pay to eBay when something sells. Final value fees = $25 to $1,000 = 5.25% of the first $25 ($1.31) plus 2.75% of the remaining closing value; over $1,000 = 5.25% of the first $25 ($1.31) plus 2.75% of the next $25 to $1,000 ($26.81), plus 1.5% of the remaining closing value balance.

7.0   FUNDING PROPOSAL

7.1   Fundraising

LA SGPW will self-fund this venture.

7.2   Early Stage Enterprise Development

The LA SGPW enterprise has nominal product revenue and limited expense history. In an early stage enterprise development, typically an incomplete management team has an idea, plan, and possibly some initial product development. Seed capital or first-round financing is usually provided by friends and family, angels, or venture capital firms focusing on early-stage enterprises. The securities issued to those investors are occasionally in the form of common stock but are more commonly in the form of preferred stock. The securities issued so far in LA SGPW comprise of none of these things.

7.3 Repeatable Business Model

This Business Model is the means by which we will develop profitable businesses in a repeatable manner. Some investors will have an appetite for businesses that require large amounts of capital, others will not. Often investors prefer businesses with high sustainable gross margins. The combination of these two factors with a high growth market supports a high, internally sustainable growth rate.

7.4 Investment Benefits

The key benefits to You as an investor include: (1) Greater visibility and insight into the publishing and fashion and luxury goods markets including new LA SGPW products, new technology developments, other ventures and alliances in the marketplace and client behavior and adoption of technology. (2) Collaboration in product development and insight into client response or consumer involvement from those product development activities. (3) Preferred client treatment in certain activities without impacting LA SGPW's growth. (4) Return on investment. (5) Seat on a Strategic Advisory Board. (6) Review sessions with LA SGPW management to gain insight into the publishing and fashion and luxury goods industry.

7.5 Redemption/Exit Strategies

We are building a company that can independently thrive and have one or many IPO scenarios. (That is, each of our divisions, salons, and businesses are unique in and of itself; each operates as a standalone business with its own set of accounting records.).Our exit strategies may include: mergers and acquisition possibilities; spin off possibilities; or IPO of the LA SGPW business units/divisions as a whole or in part. Still, our business units/divisions (companies) have been built with the flexibility to go from private to public back to private, again, wholly or in part. Other possible exit strategies include worldwide exchanges.

- **Public Companies** – NYSE: American accessories company Coach (COH) went public 12/29/2000; Polo Ralph Lauren Corp. (RL) went public in 1997; and Donna Karan went public in June 1996, however, rapid expansion plans backfired and the stock plummeted. As a result, luxury goods leader LVMH scooped up the Donna Karan Company for $643M. Fendi, also sold to LVHM for $850M.

- **Private Companies** – Attempting IPO Status: Giorgio Armani, Prada, Dolce & Gabbana, Roberto Cavalli and Salvatore Ferragamo. Going public will help companies to get the cash that is required for expansion and also to use it for acquisitions.

- **Spin Offs** – Valentino's 2005 spin-off from Manifattura Lane Gaetano Marzotto & Figlito, gave new shareholders control of Valentino, Hugo Boss, and M Missoni. Valentino retired in January 2010.

- **Emerging Markets** – With rising affluence, major Asian economies like China, India and Russia have emerged as the fastest growing market for high-end fashion and luxury goods. In order to compete with Gucci and LVHM and also to expand in the emerging markets, many family-run luxury companies are going for stock market floatation. Others are implementing growth strategies by expanding in emerging markets and controlling distribution channels.

8.0 OPERATIONAL OVERVIEW

8.1 LA SGPW Organizational Structure

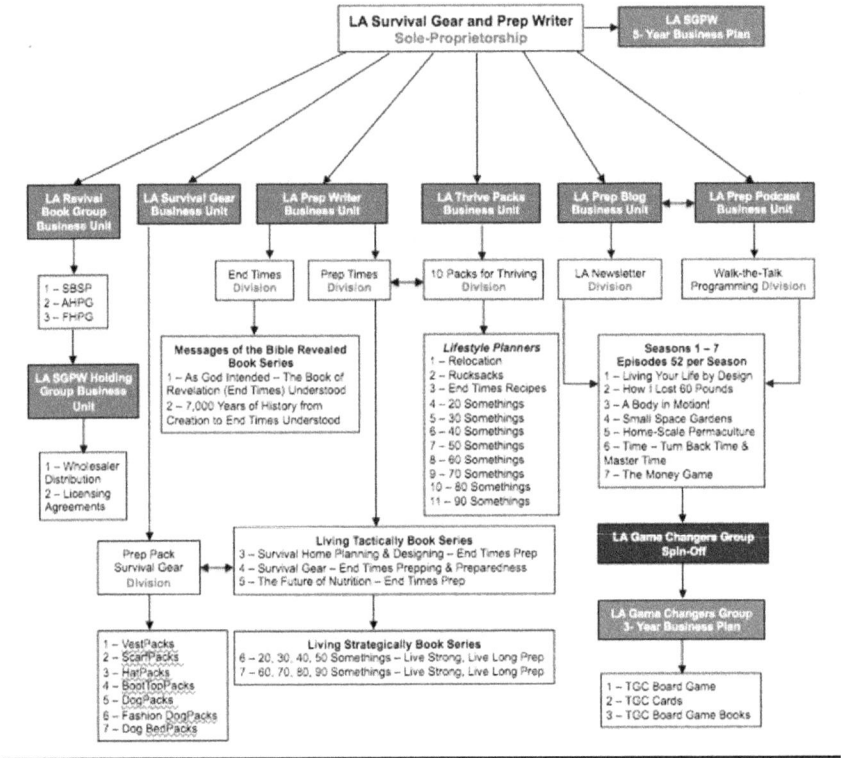

8.1.1 Employment

Our Philosophy – If you care about having a company where employees or contractors (in our case) treat work as play and regard themselves as ultimate customers for the products they produce, then you have to be careful whom you hire, treat them right, and train them to treat others right.

Compensation, Rewards – We have created our own salary/equity structure which features: salary grade ranges, initial grants, and merit grants (pre-determined compensation) paid per job category; bonus pay out (pre-determined) figures twice a year; including a minimum salary set at $25.00 per hour. All contractors will be on an annual salary plan with two reviews – primary and exception reviews. Benefits will be in the form of performance-based incentive opportunities, as well as a generous Company-wide benefit package. Our goal is to be superior among comparable companies.

Time Off, Flexible Time – All contractors will be able to participate in our flexible time off programs, including 7 named holidays, 4 company-assigned floating holidays (typically in December each year to accommodate a holiday shutdown), and 2 personal floating holidays. In addition, we offer personal time off (PTO) paid 15 days per year and a 4-week sabbatical every 4 years.

Training, Development – We encourage our contractors to participate in training seminars designed by the LA SGPW company. In addition, we offer paid job-related workshops and seminars run by professional organizations as well as classes held by local educational institutions.

8.1.2   Strategic Advisory Board Seats

LA SGPW will create a Strategic Advisory Board in 2022: Strategic Advisory Board (SAB). All Strategic Advisory Board seats will be honorary/oversight positions and non-paid. (SAB positions are appointed as acting Division General Managers (DGM) interim solutions.)

9.0   FINANCIAL PLAN

Coupled with our previously mentioned pricing structure in the *Sales & Service Plans* section, we estimate our cost and sales figures for the first three years of operations in the following sections herein.

9.1   Important Assumptions

Herein lists our main assumptions for developing our financial projections. The most sensitive assumption is the outside labor costs. For now, the business owner will solely execute all labor on her own. At some point she may look outside into cottage industries or contractors versus hiring employees. These costs may be adjusted with the amount paid for Inventory Purchases and bringing tasks in-house to balance the two costs to maintain our 80% profit margin in our cost of goods for sale. Inasmuch, the general assumption bottom line would stay the same.

9.2   Projected Personnel Plan – *assuming the above, pro forma personnel plan table available upon request.*

9.3   Projected Profit and Loss – *assuming the above, pro forma profit and loss table and charts available upon request.*

9.4   Pro Forma Statement of Cash Flows – *pro forma statement of cash flow table and chart available upon request.*

9.6   Summary Balance Sheet – *summary balance sheet table available upon request.*

9.7   Pro Forma Income Statement Summary – *assuming the above, pro forma income statement summary sample:*

3. Unilateral Nondisclosure Agreement

UNILATERAL
NONDISCLOSURE AGREEMENT

THIS AGREEMENT governs the disclosure of information to _____
(the "Company") by _____ (the "Disclosing Party") as of _____
(the "Effective Date").

1.   As used herein, "Confidential Information" shall mean the information specified below:

_____

_____

_____

_____

2.   If the Confidential Information is embodied in tangible material (including without limitation, software, hardware, drawings, graphs, charts, disks, tapes, prototypes and samples), it shall be labeled as "Confidential" or bear a similar legend. If the Confidential Information is disclosed orally or visually, it shall be identified as such at the time of disclosure.

3.   The Company agrees it will not disclose Confidential Information to any third party, except as approved in writing by the Disclosing Party, and will use the Confidential Information for no purpose other than evaluating or pursuing a business relationship with the Disclosing Party. Notwithstanding the above, Company shall not be in violation of this Section 3 with regard to a disclosure that was in response to a valid order by a court or other governmental body, provided that the Company provides the Disclosing Party with prior written notice of such disclosure in order to permit the Disclosing Party to seek confidential treatment of such information. The Company shall only permit access to Confidential Information to those of its employees or authorized representatives having a need to know and who have signed confidentiality agreements or are otherwise bound by confidentiality obligations substantially similar to those contained herein.

4.   The Company shall immediately notify the Disclosing Party upon discovery of any loss or unauthorized disclosure of any Confidential Information.

5.   The Company's obligations under this Agreement with respect to any portion of the Confidential Information shall terminate when the Company can document that: (a) it was in the public domain at the time it was communicated to the Company; (b) it entered the public domain subsequent to the time it was communicated to the Company through no fault of the Company; (c) it was in the Company's possession free of any obligation of confidence at the time it was communicated to the Company; (d) it was rightfully communicated to the Company free of any obligation of confidence subsequent to the time it was communicated to the Company; (e) it was developed by employees or agents of the Company independently of and without reference to any information communicated to the Company; (f) it was communicated by the Disclosing Party to an unaffiliated third party free of any obligation of confidence; or (g) it was not legended as Confidential Information of the Disclosing Party and if disclosed orally or visually, it was not identified as Confidential Information of the Disclosing Party at the time of such communication.

Appendix

6. Upon termination or expiration of the Agreement, or upon written request of the Disclosing Party, the Company shall promptly return to the Disclosing Party all documents, notes and other tangible materials representing the Confidential Information and all copies thereof.

7. The Company recognizes and agrees that nothing contained in this Agreement shall be construed as granting any property rights, by license or otherwise, to any Confidential Information disclosed pursuant to this Agreement, or to any invention or any patent, copyright, trademark, or other intellectual property right that has issued or that may issue, based on such Confidential Information. The Company shall not make, have made, use or sell for any purpose any product or other item using, incorporating or derived from any Confidential Information.

8. Confidential Information shall not be reproduced in any form except as required to accomplish the intent of this Agreement. Any reproduction of any Confidential Information shall remain the property of the Disclosing Party and shall contain any and all confidential or proprietary notices or legends, which appear on the original, unless otherwise authorized in writing by the Disclosing Party.

9. This Agreement shall terminate three (3) years after the Effective Date, or may be terminated by either party at any time upon thirty (30) days written notice to the other party. The Company's obligations under this Agreement shall survive termination of the Agreement between the parties and shall be binding upon the Company's heirs, successors and assigns. The Company's obligations hereunder shall continue in full force and effect with respect to non-technical sales, marketing, and financial Confidential Information for three (3) years from the date of disclosure of such Confidential Information. The Company's obligations with respect to all technical Confidential Information shall be terminated only pursuant to Section 5.

10. This Agreement shall be governed by and construed in accordance with the laws of _____ without reference to conflict of laws principles. Any disputes under this Agreement shall be subject to the exclusive jurisdiction and venue of the _____ state courts and Federal courts located in _____ County, _____, and the parties hereby consent to the personal jurisdiction and venue of these courts. This Agreement may not be amended except by a writing signed by both parties hereto.

11. If any provision of this Agreement is found by a proper authority to be unenforceable or invalid, such unenforceability or invalidity shall not render this Agreement unenforceable or invalid as a whole and, in such event, such provision shall be changed and interpreted so as to best accomplish the objectives of such unenforceable or invalid provision within the limits of applicable law or applicable court decisions.

12. Neither party will assign or transfer any rights or obligations under this Agreement without the prior written consent of the other party.

13. The Company shall not export, directly or indirectly, any technical data acquired pursuant to this Agreement or any product utilizing any such data to any country for which the U.S. Government or any agency thereof at the time of export requires an export license or other governmental approval without first obtaining such license or approval.

14. All notices or reports permitted or required under this Agreement shall be in writing and shall be delivered by personal delivery, electronic mail, facsimile transmission or by certified or registered mail, return receipt requested, and shall be deemed given upon personal delivery, five (5) days after deposit in the mail, or upon acknowledgment of receipt of electronic transmission. Notices shall be sent to the addresses set forth at the end of this Agreement or such other address as either party may specify in writing.

IN WITNESS WHEREOF, the parties hereto have caused this Nondisclosure Agreement to be executed as of the Effective Date.

COMPANY NAME   THIRD PARTY NAME

_____   _____

By: _____   By: _____

Date: _____   Date: _____

Address: _____   Address: _____

_____   _____

4. Mutual Nondisclosure Agreement

MUTUAL
NONDISCLOSURE AGREEMENT

THIS AGREEMENT governs the disclosure of information by and between the _____ and _____ as of _____, 20__ (the "Effective Date") for purposes of._____

_____

_____.

    1. As used herein, "Confidential Information" shall mean any and all technical and non-technical information provided by either party to the other, including but not limited to information regarding (a) patent and patent applications, (b) trade secret, and (c) proprietary information—mask works, ideas, samples, media, chemical compounds, assays, techniques, sketches, drawings, works of authorship, models, inventions, know-how, processes, apparatuses, equipment, algorithms, software programs, software source documents, and formulae related to the current, future, and proposed products and services of each of the parties, and including, without limitation, their respective information concerning research, experimental work, development, design details and specifications, engineering, financial information, procurement requirements, purchasing, manufacturing, customer lists, investors, employees, business and contractual relationships, business forecasts, sales and merchandising, marketing plans and information the disclosing party provides regarding third parties.

    2. If the Confidential Information is embodied in tangible material (including without limitation, software, hardware, drawings, graphs, charts, disks, tapes, prototypes and samples), it shall be labeled as "Confidential" or bear a similar legend. If the Confidential Information is disclosed orally or visually, it shall be identified as such at the time of disclosure.

    3. Each party agrees that at all times and notwithstanding any termination or expiration of this Agreement it will hold in strict confidence and not disclose to any third party Confidential Information of the other, except as approved in writing by the other party to this Agreement, and will use the Confidential Information for no purpose other than evaluating or pursuing a business relationship with the other party to this Agreement. Notwithstanding the above, the party to whom Confidential Information was disclosed (the "Recipient") shall not be in violation of this Section 3 with regard to a disclosure that was in response to a valid order by a court or other governmental body, provided that the Recipient provides the other party with prior written notice of such disclosure in order to permit the other party to seek confidential treatment of such information. Each party shall only permit access to Confidential Information of the other party to those of its employees or authorized representatives having a need to know and who have signed confidentiality agreements or are otherwise bound by confidentiality obligations at least as restrictive as those contained herein.

4.   Each party shall immediately notify the other upon discovery of any loss or unauthorized disclosure of the Confidential Information of the other party.

5.   Each party's obligations under this Agreement with respect to any portion of the other party's Confidential Information shall terminate when the Recipient can document that: (a) it was in the public domain at the time it was communicated to the Recipient by the other party; (b) it entered the public domain subsequent to the time it was communicated to the Recipient by the other party through no fault of the Recipient; (c) it was in the Recipient's possession free of any obligation of confidence at the time it was communicated to the Recipient by the other party; (d) it was rightfully communicated to the Recipient free of any obligation of confidence subsequent to the time it was communicated to the Recipient by the other party; (e) it was developed by employees or agents of the Recipient independently of and without reference to any information communicated to the Recipient by the other party; (f) it was communicated by the other party to an unaffiliated third party free of any obligation of confidence; or (g) it was not legended as Confidential Information of the disclosing party and if disclosed orally or visually, it was not identified as Confidential Information of the disclosing party at the time of such communication.

6.   Upon termination or expiration of the Agreement, or upon written request of the other party, each party shall promptly return to the other all documents, notes and other tangible materials representing the other's Confidential Information and all copies thereof.

7.   The parties recognize and agree that nothing contained in this Agreement shall be construed as granting any property rights, by license or otherwise, to any Confidential Information disclosed pursuant to this Agreement, or to any invention or any patent, copyright, trademark, or other intellectual property right that has issued or that may issue, based on such Confidential Information. Neither party shall make, have made, use or sell for any purpose any product or other item using, incorporating or derived from any Confidential Information of the other party.

8.   Confidential Information shall not be reproduced in any form except as required to accomplish the intent of this Agreement. Any reproduction of any Confidential Information of the other party by either party shall remain the property of the disclosing party and shall contain any and all confidential or proprietary notices or legends which appear on the original, unless otherwise authorized in writing by the other party.

9.   This Agreement shall terminate three (3) years after the Effective Date, or may be terminated by either party at any time upon thirty (30) days written notice to the other party. The Recipient's obligations under this Agreement shall survive termination of the Agreement between the parties and shall be binding upon the Recipient's heirs, successors and assigns. The Recipient's obligations hereunder shall continue in full force and effect with respect to non-technical sales, marketing, and financial Confidential Information for three (3) years from the date of disclosure of such Confidential Information. The Recipient's obligations with respect to all technical Confidential Information shall be terminated only pursuant to Section 5.

10.   This Agreement shall be governed by and construed in accordance with the laws of California without reference to conflict of laws principles. Any disputes under this Agreement may be brought in the state courts and the Federal courts located in Santa Clara County, California, and the parties hereby consent to the personal jurisdiction and venue of these courts. This Agreement may not be amended except by a writing signed by both parties hereto.

11.   Each party acknowledges that its breach of this Agreement will cause irreparable damage and hereby agrees that the other party shall be entitled to seek injunctive relief under this Agreement, as well as such further relief as may be granted by a court of competent jurisdiction.

12.   If any provision of this Agreement is found by a proper authority to be unenforceable or invalid, such unenforceability or invalidity shall not render this Agreement unenforceable or invalid as a whole and, in such event, such provision shall be changed and interpreted so as to best accomplish the objectives of such unenforceable or invalid provision within the limits of applicable law or applicable court decisions.

13.   Neither party shall communicate any information to the other in violation of the proprietary rights of any third party.

14.   Neither party will assign or transfer any rights or obligations under this Agreement without the prior written consent of the other party.

15.   Neither party shall export, directly or indirectly, any technical data acquired pursuant to this Agreement or any product utilizing any such data to any country for which the U.S. Government or any agency thereof at the time of export requires an export license or other governmental approval without first obtaining such license or approval.

16.   All notices or reports permitted or required under this Agreement shall be in writing and shall be delivered by personal delivery, electronic mail, facsimile transmission or by certified or registered mail, return receipt requested, and shall be deemed given upon personal delivery, five (5) days after deposit in the mail, or upon acknowledgment of receipt of electronic transmission. Notices shall be sent to the addresses set forth at the end of this Agreement or such other address as either party may specify in writing.

IN WITNESS WHEREOF, the parties hereto have caused this Mutual Nondisclosure Agreement to be executed as of the Effective Date.

PARTY: _____   PARTY: _____

By: _____   By: _____

Appendix

Name

_____
Print Title

Date: _____

_____
Address

_____
City, State, Zip code

Telephone: _____

Email: _____

Name

_____
Print Title

Date: _____

_____
Address

_____
City, State, Zip code

Telephone: _____

Email: _____

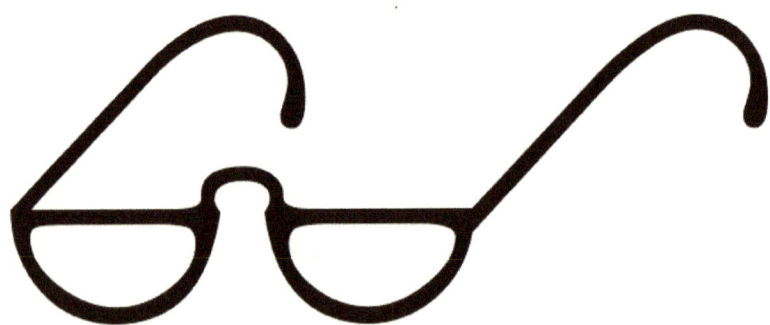

Resources

The Empire Builders and Blueprint Series

Welcome to the Resource section of the Empire Builders Series: Masterclasses in Business and Law. Here, we provide a carefully curated collection of practical tools and materials designed to complement the strategies and insights discussed throughout the series. This section is your gateway to deeper understanding and application, offering everything from sample agreements and checklists to detailed case studies and guidelines. Whether you're forging a new business, protecting intellectual property, or planning for expansion, these resources are intended to empower you with the necessary tools to effectively implement and navigate the complex landscape of business and law. Embrace these resources as your companion in building and sustaining a robust empire.

Empire Builders Series:
Masterclasses in Business and Law

In the dynamic world of business, where innovation intersects with opportunity, success often hinges not only on creativity but also on a deep understanding of the legal and operational landscapes. The Empire Builders Series is meticulously designed to arm aspiring entrepreneurs, seasoned business owners, creative professionals, and legal experts with the comprehensive knowledge and strategies needed to navigate these complexities and build lasting empires.

Each book in the series serves as a foundational pillar, offering expert guidance and actionable insights in specific areas of business and law; tailored to foster growth, innovation, and success in today's competitive marketplace:

1. **Brick by Brick**: This guide acts as your blueprint for building a business from the ground up. It offers essential strategies, legal insights, and operational tactics crucial for establishing a solid foundation for any business venture.

2. **Mark Your Territory**: Dive deep into the world of trademarks with this essential guide, designed to help you protect and effectively leverage your brand in today's competitive market.

3. **From Idea to Empire**: Transform your entrepreneurial dreams into reality with this exhaustive guide to business planning. Learn how to craft a compelling business plan that not only attracts investors but also sets the stage for a successful enterprise.

4. **Beyond the Pen**: Safeguard your creative works and master the intricacies of copyright law with this expert guide, tailored specifically for writers, artists, musicians, and digital content creators.

5. **Legal Ink**: Demystify the complex legal landscape of publishing with practical advice on negotiating contracts and protecting intellectual property, essential for authors and publishers.

The Empire Builders Series stands as a testament to the power of knowledge and the importance of mastering the strategic and legal aspects of business management. Each book is designed not merely to inform but to inspire action and lead to success. Embark on this journey to build your empire, one masterclass at a time.

Brick by Brick:
The Entrepreneur's Guide to Constructing a Company

The first book in the Empire Builders Series: Masterclass in Business and Law is "Brick by Brick: The Entrepreneur's Guide to Constructing a Company."

Summary: "Brick by Brick" is an indispensable resource for entrepreneurs who are poised to transform their innovative business ideas into successful enterprises. This comprehensive guide meticulously outlines the complexities of business formation, providing detailed, step-by-step instructions and vital insights into the legal, operational, and strategic aspects of starting and running a thriving company.

Part 1: Laying the Foundation – Focuses on selecting the appropriate business entity, delving into the legal implications of each option and the economic considerations vital for establishing a solid foundation for your business.

Part 2: Operational Mechanics – Discusses the operational aspects of setting up partnerships and LLCs, navigating corporate governance, maintaining corporate records, and managing capital and shareholder relationships effectively.

Part 3: Advanced Strategic Planning – Offers insights into managing structural changes, handling stock and ownership issues, expanding operations across state lines, and deploying tax strategies to ensure compliance and optimize financial performance.

Part 4: Implementation Tools and Resources – Provides practical tools such as sample agreements, startup task checklists, and comprehensive guidelines for drafting business plans and the incorporation process, enabling entrepreneurs to effectively implement their business strategies.

"Brick by Brick" not only serves as a guide but acts as a complete blueprint for building a robust business capable of thriving in today's competitive market. It arms aspiring entrepreneurs with the necessary knowledge and tools to navigate the complexities of business formation. From drafting your first business plan to preparing for incorporation, this book delivers invaluable insights and practical advice to establish a strong foundation and sustain growth.

Mark Your Territory:
Navigating Trademarks in the Modern Marketplace

The second book in the Empire Builders Series: Masterclass in Business and Law is "Mark Your Territory: Navigating Trademarks in the Modern Marketplace."

Summary: "Mark Your Territory" provides an indispensable resource for anyone involved in the branding and legal aspects of their business, offering a comprehensive guide to understanding, acquiring, and effectively managing trademarks. This book is crucial for ensuring that trademarks, which are vital assets to any business, are properly protected and leveraged.

Part 1: Fundamentals of Trademarks – Introduces the basics of trademarks, including their legal framework, the process of trademark selection and registration, and their importance in identifying business sources and ensuring product quality.

Part 2: Strategic Trademark Management – Focuses on the ongoing management of trademarks, detailing strategies for maintaining rights, monitoring for infringements, addressing challenges in digital marketing, and managing global trademark portfolios.

Part 3: Advanced Topics in Trademarks – Delves into more complex issues such as preventing trademark dilution, managing renewals, understanding the specific needs of service marks in advertising, and navigating the intricacies of trademark licensing and emerging legal trends.

Part 4: Practical Tools and Resources – Provides practical aids like sample trademark filings, management checklists, and insightful case studies, equipping readers with tangible tools and real-world examples to apply the concepts discussed effectively.

Designed for entrepreneurs, business owners, and legal professionals, "Mark Your Territory" equips readers with actionable strategies and essential tools for effective trademark management. It ensures that readers can maintain their brand's uniqueness and legal protections, thus securing a competitive edge in the marketplace.

From Idea to Empire:
Mastering the Art of Business Planning

The third book in the Empire Builders Series: Masterclass in Business and Law is "From Idea to Empire: Mastering the Art of Business Planning."

Summary: "From Idea to Empire" offers an indispensable roadmap for entrepreneurs eager to transform their innovative ideas into successful businesses. This comprehensive guide equips readers with a strategic blueprint for drafting robust business plans that attract investors and serve as a roadmap for navigating the transition from startup to thriving enterprise.

Part 1: Conceptualizing Your Business – This section lays the groundwork by assisting readers in defining their business vision, understanding market needs, analyzing competitors, and setting clear business objectives. It also guides readers in selecting an effective business model that aligns with their long-term goals.

Part 2: Strategic Planning – Delve into creating detailed marketing strategies, operational plans, and financial projections. This part covers risk management and technological integration, ensuring the business plan is both innovative and executable.

Part 3: Articulating Your Plan – Focuses on the actual drafting of the business plan, including how to write an engaging executive summary, develop compelling proposals, and master communication and negotiation tactics with potential investors and partners.

Part 4: Execution and Review – Outlines the necessary steps to launch the business successfully, monitor its performance, and make adjustments based on real-world feedback and market dynamics. This section also explores strategies for sustainable growth and long-term viability.

"From Idea to Empire" is more than a mere planning manual; it's a strategic guide that provides budding entrepreneurs with the necessary knowledge, tools, and confidence to build a business capable of facing today's market complexities. With practical advice, real-world examples, and essential resources, this book is a vital tool for anyone ready to evolve their business concept from idea to a profitable empire.

From Idea to Empire: Abridged Edition

The third book in the Empire Builders Series: Masterclass in Business and Law is "From Idea to Empire: Abridged Edition."

Summary: "From Idea to Empire: Abridged Edition" delivers the essential roadmap for turning business ideas into successful enterprises—streamlined for readers seeking concise and actionable insights. While the original edition provides an expansive resource with success stories and detailed case studies, this abridged version focuses solely on the strategic elements of business planning, offering the tools needed to conceptualize, design, and execute a winning business strategy.

By eliminating supplementary stories and focusing on the practical frameworks, this edition is perfect for readers eager to dive straight into the mechanics of business planning without distraction. It provides the knowledge required to develop robust business models, articulate compelling proposals, and successfully launch and grow a business in today's dynamic marketplace.

Part 1: Conceptualizing Your Business – Laying the Foundation – In this section, readers learn how to define their business idea, identify market needs, analyze competitors, and set clear objectives. It introduces essential business models and helps entrepreneurs align their vision with long-term goals.

Part 2: Strategic Planning – Mapping the Path to Success – Here, readers will discover how to design effective marketing strategies, operational plans, and financial projections. Topics like risk management and technological integration are covered to ensure every business plan is both realistic and innovative.

Part 3: Articulating Your Plan – Communicating with Precision and Impact – This section emphasizes the importance of clarity in communication. Readers will learn how to craft compelling executive summaries, develop strong proposals, and master negotiation strategies for working with investors and partners.

Part 4: Execution and Review – Launching and Scaling with Purpose – The final section covers essential steps for launching a business successfully, monitoring performance, and making real-time adjustments. It also addresses strategies for sustainable growth, long-term resilience, and market adaptation.

About This Edition:
The Abridged Edition is crafted for readers who prefer a focused, no-frills approach to business planning. By presenting the core methodologies from the original book in a concise format, this version allows entrepreneurs to absorb key concepts quickly and efficiently. Whether you're a first-time entrepreneur or a seasoned business owner, this streamlined guide provides the essential tools needed to transform an idea into a thriving business.

Why This Edition Matters:
"From Idea to Empire: Abridged Edition" underscores that great business planning doesn't require lengthy explanations—it requires clear strategies and actionable frameworks. This edition emphasizes the importance of focus, discipline, and adaptability in building a successful business.

Designed to complement busy entrepreneurs, it delivers the same powerful strategies as the original book but in a more accessible format. Readers can quickly refer to specific sections, apply the knowledge, and move forward with confidence in their business endeavors.

"From Idea to Empire: Abridged Edition" is the perfect companion for entrepreneurs who need to move swiftly from concept to execution. With straightforward advice and practical insights, this edition equips readers to create robust business plans and take decisive action toward building their own empire.

Beyond the Pen:
Copyright Strategies for Modern Creators
The fourth book in the Empire Builders Series: Masterclass in Business and Law is "Beyond the Pen: Copyright Strategies for Modern Creators."

Summary: "Beyond the Pen" serves as a crucial guide for artists, writers, musicians, and digital creators who seek to effectively navigate the complexities of copyright law and protect their creative assets. This comprehensive resource provides a deep dive into the mechanisms, legal frameworks, and strategic practices necessary to safeguard intellectual property in today's rapidly evolving digital landscape.

Part 1: Understanding Copyright Law – This section lays the groundwork by covering the essentials of copyright, including how to register works, the extent of legal protection available, and the nuances of international copyright laws. It equips creators with the crucial knowledge needed to assert and defend their rights.

Part 2: Navigating Use and Fair Use – Focuses on the vital concept of fair use, offering real-world scenarios and detailed guidance on how to handle copyright infringements and resolve disputes effectively without compromising creative freedom.

Part 3: Licensing and Monetization – Explores strategic approaches to structuring and managing licensing agreements, understanding diverse revenue models, and handling collaborations, ensuring creators can monetize their works effectively while maintaining control over their usage.

Part 4: Copyright in the Digital Age – Addresses the challenges and opportunities presented by new technologies, digital rights management, and online content sharing platforms. This part also examines the impact of social media on copyright and anticipates future trends that could influence creators' rights.

"Beyond the Pen" is more than just a legal manual; it is a strategic resource that empowers creators to protect, manage, and prosper with their intellectual property in today's interconnected market. Packed with practical examples, expert advice, and actionable strategies, this book is an indispensable tool for anyone looking to navigate the legal challenges and seize the opportunities in the modern creative landscape.

Legal Ink:
Navigating the Legalese of Publishing

The fifth book in the Empire Builders Series: Masterclass in Business and Law is "Legal Ink: Navigating the Legalese of Publishing."

Summary: "Legal Ink" offers an indispensable guide for authors seeking to navigate the complex world of publishing contracts. This comprehensive book demystifies legal jargon and provides a clear roadmap to understanding and managing the intricacies of publishing agreements effectively.

Part 1: The Grant of Rights – This section explains the various types of publishing rights, offering guidance on how to negotiate and manage these rights effectively to safeguard the author's interests.

Part 2: Your Obligations – Details the commitments authors must uphold under publishing contracts. It emphasizes the implications of these obligations for an author's literary career and advises on managing multiple contractual commitments.

Part 3: Getting Your Book to Market – Covers the practical aspects of the publishing process from the final manuscript preparation to marketing and distribution. This part ensures authors understand the steps involved and their roles in bringing their book to market.

Part 4: Follow the Money – Breaks down the financial components of publishing contracts, including advances, royalties, and accounting clauses. It offers crucial advice on how to negotiate for fair compensation.

Part 5: Parting Ways – Discusses strategies for effectively managing the conclusion of a publishing agreement, including rights reversion and contract termination, providing tactics for authors to regain control of their work.

"Legal Ink" acts as more than just a guide—it's a strategic tool for any author looking to deeply understand and master the legal framework of publishing contracts. With this book, writers are equipped to make informed decisions, negotiate better terms, and ensure their rights are protected throughout their publishing journey. It is an essential resource for anyone looking to confidently handle the legalities of publishing and secure the success of their work in the competitive marketplace.

The Empire Blueprint Series:
Case Studies for Business Success

Welcome to the Case Studies section of The Empire Blueprint Series: Case Studies for Business Success. This collection serves as an essential companion to the theoretical knowledge presented in the earlier volumes. Here, we delve into real-world applications and successful business practices through detailed case studies, showcasing how various entrepreneurs and businesses have navigated challenges, seized opportunities, and achieved success in their respective fields.

In this series, you will encounter a variety of scenarios that illustrate the practical implementation of business strategies and legal frameworks. Each case study not only highlights successes but also discusses the obstacles faced and lessons learned along the way. Whether you're a budding entrepreneur, a seasoned executive, or a legal professional, these insights will provide you with invaluable perspectives and tools to enhance your own business endeavors.

Each book in the series includes:

1. **70 Case Studies in Vision, Strategy, and Personal Branding**: This volume explores the journeys of entrepreneurs who have effectively crafted their visions and built strong personal brands. It highlights strategies for aligning personal values with business goals and creating a lasting impact in the marketplace.

2. **70 Case Studies in Leadership, Innovation, and Resilience**: This volume examines leaders who have driven innovation and fostered resilience within their organizations. The case studies showcase their approaches to overcoming challenges and inspire others to cultivate a culture of adaptability and forward-thinking.

3. **74 Case Studies in Growth, Digital Presence, and Legacy Building**: This volume delves into the strategies employed by businesses that have successfully navigated digital transformation and growth. It emphasizes the importance of establishing a strong online presence and building a legacy that resonates with future generations.

Each case study in The Empire Blueprint Series: Case Studies for Business Success is crafted to offer actionable insights and inspiration for readers. By examining these real-world examples, you will gain a deeper understanding of the strategies that drive business success and how to apply these lessons to your own ventures.

70 Case Studies in Vision, Strategy, and Personal Branding: The Foundations of Success, Volume 1

The first book in The Empire Blueprint Series: Case Studies for Business Success is "70 Case Studies in Vision, Strategy, and Personal Branding: The Foundations of Success," Volume 1

Dive deeper into the essential elements of business success with Volume 1: 70 Case Studies in Vision, Strategy, and Personal Branding. This volume not only presents a wealth of real-world examples but also serves as a practical toolkit for aspiring entrepreneurs and seasoned professionals alike. Here, you will find a curated collection of resources designed to complement the case studies and enhance your understanding of effective business practices.

From strategic planning templates and personal branding frameworks to time management guides and storytelling techniques, these resources empower you to implement the insights gleaned from the case studies. Explore practical tools for optimizing your online presence, launching impactful marketing campaigns, and engaging audiences across various platforms.

With a focus on innovation and adaptability, this resource section is your go-to companion for navigating the complexities of today's business landscape. Whether you're looking to craft an inspiring vision, develop effective strategies, or build a standout personal brand, the materials provided will equip you with the actionable insights needed to achieve meaningful success. Embrace the tools and inspiration within these pages, and take your entrepreneurial journey to new heights.

70 Case Studies in Leadership, Innovation, and Resilience: Building a Thriving Enterprise, Volume 2

The second book in The Empire Blueprint Series: Case Studies for Business Success is "70 Case Studies in Leadership, Innovation, and Resilience: Building a Thriving Enterprise," Volume 2

Enhance your understanding of effective leadership with Volume 2: 70 Case Studies in Leadership, Innovation, and Resilience: Building a Thriving Enterprise. This resource section is designed to complement the rich insights presented throughout the volume, providing you with practical tools and frameworks to elevate your leadership journey.

Within this section, you'll find a variety of resources that address the core themes of this book—leadership, innovation, and resilience. From templates for developing effective communication strategies to guides on fostering a collaborative corporate culture, these materials are crafted to support your growth as a leader. Explore negotiation techniques, emotional intelligence assessments, and frameworks for ethical leadership that will help you build trust and loyalty within your teams.

The resources also include practical tips for embracing digital transformation and integrating innovative technologies into your business practices. Learn how to leverage these tools to drive growth, enhance customer engagement, and maintain a competitive edge in today's dynamic market.

With a focus on creating lasting value and building a legacy, this section equips you with actionable insights and strategies to navigate challenges with confidence. Whether you are an entrepreneur launching a new venture or an executive steering an established enterprise, these resources will empower you to lead with purpose and resilience.

Dive into these valuable tools and insights, and discover how to turn challenges into opportunities, fostering an environment where innovation and sustainable growth thrive.

74 Case Studies in Growth, Digital Presence, and Legacy Building: Strategies for Long-Term Success, Volume 3

The third book in The Empire Blueprint Series: Case Studies for Business Success is "74 Case Studies in Growth, Digital Presence, and Legacy Building: Strategies for Long-Term Success," Volume 3

Unlock the secrets to sustainable success with Volume 3: 74 Case Studies in Growth, Digital Presence, and Legacy Building: Strategies for Long-Term Success. This resource section is designed to enhance your understanding and application of the powerful insights shared throughout the volume, providing you with practical tools and strategies for thriving in today's competitive landscape.

Resources

In this section, you'll find a wealth of resources that align with the key themes of this book—growth, digital engagement, and legacy building. From templates for strategic goal-setting and growth frameworks to guides on optimizing digital marketing efforts, these materials will help you implement the actionable insights gained from the case studies.

Explore best practices for storytelling and community engagement in the digital realm, along with practical tips for leveraging social media to amplify your brand's presence. Discover frameworks for navigating the complexities of innovation and operational efficiency, ensuring your business not only grows but flourishes sustainably.

The resource section also emphasizes the importance of legacy building, offering tools for effective succession planning and community involvement. Learn how to align your everyday decisions with your long-term vision, ensuring that your enterprise leaves a lasting impact for future generations.

Whether you are an entrepreneur embarking on a new venture, an executive scaling operations, or a professional seeking to elevate your digital presence, these resources will empower you to lead with purpose and confidence. Dive into the practical tools and insights provided here, and equip yourself to navigate challenges, innovate boldly, and create a meaningful legacy.

In conclusion, the Resource section of the Empire Builders Series and Empire Blueprint Series serves as valuable extensions of the learning journey you've embarked upon. By utilizing these carefully chosen tools and materials, you are better equipped to apply the principles and strategies discussed in the series to real-world scenarios. Each resource has been tailored to enhance your understanding and effectiveness in the realms of business and law, ensuring you have the practical support necessary to navigate challenges and seize opportunities. We hope these resources prove instrumental in helping you build and sustain your business empire, transforming knowledge into actionable success.

L. A. Moeszinger also known as simply "L" is the face behind the AuthorsDoor Leadership Program: AuthorsDoor Series: *Publisher & Her World*, AuthorsDoor Advanced Series: *Publisher & Her World*, and AuthorsDoor Masterclass Series: *Publisher & Her World*. The program comprises, books, courses, and workbooks. The courses expand upon the books. The workbooks go into further detail, outlining step-by-step instructions. Courses are *free*; books and workbooks are available for purchase on Amazon and other retailer sites. She has been launching the careers of self-publishers since 2009, and she also writes the AuthorsRedDoor.com blog on writing, publishing, and marketing. L is also the co-founder of The Ridge Publishing Group and its imprints.

She is an American author, publisher, and creator who resides in Coeur d'Alene, Idaho, with her husband and two dogs. She writes under the pseudonyms: Ann Patterson and Ann Carrington for her business law pieces; L. A. Moeszinger for her writing, publishing, and marketing pieces; Lori Ann Moeszinger for her biblical books and personal pieces; and a handful of others for her Manhattan Diaries series. She believes strongly in faith, blessings, and working her butt off . . . and she thinks one of the best things about being an author-publisher—unlike the lawyer she used to be—is that she can let her passion out.

Original Package Design
© 2024 AuthorsDoor Leadership Program
Cover Design: Eric Moeszinger
Author Photo © 2023 Edwin Wolfe

Parent Website: https://www.RidgePublishingGroup.com and

blog site https://www.PublisherAndHerWorld.com

Publisher Website: https://www.GuardiansofBiblicalTruth.com and

blog site https://www.Jesus-Says.com

Author website: https://www.LAMoeszinger.com and New Youniversity sites:

https://www.NewYouniversity.com, https://www.ManhattanChronicles.com

Bridge Website: https://www.AuthorsDoor.com and

blog site https://www.AuthorsRedDoor.com

Entertainment website: https://www.EthanFoxBooks.com and

blog site https://www.KidsStagram.com

Want More?

The ideas in this book are expanded upon throughout the AuthorsDoor Leadership Program of books, courses, and workbooks. Follow our Facebook page. Join our Facebook private group. Watch our YouTube channels (AuthorsDoor Group, Authors Red Door #Shorts, and Publisher and Her World at Ridge Publishing Group). Listen to our Podcast channel (Publisher's Circle); or email me: *Hello@AuthorsDoor.com*

AuthorsDoor Hubs

Get insights from the articles we write on our *website* (AuthorsDoor.com). You'll find more publications to help authors sell better, pitch better, recruit better, build better, create better, and connect better. You are also invited to visit our *blog* and find out what we're talking about now. Sign up for our *AuthorsDoor Leadership Program Newsletter* and join the conversations going on there with our private community (Publisher's Circle); visit: *www.AuthorsRedDoor.com*

Publisher & Her World Blogs

Enter a world where the sometimes shocking and often hilarious climb to the top as an author-publisher is exposed by a true insider. Faced with on-going trials and tribulations of the world of self-publishing, L. A. Moeszinger is witty and sometimes brutally candid in her postings. If you enjoy getting the inside scoop on the makings and thoughts behind self-publishing, this is the blog for you! *www.PublisherAndHerWorld.com*

This

book was art

directed by John Jared.

The art for both the cover and the

interior was created using pastels on toned

print making paper. The text was set in 10 point Times

New Roman, a typeface based on the sixteenth-century type designs

of Claude Garamond, redrawn by Robert Slimback in 1989.

The book was printed at Amazon and IngramSpark.

The Managing Editor was Jack Clark. The

Production was supervised by

Jason Reed and Ed

Warren.